Better Homes and Gardens®

annual**recipes**2003

Sweet Layers of
Red, White, and Blue
page 130

Better Homes and Gardens® Family Food Collection™
Des Moines, Iowa

Quick-Fried Chicken Salad
page 78

WHEN A YEAR'S WORTH OF DAYS HAVE PASSED, WHICH OF THEM INSPIRED THE MEMORIES THAT ARE NOW SAFELY STOWED IN YOUR MEMORY BANK? Chances are you'll remember the day of your family reunion when Grandma and Grandpa shared their wedding photos. Or the day you threw a surprise birthday party for your friend turning the big 5-0. Or the day of the bridal shower honoring the daughter of your close friend and your own soon-to-be daughter-in-law.

We remember the good times with family and friends. And many of those times are made up of three simple things: the people we love, time spent together—and enough good food to go around twice. While the first two take some coordination, typically the right occasion is all we need to send out the invitations. But the third element—coming up with just the right menu—can slow things down. That's where the experts at *Better Homes and Gardens*® magazine come in. For more than 80 years now, we've been bringing family and friends together around food that satisfies, delights, and says, "I'm glad you're here." In this cookbook, *Better Homes and Gardens*® *Annual Recipes 2003,* you'll find a year's worth of recipes that will keep your crowd happy and get you out of the kitchen quickly.

And the best part is that you can count on these recipes working—the first time, and every time, you try them. That's because they're tested and re-tested in America's most trusted kitchen—the Better Homes and Gardens® Test Kitchen. A recipe has to get a thumbs up from our editors and home economists before it appears in one of our magazines or books. It's this quality seal of approval that guarantees you'll get applause at the end of your next get-together. Go ahead—a year's worth of memories are waiting to happen...

Karol

KAROL DEWULF NICKELL, EDITOR IN CHIEF
Better Homes and Gardens® magazine

Better Homes and Gardens® Family Food Collection™

MICHAEL L. MAINE
Director, Editorial Administration

JOY TAYLOR
Executive Editor

BRIDGET SANDQUIST
Art Director

annual recipes 2003

JULIA MARTINUSEN
Editor

STEPHANIE HUNTER
Assistant Art Director

Contributing Recipe Editors	SHARYL HEIKEN, ELIZABETH WOOLEVER
Contributing Indexer	ROSEMARY HUTCHINSON
Contributing Copy Editors	GRETCHEN KAUFFMAN

Senior Food Editors	Sandra Mosley, Lois White
Associate Art Director	Deena Zymm
Administrative Assistants	Tamra McGee, Maria McLeese
Test Kitchen Director	Lynn Blanchard
Test Kitchen Product Supervisor	Maryellyn Krantz

VICE PRESIDENT, PUBLISHING DIRECTOR
WILLIAM R. REED

Consumer Product Associate Marketing Director	Steve Swanson
Business Director	Christy Light
Business Manager	Jie Lin
Production Director	Douglas M. Johnston
Books Production Managers	Rick von Holdt, Pam Kvitne, Marjorie J. Schenkelberg

BETTER HOMES AND GARDENS® MAGAZINE

Editor in Chief	Karol DeWulf Nickell
Executive Editor	John Riha
Managing Editor	Lamont D. Olson
Creative Director	Bradford W.S. Hong
Art Director	Michael D. Belknap
Entertaining Editor	Nancy Wall Hopkins
Nutrition Editor	Jeanne Ambrose
Associate Editors	Stephen J. Exel, Richard Swearinger
Editorial Assistants	Anna Anderson, Karen Pollock

MEREDITH PUBLISHING GROUP

President	Stephen M. Lacy
President, Magazine Group	Jack Griffin
Executive Vice President, Publishing Group	Jerry Kaplan
Corporate Solutions	Michael Brownstein
Creative Services	Ellen de Lathouder
Manufacturing	Bruce Heston
Consumer Marketing	Karla Jeffries
Finance and Administration	Max Runciman

CHAIRMAN AND CHIEF EXECUTIVE OFFICER
WILLIAM T. KERR

IN MEMORIAM   E.T. MEREDITH III (1933-2003)

Better Homes and Gardens® Annual Recipes 2003™ is published by Family Food Collection™, Publishing Group of Meredith Corp.,
1716 Locust St., Des Moines, IA 50309–3023.

ISSN: 1083-4451   ISBN: 0-696-21622-1

The Recipe Center at *www.bhg.com/siprecipe* contains more than 10,000 recipes and tips,
all tested in the Better Homes and Gardens® Test Kitchen.

As always, our seal assures you that every recipe in *Better Homes and Gardens® Annual Recipes 2003* has been
tested in the *Better Homes and Gardens®* Test Kitchen. This means that each recipe is practical and reliable,
and meets our high standards of taste appeal. We guarantee your satisfaction with this book for as long as you own it.

NEW YEAR, NEW STYLE

Polka-Dot Angel Food Cupcakes
page 105

With this 2003 edition, our Better Homes and Gardens® Test Kitchen is celebrating 75 years of cooking America's best-loved recipes. That's right—first your grandmother, then your mother, and now you can make our foolproof recipes in your kitchen and know that your family will love them because we made them here first! In *Better Homes and Gardens® Annual Recipes 2003*, you get absolutely every single recipe published in *Better Homes and Gardens®* magazine during 2003 and more, over 400 recipes in all! You'll also find:

Test Kitchen Favorites: As an extra bonus in celebration of our Test Kitchen's 75th anniversary, we've included many of our favorite recipes from previous years. These recipes, indexed under Test Kitchen Favorites, all come from the newly released *Better Homes and Gardens® Test Kitchen Favorites* cookbook, available nationwide.

Prizewinning recipes: The top winners from our monthly Prize Tested Recipes® contest are featured together in one big section beginning on page 256. And, like last year, you have all of the Honor Roll winners too—outstanding recipes from our contest that have never before been published!

Low-fat recipes and nutrition information: The low-fat symbol marks recipes that have 3 or fewer grams of fat per every hundred calories. To help you plan balanced family meals, every recipe has nutrition information. To find out how we calculate that, turn to page 335.

Preparation times and emergency substitutions: Look for recipes that fit your schedule by checking the preparation times with each recipe. And if you can't find something on your shelves, turn to our handy Emergency Substitutions chart on page 336.

Menu ideas: Throughout our month-by-month story section, you'll find deliciously flexible menus to suit the season and your lifestyle. For special-occasion menus you can serve any time of the year, plus low-fat menus, turn to page 306.

contents
2003

192

161

January

WITH GET-TOGETHERS RANGING FROM INTIMATE TO GRAND, RING IN THIS NEW YEAR IN STYLISH SIMPLICITY.

Simple Gatherings

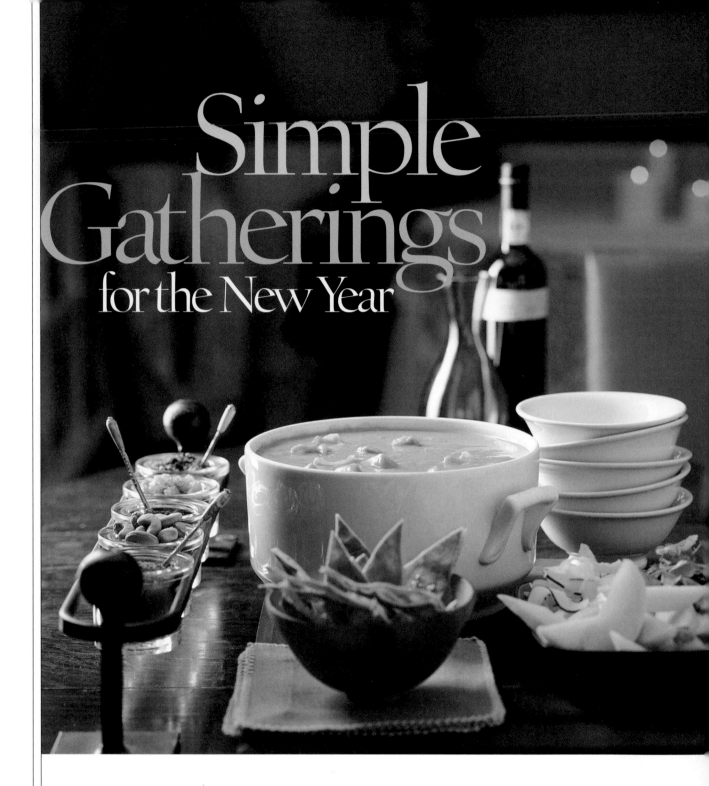

Simple Gatherings
for the New Year

KEEP THE FOOD EASY AND THE CONVERSATION LIVELY, AND THE MOOD WILL BE DELICIOUS. SERVE ONE STAR DISH TO ANCHOR THE GATHERING, THEN SURROUND IT WITH PROVOCATIVE ACCOMPANIMENTS. HERE ARE FOUR EASY IDEAS THAT INVITE EVERYONE TO DIG IN.

Soup's on!

The most memorable casual occasions often start with "Come on over." With the right menu, you can count on these friendly gatherings to be remembered for years ahead. The trick to impromptu parties is keeping them simple: White everyday dinnerware looks comfortable in any setting; layer on a touch of color with linens or tumblers. Advance prep keeps stress levels low. Make a pot of Sweet Potato Chowder ahead of time. The red curry, lemon grass, and coconut flavors of India put a spicy perspective on this warming winter party starter.

Sweet Potato Chowder

Sweet Potato Chowder

Sweet Potato Chowder beckons guests to a comfy-cozy night. They can top off mini bowls of this chunky soup appetizer as they wish—by sweetening it with sliced mango, coconut, and golden raisins; strengthening it with turmeric, cilantro, or roasted unsalted cashews; or sharpening it with paprika or toasted cumin seeds.

PREP: 30 minutes   **COOK:** 20 minutes

1 large onion, chopped (1 cup)	2 14-oz. cans chicken broth
2 Tbsp. cooking oil	1 14-oz. can unsweetened coconut milk
2 cloves garlic, minced	1 2-inch piece fresh lemon grass
1 tsp. red curry paste or 2 to 3 tsp. curry powder	2 tsp. grated fresh ginger (optional)
6 medium sweet potatoes (about 3 lb.), peeled and cut into 3/4-inch pieces (about 7 cups)	1/4 tsp. white pepper
	1/8 tsp. salt
	1 recipe Pita Crisps (below)

1. In a 4-quart Dutch oven cook onion in hot oil over medium heat for 3 minutes, stirring occasionally. Add garlic and curry paste; cook for 3 to 5 minutes more or until onion is tender, stirring occasionally. Add sweet potatoes, chicken broth, coconut milk, lemon grass, and ginger; bring to boiling. Reduce heat. Simmer, covered, for 10 to 15 minutes or until sweet potatoes are tender. Cool slightly. Discard lemon grass.

2. Remove half of the mixture (about 4 cups) from the Dutch oven. In small batches, place mixture in a blender container or food processor bowl. Cover; blend until smooth. Return pureed mixture to soup mixture in pot. Add pepper and salt; heat through. Serve with Pita Crisps. Makes 12 appetizer servings.

PITA CRISPS: Preheat oven to 350° F. In a skillet combine 1 teaspoon each cumin seeds, mustard seeds, and black caraway seeds. Heat over low heat for 2 to 4 minutes or until fragrant, stirring occasionally. Cut 2 pita bread rounds into 8 wedges each. Spread in a single layer on a cookie sheet. Brush with melted butter. Sprinkle with toasted seeds; press seeds lightly. Bake for 8 to 10 minutes or until crisp.

Each serving: 179 cal., 9 g total fat (6 g sat. fat), 0 mg chol., 271 mg sodium, 22 g carbo., 3 g fiber, 3 g pro. Daily Values: 280% vit. A, 22% vit. C, 2% calcium, 5% iron.

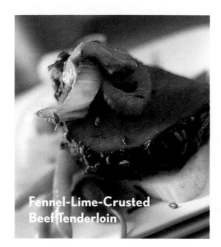

Fennel-Lime-Crusted
Beef Tenderloin

So glad you're here

Dressed to impress, and looking like it took hours of preparation, this elegant Fennel-Lime-Crusted Beef Tenderloin hors d'oeuvre can be made up to two days ahead. The chilled tenderloin sits atop a bed of crisp green beans. For crunch, offer cucumber spears dressed with gingered vinaigrette and a few graceful strands of chive. Other easy condiments include fresh green onion, sliced fresh fennel, green peppercorn mustard, and extra-large caperberries.

NEW YEAR'S COCKTAIL PARTY

Roasted Mushrooms with Fresh Sage *(page 16)*
Baguette slices or assorted small toasts and crackers
Fennel-Lime-Crusted Beef Tenderloin *(right)*
Orange-Champagne Cakes *(page 15)*
Assorted cheeses, such as Morbier, Stilton, and Manchego
Assorted fruits, including grapes, dried figs, and clementine oranges
Champagne or other sparkling wine, such as Italian Prosecco

Fennel-Lime-Crusted Beef Tenderloin

A rub of fennel seeds, lime peel, tarragon, and lime-infused olive oil crusts a beef tenderloin for this very special cocktail party dish.

PREP: 30 minutes   **ROAST:** 45 minutes   **STAND:** 10 minutes

8	Tbsp. lime-infused olive oil or olive oil (½ cup)	1	lb. peeled onions, such as cipollini, pearl, or boiling onions; or yellow onions cut into 8 wedges
¼	cup fennel seeds		
¼	cup snipped fresh tarragon		
¼	cup fresh lime peel (from about 5 or 6 limes)	3	cups sliced fennel strips
		½	cup dry red wine
2	tsp. ground black pepper	1	lb. fresh green beans, trimmed
½	tsp. salt		
1	3-lb. center-cut beef tenderloin	2	small fresh limes, halved

1. In a bowl combine 6 tablespoons of the oil, fennel seeds, tarragon, lime peel, pepper, and salt; stir well. Coat the tenderloin with seed mixture. Place meat on a nonmetal tray; cover loosely with foil. Refrigerate for 30 minutes or up to 1 hour.

2. Preheat oven to 425° F. Place roast on a rack in a shallow roasting pan. Return any coating left on tray to meat. Insert an oven-safe meat thermometer into center of meat. In a bowl toss together onions and 1 tablespoon of the remaining olive oil. Place onions on half of the roasting pan alongside meat. Roast, uncovered, for 30 minutes. Meanwhile, toss together fennel and remaining oil. Stir onions; add fennel to other half of roasting pan alongside meat. Roast for 15 to 20 minutes more or until thermometer registers 135° F for medium-rare doneness.

3. Remove roast from oven. Transfer roast to cutting board; cover with foil. Let stand 10 to 15 minutes (temperature should register 145° F for medium-rare). Wrap roast tightly in plastic wrap; refrigerate until serving time. Meanwhile, transfer onions and fennel to separate bowls. Cover tightly; refrigerate until serving time.

4. Place roasting pan on stove top over low heat. Add red wine, stirring constantly to loosen browned bits. Transfer sauce to bowl. Cover; refrigerate until serving time.

5. Cook green beans in a small amount of boiling salted water about 5 minutes or until crisp-tender. Drain. Cover; chill until serving time.

6. To serve, toss beans with reserved sauce; arrange on a platter. Slice tenderloin into thin slices; arrange on beans. Serve with roasted onion and fennel and lime halves. Makes 12 appetizer servings.

Each serving: 288 cal., 17 g total fat (4 g sat. fat), 57 mg chol., 165 mg sodium, 7 g carbo., 8 g fiber, 25 g pro. Daily Values: 2% vit. A, 15 vit. C, 6% calcium, 21% iron.

BY STEPHEN EXEL. PHOTOGRAPHS: COLLEEN DUFFLEY. FOOD STYLIST: BROOKE LEONARD.

Fennel-Lime-Crusted Beef Tenderloin

Fresh chives *(far left)* accent cucumber spears to go along with Fennel-Lime-Crusted Beef Tenderloin. Purchased green peppercorn mustard *(left)* is a spicy and colorful complement.

Horseradish-Sour Cream Dip

Relaxed, easy entertaining

Serve Roasted Mushrooms with Fresh Sage for a homey get-together where settling in for plenty of conversation is expected. Add even more flavors and textures with Horseradish-Sour Cream Dip and Red Pepper and Black Olive Tapenade. Serve it all with red endive leaves for scooping and a wedge of crumbly pecorino cheese.

Roasted Mushrooms with Fresh Sage
PREP: 30 minutes   **ROAST:** 30 minutes

1 recipe Roasted Red Pepper and Black Olive Tapenade (below)	$\frac{1}{2}$ tsp. salt
	$\frac{1}{2}$ tsp. ground black pepper
3 lb. assorted mushrooms, such as chanterelle, shiitake, button, crimini, brown and alba clamshell, morel, and/or oyster*	Dry sherry, port, or brandy
	$\frac{1}{4}$ cup fresh sage leaves, coarsely torn (leaving small leaves whole)
3 heads garlic	1 recipe Horseradish-Sour Cream Dip (below)
3 Tbsp. butter, melted	
3 Tbsp. olive oil	

1. Prepare Roasted Red Pepper and Black Olive Tapenade; set aside. Preheat oven to 450° F. Remove stems from shiitake and oyster mushrooms. Brush any dirt off mushrooms, leaving mushrooms whole (should have about 16 cups). Remove loose outer skins of garlic heads. Trim stem ends to expose cloves; break apart cloves.

2. Place mushrooms and garlic in a large roasting pan. Combine melted butter and olive oil; drizzle over mushrooms and garlic. Toss to coat. Sprinkle with salt and pepper. Roast about 30 minutes or until mushrooms are tender and garlic cloves are soft, stirring twice.

3. Remove roasted mushrooms and garlic from pan; place on a platter. Splash with sherry; sprinkle with fresh sage. Prepare Horseradish-Sour Cream Dip. Serve mushrooms with dip, tapenade, and assorted dippers. Makes 8 to 10 appetizer servings.

ROASTED RED PEPPER AND BLACK OLIVE TAPENADE: In a bowl combine $\frac{1}{2}$ cup coarsely chopped pitted ripe olives, $\frac{1}{3}$ cup coarsely chopped roasted red sweet pepper, 2 tablespoons olive oil, 1 tablespoon snipped fresh rosemary, 2 teaspoons snipped fresh oregano, and $1\frac{1}{2}$ teaspoons finely shredded lemon peel. Let stand at room temperature for 2 to 6 hours to allow flavors to blend. Serve at room temperature.

HORSERADISH-SOUR CREAM DIP: Combine one 8-ounce carton dairy sour cream and 2 to 3 tablespoons prepared horseradish; top with coarsely crushed pink peppercorns and snipped rosemary leaves.

*NOTE: Wild mushrooms are available at gourmet and specialty markets. The clamshell mushroom is distinguished by its crunchy texture even after cooking.

Each serving: 254 cal., 23 g total fat (8 g sat. fat), 25 mg chol., 301 mg sodium, 11 g carbo., 2 g fiber, 7 g pro. Daily Values: 9% vit. A, 37% vit. C, 8% calcium, 9% iron.

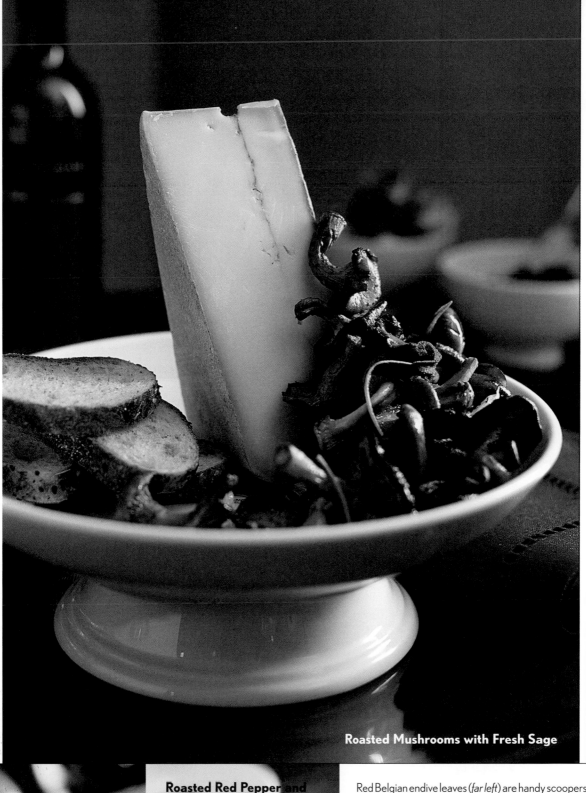

Roasted Mushrooms with Fresh Sage

Roasted Red Pepper and Black Olive Tapenade

Red Belgian endive leaves *(far left)* are handy scoopers for Roasted Mushrooms with Fresh Sage. Serve the mushrooms with Roasted Red Pepper and Black Olive Tapenade *(left)* and Horseradish-Sour Cream Dip.

Orange-Champagne Cakes

Choose an assortment of hard and soft cheeses *(far left)* as partners to polenta-based individual Orange-Champagne Cakes. Then drizzle a favorite fruit liqueur *(left)* over the small cakes to add a note of concentrated fruit.

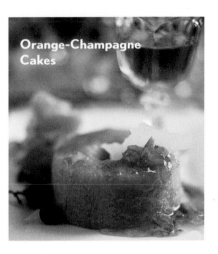

Orange-Champagne
Cakes

Orange-Champagne Cakes

A tumble of individual Orange-Champagne Cakes perches on a pedestal with room left over for fruity indulgences. The cakes' tender crumb stands alone, or provides a good foundation for piling on shards of piquant cheese or a spoonful of ginger-zapped mascarpone and marmalade.

PREP: 30 minutes **BAKE:** 30 minutes **COOL:** 10 minutes + 1 hour

1½	cups polenta cornmeal or yellow cornmeal	3	cups finely ground almonds
1	cup all-purpose flour	1	Tbsp. finely shredded orange peel
2	tsp. baking powder		
⅛	tsp. salt	1½	cups champagne or sparkling wine
1½	cups unsalted butter, softened		
		¼	cup sugar
2	cups sugar		Finely shredded orange peel (optional)
6	eggs		
1	cup orange juice		

1. Preheat oven to 325° F. Grease and flour two small angel cake pans or twelve 4-inch muffin cups; set aside. In a bowl combine polenta, flour, baking powder, and salt; set aside.

2. In a large mixing bowl beat butter with an electric mixer on medium to high speed for 30 seconds. Add the 2 cups sugar; beat until combined. Add eggs, beat until combined. Beat in orange juice (mixture may appear curdled). Beat in polenta mixture just until combined. Fold in ground almonds and 1 tablespoon finely shredded orange peel.

3. Spoon batter into pans (about ⅔ cup batter each). Bake about 30 minutes or until a wooden pick inserted near the centers comes out clean. Cool in pans on wire racks for 10 minutes.

4. Meanwhile, in a saucepan combine champagne and the ¼ cup sugar. Bring to boiling, stirring to dissolve sugar. Reduce heat; simmer, uncovered, about 10 minutes or until mixture is reduced to 1 cup.

5. Remove cakes from pans. Transfer cakes to a large platter, placing cakes bottoms up. Prick cakes with wooden toothpick. Carefully spoon or brush champagne syrup onto cakes. Immediately cover cakes with plastic wrap; cool completely. Serve cakes at room temperature. If desired, garnish with additional orange peel. Makes 12 cakes or 24 servings.

Each serving: 358 cal., 22 g total fat (9 g sat. fat), 85 mg chol., 64 mg sodium, 34 g carbo., 3 g fiber, 7 g pro. Daily Values: 12% vit. A, 9% vit. C, 8% calcium, 9% iron.

Cause for celebration

Celebrate simply, but with spirit. A late-evening dessert party needs only one star: Orange-Champagne Cakes. To serve, add Tuscan touches with a bunch of grapes, dried figs, walnuts, clementine oranges, and honey. Match sweet and savory by adding chopped crystallized ginger to softened mascarpone and topping it with orange marmalade, then pair it with grand cheeses, including a wedge of Parmesan. Finally, sprinkle the cake with a favorite liqueur, such as Grand Marnier, B&B, or cassis, and orange Muscatel dessert wine.

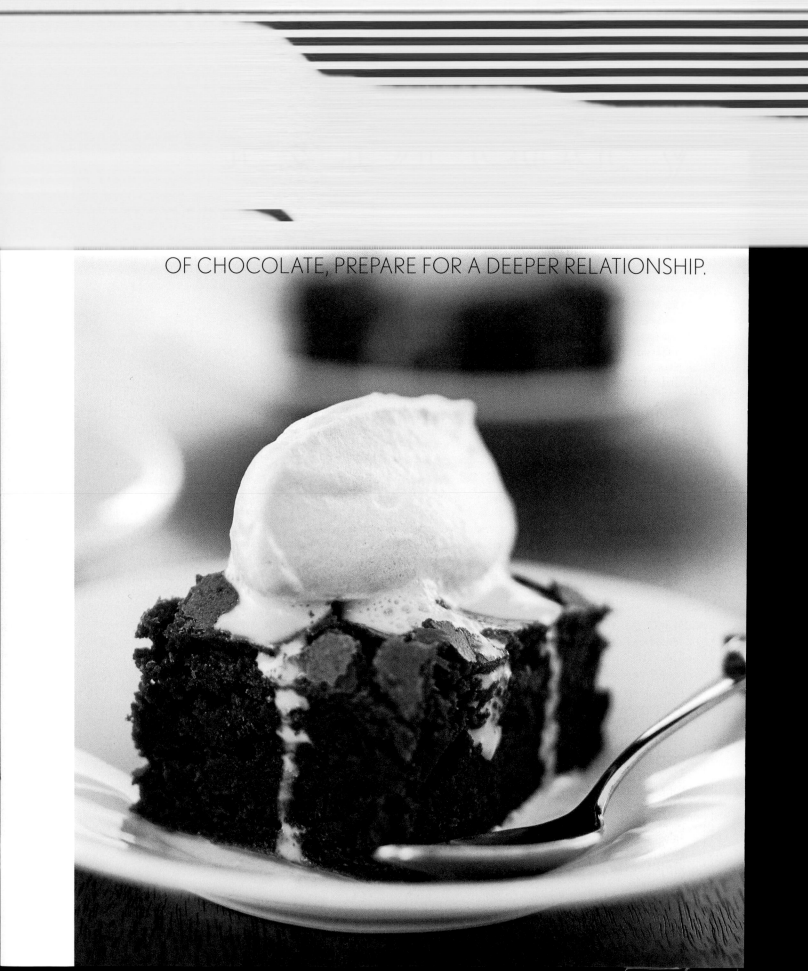
OF CHOCOLATE, PREPARE FOR A DEEPER RELATIONSHIP.

A Great Time for Chocolate

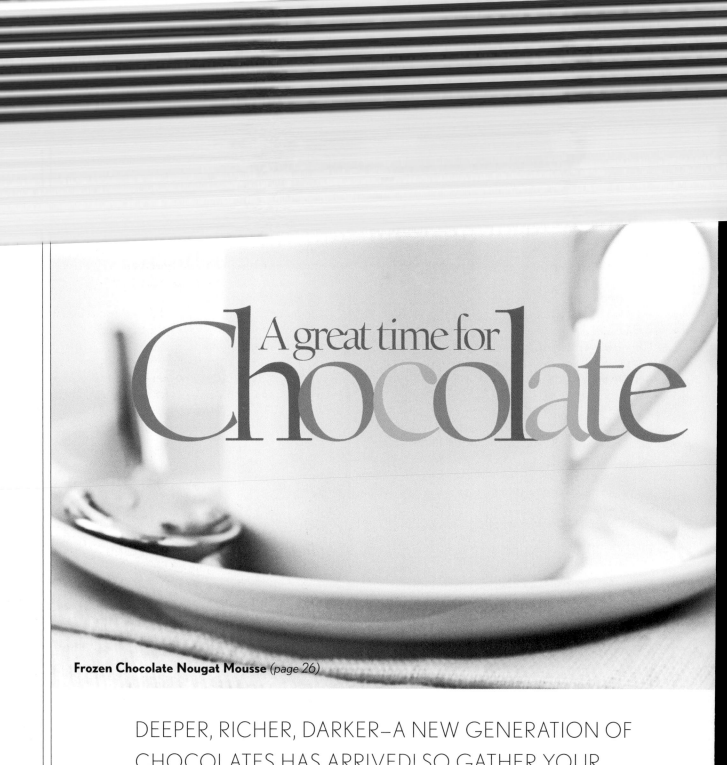

A great time for Chocolate

Frozen Chocolate Nougat Mousse *(page 26)*

DEEPER, RICHER, DARKER–A NEW GENERATION OF
CHOCOLATES HAS ARRIVED! SO GATHER YOUR
FRIENDS AND HOST A TASTING PARTY. IT PROMISES
TO BE ABOUT THE MOST FUN ANYONE'S TASTE BUDS
WILL HAVE ALL YEAR.

Double-Deck Chocolate Custard

Displaying two-toned chocolate splendor, this dessert looks best when served in a parade of small, mismatched glasses.

Prep: 15 minutes **Cool:** 5 minutes **Chill:** 2 + 4 hours

2	cups whipping cream	1	tsp. vanilla
3	oz. 30- to 40-percent-cocoa milk chocolate, chopped	3	oz. 60- to 70-percent-cocoa dark chocolate or bittersweet chocolate, chopped
6	Tbsp. sugar		
4	egg yolks		

1. In a small heavy saucepan combine 1 cup of the whipping cream, the 3 ounces milk chocolate, and 3 tablespoons of the sugar. Cook and stir over medium heat about 5 minutes or until mixture comes to a full boil and thickens. (If chocolate flecks remain, use a wire whisk to beat mixture until blended.)

2. In a medium bowl beat 2 of the egg yolks until blended. Gradually stir all of the hot mixture into the beaten egg yolks; stir in 1/2 teaspoon of the vanilla. If using glasses, cool slightly. Divide chocolate mixture evenly into 8 small glasses, dishes, pot de crème cups, or ramekins. Cover and chill for 2 hours.

3. Make second layer of dessert using the same method with the remaining whipping cream, the 3 ounces dark chocolate, remaining sugar, egg yolks, and vanilla. Divide dark chocolate mixture among chilled glasses. Cover and chill about 4 hours or until firm. Makes 8 servings.

Each serving: 384 cal., 32 g total fat (17 g sat. fat), 191 mg chol., 37 mg sodium, 23 g carbo., 1 g fiber, 4 g pro. Daily Values: 21% vit. A, 1% vit. C, 8% calcium, 4% iron.

Double-Deck Chocolate Custard

Start light

We live in tempting times, the very heart of a chocolate renaissance. Chocolatiers all over the world are turning out slabs, bars, and squares that manage to embody sublime, but surprisingly different, tastes. A single bite may reveal a refined, subdued sweetness that seems to melt into earthier flavors springing from cocoa's origins deep in equatorial jungles.

Experience this transformation by hosting a chocolate tasting party for friends. Gather the four or five people who've been nicest to you lately, and serve them some of the desserts on these pages, along with samples of the chocolate that went into each. It's just like a wine or cheese tasting. Start by trying mild chocolates, then move up the scale to a finale of the darkest, richest ones.

41-percent-cocoa milk chocolate

38-percent-cocoa milk chocolate

FAMILIAR JOYS

To begin your tasting, offer two or three samples of milk chocolate from different makers *(above)*; alongside, set out Double-Deck Chocolate Custard. It beckons with a cloudlike layer of milk chocolate perched atop or nestled below a darker, bittersweet layer. Milk chocolate is notable for such great flavors as caramel, soda-fountain chocolate malt, chocolate milk, brown sugar, and vanilla.

fruity wine or two on hand. And don't leave out one of the great joys in life—icy glasses of milk served with a plate of Milk Chocolate Mini Cookies *(page 26)*.

Take time to break off samples of raw chocolate. The sensation of pure pleasure melting on the tongue will delight your guests. They will experience surprising flavors such as cherry, jasmine, rose, almond, and raisin.

All the flavor nuances will make an invitation to your chocolate-tasting party a thing to toast.

61-percent-cocoa bittersweet chocolate

62-percent-cocoa bittersweet chocolate

NUTTY, EARTHY

When your tasting gets to midpoint, set up small plates with two or three varieties of medium (around 60 percent) chocolate. As you sample these chocolates, you'll begin entering unfamiliar territory. These are the woodsy, nuttier, darker chocolates that adults often prefer. This variety is used in these desserts: Simple Fudge *(right)*, Ultimate Chocolate Sundaes *(page 29)*, Chocolate Sherbet *(page 30)*, and Frozen Chocolate Nougat Mousse *(page 26)*.

1 tsp. vanilla
Unsweetened cocoa powder (optional)

1. Line an 8×8×2-inch baking pan with foil, extending foil over edges of pan. Butter foil; set aside.

2. Butter sides of a heavy 2-quart saucepan. (Without a heavy pan, the mixture will overcook and separate.) In saucepan combine sugar, cream, and 1/2 cup butter. Cook and stir over medium-high heat for 2 to 3 minutes or until mixture boils. Reduce heat to medium; continue cooking for 10 minutes. Boil slowly and stir constantly (mixture should not brown).

3. Remove pan from heat. Add marshmallows, chocolate, nuts (if desired), and vanilla. Stir until mixture is melted and combined. Beat by hand for 1 minute.

4. Spread fudge evenly in prepared pan. Score into squares while warm. Cover and chill for 3 to 4 hours or until firm. When firm, use foil to lift from pan. Cut fudge into squares, then cut each in half to make triangles. Store tightly covered in the refrigerator for up to 1 month. If desired, lightly sift cocoa powder over fudge before serving. Makes about 2 pounds (64 pieces).

Each piece: 53 cal., 3 g total fat (2 g sat. fat), 5 mg chol., 19 mg sodium, 8 g carbo., 0 g fiber, 0 g pro. Daily Values: 1% iron.

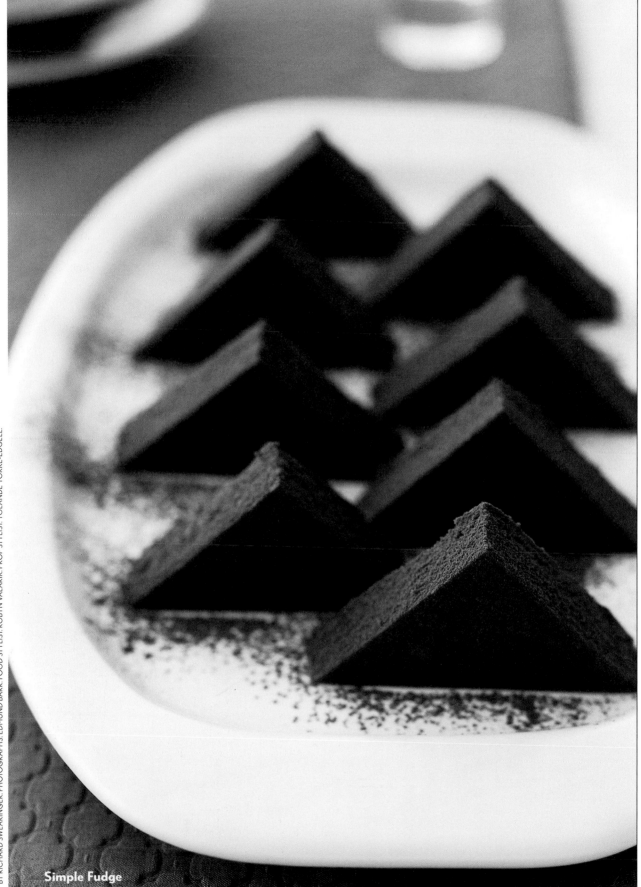

BY RICHARD SWEARINGER. PHOTOGRAPHS: EDMUND BARR. FOOD STYLIST: ROBYN VALARIK. PROP STYLIST: YOLANDE YORKE-EDGELL.

Simple Fudge

Dark Chocolate Torte

Dark Chocolate Torte
PREP: 45 minutes **BAKE:** 30 minutes **COOL:** 2 hours **CHILL:** 30 minutes

5 oz. 90- to 99-percent-cocoa chocolate or unsweetened chocolate, coarsely chopped	6 egg yolks
	1½ tsp. vanilla
	1¼ cups sugar
	¾ cup strawberry-balsamic jam*
½ cup butter	or apricot preserves
6 egg whites	1 recipe Chocolate Ganache (below)
⅔ cup all purpose flour	
½ tsp. baking powder	

1. In a medium saucepan melt chocolate and butter over low heat; transfer to a bowl and cool completely. In a large mixing bowl let egg whites stand at room temperature for 30 minutes. Grease and lightly flour a 9-inch springform pan. In a small bowl stir together the flour and baking powder. Set aside.

2. Preheat oven to 350° F. Stir egg yolks and vanilla into the cooled chocolate mixture (mixture will become stiffer); set aside.

3. Beat egg whites with an electric mixer on medium speed until soft peaks form (tips curl). Gradually add the sugar, about 1 tablespoon at a time, beating on high speed about 4 minutes or until stiff peaks form (tips stand straight).

4. Fold about one-third of the egg white mixture into chocolate mixture. Fold chocolate mixture into remaining egg white mixture. Sift about one-third of the flour mixture over egg mixture; gently fold in. Repeat twice, sifting and folding in one-third of the flour mixture at a time. Spread batter into prepared pan. Bake about 30 minutes or until wooden toothpick inserted near center comes out clean. Cool cake completely in pan on wire rack.

5. Meanwhile, stir jam to thin; set aside. Prepare Chocolate Ganache; set aside. Loosen cake from sides of pan; remove sides. Carefully remove bottom of pan from cake by loosening the cake with a knife.

6. To assemble, cut cake horizontally into 2 even layers. Place bottom layer, cut side up, on a wire rack set over waxed paper. Spread jam onto top of this layer. Top with second layer, cut side down. Pour Chocolate Ganache over torte, spreading to glaze top and sides. (If glaze drips onto the waxed paper, spoon it onto torte.) Chill cake on rack about 30 minutes or until glaze sets. Carefully transfer cake to a platter. Makes 14 to 16 servings.

CHOCOLATE GANACHE: Coarsely chop 6 ounces 70-percent-cocoa chocolate or semisweet or bittersweet chocolate; set aside. In a medium saucepan bring ½ cup whipping cream to boiling over medium-high heat; remove from heat. Add chocolate (do not stir). Let stand 5 minutes. Stir until smooth. Cool 10 minutes.

*NOTE: Find strawberry-balsamic jam at kitchen shops. Or combine ¾ cup strawberry jam and 1 tablespoon balsamic vinegar.

Each serving: 375 cal., 21 g total fat (12 g sat. fat), 122 mg chol., 122 mg sodium, 44 g carbo., 3 g fiber, 6 g pro. Daily Values: 11% vit. A, 3% vit. C, 4% calcium, 11% iron.

Finish dark

At some point during the party, give your guests a little overview on what they're tasting. Here's a short course:

Artisanal chocolatiers follow the milk, semisweet, and bittersweet labeling that larger chocolate makers use, but artisans also denote the percentage of cocoa and cocoa butter (or cacao). The higher the number, the less sweet and the more bitter and intense the chocolate. Cocoa percentages range from about 30 to 45 percent in milk chocolate to 50 to 60 percent for semisweet. Above that is bittersweet—from 61 to 80 percent. Unsweetened is 99 percent cocoa.

A big bite of 85-percent-cocoa chocolate is overwhelming, but a tiny piece melting on your tongue is a fun way to discover chocolate's complexity. These chocolates have little or no sugar and offer such aromas and flavors as cedar and coffee. The effect is an intense, lingering, but not unpleasant, bitter sensation.

85-percent-cocoa dark chocolate

85-percent-cocoa dark chocolate

BITTERSWEET AND BEYOND

Now for the tasting finale. Bring out the stoutest chocolates of all—the really dark chocolates. Offer samples of two types for tasting, followed by one last dessert. In Vienna, the locals sit at little marble tables in cafes drinking tiny cups of coffee and eating a low, dense layer cake very much like this Dark Chocolate Torte. The taste is subtle but irresistible. It is made with the most intensely complex of all chocolates: unsweetened.

bittersweet chocolate,
finely chopped

1/4 cup milk

3/4 tsp. unflavored gelatin

4 egg yolks, slightly beaten

1 1/4 cups whipping cream

1/2 tsp. vanilla

1/3 cup chopped Italian
nougat candy or almond
toffee bits

3 1 bsp. butter,
softened

1. Place finely chopped chocolate in a large bowl; set aside. In a small saucepan combine milk and gelatin. Let stand for 5 minutes. Add egg yolks, sugar, and 1/2 cup of the whipping cream. Cook and stir over medium heat about 5 minutes or until mixture coats a metal spoon (160° F).

2. Pour mixture over finely chopped chocolate. Let stand for 5 minutes. Gently stir to incorporate chocolate. Stir in vanilla. Place in freezer; chill for 30 minutes or until mixture thickens and cools, stirring after 15 minutes.

3. Meanwhile, place six 3-ounce small cups or soufflé dishes on a tray (or use 4-ounce dessert dishes and do not add collars). To prepare collars, cut six 12×6-inch pieces of foil. Fold lengthwise into thirds to form 12×2-inch strips. Wrap each collar tightly around the cups with one edge extending 1 inch above the top of the cups. Secure with tape. Place cups in freezer to chill.

4. Meanwhile, beat chocolate mixture with an electric mixer on high speed about 3 minutes or until light and fluffy. In a small bowl beat the remaining 3/4 cup whipping cream until soft peaks form (tips curl). Gently fold whipped cream and nougat candy or toffee bits into chocolate mixture. Divide chocolate mixture evenly among the chilled cups, filling 1/2 to 1 inch over the top of each dish, if collar is present. Cover and freeze for 3 to 24 hours or until firm.

5. To serve, remove tape and gently peel away collars. Let mousse stand for 10 to 15 minutes at room temperature before serving. Makes 6 servings.

Each serving: 395 cal., 29 g total fat (16 g sat. fat), 212 mg chol., 0 mg sodium, 33 g carbo., 1 g fiber, 5 g pro. Daily Values: 20% vit. A, 1% vit. C, 8% calcium, 5% iron.

1. In a medium bowl combine flour, baking powder, and salt; set aside.

2. In a small heavy saucepan heat the chocolate over low heat until melted, stirring constantly; set aside.

3. In a medium mixing bowl beat butter with electric mixer on medium speed for 30 seconds. Beat in sugar until fluffy. Beat in melted chocolate, egg, and vanilla until combined.

4. Gradually beat in the flour mixture. Divide dough into 4 equal portions. Wrap each portion in plastic wrap. Chill in the freezer for 20 to 30 minutes or until firm enough to handle. (Or, chill in the refrigerator for 1 hour.)

5. Preheat oven to 350° F. Removing 1 portion of dough from freezer at a time, roll each portion into a 10-inch-long roll.* Cut each roll crosswise into 1/4-inch-thick slices. Place slices 1 inch apart on ungreased cookie sheets. Bake for 9 to 10 minutes or until edges are set. Let cool on cookie sheet for 2 minutes. Gently remove from sheets (cookies will be brittle). Transfer to a wire rack to cool completely.

6. If desired, spread 1/2 teaspoon of frosting on half of the cookies; top with remaining cookies. Serve the same day. To store, place plain cookies in airtight containers at room temperature for up to 3 days or freeze in a freezer container for up to 3 months. Thaw, then fill, if desired. Makes 72 sandwich cookies or 144 unfrosted cookies.

MILK CHOCOLATE-SOUR CREAM FROSTING: In a medium saucepan melt 3 ounces chopped 30- to 40-percent-cocoa chocolate or milk chocolate and 2 tablespoons butter over low heat, stirring frequently. Cool for 5 minutes. Stir in 1/4 cup dairy sour cream. Gradually stir in 1 to 1 1/4 cups sifted powdered sugar until spreadable.

*NOTE: It helps to place the dough on a sheet of waxed paper and use the paper to help shape the roll. If dough becomes too sticky, return it to freezer for a few minutes.

Each sandwich cookie: 45 cal., 2 g total fat (1 g sat. fat), 6 mg chol., 21 mg sodium, 6 g carbo., 0 g fiber, 0 g pro. Daily Values: 1% vit. A, 1% calcium, 1% iron.

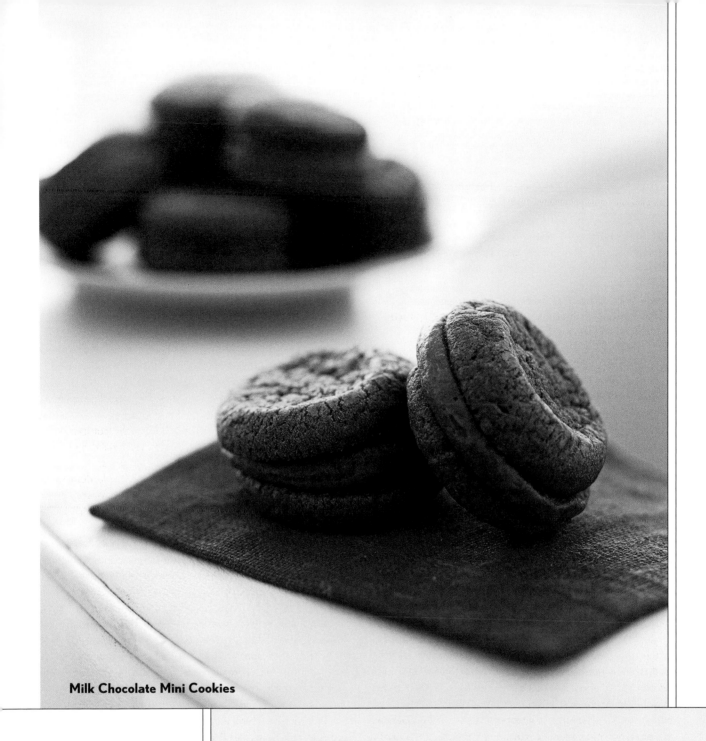

Milk Chocolate Mini Cookies

THE ART OF THE BUNNY SNIFF

Here's how to get the most out of your chocolate-tasting experience.

LOOK: Chocolate should be shiny, but sometimes has a slightly grayish cast. This is called "bloom" and indicates that the chocolate has experienced temperature fluctuations. Luckily, bloom doesn't usually affect flavor. Examine the color of chocolate, but don't let hue be your only guide; darkness varies by the type of beans used and how they're processed.

BUNNY SNIFFS: Break off a small piece and rub gently until the chocolate just begins to soften. Then take tiny sniffs. In addition to chocolate, you'll discover such aromas as apple pie, flowers, caramel, citrus, berries, grass, and cedar.

TASTE: Pop the piece into your mouth, but don't chew! Let it melt on your tongue for 20 seconds. Some of the flavors you'll encounter include vanilla, fruit, and nuts. Other words that might come to mind: fudgy, smoky, malty, earthy, and tart. Savor the balance of nuttiness, acidity, sweetness, and bitterness.

TEXTURE: Is it smooth, velvety, creamy, soft? Or is it a little gritty? All these textures can be wonderful in chocolate because of the way they interact with the flavors. Smooth chocolates emphasize the fruity, flowery flavors, while gritty chocolates bring out the earthy, nutty side.

Ultimate Chocolate Sundaes

Chocolate-Crusted Chocolate Tarts

STORING CHOCOLATE

- Chocolate must be stored below 70° F—which means in your refrigerator or freezer, especially in summer. It has to be tightly wrapped and kept away from strong-smelling foods.

- When you remove it from the fridge, leave it in its wrapping until it's at room temperature. Water condensing on the surface can cause problems in melting and cooking.

- Dark chocolate candy will keep in the refrigerator for up to one year; milk chocolate will keep for six months. Filled chocolate candy can be stored for up to three months. All chocolate will keep in the freezer up to one year.

Chocolate-Crusted Chocolate Tarts

Work carefully to get an even layer of crust in the muffin tins.

Prep: 20 minutes **Bake:** 25 minutes

1	recipe Chocolate-Hazelnut Tart Shells (below)
10	to 10½ oz. 85-percent-cocoa chocolate or bittersweet chocolate, finely chopped
¾	cup whipping cream
½	cup milk
3	Tbsp. flavored honey (raspberry, cinnamon, or ginger)
1	egg
	Halved or chopped hazelnuts (filberts) (optional)

1. Prepare Chocolate-Hazelnut Tart Shells; set aside to cool.

2. Preheat oven to 325° F. In a 1-quart casserole combine chocolate, whipping cream, and milk. Microwave, uncovered, on 100 percent power (high) for 3 to 4 minutes or until chocolate is melted and mixture is smooth, stirring once each minute. Stir in honey. (Or, place chocolate in a medium bowl. Set aside. In a small saucepan combine cream and milk. Bring to boiling. Pour over chocolate. Stir until chocolate is melted. Stir in honey.)

3. In another medium bowl beat egg. Gradually stir in hot chocolate mixture. Pour into tart shells.

4. Bake for 25 minutes. Cool slightly on a wire rack. Serve warm. If desired, garnish with nuts. Makes 8 servings.

CHOCOLATE-HAZELNUT TART SHELLS: Preheat oven to 375° F. Lightly coat twelve 2½-inch muffin pans with nonstick cooking spray. In a small bowl stir together 1 cup crushed chocolate wafer crumbs, ⅓ cup ground hazelnuts (filberts), ⅓ cup melted butter, and 1 tablespoon sugar. Press onto the bottom and sides of prepared muffin cups. Bake for 5 minutes. Cool on a wire rack.

Each tart: 378 cal., 28 g total fat (14 g sat. fat), 60 mg chol., 217 mg sodium, 33 g carbo., 3 g fiber, 5 g pro. Daily Values: 11% vit. A, 1% vit. C, 4% calcium, 10% iron.

CHOCOLATE DESSERT TASTING

Double-Deck Chocolate Custard *(page 21)*
Milk Chocolate Mini Cookies *(page 26)*
Chocolate Sherbet *(page 30)*
Dark Chocolate Torte *(page 25)*
Assorted broken pieces of 40- to 80-percent-cocoa chocolate
Cold milk and dark-roast coffee, such as French or Italian roast

Ultimate Chocolate Sundaes

It is essential that the water and chocolate are together from the very beginning of cooking; otherwise, they won't blend properly when heated.

Start to Finish: 30 minutes

8	oz. 65-percent-cocoa chocolate or bittersweet chocolate, coarsely chopped
⅓	cup water
¼	cup sugar
¼	cup pear liqueur or pear nectar
4	small fresh Forelle or Bosc pears (1 lb. total)
3	Tbsp. butter
2	Tbsp. sugar
1	qt. vanilla ice cream

1. For chocolate sauce, in a small saucepan combine chocolate, water, and the ¼ cup sugar. Melt chocolate over low heat, stirring slowly and constantly. Stir in pear liqueur or nectar. Set aside to cool slightly.

2. Peel pears, if desired; cut into halves and remove cores.* Leave stem on one portion, if desired. In a large skillet melt butter. Add pear halves; cook over medium heat about 12 minutes or until brown and tender, turning once. Add the 2 tablespoons sugar, stirring gently until sugar is dissolved and pears are glazed.

3. To assemble, place scoops of ice cream in 8 bowls. Spoon a pear half and some butter mixture around the ice cream in each bowl. Top with the chocolate sauce. Makes 8 servings.

*NOTE: If using large pears, use only 2 pears and cut them into fourths.

Each serving: 538 cal., 33 g total fat (20 g sat. fat), 132 mg chol., 119 mg sodium, 56 g carbo., 3 g fiber, 7 g pro. Daily Values: 19% vit. A, 4% vit. C, 17% calcium, 6% iron.

Dark Chocolate Brownies

Chocolate Sherbet

The chocolate mixture needs to chill overnight in order to freeze properly. What differentiates a sherbet from a sorbet is the use of a milk product—in this case it's cream.

PREP: 25 minutes **CHILL:** overnight **FREEZE:** 30 minutes + 4 hours

6 to 7 oz. 60-percent-cocoa chocolate or bittersweet chocolate, chopped	1/2 cup whipping cream
	1 tsp. vanilla
	Pomegranate seeds
2 cups water	(optional)
2/3 cup sugar	

1. In a medium saucepan stir together chopped chocolate, water, sugar, and whipping cream. Bring to boiling, whisking constantly. Boil gently for 1 minute. Remove from heat; stir in vanilla. Cover and chill overnight.

2. Freeze mixture in a 1-quart ice cream freezer according to manufacturer's directions. Allow to firm up in freezer for 4 hours before serving. To serve, scoop into 12 bowls. If desired, garnish with pomegranate seeds. Makes 12 servings.

Each serving: 157 cal., 9 g total fat (6 g sat. fat), 14 mg chol., 6 mg sodium, 20 g carbo., 1 g fiber, 1 g pro. Daily Values: 3% vit. A, 1% calcium, 3% iron.

Dark Chocolate Brownies

As our recipe demonstrates, it's OK to melt chocolate in a microwave oven. The key is to heat it for a short time, then to stir to complete the melting process.

PREP: 20 minutes **FREEZE:** 3 hours
BAKE: 25 minutes **COOL:** 30 minutes

1 recipe Frozen Coffee Whipped Cream (below)	1 cup granulated sugar
	3/4 cup packed brown sugar
7 oz. 99-percent-cocoa chocolate or unsweetened chocolate, coarsely chopped	2 eggs
	1 tsp. vanilla
	1 1/3 cups all-purpose flour
	1/8 tsp. salt
3/4 cup butter	1/8 tsp. ground cinnamon
1/4 cup water	

1. Prepare Frozen Coffee Whipped Cream. For brownies, lightly grease a 9×9×2-inch baking pan; set pan aside. Preheat oven to 350° F.

2. In a large microwave-safe mixing bowl combine chocolate, butter, and water. Microwave, uncovered, on 100 percent power (high) for 2 to 3 minutes or until butter is melted, stirring once or twice. Remove bowl from microwave oven. Stir until chocolate is completely melted. (Or, combine chocolate, butter, and water in a medium saucepan; cook and stir over low heat until chocolate is melted. Transfer to a mixing bowl.)

3. Beat in granulated sugar and brown sugar with an electric mixer on low to medium speed until combined. Add eggs and vanilla; beat on medium speed for 2 minutes. Add flour, salt, and cinnamon. Beat on low speed until combined. Spread batter in prepared pan.

4. Bake about 25 minutes or until a toothpick inserted near center comes out clean. Cool on a wire rack about 30 minutes (or until brownies hold a cut edge). Cut into bars.

5. To assemble, while brownie is still warm, place a bar on each plate. Top with a scoop of Frozen Coffee Whipped Cream. Makes 20 to 25 brownies.

FROZEN COFFEE WHIPPED CREAM: Chill a medium mixing bowl and the beaters of an electric mixer. In the chilled bowl combine 2/3 cup whipping cream, 4 teaspoons sugar, and 4 teaspoons cooled brewed espresso or 1/2 teaspoon vanilla. Beat on medium speed until soft peaks form (tips curl). Cover and freeze for 2 to 3 hours or until firm. Let stand at room temperature for 10 minutes to soften slightly. Using 2 teaspoons, shape small ovals of frozen whipped cream, dipping spoons into hot water if necessary.

Each brownie with whipped cream: 304 cal., 19 g total fat (10 g sat. fat), 52 mg chol., 121 mg sodium, 35 g carbo., 2 g fiber, and 3 g pro. Daily Values: 9% vit. A, 4% calcium, and 8% iron.

Chocolate Sherbet

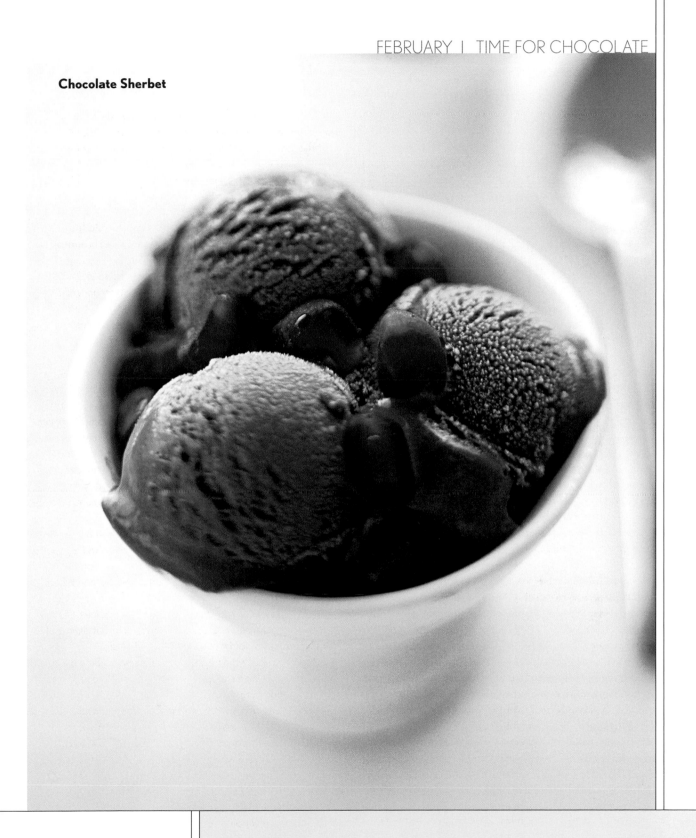

HOW TO MEASURE CHOCOLATE

All the recipes in this story were created and tested to be made with either standard 1-ounce squares or 3.5-ounce (100-gram) bars. Recipes work equally well with either. If you buy 250-gram (8.75-oz.) bars or 275-gram (9.7-oz. bars), fear not. They're usually scored in convenient measurements that will allow you to break off what you need. In these recipes, there's some wiggle room, so you can be off by a square or two without affecting the final product.

March

SPRING IS HERE, SO MAKE A LITTLE TIME FOR COOKING WITH FAMILY AND FRIENDS, AND TAKE A FRESH LOOK AT THE SIGNATURE INGREDIENTS OF THE COMING SEASON.

The Comforts of Home

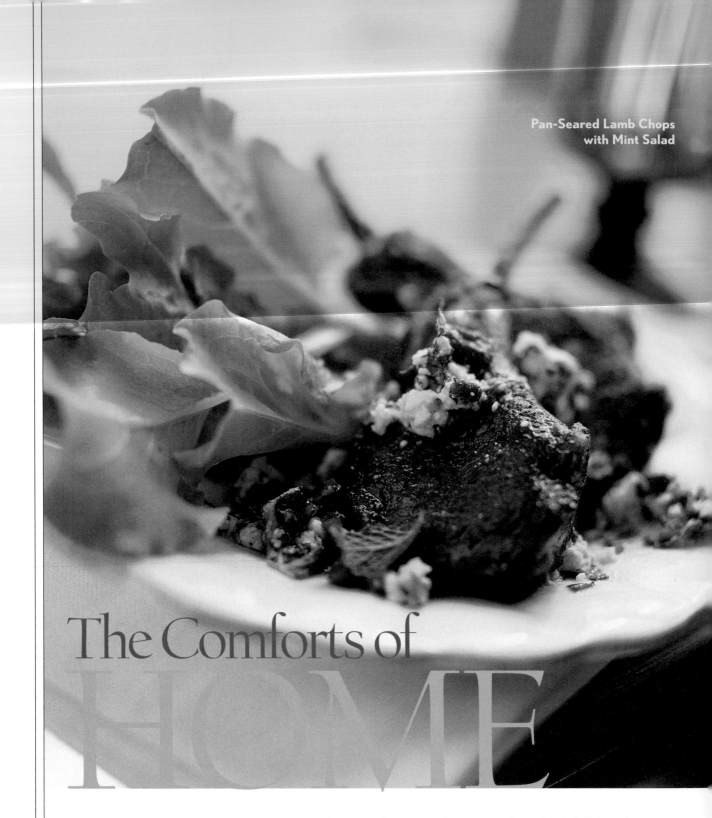

Pan-Seared Lamb Chops
with Mint Salad

The Comforts of
HOME

COMFORT FOOD'S FAMILIARITY AND HOMEY APPEAL
MAKE IT PERFECT FOR COOKING TOGETHER WITH
FAMILY—A LESSON CHEF-IN-TRAINING MATTHEW
BUCHANAN TOOK TO HEART AT AN EARLY AGE.

Pan-Seared Lamb Chops with Mint Salad

To achieve optimum color and flavor, let the chops sizzle in the skillet without moving or stirring—except when it's time to turn them.

START TO FINISH: 30 minutes

¼	cup snipped fresh mint	2	tsp. olive oil
¼	cup snipped fresh Italian parsley	¼	tsp. salt
¼	cup crumbled feta cheese (1 oz.)	⅛	tsp. ground black pepper
¼	cup toasted chopped pecans		Olive oil (optional)
8	lamb rib chops or loin chops, cut 1 inch thick (about 2 lb.)		Lemon juice (optional)
			Mixed salad greens (optional)

1. In a small bowl combine mint, parsley, feta cheese, and pecans; set aside.

2. Trim fat from chops. Rub chops with 2 teaspoons olive oil, salt, and pepper. Preheat a large heavy skillet over medium-high heat until very hot. Add chops. For medium-rare doneness, cook over medium-high heat for 8 to 10 minutes or until brown and an instant-read thermometer inserted in thickest portion registers 145° F, turning chops once halfway through cooking.

3. To serve, sprinkle chops with mint mixture. If desired, drizzle with oil and lemon juice; serve with salad greens. Makes 4 servings.

Each serving: 252 cal., 17 g total fat (5 g sat. fat), 72 mg chol., 311 mg sodium, 2 g carbo., 1 g fiber, 22 g pro. Daily Values: 6% vit. A, 9% vit. C, 7% calcium, 12% iron.

Kitchen comfort

There's comfort to be found in the kitchen. Matthew Buchanan discovered that at age 10 or so when he first began bumping elbows with his mother, Missy, during meal preparations. He was the potato kid, often in charge of spuds for dinner.

"Boy, did my family have to eat 100 varieties of au gratin," says Matthew (shown at left with his mother). Now as a 25-year-old student at the Culinary Institute of America (CIA) in New York, Matthew's alchemy continues as he transforms a cup of this and a dash of that into nouveau comfort food.

Even when he takes over the kitchen during visits to his parents' home near Dallas, Missy doesn't mind at all. "Matthew is so inventive with food," she says. When Matthew was a boy, he and his mom shared a lot of kitchen time. Meals tended to be simple and quick—something to eat together as a family before it was time to rush off. Matthew's sisters, Mindy and Beth, and father, Barry, were part of the dine-and-dash whirlwind. But Matthew loved helping out in the kitchen. He got upset when his mom went grocery shopping while he was in school.

Puttering in the kitchen at an early age led to advanced puttering in college. While a student at Texas A&M University, Matthew cooked for his roommates. And every year he concocted a "gigantic" post-Thanksgiving feast for his friends. "It was our last hurrah before finals and the Christmas break," he said. After graduating with a degree in psychology, he decided he'd rather be a chef. So, after a year in Italy with his wife, Rachel, he headed for the CIA.

But there's no place like home. Visiting his parents sparks the familiar mom-and-son sessions in the kitchen. Matthew takes his family favorites to new levels, punching up the freshness and adding zings of flavor. See for yourself by trying Matthew's recipes on the following pages.

COOKING FISH

Fish cooks pretty quickly, but just how quick depends on the thickness of the fillet. Measure the height at the thickest part of the fillet before you put the fish on the grill. Expect a 1/2-inch-thick piece to cook in 4 to 6 minutes over direct heat. Indirect heat will take a little longer. To see if fish is done, insert a fork into the thickest part and twist gently. If the fish flakes, it is done. If it doesn't separate into flakes and is still translucent, cook it a little longer.

Smoked Trout with Mango-Avocado Salsa

Wood chips come in several varieties, including apple, cherry, maple, and mesquite. They may be large or could be ground to a fine consistency. Larger wood chips work in most smokers, but must be soaked in water before they're used.

PREP: 20 minutes **COOK:** 20 minutes

Wood chips for smoking	Ground black pepper
1 lb. fresh trout fillets,	1 recipe Mango-Avocado
1/2 to 1 inch thick	Salsa (below)
Salt	Tortilla chips

1. At least 1 hour before smoke cooking, soak 1 cup wood chips in enough water to cover. Drain wood chips. In a charcoal grill arrange medium-hot coals around a drip pan. Test for medium heat above the pan. Sprinkle the drained wood chips over the coals.

2. Rinse fish and pat dry with paper towels. Sprinkle fish with salt and pepper. Place fish on foil on the grill rack over drip pan. Cover and smoke for 25 to 30 minutes or until fish flakes easily when tested with a fork. Cool.

3. Meanwhile, prepare Mango-Avocado Salsa. Use a fork to break trout into large chunks. Serve trout pieces on tortilla chips with salsa. Makes 4 servings.

MANGO-AVOCADO SALSA: In a medium bowl combine 1 medium mango,* seeded, peeled, and chopped (1 cup); 1 small avocado, seeded, peeled, and chopped (3/4 cup); 1/4 cup chopped red sweet pepper; 2 tablespoons chopped red onion (a quarter of a small onion); 1/2 of a fresh jalapeño pepper,** seeded and finely chopped; 1 clove garlic, minced; 2 teaspoons lime juice; 1 teaspoon sugar; 1/4 teaspoon salt; and 1/4 teaspoon ground cumin. Cover and chill for up to 2 hours.

*NOTE: To cut a mango, start on one of the wider sides of the mango and cut from the stem down, following the curve of the pit. Repeat on other sides. With pieces skin side down, make crosshatch cuts through the flesh and down to the peel. Slice close to peel to remove fruit.

**NOTE: Because hot chile peppers contain volatile oils that can burn your skin and eyes, wear plastic or rubber gloves when working with chile peppers. If your bare hands do touch the chile peppers, wash your hands well with soap and water.

Each serving: 408 cal., 19 g total fat (3 g sat. fat), 65 mg chol., 370 mg sodium, 33 g carbo., 4 g fiber, 27 g pro. Daily Values: 56% vit. A, 62% vit. C, 10% calcium, 14% iron.

BY JEANNE AMBROSE. PHOTOGRAPHS: COLLEEN DUFFLEY. FOOD STYLIST: BROOKE LEONARD. PROP STYLIST: NICK HAMBLEN.

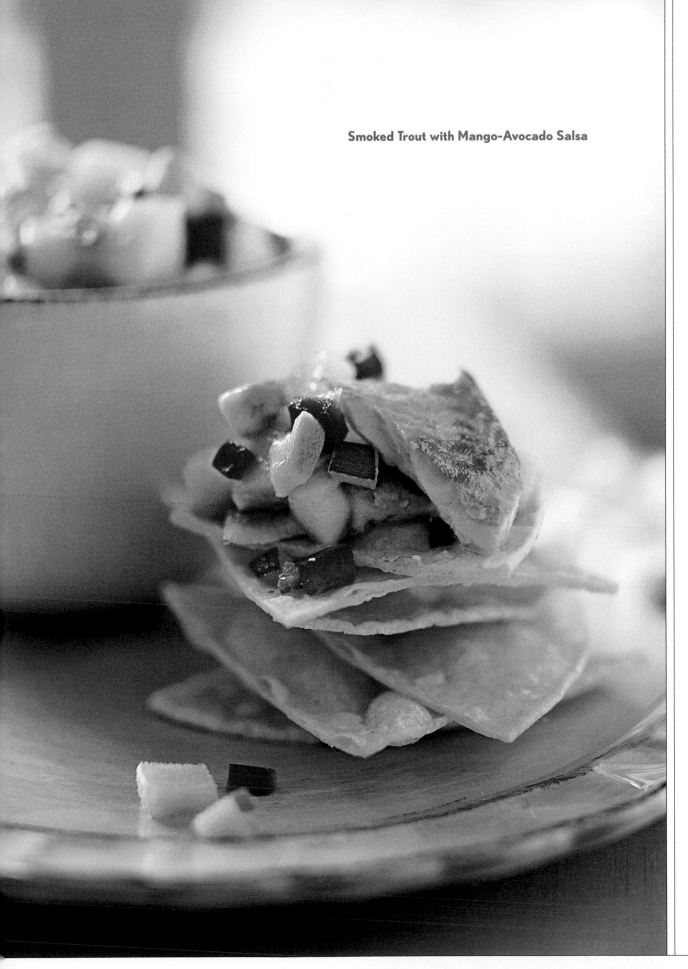

Smoked Trout with Mango-Avocado Salsa

Jicama Slaw with Jalapeño Dressing

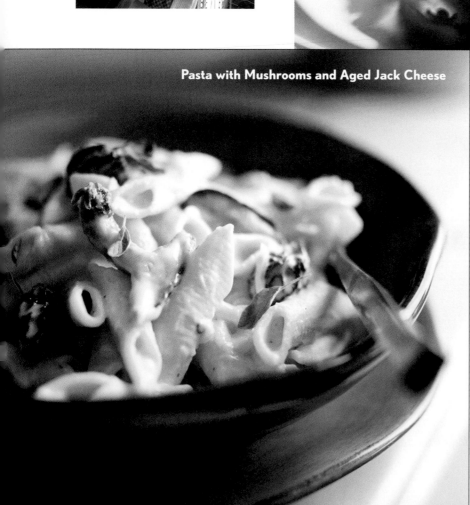

Pasta with Mushrooms and Aged Jack Cheese

PERFECT PASTA

To get the best flavor from your pasta, cook it only until it is *al dente* (al DEN-tay), which means it is still slightly firm and a little chewy. In Italian, *al dente* means "to the tooth" and describes the doneness of pasta and other foods, such as vegetables. For the best results, carefully follow the cooking directions on the package of dried or fresh pasta.

Pasta with Mushrooms and Aged Jack Cheese

Aged Jack cheese is not to be confused with Monterey Jack cheese, which is mild and semisoft. The aged version has a pale buttery color, a rich flavor, and a dry texture.

START TO FINISH: 35 minutes

8 oz. dried penne or campanelle pasta (2½ cups)	½ cup whipping cream
	¼ cup chicken broth
1 Tbsp. butter	4 oz. aged Jack cheese, finely shredded (1 cup firmly packed)
1 large Walla Walla onion or other sweet onion, cut into thin wedges	
4 cloves garlic, minced	Salt
2 Tbsp. butter	Ground black pepper
3 cups fresh spring mushrooms, such as whole or halved morel mushrooms*, sliced shiitake mushrooms, and/or sliced oyster mushrooms	Fresh thyme leaves (optional)

1. In a large saucepan cook pasta according to package directions. Drain; return to saucepan. Stir in the 1 tablespoon butter. Cover and keep warm.

2. In a large skillet cook and stir the onion and the garlic in the 2 tablespoons hot butter over medium heat for 4 to 5 minutes or until tender. Stir in mushrooms; cook about 3 minutes more or until tender.

3. Meanwhile, in a small saucepan heat whipping cream and broth over medium heat just to boiling. Reduce heat to low; stir in cheese. Continue stirring until cheese is almost melted.

4. Add mushroom mixture and cream mixture to pasta. Toss gently to combine; heat through. Season to taste with salt and pepper. If desired, sprinkle with thyme leaves before serving. Makes 4 servings.

*NOTE: To clean morel mushrooms, set the mushrooms in a pan or bowl. Cover with water; add a dash of salt. Soak for 10 to 15 minutes. Drain and rinse. Repeat twice. Pat mushrooms dry.

Each serving: 586 cal., 36 g total fat (18 g sat. fat), 76 mg chol., 352 mg sodium, 50 g carbo., 4 g fiber, 19 g pro. Daily Values: 24% vit. A, 5% vit. C, 25% calcium, 15% iron.

Jicama Slaw with Jalapeño Dressing

Great as a solo side dish, this slaw is also adaptable. Pile the jicama mixture onto chicken sandwiches, use it to make spring rolls, or place a spoonful on top of tortilla soup or other thick soups.

PREP: 20 minutes **CHILL:** 1 hour

2 cups peeled jicama,* cut into thin matchstick strips (about 6½ oz.)	1 small red onion, thinly sliced and halved
3 small red, yellow, and/or green sweet peppers, cut into thin matchstick strips (1½ cups)	1 recipe Jalapeño Dressing (below)

1. In a large salad bowl combine jicama strips, sweet pepper strips, and onion slices. Prepare Jalapeño Dressing. Pour dressing over jicama mixture; toss gently to coat. Cover; chill for 1 to 6 hours, stirring occasionally. Makes 6 servings.

JALAPEÑO DRESSING: In a screw-top jar combine ¼ cup peanut oil or olive oil; ⅓ cup snipped fresh cilantro; 2 tablespoons red wine vinegar; 1 small fresh jalapeño chile pepper (see note, page 36), seeded and finely chopped; 1 clove garlic, minced; 1 teaspoon sugar; ⅛ teaspoon black pepper; and a dash each of salt and cayenne pepper. Cover and shake well.

*NOTE: You can make cutting up a large jicama less daunting if you cut it in half after you peel it. Place the flat side down on your cutting board so it won't wobble. (All round vegetables are easier to work with when you cut them in half.) Next, cut each jicama half vertically into thin slices. Stack several slices. Cut the stack vertically into thin strips, then trim the strips so you have matchstick-size pieces.

Each serving: 120 cal., 9 g total fat (2 g sat. fat), 0 mg chol., 27 mg sodium, 9 g carbo., 1 g fiber, 1 g pro. Daily Values: 46% vit. A, 146% vit. C, 1% calcium, 5% iron.

FLAVORS OF SPRING DINNER

Pan-Seared Lamb Chops with Mint Salad *(page 35)*
Spring Greens with Shortcut Lemon Sauce *(page 40)*
Pita Crisps *(page 11)*
Banana Split Sundaes *(page 40)*
Iced tea

Banana Split Sundaes

For a special touch, Matthew likes to caramelize the bananas to achieve a brittle brûlée-like crunch. He works with a chef's torch to achieve the effect, but you can also caramelize sugar in a skillet and quickly pour it over the bananas.

START TO FINISH: 35 minutes

3	1-inch-thick slices angel food cake, purchased or homemade (right), torn into 1/2- to 1-inch cubes	3	Tbsp. light-colored corn syrup
2	Tbsp. butter, melted	1	Tbsp. butter
3/4	cup packed brown sugar	1/2	tsp. vanilla
4	tsp. cornstarch	1	recipe Caramelized Sugar (below) (optional)
1/3	cup water	2	bananas
1/2	cup half-and-half or light cream	1	pt. vanilla, chocolate, and/or strawberry ice cream

1. Preheat oven to 400° F. Place cake cubes in an 8×8×2-inch baking pan. Drizzle with the 2 tablespoons melted butter; toss gently to coat. Bake, uncovered, for 10 minutes, stirring twice. Cool. (The cake croutons will crisp as they cool.)

2. For caramel sauce, in a large skillet combine brown sugar and cornstarch. Stir in the water. Stir in cream, corn syrup, and the 1 tablespoon butter. Cook and stir over medium heat until bubbly (mixture may appear curdled). Cook and stir for 2 minutes more. Remove from heat; stir in vanilla. Meanwhile, begin preparing Caramelized Sugar, if using.

3. Cut each banana in half both vertically and horizontally so you have four equal pieces from each. Place bananas in an even layer in the skillet, turning to coat with sauce; cook for 1 to 2 minutes.

4. Scoop ice cream into 4 bowls; top with bananas, cake croutons, and remaining caramel sauce. If desired, drizzle with Caramelized Sugar. Makes 4 servings.

CARAMELIZED SUGAR: Place 1/3 cup sugar in an 8-inch heavy skillet. Heat over medium-high heat until sugar begins to melt, shaking skillet occasionally. Do not stir. Once the sugar starts to melt, reduce heat to low. Cook about 5 minutes more or until sugar is melted and golden, stirring as necessary.

Each serving: 628 cal., 25 g total fat (15 g sat. fat), 81 mg chol., 343 mg sodium, 101 g carbo., 2 g fiber, and 6 g pro. Daily Values: 20% vit. A, 10% vit. C, 19% calcium, 7% iron.

Spring Greens with Shortcut Lemon Sauce

START TO FINISH: 25 minutes

1	lb. baby broccoli and/or asparagus spears and/or pea pods	3/4	tsp. snipped fresh thyme
2	oz. mascarpone cheese	1/2	tsp. finely shredded lemon peel
2	Tbsp. dairy sour cream	1 1/2	tsp. lemon juice
2	Tbsp. milk		Salt
			Ground white pepper

1. In a Dutch oven or large saucepan bring a small amount of salted water to boiling. Cook vegetables, covered, until crisp-tender, allowing 5 to 7 minutes for baby broccoli, 3 to 5 minutes for asparagus, and 2 to 4 minutes for pea pods. Drain.

2. For the lemon sauce, in a small bowl combine mascarpone cheese, sour cream, milk, thyme, lemon peel, and lemon juice. Season sauce to taste with salt and pepper. To serve, spoon lemon sauce over the vegetables. Makes 4 servings.

Each serving: 111 cal., 8 g total fat (5 g sat. fat), 21 mg chol., 117 mg sodium, 8 g carbo., 3 g fiber, 7 g pro. Daily Values: 33% vit. A, 135% vit. C, 7% calcium, 6% iron.

Angel Food Cake

Loosen the cooled cake from the pan by sliding a metal spatula between the pan and cake in a continuous—not sawing—motion.

PREP: 50 minutes **BAKE:** 40 minutes **COOL:** 2 hours

1 1/2	cups egg whites (10 to 12 large)	1 1/2	tsp. cream of tartar
1 1/2	cups sifted powdered sugar	1	tsp. vanilla
1	cup sifted cake flour or sifted all-purpose flour	1	cup granulated sugar

1. In a very large mixing bowl let egg whites stand at room temperature for 30 minutes. Meanwhile, sift powdered sugar and flour together 3 times; set aside.

2. Preheat oven to 350° F. Add cream of tartar and vanilla to egg whites. Beat with an electric mixer on medium speed until soft peaks form (tips curl). Gradually add granulated sugar, 2 tablespoons at a time, beating until stiff peaks form (tips stand straight).

3. Sift about one-fourth of the flour mixture over beaten egg whites; fold in gently. (If bowl is too full, transfer to a larger bowl.) Repeat, folding in remaining flour mixture by fourths. Pour into an ungreased 10-inch tube pan. Gently cut through batter to remove any large air pockets.

4. Bake on lowest rack for 40 to 45 minutes or until top springs back when lightly touched. Immediately invert cake (in pan); cool thoroughly. Loosen sides of cake from pan; remove cake. Makes 12 servings.

low fat Each serving: 161 cal., 0 g total fat (0 g sat. fat), 0 mg chol., 51 mg sodium, 36 g carbo., 0 g fiber, 4 g pro. Daily Values: 4% iron.

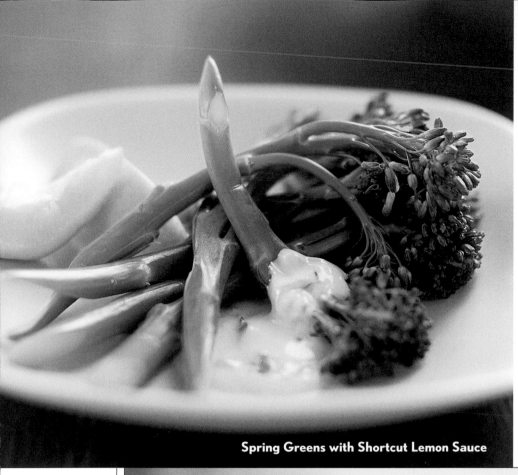

Spring Greens with Shortcut Lemon Sauce

KEEPING GREENS BRIGHT

To keep green vegetables vivid, avoid overcooking them. Give the veggies a quick dip in a large pot of boiling salted water. Stop the bright color from cooking away by plunging the vegetables into ice water as soon as they're crisp-tender. Cover and store in the refrigerator until serving time. Reheat by dropping them briefly into boiling water.

Banana Split Sundae

EXCELLENT Eggplant

Historically, the 5th-century Chinese were the first to write about eggplants. No wonder the ancient Chinese found eggplant useful—its mild flavor adds a harmonious accent to the spicy overtones of Asian cooking. When eggplants eventually found their way to the Mediterranean, they fit well with the equally zesty cuisines of Spain, Italy, and Greece and became part of many recipes we know today, such as Lemon-Scented Eggplant Tart.

For best results with the tart and other recipes, choose the right eggplant and handle it with care. Select small to medium sizes or try one of the small varieties pictured *left*. The skin of young eggplant is very flavorful but gets bitter as it ages. Small varieties are also more tender than the large types. Store eggplants in a cool, dry place and use them within two days. Because they soak up oils during cooking, bread them to keep them from becoming mushy. Cook small varieties the same way you would cook regular eggplant, but for shorter lengths of time.

Baby White Eggplant

Japanese Eggplant

Chinese Eggplant

Thai Eggplant

Western Eggplant

BY STEPHEN EXEL. PHOTOGRAPHS: COLLEEN DUFFLEY. FOOD STYLIST: BROOKE LEONARD.

Lemon-Scented Eggplant Tart

If it's available, substitute white eggplant for purple.

PREP: 45 minutes   **BAKE:** 22 minutes

1	recipe Butter Pastry (below)	1½	tsp. minced fresh garlic (3 large cloves)
12	oz. Japanese eggplant	2	Tbsp. olive oil
	Salt	¼	cup purchased black olive pâté
⅓	cup snipped fresh cilantro		
4	tsp. shredded lemon peel	2	Tbsp. lemon juice

1. Preheat oven to 450° F. For crust, on a lightly floured surface roll the Butter Pastry to a 16×5-inch rectangle. Ease pastry into an ungreased 13¾×4-inch tart pan with a removable bottom, pressing into sides of pan and trimming to edge of pan to remove excess. Generously prick the bottom of the pastry. Line with a double thickness of foil. Bake for 10 minutes. Remove foil; bake for 4 to 5 minutes more or until golden brown. Cool on a wire rack.

2. Halve eggplant lengthwise and slice into ¼-inch-thick slices. Sprinkle slices with salt on both sides; set between two paper towels. Place a cookie sheet on top of the paper towel. Weigh down with a heavy bowl for 20 minutes. Meanwhile, in a bowl combine cilantro, lemon peel, and garlic; set aside.

3. Place eggplant slices in a colander; rinse and drain well. In a skillet heat 1 tablespoon of the oil over medium-high heat. Cook and stir eggplant, half at a time, for 3 to 5 minutes or until eggplant has softened and is light brown. Remove slices from skillet; drain on paper towels. Repeat with remaining oil and eggplant.

4. Stir together the olive pâté and 1 tablespoon of the lemon juice. Spread olive mixture onto baked pastry. Arrange eggplant on top. Sprinkle evenly with cilantro mixture. Bake, uncovered, about 8 minutes or until heated through.

5. Remove from oven; cool slightly on a wire rack. Remove sides of pan. Cut into 1-inch-thick slices; drizzle with remaining lemon juice. Serve warm. Makes 12 appetizer servings.

BUTTER PASTRY: In a mixing bowl combine 1 cup all-purpose flour and ¼ teaspoon salt. Using a pastry blender, cut in ⅓ cup unsalted butter until pieces are pea-size. Sprinkle 1 teaspoon cold water over part of the mixture; gently toss with a fork. Push the moistened dough to side of bowl. Repeat with additional cold water, using 1 tablespoon at a time, until all the dough is moistened. Form dough into a ball.

Each serving: 117 cal., 8 g total fat (4 g saturated fat), 14 mg chol., 106 mg sodium, 10 g carbo., 1 g fiber, 1 g protein. Daily Values: 10 % vit. C, 1 % calcium, 3 % iron.

Lemon-Scented Eggplant Tart

EGGPLANT EXAMPLES

BABY WHITE EGGPLANT: Small, firm, and with a sweet flesh. Its thick skin should be peeled before use. A quick glance at this variety lets one know the probable derivation of eggplant's name.

JAPANESE EGGPLANT: Long, slender, and a deep purple color. Its flesh is tender and slightly sweet. This delicate variety is specified for use in Lemon-Scented Eggplant Tart.

CHINESE EGGPLANT: Resembles a small zucchini. This version has a thin, pleasant-tasting skin, so there's no need to peel it. Its slender shape and size make this eggplant practical and easy to use.

THAI EGGPLANT: Look for golf-ball-size fruits, although occasionally, grape-sized Thai eggplants have been spotted. This one is a natural for grilling, stir-frying, or frying in tempura.

WESTERN EGGPLANT: This larger version is the one most of us know. Look for a smooth, glossy surface and a heavy-in-the-hand weight. Seek out the very freshest eggplant for the sweetest, least bitter flavor.

Egg-Poaching PANS

In a world of kitchen multitaskers, here's a pan designed to do just one thing: poach an egg. Because poached egg dishes are popular again, the *Better Homes and Gardens®* Test Kitchen decided to put a slew of poaching pans through their paces. Here are some tips for picking a great pan.

- Look for nonstick egg cups, although you should coat these cups with butter or oil before filling.
- Cups with perforated bottoms let water enter cups for even poaching.
- Be sure cups can be easily removed from a hot pan, either with easy-access handles on the individual cups or with a knob or handle for lifting out the entire tray.
- Most pans are made of good quality 18/10 stainless steel. Some have a copper or an aluminum disc on the bottom for better heat conduction. Heavier pans typically have thicker discs (a plus) and better heat distribution. However, when considering choices, be sure you're comparing the same kind of pans: copper to copper and aluminum to aluminum.
- A glass lid lets you monitor cooking.
- The dishwasher-safe capabilities of poaching pans differ from manufacturer to manufacturer. Choose the pan that best meets your needs.
- Avoid microwave poachers. During our cooking tests, the pans repeatedly popped open.
- When you are ready to poach, break eggs one at a time into a measuring cup. Pour the egg into a poaching cup and proceed with cooking according to manufacturer's directions.

Poached Eggs with Grainy Mustard Vinaigrette

BY STEPHEN EXEL. PHOTOGRAPHS: COLLEEN DUFFLEY. FOOD STYLIST: BROOKE LEONARD.

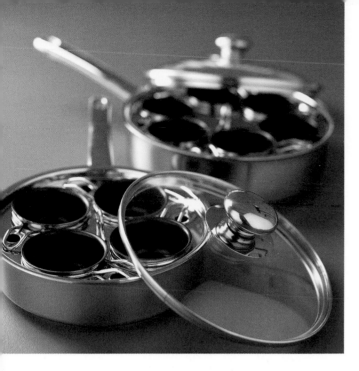

Poached Eggs with Grainy Mustard Vinaigrette

Put your poaching pan to the test with this quick preparation. Fresh mixed greens provide a cozy nest.

START TO FINISH: 20 minutes

1 Tbsp. coarse-grain brown mustard	2 slices dark rye bread, toasted and halved diagonally
2 Tbsp. vinegar	Salt
2 Tbsp. olive oil	Ground black pepper
4 large eggs	
2 cups fresh assorted greens; or 8 cups torn spinach, sautéed in 1 Tbsp. butter	

1. In a small saucepan combine mustard, vinegar, and olive oil. Bring to boiling, stirring to combine. Reduce heat and keep warm, stirring again just before serving.

2. Grease 4 cups of an egg-poaching pan with oil. Place poacher cups over pan of boiling water (water should not touch the bottoms of the cups). Reduce heat to simmering. Break one of the eggs into a measuring cup. Carefully slide egg into a poacher cup. Repeat with remaining eggs. Cover and cook for 6 to 9 minutes or until the whites are completely set and yolks begin to thicken but are not hard.

3. To serve, loosen eggs by running a knife around poaching cups. Place greens or sautéed spinach over toasted rye bread. Top with poached egg by inverting poaching cups. Drizzle with warm mustard vinaigrette. Season to taste with salt and pepper. Makes 4 servings.

Each serving: 183 cal., 13 g total fat (3 g sat. fat), 213 mg chol., 257 mg sodium, 10 g carbo., 1 g dietary fiber, 8 g protein. Daily Values: 8% vit. A, 2% vit. C, 5% calcium, 8% iron.

Eggs Benedict

STAND: 45 minutes **PREP:** 30 minutes **COOK:** 20 minutes

4 eggs	4 slices Canadian-style bacon
1 recipe Hollandaise Sauce (below)	Paprika (optional)
2 English muffins, split	

1. Grease 4 cups of an egg-poaching pan with oil. Place poacher cups over pan of boiling water (water should not touch the bottoms of the cups). Reduce heat to simmering. Break one of the eggs into a measuring cup. Carefully slide egg into a poacher cup. Repeat with remaining eggs. Cover and cook 6 to 9 minutes or until the whites are completely set and yolks begin to thicken but are not hard.

2. Loosen eggs by running a knife around poaching cups. Remove eggs with a slotted spoon; place in a large pan of warm water to keep them warm. Prepare Hollandaise Sauce.

3. Meanwhile, place muffin halves, cut sides up, on a baking sheet. Broil 3 to 4 inches from the heat about 2 minutes or until toasted. Top each muffin half with a slice of Canadian-style bacon; broil about 1 minute more or until meat is heated.

4. To serve, top each bacon-topped muffin half with an egg; spoon Hollandaise Sauce over eggs. If desired, sprinkle with paprika. Makes 4 servings

HOLLANDAISE SAUCE: Cut 1/2 cup unsalted butter into thirds and bring it to room temperature (allow about 45 minutes). In the top of a double boiler combine 3 beaten egg yolks, 1 table-spoon lemon juice, and 1 tablespoon water. Add a piece of the butter. Place over gently boiling water (upper pan should not touch water). Cook, stirring rapidly with a whisk, until butter melts and sauce begins to thicken. (Sauce may appear to curdle at this point but will smooth out when remaining butter is added). Add remaining butter, a piece at a time, stirring constantly until melted. Continue to cook and stir for 2 to 2 1/2 minutes more or until sauce thickens. Immediately remove from heat. If sauce is too thick or curdles, immediately whisk in 1 to 2 tablespoons hot water. Season to taste with salt and ground white pepper. Makes 3/4 cup sauce.

Each serving: 442 cal., 36 g total fat (19 g sat. fat), 451 mg chol., 836 mg sodium, 14 g carbo., 1 g fiber, 16 g pro. Daily Values: 30% vit. A, 3% vit. C, 10% calcium, 12% iron.

April

CELEBRATE SPRING'S RENEWED SUNSHINE AND WARMTH
WITH A FRESH APPROACH TO ITS BEST-LOVED FLAVORS.

A Parade of Easter Breads

Plus...

A Parade of
Easter Breads

THERE'S AS MUCH TRADITION IN OUR HOT CROSS BUNS AS THERE IS PLAYFULNESS IN OUR GARDEN BUNNY BREAD. HOP TO THE BEST IN SPRING BAKING.

Hot Cross Buns

Hot Cross Buns

Soaking the currants in balsamic vinegar gives them a slightly tangy flavor that contrasts well with the rich dough.

PREP: 45 minutes **RISE:** 2 hours
CHILL: 6 hours **BAKE:** 12 minutes

2/3	cup dried currants or raisins	1 1/2	cups mascarpone cheese (12 oz.)
2	Tbsp. balsamic vinegar	1/3	cup sugar
3 1/4	to 3 3/4 cups all-purpose flour	1/2	tsp. salt
1	pkg. active dry yeast	3	eggs
1	tsp. ground cardamom	1	egg white
1/8	tsp. ground cloves	1	Tbsp. water
2/3	cup milk	1/4	cup sugar
			Milk

1. Place the currants in a small bowl; add vinegar. Cover; let stand. In a large mixing bowl stir together 2 cups of the flour, the yeast, cardamom, and cloves; set aside.

2. In a saucepan heat and stir 2/3 cup milk, 1/2 cup of the mascarpone cheese, 1/3 cup sugar, and salt just until warm (120° F to 130° F) and mascarpone almost melts. Add milk mixture to flour mixture along with eggs. Beat with an electric mixer on low to medium speed for 30 seconds, scraping sides of bowl constantly. Beat on high speed for 3 minutes. Using a wooden spoon, stir in currant mixture and as much of the remaining flour as you can.

3. Turn dough out onto a lightly floured surface. Knead in enough remaining flour to make a moderately soft dough (3 to 5 minutes). (The dough will be sticky.) Shape into a ball. Place in a lightly greased bowl; turn once to grease the surface. Cover; let rise in a warm place until double (about 1 hour). Chill dough for 6 hours. (Or omit rising time and chill dough for 12 to 24 hours.)

4. Punch dough down; turn out onto a lightly floured surface. Cover; let rest for 10 minutes. Meanwhile, lightly grease 2 baking sheets; set aside. Divide dough into 24 portions. Gently shape each portion into a ball, tucking edges under to make smooth tops. Arrange balls on prepared baking sheets so edges are almost touching. Cover; let rise until nearly double (1 to 1 1/2 hours).

5. Preheat oven to 375° F. Using a sharp knife, make a crisscross slash across the top of each bun. In a small bowl beat egg white; stir in water. Brush onto rolls. Bake for 12 to 15 minutes or until golden brown. Immediately remove buns from baking sheets. Cool slightly on a wire rack.

6. In a small bowl stir together remaining mascarpone cheese, 1/4 cup sugar, and enough milk to make a frosting of a thick drizzling consistency. Drizzle icing into a cross on each bun. Pass additional icing for dipping. Serve warm. Makes 24 buns.

Each bun: 168 cal., 7 g total fat (4 g sat. fat), 45 mg chol., 71 mg sodium, 22 g carbo., 1 g fiber, 6 g pro. Daily Values: 1% vit. A, 2% calcium, 6% iron.

History of bread

Whether they're crusty loaves that tug apart into a dozen fragrant portions or trays stacked high with sweet muffins, breads are meant as a communal blessing—particularly at this time of year. People have long gathered to share and celebrate the dawn of spring. Ever since we began reckoning that the dark days of winter were over and nature was reawakening, we've enjoyed spring feasts.

We're especially lucky in America because we're adept at striking a respectful balance between observing Easter and pursuing a day of whimsical fun to celebrate the beginning of spring. Thankfully, bread has been a staple of both occasions.

The breads presented here—many with long traditions and deep connections to our culture—strike a similar balance. Take Hot Cross Buns, for example. The cross imagery may appeal to devout Christians, while children just love to giggle and recite "one a penny, two a penny, hot cross buns."

Historians believe these rolls predate Christianity and were enjoyed by ancient Greeks, Romans, and Britons. To them, the round shape represented the sun. The cross stood for the four seasons or the moon's four phases.

As the centuries passed, Hot Cross Buns became associated with Good Friday and its community meals. The rest of the year, the buns were used as a kind of magical talisman to ward off everything from fires to shipwrecks.

Regardless of historical context, anytime is a good time to bake bread with family. A sunny spot in the kitchen and a new bag of flour are God's gifts to the baker. And never are these blessings more welcome than at Eastertime. The pace of life slows, the yearning for connection grows, and the prospect of a quiet hour or two of baking seems suddenly irresistible.

HOW TO TELL BREAD IS DONE

To tell when bread is ready to come out of the oven, you can tap the bottom and listen for a hollow sound, something like knocking on a wooden box. Or you can take the bread's temperature with an instant-read thermometer. Insert it into the thickest part of the loaf and look for a temperature of 195° F to 200° F.

"Using a thermometer is an excellent way to tell when bread is done," says Glenna Vance, spokesperson for Red Star Yeast, "especially for younger bakers who don't know how that thump on the bottom sounds."

Red Star also has a baker's help line: 800/445-4746.

CREATING THE EASTER LATTICE

With hands lightly floured, and working on a lightly floured surface, weave strips together by crossing short strips of dough under and over long strips. Try not to stretch the dough too much as you work.

PURCHASING QUAIL EGGS

Find quail eggs in Asian grocery stores, farmers' markets, health food stores, and some supermarkets. You can also call Rosi's Game Bird Farm at 800/969-9970.

EASTER BRUNCH

Asparagus-Salmon Scramble (page 84)
Hot Cross Buns (page 49) or Easter Lattice (right)
Assorted fresh fruit such as sliced melon, kiwifruit, strawberries, and pineapple
Coffee or tea

Easter Lattice

PREP: 45 minutes **RISE:** 1³/₄ hours **BAKE:** 25 minutes

4¼	to 4³/₄ cups all-purpose flour	2	tsp. fennel seeds, toasted and crushed
1	pkg. active dry yeast		Cooking oil
1	cup milk		Hard-cooked and dyed
⅓	cup sugar		quail eggs* (see tip, left),
¼	cup butter		eggs, or egg-shaped
1¼	tsp. salt		colored candies, such as
2	eggs		Jordan almonds or malted
3	Tbsp. flaxseeds, poppy seeds, and/or toasted sesame seeds		milk eggs
			Crème fraîche or butter

1. In a large mixing bowl stir together 2 cups of the flour and the yeast; set aside. In a medium saucepan heat and stir milk, sugar, the ¼ cup butter, and salt just until warm (120° F to 130° F) and butter almost melts. Add milk mixture to flour mixture along with eggs. Beat with an electric mixer on low to medium speed for 30 seconds, scraping sides of bowl constantly. Beat on high speed for 3 minutes. Stir in seeds. Using a wooden spoon, stir in as much of the remaining flour as you can.

2. Turn dough out onto a lightly floured surface. Knead in enough remaining flour to make a moderately stiff dough that is smooth and elastic (6 to 8 minutes). Shape dough into a ball. Place in a lightly greased bowl; turn once to grease the surface. Cover; let rise in a warm place until double in size (about 1 hour).

3. Punch dough down; turn onto a lightly floured surface. Divide in half. Cover and let rest for 10 minutes. Meanwhile, lightly grease a large baking sheet. Roll half of dough into a 12×6-inch rectangle. Cut into three 12×2-inch strips; arrange 1 inch apart on the prepared baking sheet. Roll remaining dough into a 10×8-inch rectangle; cut into five 8×2-inch strips. Arrange shorter strips crosswise over longer ropes, weaving under and over longer strips (see photo, left). Cover; let rise in warm place until nearly double (45 minutes).

4. Preheat oven to 350° F. Bake for 25 to 30 minutes or until bread is brown and sounds hollow when tapped. Lightly brush bread with cooking oil. Cool on a wire rack. Arrange eggs on top of bread. Serve with crème fraîche or butter. Makes 15 servings.

BREAD MACHINE METHOD: Use 4½ cups all-purpose flour. In a 2-pound bread machine combine first 9 ingredients. Select dough cycle according to manufacturer's directions. When cycle finishes, remove dough. Shape and bake as in Steps 3 and 4, above.

***NOTE:** To hard-cook quail eggs, place eggs in a single layer in a medium saucepan. Cover eggs with cold water. Bring to a rapid boil over high heat (water will have large, rapidly breaking bubbles). Cook for 3 minutes; remove from heat. Drain; cool.

low fat Each serving (bread): 201 cal., 6 g total fat (3 g sat. fat), 38 mg chol., 245 mg sodium, 31 g carbo., 2 g fiber, 5 g pro. Daily Values: 4% vit. A, 4% calcium, 11% iron.

BY RICHARD SWEARINGER. PHOTOGRAPHS: CHARLES MARAIA. FOOD STYLIST: ANNE DISRUDE. PROP STYLIST: BARBARA FRITZ.

Easter Lattice

Adorned with tiny quail eggs, Easter Lattice is another version of the many golden braids, rings, and crowns that bakers have long created for Easter.

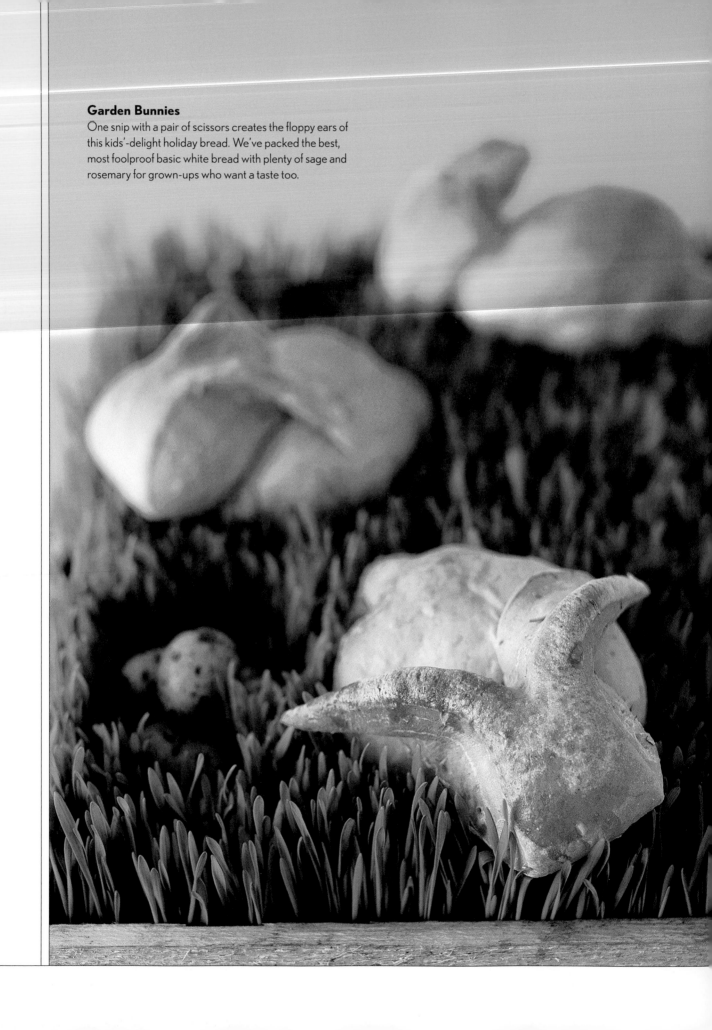

Garden Bunnies
One snip with a pair of scissors creates the floppy ears of this kids'-delight holiday bread. We've packed the best, most foolproof basic white bread with plenty of sage and rosemary for grown-ups who want a taste too.

Garden Bunnies

Rosemary and sage are strong-flavored herbs. If using them alone, add only 2 tablespoons fresh or 2 teaspoons dried.

PREP: 30 minutes **RISE:** 1¼ hours **BAKE:** 40 minutes

5½	to 6 cups all-purpose flour	2	Tbsp. sugar
1	pkg. active dry yeast	1	Tbsp. butter
2¼	cups milk or buttermilk	1½	tsp. salt
¼	cup mixed snipped fresh herbs such as sage, rosemary, parsley, and thyme; or 3 to 4 tsp. dried herbs, crushed	1	recipe Sugar-Sage Topping or Rosemary-Cheese Topping (right)
		1	egg white
		1	Tbsp. water

1. In a large mixing bowl combine 2½ cups of the flour and the yeast; set aside. In a medium saucepan heat and stir milk, herbs, sugar, butter, and salt just until warm (120° F to 130° F) and butter almost melts. Add milk mixture to flour mixture. Beat with an electric mixer on low to medium speed for 30 seconds, scraping sides of bowl constantly. Beat on high speed for 3 minutes. Using a wooden spoon, stir in as much of the remaining flour as you can.

2. Turn dough out onto a lightly floured surface. Knead in enough of the remaining flour to make a moderately stiff dough that is smooth and elastic (6 to 8 minutes). Shape into a ball. Place in a lightly greased bowl; turn once to grease surface. Cover; let rise in a warm place until double (45 to 60 minutes).

3. Punch dough down; turn out onto a lightly floured surface. Divide in half; cover and let rest for 10 minutes. Meanwhile, lightly grease a baking sheet; set aside.

4. To form bunnies, roll a portion of dough into an 8-inch circle. With a sharp knife, cut into 6 wedges (see photo 1, *above right*). From 4 wedges, snip a small amount of dough to make tails for bunnies. Gently shape the 4 wedges into ovals by pulling edges under and pinching together. Place ovals, pinched side down, on prepared baking sheet. Flatten slightly to 4 inches long.

5. Form snipped pieces of dough into tails; press onto one end of dough ovals. To make heads and ears, divide the remaining 2 wedges in half, making 4 small wedges total. Shape each wedge into a teardrop shape, about 4 inches long. With kitchen shears, cut into the pointed end of each, making cuts about 2½ inches long (see photo 2, *above center*). Lay each set of ears on top of an oval shape, near end opposite tail (see photo 3, *above right*). If necessary, brush with water to help dough stick together. Gently give the ears a half twist so the cut edge is facing up.

6. Repeat rolling and shaping with the other portion of dough. Cover and let rise in a warm place until nearly double in size (about 30 minutes).

7. Preheat oven to 350° F. Prepare Sugar-Sage Topping or Rosemary-Cheese Topping; set toppings aside. In a small bowl

MAKING THE BUNNIES

Cut two of the six wedges in half to make four small and four big wedges (photo 1) from each half of the dough. Create the ears by snipping the point of the triangle of the small wedges (photo 2). To give the ears surface texture, twist slightly outward (photo 3).

beat together egg white and water. Brush bunnies with egg mixture. Sprinkle (or rub) with topping. Bake for 15 to 20 minutes or until done, covering with foil the last half of baking to prevent overbrowning. Serve warm. Makes 8 bunnies.

SUGAR-SAGE TOPPING: In a small bowl stir together ⅓ cup fine sanding sugar or granulated sugar and 1 tablespoon finely snipped fresh sage.

ROSEMARY-CHEESE TOPPING: In a small bowl stir together ⅓ cup grated Parmesan cheese and 1 tablespoon finely snipped fresh rosemary.

low fat Each serving: 390 cal., 4 g total fat (2 g sat. fat), 18 mg chol., 495 mg sodium, 75 g carbo., 2 g fiber, 12 g pro. Daily Values: 6% vit. A, 3% vit. C, 9% calcium, 24% iron.

EASTER BUNNY BRUNCH

Scrambled eggs
Sausage
Garden Bunnies *(left)* or Lemon Muffins *(page 60)*
Strawberries or grapes
Fruit juice

Easter Rings

This rich Easter bread hails from Bologna, Italy. The round shape is said to represent the unity of the family.

PREP: 30 minutes **RISE:** 1½ hours + 40 minutes
STAND: 10 minutes **BAKE:** 25 minutes

3¼ to 3¾ cups all-purpose flour	1 tsp. salt
1 pkg. active dry yeast	2 eggs
½ tsp. ground cinnamon (optional)	¾ cup chopped almonds, toasted
¾ cup milk	¼ cup sugar
¼ cup butter	¼ cup almond toffee pieces
¼ cup sugar	2 egg yolks, slightly beaten
	1 egg white, slightly beaten

1. In a large mixing bowl combine 1½ cups of the flour, the yeast, and cinnamon, if desired; set aside. In a small saucepan heat and stir together the milk, butter, ¼ cup sugar, and salt just until warm (120° F to 130° F) and butter almost melts. Add milk mixture to flour mixture along with eggs. Beat with an electric mixer on low speed for 30 seconds, scraping sides of bowl constantly. Beat on high speed for 3 minutes. Using a wooden spoon, stir in as much of the remaining flour as you can.

2. Turn dough out onto a lightly floured surface. Knead in enough of the remaining flour to make a moderately soft dough that is smooth and elastic (3 to 5 minutes total). Shape dough into a ball. Place in a lightly greased bowl; turn once to grease surface. Cover; let rise in a warm place until double in size (about 1½ hours).

3. Punch dough down. Turn dough out onto a lightly floured surface. Cover and let rest for 10 minutes. Meanwhile, lightly grease a baking sheet; set aside.

4. Divide dough in half. Roll each dough half into a rope about 20 inches long. Shape each half into 2 rings; place on prepared baking sheet. Pinch ends to seal. Cover and let rise in a warm place until nearly double in size (about 40 minutes).

5. Preheat oven to 350° F. In a small bowl combine almonds, ¼ cup sugar, and toffee bits; stir in egg yolks. Brush rings with egg white. Sprinkle almond mixture evenly onto the tops and sides of rings, lightly pressing almond mixture into sides as necessary. Bake about 25 minutes until golden brown and a thermometer registers 195° F in the thickest part of the bread. Serve warm. Makes 4 rings (20 to 24 servings).

Each serving: 177 cal., 7 g total fat (2 g sat. fat), 51 mg chol., 172 mg sodium, 24 g carbo., 1 g fiber, 5 g pro. Daily Values: 4% vit. A, 3% calcium, 8% iron.

Orange-Saffron Bread

PREP: 1 hour **RISE:** 1¾ hours **BAKE:** 35 minutes

1 recipe Candied Orange Slices (below)	¼ tsp. thread saffron, ⅛ tsp. ground saffron, or ¼ tsp. ground turmeric
4¼ cups all-purpose flour	1 egg
1 pkg. active dry yeast	½ cup pine nuts or chopped almonds, toasted
¾ cup water	½ cup Candied Orange Syrup (below)
½ cup packed brown sugar	
½ cup orange juice	
⅓ cup butter	
½ tsp. salt	

1. Prepare Candied Orange Slices; set aside.

2. In a large mixing bowl, combine 1½ cups of the flour and the yeast; set aside. In a medium saucepan heat and stir water, brown sugar, orange juice, butter, salt, and saffron just until warm (120° F to 130° F) and butter almost melts. Add to flour mixture along with egg. Beat with an electric mixer on low to medium speed for 30 seconds, scraping sides of bowl constantly. Beat on high speed for 3 minutes. Using a wooden spoon, stir in the remaining flour and pine nuts. Cover and let rise in a warm place until double in size (about 1 hour).

3. Grease a 9x1½-inch round or 8×8×2-inch square baking pan; set aside. Lightly grease a spoon; stir dough down. Transfer batter to pan; use back of spoon to pat dough into corners. Cover; let rise in a warm place until double in size (about 45 minutes).

4. Preheat oven to 350° F. Bake about 35 minutes or until bread sounds hollow when lightly tapped and a thermometer registers 195° F in the thickest part of bread. Cover with foil after 20 minutes of baking to prevent overbrowning. Remove from pan; cool on a wire rack.

5. To serve, place half of the candied orange slices on top of the bread; drizzle with ½ cup of the candied orange syrup. Remove remaining orange slices from syrup; coarsely chop. Pass chopped orange slices with bread. (Reserve remaining syrup to brush onto chicken, turkey, or pork during the last 5 minutes of broiling or grilling.) Makes 12 servings.

CANDIED ORANGE SLICES AND SYRUP: Cut 3 oranges crosswise into ¼-inch-thick slices; remove seeds. In a large skillet that's at least 2 inches deep combine 3½ cups water, 3 cups sugar, one 1-inch piece of peeled fresh ginger, and ¼ teaspoon crushed red pepper. Bring to boiling. Add orange slices. Simmer, uncovered, about 1 hour until rinds become very tender. Transfer slices and syrup to a glass bowl. Remove ginger. Cool.

Each serving: 367 cal., 10 g total fat (4 g sat. fat), 32 mg chol., 163 mg sodium, 65 g carbo., 2 g fiber, 7 g pro. Daily Values: 6% vit. A, 38% vit. C, 4% calcium, 17% iron.

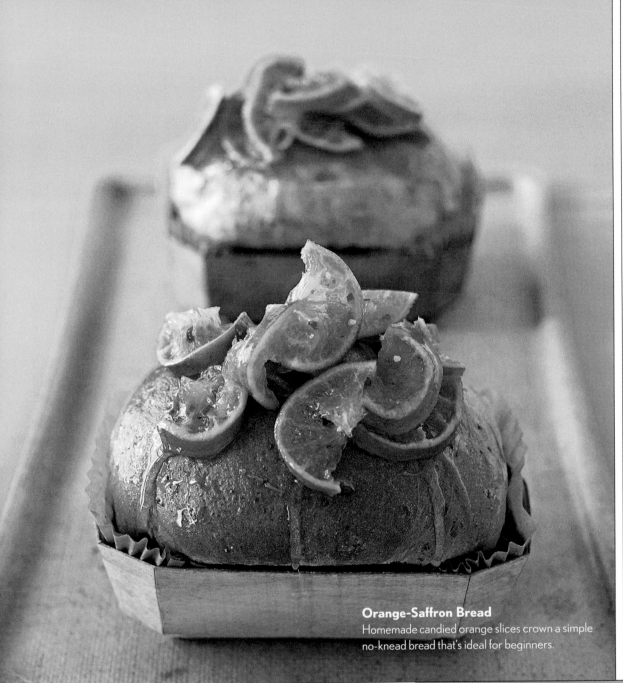

Orange-Saffron Bread
Homemade candied orange slices crown a simple
no-knead bread that's ideal for beginners.

WOODEN MOLDS ADD CHARM

Baking Orange-Saffron Bread in wooden molds gives it a timeless,
old-world appearance. Line three 5⅛×3¾×2-inch wooden bread
molds with parchment paper. Prepare the dough through Step 3, then
turn it onto a lightly floured surface. With a floured knife, divide the dough
into three portions. With floured hands, transfer the dough to prepared
molds; cover and let rise in a warm place until double (about 45 minutes). Bake as directed in Step 4.

Easter Rings

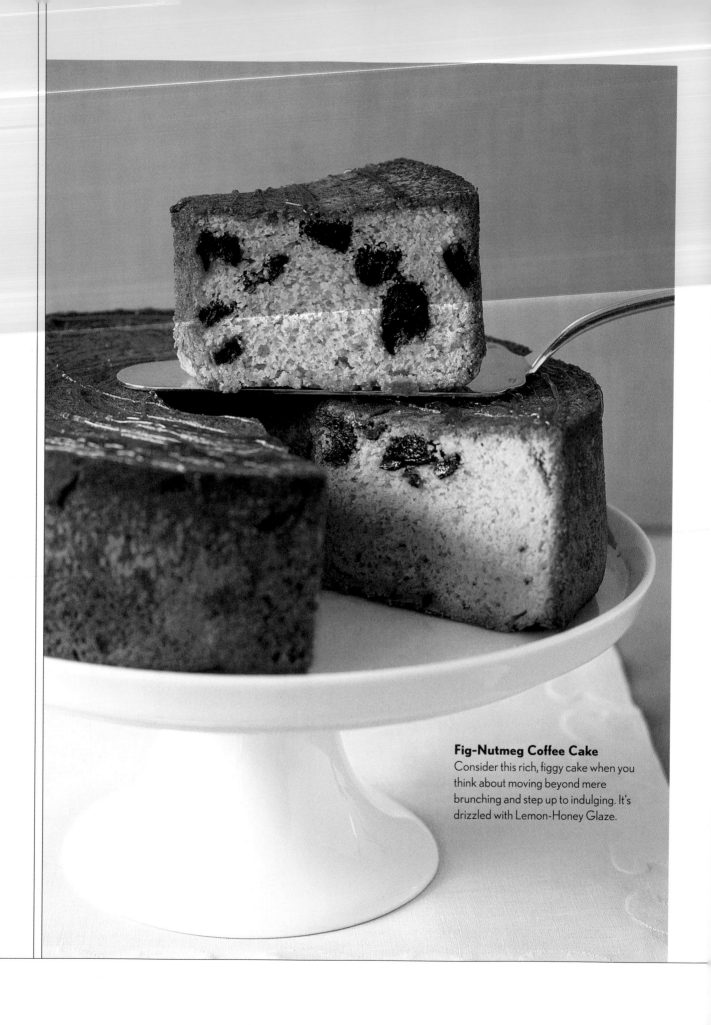

Fig-Nutmeg Coffee Cake
Consider this rich, figgy cake when you think about moving beyond mere brunching and step up to indulging. It's drizzled with Lemon-Honey Glaze.

Rhubarb-Strawberry Coffee Cake

The tantalizing filling of strawberries and rhubarb makes a scarlet ribbon in this rich and tangy coffee cake.

PREP: 35 minutes **BAKE:** 40 minutes

1	recipe Rhubarb-Strawberry Filling (below)	2	eggs
3	cups all-purpose flour	1	cup buttermilk or sour milk*
1	cup sugar	1	tsp. vanilla
1	tsp. baking soda	1/2	cup sugar
1	tsp. baking powder	1/2	cup all-purpose flour
1	tsp. salt	1/4	cup butter
1	cup butter		

1. Prepare Rhubarb-Strawberry Filling; set aside to cool.
2. Preheat oven to 350° F. In a large mixing bowl stir together the 3 cups flour, the 1 cup sugar, the baking soda, baking powder, and salt. Cut in the 1 cup butter until mixture resembles fine crumbs. In a small bowl beat eggs; stir in buttermilk or sour milk and vanilla. Add to flour mixture; stir to moisten.
3. Lightly grease a 13×9×2-inch baking pan; spread half of the batter in pan. Spread cooled filling over batter in pan. Spoon remaining batter in small mounds on filling.
4. In a small bowl combine the 1/2 cup sugar and the 1/2 cup flour. Cut in the 1/4 cup butter until mixture resembles fine crumbs. Sprinkle crumb mixture over batter in pan. Bake for 40 to 45 minutes or until golden. Serve warm. Makes 15 servings.

RHUBARB-STRAWBERRY FILLING: In a medium saucepan combine 3 cups fresh rhubarb or one 16-ounce package frozen unsweetened sliced rhubarb, and 4 cups hulled fresh strawberries or one 16-ounce package frozen unsweetened whole strawberries, thawed and halved. Cook fruit, covered, for 5 minutes. Add 2 tablespoons lemon juice. Combine 1 cup sugar and 1/3 cup cornstarch; add to rhubarb mixture. Cook and stir for 4 to 5 minutes until thickened and bubbly; cool.

*NOTE: For each cup of sour milk needed, place 1 tablespoon lemon juice or vinegar in a glass measuring cup. Add enough milk to make 1 cup total liquid; stir. Let mixture stand for 5 minutes before using.

low fat Each serving: 410 cal., 17 g total fat (10 g sat. fat), 73 mg chol., 458 mg sodium, 60 g carbo., 2 g fiber, 5 g pro. Daily Values: 14% vit. A, 41% vit. C, 7% calcium, 9% iron.

Fig-Nutmeg Coffee Cake

For fresh nutmeg flavor, use whole nutmeg and grate it yourself.

PREP: 20 minutes **BAKE:** 65 minutes **COOL:** 10 + 30 minutes

2	cups all-purpose flour	1 1/2	cups sugar
1	Tbsp. freshly grated nutmeg or 1 1/2 tsp. ground nutmeg	2	eggs
		1	8-oz. carton dairy sour cream
1	tsp. baking powder	1 1/2	cups snipped dried figs
1/4	tsp. salt	1	recipe Lemon-Honey Glaze (below)
1/2	cup butter, softened		

1. Preheat oven to 350° F. Grease and lightly flour a 9-inch springform pan with flat-bottom tube insert or an 8- to 10-cup fluted tube pan; set aside. In a medium bowl stir together flour, nutmeg, baking powder, and salt; set aside.
2. In a large bowl beat butter with an electric mixer on medium speed for 30 seconds. Add sugar; beat until combined. Add eggs, 1 at a time, beating well after each addition. Alternately add the flour mixture and the sour cream, beating after each addition until combined (batter will be thick). Stir in figs. Spoon batter into prepared pan, spreading evenly.
3. Bake for 65 to 70 minutes or until a wooden toothpick inserted near center comes out clean. Cool in pan on a wire rack over waxed paper for 10 minutes. Remove from pan. Cool slightly on the rack, about 30 minutes.
4. Prepare Lemon-Honey Glaze. Drizzle glaze onto slightly cooled cake, spooning any glaze that drips onto waxed paper back onto the cake. Serve warm or at room temperature. Makes 10 to 12 servings.

LEMON-HONEY GLAZE: In a small bowl combine 1/3 cup honey and 1/2 teaspoon finely shredded lemon peel.

Each serving: 465 cal., 16 g total fat (10 g sat. fat), 79 mg chol., 227 mg sodium, 78 g carbo., 4 g fiber, 6 g pro. Daily Values: 13% vit. A, 1% vit. C, 11% calcium, 12% iron.

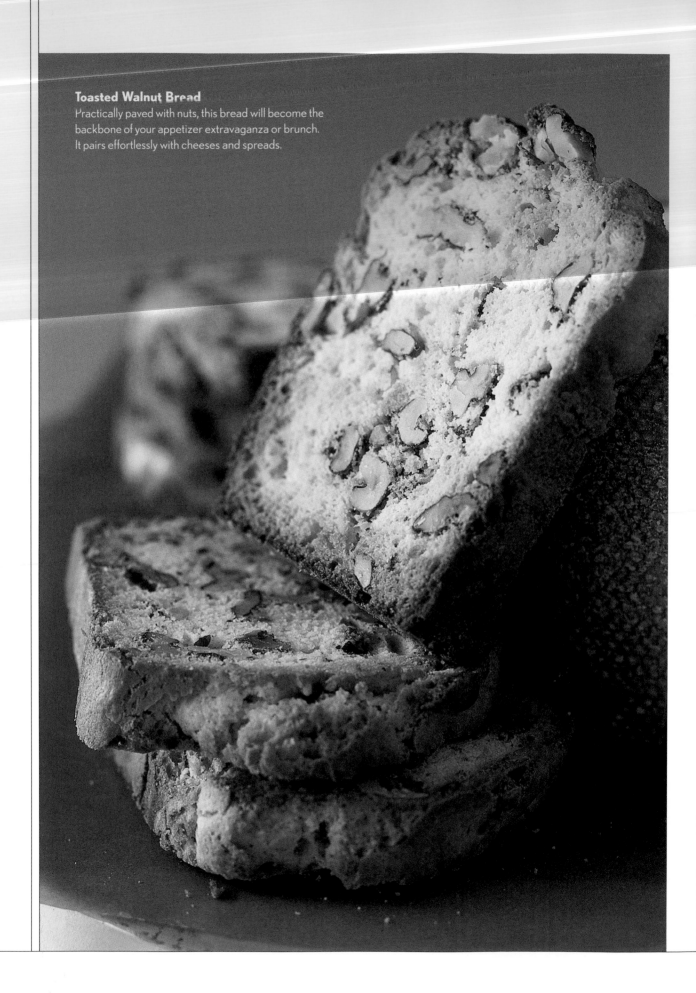

Toasted Walnut Bread
Practically paved with nuts, this bread will become the backbone of your appetizer extravaganza or brunch. It pairs effortlessly with cheeses and spreads.

Blueberry Rolls

Although shaped and baked like cinnamon rolls, this recipe offers a richer dough. Blueberry Rolls are scrumptious alone for breakfast or brunch or with ice cream for dessert.

Prep: 25 minutes **Bake:** 20 minutes

2	16 1/2-oz. cans blueberries	1/2	tsp. ground cinnamon
1	recipe Rich Shortcake (below)	1/4	cup sugar
1	Tbsp. butter, melted	2	Tbsp. all-purpose flour
2	Tbsp. sugar	2	tsp. lemon juice
			Vanilla ice cream (optional)

1. Drain blueberries, reserving juice; set aside. Grease a 2-quart square baking dish; set aside.

2. Prepare Rich Shortcake dough. On a lightly floured surface roll dough into an 11×9-inch rectangle. Brush dough with melted butter. In a small bowl combine the 2 tablespoons sugar and the cinnamon; sprinkle onto dough. Sprinkle with 1 cup of the drained blueberries. Roll up, starting from a short side. Seal seam. Slice roll into 9 equal pieces.

3. Preheat oven to 425° F. In a small saucepan combine the 1/4 cup sugar and the flour. Add remaining blueberries and reserved juice. Cook and stir until thickened and bubbly. Remove from heat; stir in lemon juice.

4. Pour blueberry mixture into prepared baking dish. Place rolls, cut sides down, on top of blueberry mixture. Bake about 20 minutes or until rolls are golden. Invert rolls onto a round platter; remove pan. If desired, serve warm with vanilla ice cream. Makes 9 servings.

RICH SHORTCAKE: In a medium mixing bowl stir together 2 cups all-purpose flour, 4 teaspoons baking powder, 1 tablespoon sugar, and 1/2 teaspoon salt. Using a pastry blender, cut in 1/3 cup shortening until mixture resembles coarse crumbs. Make a well in the center. Add 2/3 cup milk and 1 beaten egg all at once. Stir just until dough clings together. On a heavily floured surface coat the dough lightly with flour. Knead gently for 10 to 12 strokes.

Each serving: 284 cal., 10 g total fat (3 g sat. fat), 29 mg chol., 339 mg sodium, 44 g carbo., 2 g fiber, 5 g pro. Daily Values: 157% vit. A, 2% vit. C, 145% calcium, 2% iron.

Toasted Walnut Bread

Toasting the walnuts before adding them to the dough intensifies their flavor, providing greater richness and depth to the finished bread.

Prep: 20 minutes **Bake:** 50 + 20 minutes

2	cups all-purpose flour	2	cups coarsely chopped walnuts, toasted*
1/3	cup sugar		Slices of firm cheese, such as white or orange farmhouse cheddar, Appenzell, Edam, or Gouda (optional)
1	Tbsp. baking powder		
1/2	tsp. salt		
1	egg		
1	cup milk		
1/3	cup cooking oil		

1. Preheat oven to 350° F. Grease the bottom and 1/2 inch up sides of an 8×4×2-inch loaf pan; set aside. In a large bowl stir together flour, sugar, baking powder, and salt. Make a well in center of flour mixture; set aside.

2. In a medium bowl beat egg; stir in milk and oil. Add egg mixture all at once to flour mixture. Stir just until moistened (batter should be lumpy). Fold in nuts. Spoon batter into prepared pan; spreading evenly.

3. Bake for 50 to 55 minutes or until a wooden toothpick inserted near center comes out clean. Cool in pan on a wire rack for 10 minutes. Remove from pan. Cool on the wire rack.

4. Preheat oven to 375° F. Cut bread into 3/4-inch-thick slices. Arrange slices in a single layer on a baking sheet. Bake about 20 minutes or until brown on both sides, turning once. If desired, serve warm with cheese slices. Makes 1 loaf (10 servings).

***NOTE:** To toast nuts, bake in a 350° F oven for 5 to 10 minutes or until golden, stirring once or twice.

Each serving (without cheese): 355 cal., 24 g total fat (3 g sat. fat), 23 mg chol., 256 mg sodium, 30 g carbo., 2 g fiber, 8 g pro. Daily Values: 2% vit. A, 1% vit. C, 14% calcium, 11% iron.

EASTER DINNER

Roasted Asparagus Soup *(page 67)*
Baked ham
Zucchini-Olive Couscous *(page 296)*
Toasted Walnut Bread *(above)*
Cornbread Cassata *(page 60)*
Coffee or tea

Lemon Muffins

Lemon curd is a smooth, sweet spread popular in Britain. You can find it in the preserves section of grocery stores or specialty food shops. Spread any leftover curd onto toasted English muffins.

PREP: 25 minutes **BAKE:** 18 minutes **COOL:** 5 minutes

1½	cups all-purpose flour	¾	cup milk
½	cup sugar	¼	cup cooking oil
¼	cup whole wheat flour	⅔	cup purchased lemon
2	tsp. baking powder		curd
¼	tsp. salt	2	Tbsp. toasted coconut
1	egg		

1. Preheat oven to 400° F. Grease 6 popover pans and line with paper bake cups; set aside. (See directions for baking in muffin cups, below.) In a medium bowl stir together all-purpose flour, sugar, whole wheat flour, baking powder, and salt. Make a well in the center of the flour mixture; set aside.

2. In a small mixing bowl beat the egg; stir in milk and oil. Add egg mixture all at once to flour mixture. Stir just until moistened (batter should be lumpy).

3. Spoon half of the batter into the prepared popover pans (2 rounded tablespoons in each cup). Spoon 2 rounded teaspoons lemon curd into each cup. (There will be some remaining for topping.) Spoon remaining batter into popover pans, filling each cup two-thirds full.

4. Bake for 18 to 20 minutes or until golden. Cool in popover pans on a wire rack for 5 minutes. Remove from popover pans. Spread with remaining lemon curd; top with toasted coconut. Serve warm, or cool on a wire rack. If desired, slip muffins into fresh paper bake cups and tie with string. Makes 6 tall muffins.

NOTE: To bake in muffin cups, grease twelve 2½-inch muffin cups and line with paper bake cups; set aside. Prepare muffin batter through Step 2. Spoon half the batter into prepared muffin cups (a rounded tablespoon in each muffin cup). Spoon a rounded teaspoon of lemon curd onto the batter in each cup. (There will be some remaining for topping.) Spoon remaining batter into muffin cups, filling each cup two-thirds full. Bake, cool, and serve as directed. Makes 12 muffins.

Each tall muffin: 419 cal., 13 g total fat (4 g sat. fat), 65 mg chol., 291 mg sodium, 47 g carbo., 5 g fiber, 6 g pro. Daily Values: 2% vit. A, 1% vit. C, 13% calcium, 9% iron.

Corn Bread Cassata

PREP: 30 minutes **BAKE:** 20 minutes **COOL:** 2 hours

2	8½-oz. pkg. corn muffin mix	1½	cups whipping cream
1	8-oz. can crushed pineapple (juice pack)	1	Tbsp. packed brown sugar
2	Tbsp. rum or brandy	½	cup chopped white chocolate chunks
1½	cups chopped, dried cherries and/or golden raisins		Dried cherries (optional) White chocolate chunks (optional)

1. Preheat oven to 350° F. Chill a large mixing bowl and beaters of an electric mixer. Grease and flour 8 nonstick popover or 2½-inch muffin cups or two 9×1½- or 8×1½-inch round cake pans. Line pans with waxed paper or parchment paper; set aside.

2. In 2 medium bowls prepare each muffin mix according to package directions, except stir half of the undrained pineapple into each bowl along with the milk and egg. Spoon a scant ½ cup batter into each popover or muffin cup* or spread the batter into prepared 8- or 9-inch pans, using 1 pan for each mix.

3. Bake until a wooden toothpick inserted near the center comes out clean, allowing 20 minutes for popover pans, 2½-inch muffin cups, or 9-inch pans, and 20 to 22 minutes for 8-inch pans. Cool in pans on a wire rack for 5 minutes for smaller pans and 10 minutes for larger pans. Remove cakes from pans; remove paper. Cool for 2 hours on the wire rack.

4. Meanwhile, in a small saucepan heat rum over low heat until warm. Add the 1½ cups dried fruit. Let stand for 20 minutes; drain off any excess liquid.

5. In the chilled mixing bowl beat whipping cream and brown sugar with chilled beaters of an electric mixer on medium speed until soft peaks form (tips curl). Fold in fruit mixture and the ½ cup white chocolate chunks. Cover and chill for up to 2 hours.

6. Trim rounded cake tops so inverted cakes will be flat. Split cakes horizontally at a slight diagonal. Place 1 layer on a dessert plate. Top with some of the filling, cake top, and more filling. If desired, top with additional cherries and white chocolate chunks. Makes 8 to 12 servings.

*NOTE: You have enough batter to make 8 individual cakes. If you don't have 8 of the smaller pans, refrigerate the remaining batter while the first cakes bake. Cool pans; wash and prepare pans as above to bake remaining cakes.

Each serving: 604 cal., 30 g total fat (13 g sat. fat), 104 mg chol., 510 mg sodium, 76 g carbo., 1 g fiber, 9 g pro. Daily Values: 13% vit. A, 5% vit. C, 15% calcium, 7% iron.

Lemon Muffins
An Easter bonnet of coconut and a heart of lemon make these tall, filled muffins just the thing to savor after a little post-dinner stroll. Go out and discover which flowers have won the race to be first out of the ground.

Corn Bread Cassata
Our spin on an Italian classic, this pineapple corn bread is stacked high with nuts, brown-sugar whipped cream, and rum-drenched dried cherries.

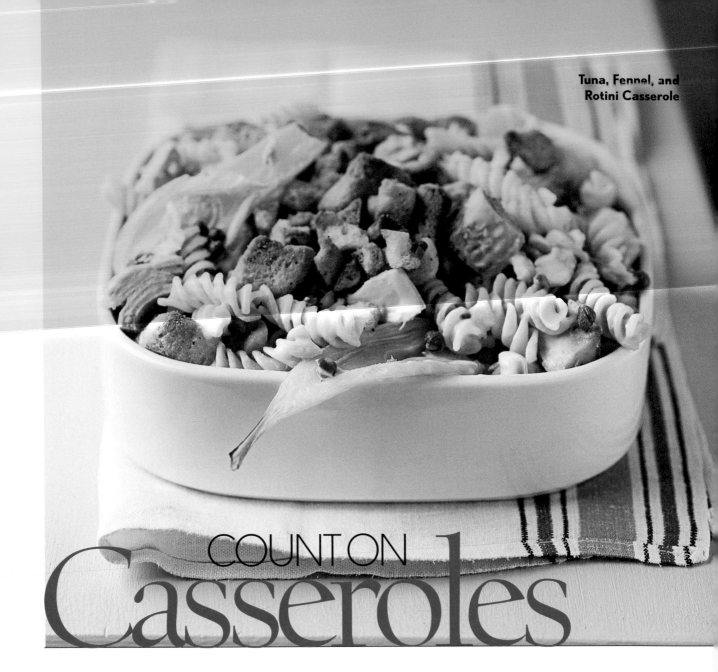

COUNT ON Casseroles

HERE ARE THREE HOMESPUN CASSEROLES TO FEED CROWD-SIZE APPETITES. JUST ADD A SALAD AND A LOAF OF CRUSTY BREAD.

Remember the good old days when Mom would say to friends, "We'd love to have you over. I've got a casserole in the oven"? It sounded so simple and inviting, and tasted so good. Now, with the help of these updated classics, you can serve your family and friends an impromptu feast with the same ease. Consider these delicious spins on tried-and-true favorites. They're big on flavor and perfect for those days when carpool conversation turns into an invitation for supper. Plus, they go together with a minimum of effort and require only ingredients you probably have on hand. Even better, they're out of the oven in 30 minutes or less and register a big 10 in the flavor department. And while you're at it, why not make an extra casserole and tuck it in the freezer so you're always ready for company?

BY STEPHEN EXEL. PHOTOGRAPHS: JOYCE OUDKERK POOL. FOOD STYLIST: POUKÉ. PROP STYLIST: CAROL HACKER.

Tuna, Fennel, and Rotini Casserole

It's tuna-noodle casserole like your mom never made, tossed with fennel and capers and coated in a creamy light alfredo sauce.

PREP: 20 minutes **BAKE:** 20 minutes

1½ cups dried rotini	2 Tbsp. capers, drained
2 Tbsp. butter	(optional)
¾ cup seasoned croutons, slightly crushed	2 6-oz. cans tuna (packed in oil), drained and broken into chunks
2 small fennel bulbs, sliced (2 cups)	
1 10-oz. container refrigerated light Alfredo sauce	

1. Preheat oven to 375° F. Cook rotini according to package directions; drain.

2. Meanwhile, in a medium saucepan melt butter. In a bowl combine croutons with 1 tablespoon of the melted butter; toss gently to coat.

3. Add fennel to remaining butter in saucepan. Cover; cook for 6 to 8 minutes or until fennel is just tender, stirring occasionally. Stir in Alfredo sauce, cooked rotini, and capers, if desired. Fold in tuna.

4. Transfer tuna mixture to an ungreased 1½-quart casserole. Top with croutons. Bake, uncovered, about 20 minutes or until heated through. Serve warm. Makes 6 servings.

Each serving: 306 cal., 11 g total fat (6 g sat. fat), 44 mg chol., 527 mg sodium, 29 g carbo., 9 g dietary fiber, 20 g protein. Daily Values: 4% vit. A, 6% vit. C, 13% calcium, 10% iron.

Chicken and Orzo Casserole

To boost the heat, choose the serrano peppers. They provide more kick than jalapeño peppers.

PREP: 15 minutes **BAKE:** 20 minutes **STAND:** 10 minutes

2 tsp. cumin seeds	2 9-oz. pkg. frozen cooked southwest-flavored chicken breast strips, thawed, or two 6-oz. pkg. refrigerated cooked southwest-flavored chicken breast strips
1 14-oz. can chicken broth	
1 14½-oz. can Mexican-style stewed tomatoes or one 10-oz. can diced tomatoes and green chile peppers	
¼ cup oil-packed dried tomatoes, drained and cut up	Seeded and chopped jalapeño or serrano chile peppers (optional)*
1 cup dried orzo pasta	Paprika (optional)

1. Preheat oven to 350° F. In a large saucepan heat cumin seeds over medium heat for 3 to 4 minutes or until fragrant and toasted, shaking pan occasionally. Carefully stir in broth, undrained tomatoes, dried tomatoes, and orzo. Bring to boiling. Transfer mixture to an ungreased 2-quart baking dish. Top with chicken breast strips.

2. Bake, covered, for 20 minutes or until orzo is tender. Let casserole stand, covered, for 10 minutes. If desired, top with jalapeño peppers; sprinkle with paprika. Serve warm. Makes 4 to 6 servings.

***NOTE:** Because hot chile peppers, such as jalapeños, contain volatile oils that can burn your skin and eyes, avoid direct contact with chiles as much as possible. When working with chile peppers, wear plastic or rubber gloves. If your bare hands do touch the chile peppers, wash your hands well with soap and water.

low fat Each serving: 388 cal., 7 g total fat (2 g sat. fat), 60 mg chol., 1,227 mg sodium, 44 g carbo., 3 g dietary fiber, 35 g protein. Daily Values: 14% vit. A, 15% vit. C, 9% calcium, 24% iron.

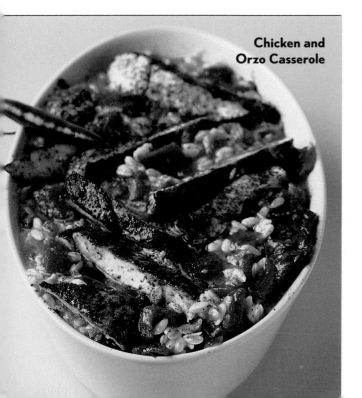

Chicken and Orzo Casserole

MAKE-AHEAD TIPS

Make-ahead cooking—whether you're stashing leftovers in the freezer or baking ahead for busy days—is a great way to get the most out of your time in the kitchen. You can store most casseroles in the fridge for three to four days or in the freezer up to three months.

SEAL IT TIGHTLY

Most food-storage containers that have tight-fitting lids—even disposables—provide adequate protection in the refrigerator. However, when you're shopping for freezer-safe containers, look for a phrase or icon indicating the container is designed for freezer use. Be sure to use freezer-to-oven dishes when you want to store an entire casserole in its baking dish. If your casserole doesn't have its own tight-fitting lid, cover the surface with heavy-duty foil or plastic freezer wrap. Do not use foil to wrap foods that contain acidic ingredients. To freeze a casserole that contains tomatoes or other acidic ingredients, cover with plastic freezer wrap, then with foil. Remove the plastic wrap before reheating in the oven.

COOL IT QUICKLY

Hot casseroles bound for the refrigerator or freezer must be cooled rapidly. A quick chill decreases the chance that harmful bacteria will grow. Cooling food quickly before popping the sealed containers into the freezer allows the food to freeze faster. This also helps to prevent the formation of large ice crystals that may ruin the flavor and texture. When freezing leftovers, the quickest way to cool down a casserole is to divide it into individual portions and place them in shallow containers. Put these into the refrigerator. Once thoroughly chilled, transfer the cold containers to the freezer. Arrange the containers in a single layer until frozen. Stack after they're frozen solid.

KEEP IT COLD

When you store casseroles in the refrigerator or freezer, it's important to make sure they are kept cold enough. Maintain a refrigerator temperature of 40° F or below. Freezers should be kept at a temperature of 0° F or below.

Creamy Macaroni and Cheese

You can use cavatelli or campanelle pasta instead of the elbow macaroni called for in this hearty macaroni and cheese.

PREP: 10 minutes **BAKE:** 30 minutes
COOK: 10 minutes **STAND:** 10 minutes

4	slices bacon	2	to 4 oz. blue cheese,
1	large sweet onion,		crumbled ($1/2$ to 1 cup)
	thinly sliced	1	cup half-and-half or
6	oz. dried elbow macaroni		light cream
8	oz. mozzarella cheese,	$1/8$	tsp. ground black pepper
	shredded (2 cups)		

1. Preheat oven to 350° F. In a large skillet cook bacon over medium heat until crisp, turning once. Drain bacon on paper towels; crumble. Reserve bacon drippings in skillet.

2. Cook onion in reserved bacon drippings for 5 to 8 minutes or until onion is tender and golden brown. Set aside.

3. Cook elbow macaroni according to package directions. Drain and place in an ungreased $1^{1}/2$-quart casserole. Add the crumbled bacon, onion, $1^{1}/2$ cups of the mozzarella cheese, the blue cheese, half-and-half, and pepper. Toss gently to combine.

4. Bake, uncovered, for 20 minutes. Stir gently. Top with the remaining mozzarella cheese. Bake for 10 minutes more or until top is brown and bubbly. Let stand for 10 minutes. Serve warm. Makes 6 servings.

Each serving: 331 cal., 18 g total fat (9 g sat. fat), 45 mg chol., 280 mg sodium, 26 g carbo., 1 g dietary fiber, 16 g protein. Daily Values: 8% vit. A, 3% vit. C, 30% calcium, 6% iron.

COMFORTING CASSEROLE SUPPER

Creamy Macaroni and Cheese (*above*)
Apple wedges
Dinner rolls
Ultimate Chocolate Sundaes (*page 29*)
Milk

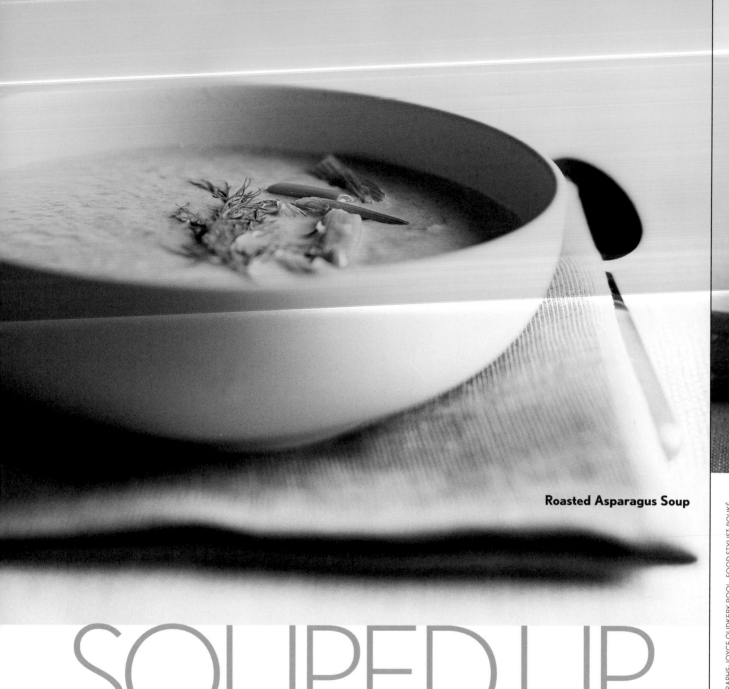

Roasted Asparagus Soup

BY STEPHEN EXEL. PHOTOGRAPHS: JOYCE OUDKERK POOL. FOOD STYLIST: POUKÉ.

SOUPED UP
AND READY TO GO

USE APRIL'S SHOWER OF TENDER GREENS TO THEIR BEST
ADVANTAGE IN THESE LIGHT-AS-AIR SPRING SOUPS.

Soups are the best way to bridge this changeable season. Caught between winter's last gasp
and springtime's first fertile breath, we turn to soups to both warm chilled souls and
rejuvenate spirits still caught in the winter doldrums. Thankfully, as we start to pick up
the threads of outdoor life again, these soups are ready. They're quick to prepare and use
a minimum number of ingredients, with a big nod toward spring's tenderest greens—
spinach, asparagus, baby green beans, green onions, chives, and fresh herbs.

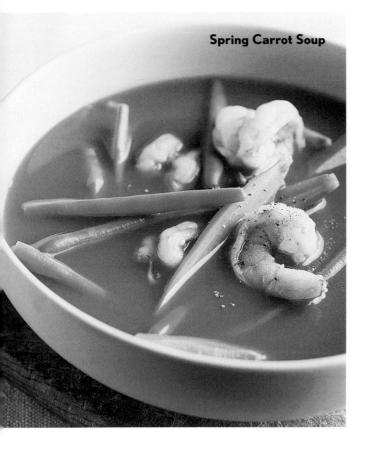

Spring Carrot Soup

Roasted Asparagus Soup

Roasted green onions give this soup smoky depth. Their dark green tops, along with fresh dill, brighten the soup with a splash of color.

START TO FINISH: 25 minutes

2	bunches green onions	2	14-oz. cans reduced-sodium chicken broth
1½	lb. asparagus, trimmed and cut into 2- to 3-inch pieces	¼	tsp. kosher salt
		¼	tsp. ground black pepper
1	medium onion, cut into thin wedges	½	cup half-and-half, light cream, or milk
2	Tbsp. olive oil	1	Tbsp. snipped fresh dill

1. Preheat oven to 450° F. Trim root ends from green onions. Cut white parts into 1-inch lengths. Cut green tops into 1-inch lengths and reserve. Place the white parts of green onions, asparagus, and onion wedges in an even layer in a shallow large roasting pan. Drizzle vegetables with olive oil. Roast, uncovered, for 15 to 20 minutes or until vegetables are charred and tender.

2. Place half of the roasted vegetables in a food processor or blender. Add half a can of broth. Cover; process or blend until smooth. Transfer to a large saucepan. Repeat with remaining asparagus, onion wedges, and half a can of broth.

3. Stir in remaining can of broth, salt, and pepper. Bring to boiling; reduce heat. Stir in half-and-half and snipped fresh dill; heat through, but do not boil.

4. To serve, ladle soup into 6 bowls. Top with green onion tops and dill sprigs, if desired. Makes 6 appetizer servings.

Each serving: 128 cal., 8 g total fat (3 g sat. fat), 9 mg chol., 598 mg sodium, 10 g carbo., 3 g fiber, 6 g pro. Daily Values: 14% vit. A, 28% vit. C, 8% calcium, 8% iron.

Spring Carrot Soup

You'll find *haricots vert,* which are tiny French green beans, in the specialty section of the produce aisle.

START TO FINISH: 25 minutes

1	14-oz. can vegetable broth	6	oz. fresh or frozen peeled, deveined medium shrimp
8 to 10	small carrots with tops, trimmed, scrubbed, halved lengthwise, and cut in half crosswise (4 oz.)	1	12-oz. can carrot juice
		¼	tsp. bottled hot pepper sauce
½	cup haricots vert or baby green beans, trimmed		Salt
			Ground black pepper

1. In a large saucepan bring vegetable broth to boiling. Add carrots.* Bring to boiling; reduce heat. Cover and simmer for 4 minutes.

2. Add haricots vert and shrimp. Bring to boiling; reduce heat. Cover and simmer about 3 minutes or until shrimp turn pink.

3. Add carrot juice and hot pepper sauce; heat through (do not boil). Season to taste with salt and pepper. To serve, ladle soup into 4 to 6 bowls. Makes 4 to 6 appetizer servings.

*NOTE: If you prefer green beans to be more than crisp-tender, add them with the carrots.

low fat Each serving: 104 cal., 1 g total fat (0 g sat. fat), 65 mg chol., 586 mg sodium, 13 g carbo., 2 g fiber, 11 g pro. Daily Values: 351% vit. A, 21% vit. C, 6% calcium, 9% iron.

Country Potato Soup with Chives and Garlic Olive Oil

This soup is equally delicious hot or chilled. Garlic Olive Oil is not only great in the soup, it's marvelous as a dipper for crusty bread.

START TO FINISH: 20 minutes

1½ cups refrigerated diced red-skinned potatoes or new potatoes, peeled and quartered	6 fresh chives, cut into 1-inch pieces
½ cup chopped leek*	⅛ tsp. ground white pepper
1 clove garlic, minced	1 cup half-and-half, light cream, or milk
2 14-oz. cans reduced-sodium chicken broth	Snipped fresh chives
	1 recipe Garlic Olive Oil (below)

1. In a large saucepan combine potatoes, leek, garlic, and 1 cup of the broth. Bring to boiling; reduce heat. Cover and simmer until potatoes are tender, allowing 5 minutes for diced potatoes or 10 minutes for quartered potatoes.

2. Using a hand-held mixer, puree undrained potato mixture. (Or, add potato mixture to a blender. Cover; blend on low speed until nearly smooth, adding additional broth if necessary. Return mixture to saucepan.)

3. Add cut chives and white pepper. Whisk in remaining broth and half-and-half. Heat through.

4. To serve, ladle soup into 6 bowls. Top with snipped chives and a few drops of Garlic Olive Oil. Makes 6 appetizer servings.

GARLIC OLIVE OIL: In a small skillet heat 1 clove minced garlic in 2 tablespoons olive oil until garlic begins to brown. Strain to remove garlic. Discard any unused oil (do not store).

*NOTE: Use the white part of the leek plus a little of the green top to give the soup a pleasant hint of color.

Each serving: 96 cal., 5 g total fat (3 g sat. fat), 15 mg chol., 424 mg sodium, 10 g carbo., 1 g fiber, 4 g pro. Daily Values: 4% vit. A, 8% vit. C, 5% calcium, 2% iron.

Spring Salmon Chowder

This broth-based chowder sings with spring flavors. Baby spinach, thyme, and green onions nicely accent sweet new potatoes and salmon.

START TO FINISH: 25 minutes

6 tiny new potatoes, quartered	12 oz. fresh or frozen skinless, boneless salmon, cut into 1-inch chunks
2 14-oz. cans vegetable broth	1 cup packed baby spinach leaves
1 ear fresh corn, kernels removed and reserved, or ½ cup frozen whole kernel corn, thawed	¼ cup sliced green onion
	Salt
6 2-inch sprigs fresh thyme, or ½ tsp. dried thyme, crushed	Ground black pepper

1. In a large saucepan cook potatoes, covered, in boiling vegetable broth about 5 minutes or until potatoes are tender but not cooked through.

2. Add corn and thyme. Return to boiling; reduce heat. Cover and cook about 4 minutes or until vegetables are crisp-tender; reduce heat.

3. Carefully add salmon to saucepan. Simmer, uncovered, for 3 to 5 minutes or until salmon flakes easily with a fork.

4. Remove thyme sprigs, if desired. Stir in spinach and green onion; cook about 1 minute or until spinach begins to wilt.

5. To serve, ladle chowder into 6 cups or bowls. Season to taste with salt and pepper. Makes 6 main-dish servings.

Each serving: 169 cal., 7 g total fat (1 g sat. fat), 37 mg chol., 639 mg sodium, 14 g carbo., 2 g fiber, 14 g pro. Daily Values: 14% vit. A, 22% vit. C, 3% calcium, 9% iron.

A SOUPER SUPPER

Spring Salmon Chowder (*above*)
Tossed green salad
Mom's Bread (*page 288*)
Nutty Berry-Chip Squares (*page 301*)
Sparkling water

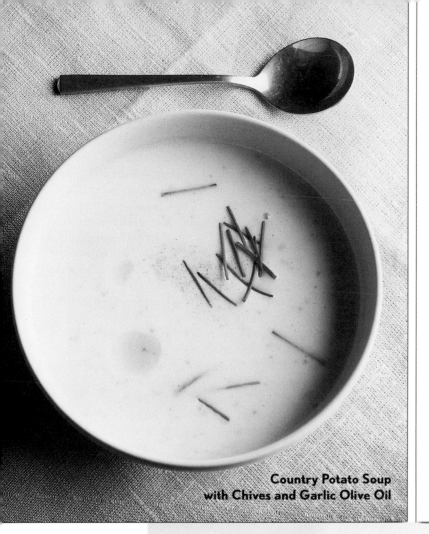

**Country Potato Soup
with Chives and Garlic Olive Oil**

SOUP TOPPERS

Sometimes a quick little sprinkle of something special can bring a soup to life—not only its flavor, but also its appearance. To find ideal toppers and garnishes, start by looking at the soup recipe itself.

First, consider classic complements such as shredded cheese, snipped herbs, croutons or toast, or coarsely cracked peppercorns—in fact, a colorful mix of peppercorns is often pretty and peppy. But if none of the classic toppers sounds appealing, take one more look at the recipe's ingredient list. Is there something you can chop, slice, or julienne into a garnish—and perhaps even use in a different form than in the recipe?

In a soup featuring cooked carrots, you can float a simple sprinkling of raw, julienne-cut carrot for contrasting color and flavor. In a beet soup, you might do the same with blanched or even pickled beets.

Don't be afraid of a mess when garnishing wide-rimmed soup bowls—many garnishes, particularly herbs, look great sprinkled not only on the soup, but on the bowl rim as well.

Spring Salmon Chowder

Alesia Lacina *(left)* and her sister, Francene Coons, stand in their Iowa field of soybeans. The sisters follow their soybeans from field to factory, where they make tofu that they include in recipes such as Thai Noodles. The young green soybeans *(below left)* look similar to peas in a pod.

The Soy SISTERS

TWO SISTERS—WHO ADMIT TO BEING SOY NUTS—ADD A HEALTHY BOOST OF SOY FOODS TO NEARLY EVERYTHING THEY EAT.

Thai Noodles

Featuring soy in three ways—soy nut butter, soy sauce, and tofu—this dish showcases the delicious versatility of the nutritious bean.

PREP: 15 minutes   **COOK:** 15 minutes

½	cup soy nut butter or creamy peanut butter	1	14- to 16-oz. pkg. firm tofu
⅓	cup water	1	Tbsp. cooking oil
⅓	cup reduced-sodium soy sauce	8	oz. Chinese egg noodles or fine egg noodles
3	Tbsp. lime juice	2	Tbsp. snipped fresh cilantro
3	cloves garlic, quartered	¼	tsp. crushed red pepper
1	Tbsp. grated fresh ginger	¼	cup chopped unsalted peanuts
1	Tbsp. sesame oil		

1. In a food processor or blender combine soy nut butter, water, soy sauce, lime juice, garlic, ginger, and sesame oil. Cover and process or blend until smooth; set aside.

2. Drain tofu; pat dry with paper towels. Cut tofu into ½-inch-thick slices. In a 12-inch nonstick skillet heat cooking oil over medium-high heat. Add tofu; cook for 5 minutes or until brown. Turn slices. Cook for 5 minutes more. Remove from heat. Transfer slices to a cutting board. Cut each slice into 1½- to 2-inch triangles or squares; set aside.

3. Meanwhile, cook noodles according to package directions; drain and add to skillet.

4. Add soy nut butter mixture to skillet; heat through. Add tofu, noodles, cilantro, and pepper to skillet. Toss gently to coat. Sprinkle with peanuts. Serve warm. Makes 4 to 6 main-dish servings.

Each serving: 582 cal., 28 g total fat (4 g sat. fat), 54 mg chol., 972 mg sodium, 58 g carbo., 3 g fiber, 27 g pro. Daily Values: 4% vit. A, 12% vit. C, 6% calcium, 18% iron.

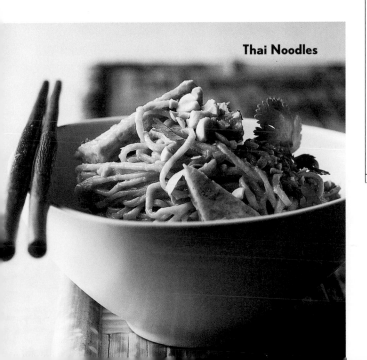

Thai Noodles

Sisters' story

It all began when Alesia Lacina and her husband, Tom, an attorney and Iowa soybean farmer, experienced a "eureka" moment one evening. At the time, they were growing and shipping food-grade soybeans to Japan, where the beans were used to make tofu.

"We thought—why can't we do that here?" says Alesia. So she and Tom teamed up with her sister, Francene Coons, and Francene's husband, Dave, to immerse themselves in everything tofu. Alesia and Francene—they call themselves the Soy Sisters—tried making tofu in their kitchens, but it "was a real mess," Alesia says. So they studied with soy experts at Iowa State University and the University of Illinois at Urbana-Champaign.

In 1999, the family-run company, Midwest Harvest, started producing organic tofu. The sisters' tofu consumption skyrocketed as their knowledge of the health benefits of soy foods increased. The sisters say they consume 25 grams of soy protein daily—the amount reported to reduce the risk of heart disease. Soy foods, which are high in protein and low in saturated fat, also may alleviate hot flashes and other menopausal symptoms, as well as reduce the risk of osteoporosis. Research also shows soy foods may fight prostate, colon, and breast cancers.

The Soy Sisters compiled their recipes into *A Tofu Cookbook* in an effort to move tofu into the mainstream. "There's a tremendous misconception about soy," says Francene. "You don't have to go vegetarian. The recipes may not be low in fat, but they are comfort foods with the added benefits of soy." Recipes for some of their favorite dishes begin here. Their cookbook, $20 including shipping, is available by calling 888/766-0051 or by sending e-mail requests to: orders@wildwoodharvestfoods.com.

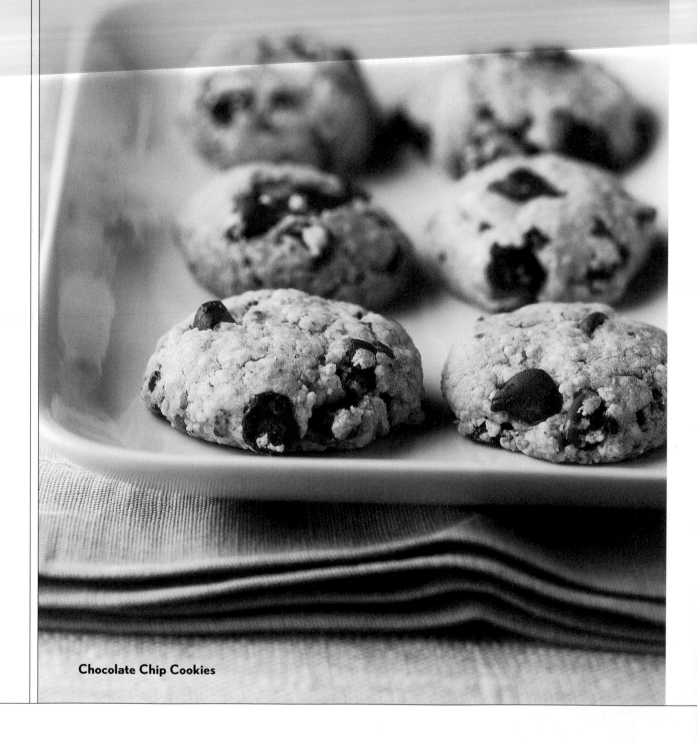

"THE RECIPES MAY NOT BE LOW IN FAT, BUT THEY'RE COMFORT FOODS WITH THE ADDED BENEFITS OF SOY."

Francene Coons

Chocolate Chip Cookies

Chocolate Chip Cookies

What better way to introduce tofu to your diet than through chocolate chip cookies?

PREP: 30 minutes **BAKE:** 8 minutes per batch

2½ cups quick-cooking rolled oats	1 cup granulated sugar or maple sugar
2 cups all-purpose flour	1 tsp. vanilla
1 tsp. baking powder	1 12-oz. pkg. semisweet chocolate pieces
1 tsp. baking soda	
8 oz. soft tofu	4 oz. semisweet chocolate, coarsely chopped
1 cup butter or margarine, softened	
1 cup packed brown sugar	

1. Preheat oven to 375° F. Process oats in small batches in a food processor until oatmeal resembles coarse flour. In a medium bowl stir together the oatmeal, flour, baking powder, and baking soda; set aside. Place tofu in food processor; cover and process until smooth. Set aside.

2. In a very large bowl beat butter with an electric mixer on medium to high speed for 30 seconds. Add sugars; beat until combined. Beat in vanilla and tofu until combined. Beat in as much of the flour mixture as you can with the mixer. Stir in any remaining flour mixture. Stir in chocolate pieces and chopped chocolate.

3. Form dough into 1½-inch balls. Place 3 inches apart on an ungreased cookie sheet. Slightly flatten dough. Bake for 8 to 10 minutes or until cookies are golden brown around the edges; cool on a wire rack. Makes about 52 cookies.

Each cookie: 131 cal., 6 g total fat (4 g sat. fat), 10 mg chol., 70 mg sodium, 19 g carbo., 1 g fiber, 2 g pro. Daily Values: 3% vit. A, 1% calcium, 4% iron.

TOFU IS SOY GOOD

Besides being good for you—cholesterol-free, low-calorie, high-protein—tofu is surprisingly fun and easy to use in cooking. Originating in China as early as the 2nd century B.C., tofu is made from soy bean curd in a process similar to cheesemaking. In fact, many of the historic uses of tofu in Asia compare well to Western uses of dairy products. Tofu is easy to use because it takes on the flavors of other ingredients. Yet, because tofu is available in textures ranging from soft to extra firm, it's important to select the texture specified in the recipe you're preparing.

Garlic Mashed Potatoes with Tofu and Feta

Tofu lends smooth creaminess while feta cheese and garlic add flavorful accents to comfy mashed potatoes.

PREP: 20 minutes **COOK:** 20 minutes

8 oz. soft tofu, drained	1 Tbsp. olive oil
½ cup crumbled basil-and-tomato feta cheese	½ tsp. salt
	¼ tsp. ground black pepper
6 medium red potatoes (about 2 lb.)	Milk (optional)
	2 Tbsp. finely shredded Parmesan cheese
8 cloves garlic, peeled	

1. Let tofu and feta cheese stand at room temperature while preparing the potatoes. Quarter potatoes. In a large saucepan cook potatoes and garlic, covered, in lightly salted boiling water for 20 to 25 minutes or until tender.

2. Meanwhile, place tofu in a blender or food processor. Cover; blend or process tofu until smooth. Set aside.

3. Drain potatoes and garlic; transfer to a large bowl. Mash potatoes and garlic with a potato masher or beat with an electric mixer on low speed. Stir in pureed tofu, olive oil, salt, and pepper. If needed, add milk, 1 tablespoon at a time, until potatoes are light and fluffy. Stir in feta and Parmesan cheeses. Makes 6 servings.

Each serving: 229 cal., 9 g total fat (4 g sat. fat), 16 mg chol., 499 mg sodium, 28 g carbo., 3 g fiber, 11 g pro. Daily Values: 2% vit. A, 39% vit. C, 22% calcium, 14% iron.

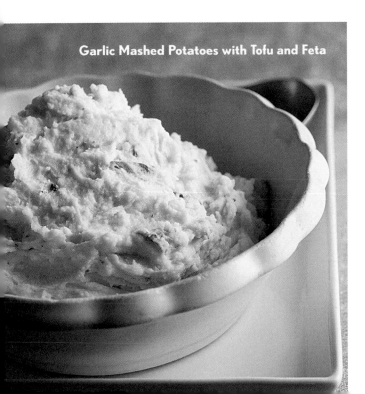

Garlic Mashed Potatoes with Tofu and Feta

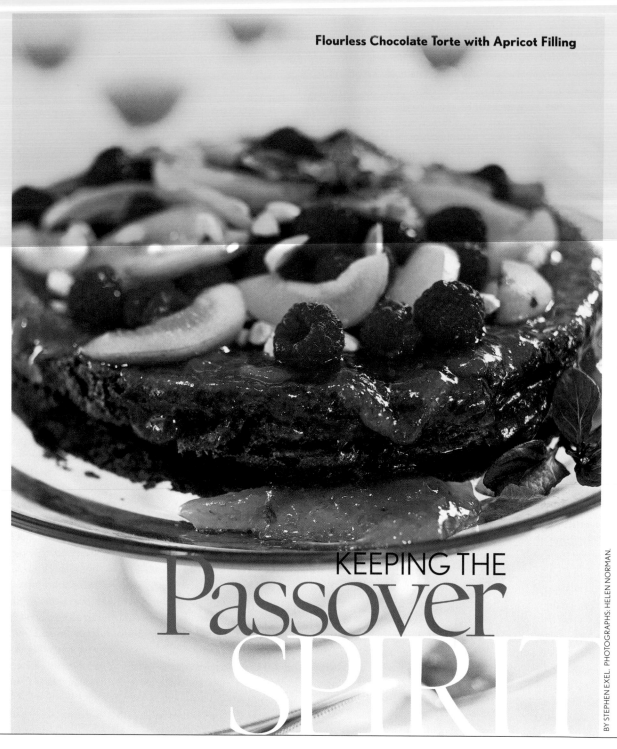

Flourless Chocolate Torte with Apricot Filling

KEEPING THE
Passover
SPIRIT

BY STEPHEN EXEL. PHOTOGRAPHS: HELEN NORMAN.

COOKBOOK AUTHOR JOAN NATHAN'S PASSOVER
SEDER SETS THE STAGE FOR A HARMONIOUS
BLEND OF RITUAL AND FAMILY TRADITION.

Flourless Chocolate Torte with Apricot Filling

Joan's chocolate torte is made with potato starch instead of flour, which is forbidden for use during the eight days of Passover.

PREP: 40 minutes **BAKE:** 30 minutes
STAND: 30 minutes **COOL:** 2 hours

6 egg yolks	2 Tbsp. potato starch
8 egg whites	1 recipe Apricot Filling
1 Tbsp. unsweetened	(below)
cocoa powder	½ cup toasted chopped
8 oz. bittersweet chocolate,	almonds
chopped	1 cup fresh red raspberries
1 cup unsalted butter or	½ cup sliced, pitted, fresh
parve margarine, softened	apricots or dried apricots,
1 cup sugar	cut into slivers

1. Let egg yolks and whites stand at room temperature for 30 minutes. Meanwhile, grease two 9-inch round cake pans. Line the bottoms of the pans with waxed paper; grease the waxed paper. Dust the insides of the pans with the cocoa powder; set aside.

2. In a small saucepan cook and stir bittersweet chocolate over low heat until melted. Let cool for 10 minutes.

3. Preheat oven to 350° F. In a large bowl beat butter with an electric mixer on medium to high speed for 30 seconds. Add sugar and potato starch; beat until combined. Beat in the melted chocolate until combined. Add egg yolks, 2 at a time, beating well after each addition until combined.

4. Thoroughly wash beaters. In another large bowl beat the egg whites with an electric mixer on medium speed until stiff peaks form (tips stand straight).

5. Stir some of the egg white into the chocolate mixture to lighten. Fold remaining egg white into chocolate mixture. Divide batter evenly between prepared pans. Bake for 30 to 35 minutes or until tops spring back when lightly touched and a toothpick inserted near the centers comes out clean. Cool in pans on a wire rack for 10 minutes. Remove from pans; cool completely. (Centers will sink slightly as cakes cool.) Remove waxed paper.

6. Meanwhile, prepare Apricot Filling. To assemble, place one cake layer on a plate, top side up. Top with half of the filling and half of the almonds. Top with remaining cake layer, filling, and almonds. Mound raspberries and fresh or dried apricot slivers on top. Chill to store for up to 3 days. Makes 12 to 16 servings.

APRICOT FILLING: In a small saucepan combine one 18-ounce jar apricot preserves (1½ cups), ½ cup snipped dried apricots, and 3 tablespoons lemon juice. Cook and stir over low heat until melted. Set aside to cool.

Each serving: 549 cal., 31 g total fat (15 g sat. fat), 150 mg chol., 58 mg sodium, 66 g carbo., 4 g fiber, 8 g pro. Daily Values: 27% vit. A, 15% vit. C, 7% calcium, 12% iron.

Passover tradition

"The seder is absolutely my favorite night of the year," says Joan Nathan, award-winning author of cookbooks on Jewish cooking. "The most important part of the holiday is to relate the story of Passover to your children. It provides a direct connection to ancient Israel—and could be the oldest theatrical event in history. We put on a Passover play every year, a tradition that started 23 years ago when my eldest daughter was two."

In addition to hosting the annual play, Joan creates a happy medley of dishes for her Passover seder guests, incorporating everything from recipes that are hundreds of years old to her own version of Flourless Chocolate Torte with Apricot Filling. On the first night of Passover, you'll find at least 40 relatives and friends gathering at the Nathans' table for seder. The event combines food, ritual, and storytelling to commemorate the flight from Egypt by Moses and the people of Israel, as told in the Book of Exodus.

Joan is shy when asked to talk about her writing accomplishments, but her expertise and enthusiasm for

cooking and her faith are plain to see. Her book *Jewish Cooking in America* won the Julia Child Cookbook Award and the James Beard Award for Food of the Americas. She also has written *The Jewish Holiday Baker* and *The Jewish Holiday Kitchen*.

May

SAVOR THE GENTLE, SWEET DAYS OF MAY WITH SIMPLE MEALS SHARED OUTDOORS WITH FRIENDS AND FAMILY.

Together on Sunday

Together on Sunday

**Quick-Fried Chicken Salad
with Strawberries**

SUNDAY DINNER HAS A COMFY MOOD OF ITS OWN. WE PILE
PLATES HIGH WITH FAMILY FAVORITES AND SERVE THEM
WITH HEAPS OF LOVE AND MAYBE A GOOFY JOKE OR TWO.
IT'S A TRADITION THAT FEEDS THE HEART AND SOUL.

Quick-Fried Chicken Salad with Strawberries

Chicken breast strips double-dipped in a lemon-and-herb flour, then flash-fried in a skillet have all the crunch of the traditional fried chicken. And it's ready in half the time.

START TO FINISH: 30 minutes

¾ cup all-purpose flour	1 head radicchio, torn into
4 Tbsp. snipped fresh purple	bite-size pieces
or green basil	2 cups sliced fresh
1 Tbsp. finely shredded	strawberries
lemon peel	½ cup bottled balsamic
2 eggs, slightly beaten	vinaigrette salad dressing
1 lb. skinless, boneless	6 Bibb or butterhead lettuce
chicken breast strips	leaves
2 Tbsp. cooking oil	Purple or green basil leaves
4 cups mixed spring salad	(optional)
greens	

1. In a shallow dish combine flour, 2 tablespoons of the basil, and the lemon peel. Place eggs in another shallow dish. Dip chicken into flour mixture, then into the eggs, and then again into flour mixture to coat.

2. In a 12-inch heavy skillet heat cooking oil over medium-high heat. Add chicken breast strips to skillet. Cook, uncovered, for 6 to 8 minutes or until chicken is no longer pink, turning once. (If necessary, reduce heat to medium to prevent overbrowning and add more oil as needed during cooking.) Cool slightly.

3. Meanwhile, in a large bowl toss together greens, radicchio, strawberries, and remaining 2 tablespoons basil. Drizzle vinaigrette over salad mixture; toss gently to coat.

4. To serve, line 6 bowls with lettuce leaves. Add salad mixture. Top with chicken and, if desired, basil leaves. Makes 6 main-dish servings.

Each serving: 261 cal., 13 g total fat (2 g sat. fat), 79 mg chol., 295 mg sodium, 16 g carbo., 2 g fiber, 21 g pro. Daily Values: 14% vit. A, 60% vit. C, 5% calcium, 10% iron.

SUNDAY DINNER

Salt-and-Pepper Trout with
Caramelized Red Onion Polenta *(page 84)*
Steamed peas
Biscuits
Good Thyme Lemon Cups *(page 296)*
Iced tea

Dinner Traditions

It doesn't seem to matter whether supper is pasta, fried chicken, rack of lamb, or even hot dogs. The Sunday tradition of puttering together in the kitchen and sharing a relaxing family meal holds meaning beyond the menu. If you haven't yet started your own Sunday family dinner tradition, now's the time. The pace is more leisurely than the grab-and-go weeknight dinner and the food can be more carefully planned. It's the perfect combination to draw the family together.

As you might discover, when your family eats together, you share more than just a meal. Sitting down for dinner together nourishes body and soul. Indeed, psychologists have confirmed what most of us have always known in our hearts: Dinnertime rituals are associated with better health, both physical and mental. Such rituals even provide a beneficial boost to marriages. (That information comes from a review of 50 years' worth of studies scrutinized by a group of psychologists led by Barbara Fiese, Ph.D., professor and chair of psychology at Syracuse University in New York.)

The ritual of Sunday dinner gives families an opportunity to bond in ways that often only make sense to members of that family. "There are inside jokes. A lot of shorthand communication tends to go on. It helps you feel like you belong to something bigger than yourself," Fiese says.

Although food links the family in a special way on Sunday, your meal doesn't have to be a major production. Our spring-fresh recipes will help you. Each recipe is a fairly complete meal in itself. The only things you may want to go with Quick-Fried Chicken Salad with Strawberries are tall glasses of icy lemonade or tea and bakery-fresh rolls slathered with honey butter. And you'll be in comfort-food nirvana if you add some homemade mashed potatoes to Grilled Pork with Melon-Tomato Tumble on *page 87.* Just remember: The more relatives you can squeeze around the table, the more memories you'll be making.

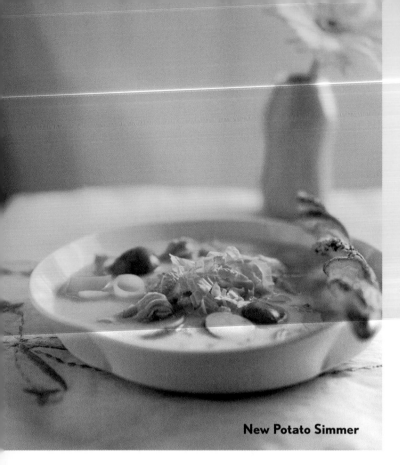

New Potato Simmer

Spring Pea Soup

A subtle touch of tarragon enhances the flavor of this chunky pea soup—a hearty spring meal when you top it with a baguette slice piled high with prosciutto and feta cheese.

PREP: 25 minutes **COOK:** 10 minutes

5 cups fresh shelled peas or two 1-lb. pkg. frozen baby peas	Salt Ground black pepper
2 14-oz. cans chicken broth	6 slices French bread or baguette, brushed with olive oil and oven-toasted or grilled
2 small heads butterhead or Bibb lettuce, ribs discarded, and torn into small pieces	
12 green onions, sliced	2 oz. prosciutto, cut into thin strips
3 Tbsp. snipped fresh tarragon	⅓ cup crumbled feta cheese Fresh tarragon sprigs (optional)
1½ to 2 cups half-and-half or milk	

1. If using fresh peas, in a 4-quart Dutch oven combine peas and broth. Bring to boiling; reduce heat. Cover and simmer for 6 minutes. Add lettuce and green onions. Bring to boiling; reduce heat. Cover and simmer for 4 to 6 minutes more or until peas are tender. If desired for garnish, use a slotted spoon to remove ⅓ cup peas. (If using frozen peas, thaw ⅓ cup of peas; set aside for garnish. In a Dutch oven combine remaining frozen peas, lettuce, green onions, and broth. Bring to boiling; reduce heat. Cover and simmer for 4 to 6 minutes or until peas are tender.)

2. Stir tarragon into soup mixture in Dutch oven. Cool slightly. Place one-fourth of the soup mixture in a blender or food processor. Cover and blend or process until nearly smooth. Repeat with remaining soup mixture, blending or processing one-fourth at a time. Return all of the soup to the Dutch oven. Stir in enough half-and-half to reach desired consistency; heat through, but do not boil. Add salt and pepper to taste.

3. To serve, ladle soup into 6 bowls. Top each serving with a slice of French bread, some prosciutto, and some feta cheese. Sprinkle with reserved peas and add a tarragon sprig, if desired. Makes 6 main-dish servings.

Each serving: 341 cal., 12 g total fat (6 g sat. fat), 36 mg chol., 1,120 mg sodium, 41 g carbo., 9 g fiber, 20 g pro. Daily Values: 41% vit. A, 63% vit. C, 20% calcium, 22% iron.

New Potato Simmer

There's nothing complicated about this savory potato soup enhanced with a splash of cream for a rich flavor. We love the bright yellow-green color of napa cabbage on each serving, but a little pile of baby spinach leaves is a great option.

PREP: 10 minutes **COOK:** 20 minutes

1½ lb. tiny new potatoes	3 Tbsp. Dijon-style mustard
1 lb. smoked turkey or chicken breast, shredded	1 Tbsp. snipped fresh lemon thyme
2 14-oz. cans reduced-sodium chicken broth	1½ cups napa cabbage, cut into ¼-inch-wide strips
1 medium leek, sliced	Breadsticks (see tip, page 83) (optional)
⅓ cup whipping cream	

1. Cut any large potatoes in half. In a 4-quart Dutch oven combine potatoes, turkey, broth, and leek. Bring to boiling; reduce heat. Simmer, covered, for 15 minutes.

2. In a small bowl stir together cream and mustard. Add cream mixture and thyme to Dutch oven. Simmer, uncovered, for 5 minutes more or until potatoes are tender, stirring occasionally.

3. To serve, ladle soup into 6 bowls. Top each serving with ¼ cup of cabbage. If desired, serve with breadsticks. Makes 6 main-dish servings.

Each serving: 243 cal., 8 g total fat (4 g sat. fat), 57 mg chol., 1,297 mg sodium, 23 g carbo., 3 g fiber, 19 g pro. Daily Values: 9% vit. A, 41% vit. C, 5% calcium, 13% iron.

BY JEANNE AMBROSE. PHOTOGRAPHS: COLLEEN DUFFLEY. FOOD STYLIST: BROOKE LEONARD. RECIPES: JUDITH FERTIG.

Spring Pea Soup

Flash-Roasted
Vegetables and Pasta

Flash-Roasted Vegetables and Pasta

Pappardelle pasta is a fantastically wide (about 1-inch) egg noodle, while mafalda pasta is narrower with rippled edges similar to lasagna. In a pinch, you can use any wide noodle, such as fettuccine.

PREP: 20 minutes **ROAST:** 35 minutes

2	Tbsp. Fennel-Spice Mix (below)	1	large red onion, cut into 6 or 8 wedges
2	lb. assorted fresh mushrooms, such as chanterelles, crimini, and/or oyster, cut into chunks	8	oz. baby carrots with tops, trimmed
		1/4	cup olive oil
2	medium fennel bulbs, trimmed and cut into wedges (about 1 lb. trimmed)	8	oz. dried pappardelle or mafalda pasta
		3/4	cup dry white wine
			Shredded Parmesan cheese (optional)

1. Prepare Fennel-Spice Mix; set aside. Preheat oven to 425° F. Place mushrooms, fennel, onion, and carrots in a large roasting pan. Combine oil and Fennel-Spice Mix; drizzle over vegetables. Toss gently to coat.

2. Roast, uncovered, for 35 minutes or until vegetables are tender, stirring twice. Transfer roasted vegetables to a very large bowl, leaving juices in pan.

3. Meanwhile, cook pasta according to package directions; drain well.

4. Add pasta to roasted vegetables. Add wine to roasting pan. Cook and stir over medium-high heat, scraping up any browned bits, about 3 minutes or until wine is slightly reduced. Pour wine over pasta mixture; toss well to coat. Top with cheese. Makes 6 to 8 main-dish servings.

FENNEL-SPICE MIX: In a small skillet over medium heat toast 1/4 cup fennel seeds, 1 tablespoon coriander seeds, and 1/4 teaspoon cracked peppercorns about 1 minute or until fragrant, shaking the pan occasionally. Cool thoroughly. When completely cool, grind in a spice grinder or blender with 1 teaspoon coarse sea salt or kosher salt.

Each serving: 336 cal., 13 g total fat (2 g sat. fat), 0 mg chol., 197 mg sodium, 45 g carbo., 24 g fiber, 12 g pro. Daily Values: 213% vit. A, 24% vit. C, 9% calcium, 15% iron.

DO-IT-YOURSELF BREADSTICKS

Dressing up breadsticks with a twist of your own is a simple technique that produces impressively tasty results.

Here's how you can create your own: Start with purchased breadstick dough. Preheat the oven according to package directions. Separate breadstick dough and lay flat. Brush the dough with melted butter or olive oil. Add a generous sprinkling of toasted seeds, such as sesame or poppy; snipped parsley and thyme; and/or coarse sea salt and cracked peppercorns. Twist dough strips; transfer twisted strips to a foil-lined baking sheet. Bake as directed.

Spaghetti Pie

PREP: 30 minutes **BAKE:** 20 minutes

4	oz. dried spaghetti	1/2	tsp. fennel seeds, crushed
1	Tbsp. butter or margarine	1	8-oz. can tomato sauce
1	egg, beaten	1	tsp. dried oregano, crushed
1/4	cup grated Parmesan cheese		Nonstick cooking spray
8	oz. ground beef	1	cup low-fat cottage cheese, drained
1/2	cup chopped onion (1 medium)	1/2	cup shredded part-skim mozzarella cheese
1/2	cup chopped green sweet pepper		
1	clove garlic, minced		

1. Cook spaghetti according to package directions; drain.

2. Return spaghetti to warm saucepan. Stir butter into hot pasta until melted. Stir in egg and Parmesan cheese; set aside.

3. Preheat oven to 350° F. In a medium skillet cook ground beef, onion, sweet pepper, garlic, and fennel seeds until meat is brown and onion is tender. Drain off fat. Stir in tomato sauce and oregano; heat through.

4. Coat a 9-inch pie plate with nonstick cooking spray. Press spaghetti mixture onto bottom and up sides of pie plate to form a crust. Spread cottage cheese on the crust, spreading it up the sides. Spread meat mixture onto cottage cheese. Sprinkle with shredded mozzarella cheese.

5. Bake for 20 to 25 minutes or until bubbly and heated through. To serve, cut into wedges. Makes 6 servings.

Each serving: 270 cal., 11 g total fat (6 g sat. fat), 76 mg chol., 500 mg sodium, 20 g carbo., 1 g fiber, 21 g pro. Daily Values: 7% vit. A, 17% vit. C, 16% calcium, 11% iron.

Asparagus-Salmon Scramble

PREP: 25 minutes **STAND:** 1 hour **BAKE:** 18 minutes per batch

1 17-oz. pkg. (2 sheets) frozen puff pastry	1/2 tsp. salt
1 egg yolk	1/8 tsp. ground black pepper
1 lb. fresh asparagus, trimmed	1 Tbsp. butter
8 eggs	4 oz. Havarti cheese with dill, shredded (1 cup)
1/2 cup milk, half-and-half, or light cream	1 4-oz. piece smoked salmon, broken into chunks, with skin and bones removed
1 tsp. snipped fresh dill or 1/4 tsp. dried dillweed	Fresh dill sprigs (optional)

1. Thaw the pastry sheets at room temperature for 1 hour.

2. Preheat oven to 400° F. In a small bowl mix egg yolk with 1 teaspoon water; set aside. Unfold pastry sheets on a lightly floured surface. Roll gently to flatten creases (you should have a 10-inch square). Cut 1/2-inch-wide strips from all 4 sides of each pastry sheet. Brush edges of pastry sheets with egg mixture. Place the cut strips along edges on top of the pastry sheets, gently pressing in place to form a raised rim; trim ends. Place pastries on 2 baking sheets. Prick centers with a fork. Brush pastries with egg mixture. Bake, 1 sheet at a time, about 15 minutes or until puffed and golden brown. Cool on baking sheets on wire racks.

3. Meanwhile, in a large skillet bring 1 cup water and a dash salt to boiling. Add asparagus and cook, covered, for 1 minute. Drain. Rinse asparagus with cold water; drain well. Transfer the asparagus to a cutting board. Slice 3-inch pieces from the tips of asparagus; set aside. Cut remaining asparagus into 2-inch pieces.

4. In a large mixing bowl whisk together eggs, milk, snipped dill, salt, and pepper until combined. In the large skillet melt butter over medium heat. Add egg mixture to skillet. Cook over medium heat, without stirring, until mixture begins to set on bottom and around edges. With a spatula or a large spoon, lift and fold the partially cooked egg mixture so the uncooked portion flows underneath. Continue cooking over medium heat for 2 to 3 minutes or until egg mixture is cooked but still glossy. Remove from heat; fold in 1/2 cup of the cheese.

5. Spoon egg mixture into baked pastry shells on baking sheets. Top with the 2-inch asparagus pieces, salmon, and remaining 1/2 cup cheese. Arrange asparagus tips over all. Return 1 baking sheet at a time to oven and bake 3 to 5 minutes or until cheese is melted and filling is heated through. If desired, garnish with fresh dill sprigs. Makes 8 main-dish servings.

Each serving: 524 cal., 37 g total fat (9 g sat. fat), 266 mg chol., 567 mg sodium, 30 g carbo., 2 g fiber, 18 g pro. Daily Values: 13% vit. A, 6% vit. C, 14% calcium, 15% iron.

Salt-and-Pepper Trout with Caramelized Red Onion Polenta

For a splash of color, rescue a few red onions from the skillet after they've softened slightly, but while they still have a pretty tint. Let the rest of the onions cook until they're caramelized and golden brown. Stir all of the onions into the creamy soft polenta and use it as a bed for the broiled trout.

PREP: 30 minutes **COOK:** 30 minutes **BROIL:** 8 minutes

1 medium red onion, cut into 1/4-inch-thick slices and separated into rings (3/4 cup)	4 fresh or frozen boned, pan-dressed trout (6 to 7 oz. each) or 4 fresh trout fillets (about 4 oz. each)
4 tsp. butter	Citrus-flavored olive oil (such as lime, lemon, or grapefruit) or olive oil
2/3 cup stone-ground cornmeal	Coarse sea salt
2 1/2 cups chicken broth	Ground black pepper
3 Tbsp. grated Parmesan cheese	1 bunch watercress
1/8 tsp. ground black pepper	

1. In a medium covered skillet cook onion in hot butter over medium-low heat for 13 to 15 minutes or until onion is tender. Uncover and stir over medium-high heat for 4 to 5 minutes or until onions are golden brown. Set aside.

2. In a small bowl combine cornmeal and 1 cup of the chicken broth; set aside. In a medium saucepan bring the remaining 1 1/2 cups chicken broth to boiling over medium-high heat. Slowly add cornmeal mixture, stirring constantly. Return to boiling; reduce heat to low. Cook for 10 to 15 minutes or until mixture is very thick, stirring occasionally. Add the caramelized onion, Parmesan cheese, and the 1/8 teaspoon pepper; stir until the cheese is melted. Set aside and keep warm.

3. Preheat broiler. If using pan-dressed trout, spread open fish; brush with olive oil and sprinkle with salt and pepper. Close fish and place on greased, unheated rack of a broiler pan. Measure thickness of fish at the thickest spot. Broil 4 inches from the heat for 4 to 6 minutes per 1/2-inch thickness or until fish flakes easily when tested with a fork, turning after 4 minutes. (If using fillets, place fish, skin side down, on ungreased rack of broiler pan. Measure thickness of fish at the thickest spot. Brush with flavored olive oil and sprinkle with salt and pepper. Broil 4 inches from the heat for 4 to 6 minutes per 1/2-inch thickness or until fish flakes easily when tested with a fork.)

4. To serve, spoon polenta onto 4 plates. Top with fish and some watercress. Makes 4 main-dish servings.

Each serving: 425 cal., 18 g total fat (6 g sat. fat), 114 mg chol., 859 mg sodium, 21 g carbo., 2 g fiber, 43 g pro. Daily Values: 18% vit. A, 12% vit. C, 18% calcium, 7% iron.

Asparagus-Salmon Scramble

"SUNDAY DINNER IS THE ESSENCE OF THE DINNERS WE HAVE THE REST OF THE WEEK. I MAKE THINGS THE FAMILY REALLY LOVES. THE KIDS MIGHT HELP ME COOK. DINNER IS MUCH MORE LEISURELY."

SARA MOULTON, TV CHEF, COOKBOOK AUTHOR

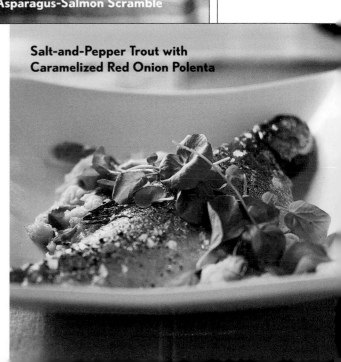

Salt-and-Pepper Trout with Caramelized Red Onion Polenta

**Grilled Pork with
Melon-Tomato Tumble**

Grilled Pork with Melon-Tomato Tumble

Although the colorful pear-shape cherry tomatoes make a stunning statement in the melon-tomato mixture, chopped roma tomatoes work well too. The mixture makes a standout accompaniment to a simple grilled pork tenderloin.

PREP: 20 minutes **GRILL:** 30 minutes **STAND:** 10 minutes

3 Tbsp. olive oil	1 1-lb. pork tenderloin
3 Tbsp. white wine vinegar	1 recipe Melon-Tomato
1/4 tsp. salt	Tumble (below)
1/8 tsp. ground black pepper	

1. In a small mixing bowl whisk together oil, vinegar, salt, and pepper. Remove 1 tablespoon of the mixture for pork. Reserve remaining oil-and-vinegar mixture for Melon-Tomato Tumble.

2. Brush reserved 1 tablespoon oil-and-vinegar mixture onto pork. Place pork tenderloin on a grill rack directly over medium coals. Grill, uncovered, about 30 minutes or until an instant-read thermometer inserted into the center of meat registers 160° F, turning every 5 to 6 minutes.

3. Meanwhile, prepare Melon-Tomato Tumble. Transfer the pork to a cutting board. Cover and let pork rest for 10 minutes. Slice meat diagonally; serve with Melon-Tomato Tumble spooned onto melon wedges. Makes 4 main-dish servings.

MELON-TOMATO TUMBLE: Cut 1 small cantaloupe or honeydew melon in half. Cut one of the melon halves into bite-size pieces. Cut remaining melon half into 4 wedges; cover and chill wedges in the refrigerator until serving time. In a medium bowl combine melon pieces; 1 cup yellow, red, and/or orange pear-shape cherry and/or grape tomatoes, halved or quartered; 1 small red onion, thinly sliced and halved; and 1/3 cup small fresh mint leaves. Add remaining oil-and-vinegar mixture; toss gently to coat.

Each serving: 292 cal., 14 g total fat (3 g sat. fat), 73 mg chol., 211 mg sodium, 15 g carbo., 2 g fiber, 26 g pro. Daily Values: 88% vit. A, 122% vit. C, 3% calcium, 19% iron.

FAMILY DINNER ALFRESCO

Chive-Yogurt Cheese Spread *(page 91)*
Grilled Pork with Melon-Tomato Tumble *(above)*
Grilled corn on the cob
Angel Food Cake *(page 40)* with strawberries
Iced tea or Watermelon Lemonade *(page 106)*

Campfire-Style Pot Roast

PREP: 30 minutes **GRILL:** 2 1/2 hours

1 3 1/2- to 4-lb. boneless beef chuck pot roast	2 stalks celery, bias-sliced into 1-inch pieces
1 Tbsp. cooking oil	6 small whole carrots, peeled and halved
Salt	1 medium green sweet pepper, cut into rings
Ground black pepper	2 medium onions, quartered
Nonstick cooking spray	2 medium tomatoes, cut into wedges
1 recipe Mustard Barbecue Sauce (below)	

1. Trim fat from roast. In a 4-quart Dutch oven brown pot roast in hot oil on all sides. Season with salt and pepper.

2. Meanwhile, fold two 5-foot lengths of heavy foil in half crosswise. Place one on top of the other, forming a cross shape. Lightly coat center of foil with cooking spray. Top with meat. Spread 3/4 cup sauce onto meat (cover and chill remaining sauce). Top with vegetables. Season with salt and pepper. Seal each piece of foil securely, allowing room for expansion.

3. For a charcoal grill, arrange medium coals around edge of grill. Test for medium heat in the center of the grill. Place foil packet on grill rack in center of grill. Cover and grill for 2 1/2 hours, adding additional charcoal as needed to maintain heat. (For a gas grill, preheat grill. Reduce heat to medium-low. Adjust for indirect cooking. Grill as above, except place packet in a roasting pan.)

4. To serve, transfer meat and vegetables to a platter. Heat remaining sauce; pass with meat. Makes 8 main-dish servings.

OVEN METHOD: Preheat oven to 350° F. Trim fat from roast and brown as above. Drain off fat; season roast with salt and pepper. Spread 3/4 cup of the sauce on meat in Dutch oven; add vegetables. Cover Dutch oven; roast for 2 1/2 hours. Serve as above.

MUSTARD BARBECUE SAUCE: In a medium saucepan stir together 2 tablespoons dried minced onion; 2 tablespoons packed brown sugar; 1 tablespoon mustard seeds, slightly crushed; 2 teaspoons paprika; 1 teaspoon dried oregano, crushed; 1 teaspoon chili powder; 1 teaspoon cracked black pepper; 1/2 teaspoon salt; 1/2 teaspoon ground cloves; 1 bay leaf; 1 clove garlic, minced. Stir in 1 cup catsup, 1/2 cup water, 2 tablespoons olive oil or cooking oil, 2 tablespoons red wine vinegar or cider vinegar, 2 tablespoons Worcestershire sauce, and 2 or 3 drops liquid smoke. Bring to boiling; reduce heat. Simmer, uncovered, for 20 to 25 minutes or until desired consistency, stirring often. Remove bay leaf.

Each serving: 395 cal., 14 g total fat (3 g sat. fat), 118 mg chol., 790 mg sodium, 24 g carbo., 4 g fiber, 44 g pro. Daily Values: 251% vit. A, 47% vit. C, 6% calcium, 41% iron.

Game Hens with
Rhubarb Barbecue Glaze

Game Hens with Rhubarb Barbecue Glaze

Bottled barbecue sauce gets taken in a grand new direction when simmered with chopped rhubarb. The garden-fresh tangy sauce provides a spectacular glaze of flavor and color for Cornish game hens.

PREP: 30 minutes **COOK:** 20 minutes **ROAST:** 55 minutes

3 1¼- to 1½-lb. Cornish game hens	1 cup bottled tomato-based barbecue sauce
Olive oil	¼ cup water
Salt	8 oz. dried orzo (rosamarina)
Ground black pepper	1 cup shredded carrots
3½ to 4 cups chopped fresh or frozen rhubarb	¼ cup sliced green onions

1. Preheat the oven to 375° F. Using a long, heavy knife or kitchen shears, halve Cornish hens lengthwise, cutting through the breast bone, just off-center, and through the center of the backbone. (Or ask the butcher to cut hens into halves.) Twist wing tips under back. Rub the olive oil onto the surface and in the cavity of each hen half; sprinkle generously with salt and pepper. Place hen halves, cut side down, in a 15×10×1-inch baking pan. Roast, uncovered, for 40 minutes.

2. Meanwhile, for sauce, in a medium saucepan bring rhubarb, barbecue sauce, and water to boiling over medium-high heat. Reduce heat to medium-low and cook, covered, for 20 minutes or until rhubarb loses its shape. Remove from heat; coarsely mash rhubarb. Remove and reserve 1 cup of the sauce.

3. Brush surface of game hens with some of the remaining sauce. Roast for 15 to 20 minutes more, brushing every 5 minutes, or until hens are glazed, tender, no longer pink, and an instant-read thermometer inserted into thigh muscle registers 180° F.

4. Meanwhile, cook orzo according to package directions; drain. Transfer orzo to a large bowl. Stir in the additional reserved sauce, carrots, and green onions. Season to taste with salt and pepper. Spoon orzo mixture onto a large platter; top with hen halves. Pass the remaining sauce. Makes 6 main-dish servings.

low fat Each serving: 375 cal., 10 g total fat (2 g sat. fat), 111 mg chol., 609 mg sodium, 39 g carbo., 4 g fiber, 31 g pro. Daily Values: 124% vit. A, 18% vit. C, 10% calcium, 17% iron.

German Meatballs with Spaetzle

If you've never made pasta from scratch, consider spaetzle a good place to start. These chewy homemade egg noodles are easy to make and worth the effort.

PREP: 20 minutes **COOK:** 25 minutes **STAND:** 5 minutes

1 egg	½ cup chopped onion
¼ cup milk	1 8-oz. carton dairy sour cream
¼ cup fine dry bread crumbs	
1 Tbsp. snipped fresh parsley	2 Tbsp. all-purpose flour
½ tsp. salt	½ to 1 tsp. caraway seeds
Dash ground black pepper	1 recipe Spaetzle (below)
1 lb. ground beef	Snipped fresh parsley (optional)
1⅓ cups beef broth	
1 4-oz. can mushroom pieces and stems, drained	

1. In a large bowl beat egg; stir in milk, bread crumbs, the 1 tablespoon parsley, salt, and pepper. Add ground meat; mix well. Shape mixture into twenty-four 1½-inch meatballs.

2. In a large nonstick skillet brown meatballs; drain off fat. Add broth, mushrooms, and onion. Simmer, covered, about 20 minutes or until an instant-read thermometer inserted into meatballs registers 160° F.

3. In a small bowl combine sour cream, flour, and caraway seeds; stir into broth. Cook and stir until mixture is thickened and bubbly. Cook and stir for 1 minute more.

4. Meanwhile, prepare Spaetzle. To serve, spoon spaetzle onto 6 plates; top with meatballs and sauce. If desired, sprinkle with snipped parsley. Makes 6 servings.

SPAETZLE: In a medium bowl combine 2 cups all-purpose flour and 1 teaspoon salt. Add 2 slightly beaten eggs and 1 cup milk; beat well. Let rest for 5 minutes. Bring a large kettle of lightly salted water to boiling. Holding a coarse-sieved colander (such as the basket for a deep-fat fryer) over rapidly boiling water, pour batter into colander. Press batter through colander with back of wooden spoon or rubber spatula. Cook and stir for 5 minutes; drain.

Each serving: 465 cal., 21 g total fat (10 g sat. fat), 175 mg chol., 1,049 mg sodium, 40 g carbo., 2 g fiber, 26 g pro. Daily Values: 12% vit. A, 5% vit. C, 14% calcium, 23% iron.

BY JOHN SCHIESZER. PHOTOGRAPHS: GREG SCHEIDEMANN [N] HAUS FOTO. FOOD STYLIST: CHARLES WORTHINGTON.

GO FOR
YOGURT

GOBBLING GOOD BACTERIA MAY HEAL STOMACH WOES.

Foods you already know are good for your bones are proving to be good for your digestive tract as well. Eating certain calcium-rich dairy products, such as yogurt, provides you with a boost of "good" bacteria that may prevent a host of health problems. These good bacteria, called probiotics, bind to intestinal tissues and crowd out less-friendly bugs that might be present. A daily helping of foods enhanced with probiotics could keep you from suffering some stomach and gastro-intestinal problems. Yogurt that contains added probiotics can improve the balance between good bacteria and bad bacteria in the gut.

At Johns Hopkins Children's Center in Baltimore, Maryland, researchers have found that children with symptoms of lactose intolerance (the inability to break down lactose, the sugar in many dairy products) experience fewer side effects when they eat yogurt containing *Lactobacillus bulgaricus* and *Streptococcus thermophilus*. After eating the bacteria-enhanced yogurt, children in the study could drink milk with less pain and discomfort. However, despite the potential health benefits, people with health problems should consult their doctors before consuming products enhanced with probiotics.

Orange-Yogurt Cheese Spread

PREP: 5 minutes **CHILL:** 24 hours

1 recipe Yogurt Cheese
   (below)
¼ cup orange marmalade
   or lemon curd
1 tsp. finely shredded
   orange or lemon peel

Thin spice cookies
Fresh or canned mandarin
   orange slices or
   fresh berries

1. In a small bowl combine Yogurt Cheese, orange marmalade, and orange peel. Stir to combine. Place cheese spread on cookie; top with orange slices.

low fat Each tablespoon of orange-yogurt spread: 27 cal., 1 g total fat (0 g sat. fat), 4 mg chol., 19 mg sodium, 2 g carbo., 0 g dietary fiber, 1 g protein. Daily Values: 1% vit. C, 4% calcium.

YOGURT CHEESE: Line a sieve or small colander with 3 layers of 100-percent-cotton cheesecloth or a clean paper coffee filter. Suspend lined sieve or colander over a bowl. (Or use a yogurt strainer.) Spoon in one 16-ounce carton plain yogurt.* Cover with plastic wrap. Chill for at least 24 hours. Remove from refrigerator. Discard liquid. Transfer yogurt cheese to a bowl. Cover and store in the refrigerator for up to 1 week.

*Note: Use a brand of yogurt that contains no gums, gelatin, or fillers. These ingredients may prevent the whey from separating from the curd to make cheese.

ONE A DAY

Researchers say one to two 1-cup daily servings of yogurt with probiotics are enough to be beneficial for adults. Children should stick to 1 cup of yogurt each day. "I think a probiotic a day is like a multi-vitamin a day. It offers protection against viruses," says Rosemary Young, pediatric gastroenterology nurse specialist at the University of Nebraska Medical Center in Omaha.

Studies show that probiotics also prevent diarrhea. "From human studies, we know that probiotics are very effective for diarrhea from viral illnesses. Seventy percent of all traveler's diarrhea is viral in nature," says Rosemary.

Probiotics are added to—or found in—such foods as some rice and soy "milks" as well as acidophilus milks, yogurt, and some cottage cheeses. If the products contain probiotics, they will be listed on the label, typically as acidophilus or bifidus.

Yogurt, drinkable yogurt, and fermented milk that list probiotics on the label are among the best food sources of the helpful bacteria.

Besides being in foods, probiotics are sold in pills, powders, and suppositories. But experts caution that dietary supplements are not closely regulated, so there is no guarantee that labels are accurate.

Chive-Yogurt Cheese Spread

PREP: 5 minutes **CHILL:** 24 hours

1 recipe Yogurt Cheese
   (left)
2 Tbsp. chopped dried
   tomatoes
2 Tbsp. finely snipped
   fresh chives
1 small clove garlic, minced
   (optional)

¼ tsp. salt
   Crackers or fresh
   vegetables, such as
   carrots, broccoli, and
   cucumber spears
   (optional)

1. In a small bowl combine Yogurt Cheese, dried tomatoes, chives, garlic (if desired), and salt. Stir to combine. Spoon the spread onto crackers or use it as a dip for fresh vegetables.

low fat Each tablespoon of chive-yogurt spread: 15 cal., 0 g total fat (0 g sat. fat), 1 mg chol., 52 mg sodium, 2 g carbo., 0 g dietary fiber, 1 g protein. Daily Values: 1% vit. A, 1% vit. C, 4% calcium.

June

ENJOY THE MAGICAL SEASON OF BACKYARDS,
BARBECUES, AND RELAXED GOOD TIMES,
BY CASTING FAMILIAR FAVORITES IN ENTICING NEW GUISES.

Easy-Does-It-Summer

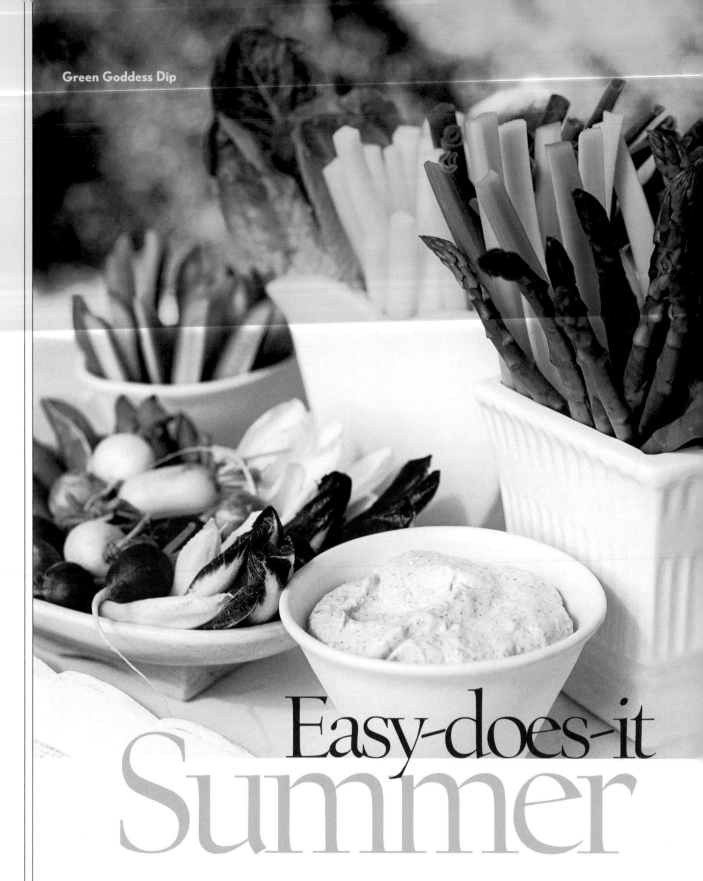

Green Goddess Dip

Easy-does-it Summer

A SPIRIT OF SPONTANEITY, A MOOD OF PLENTY,
WILLING HANDS, AND A BIT OF PLANNING MAKE IT
ALL HAPPEN AT A CASUAL GATHERING FOR FRIENDS.

Green Goddess Dip

A 1920s San Francisco chef gave the name "green goddess" to a unique salad dressing to honor an actor appearing in a play of the same name.

START TO FINISH: 30 minutes

⅓	cup refrigerated or frozen egg product, thawed
3	Tbsp. lemon juice
2	tsp. Dijon-style mustard
1	clove garlic, minced
1	cup canola oil
4	to 5 anchovy fillets, drained and chopped (1 Tbsp.)
1	cup loosely packed fresh parsley leaves
¼	cup loosely packed fresh tarragon leaves
¼	cup snipped fresh chives
2	green onions, chopped
4	oz. cream cheese, cubed and softened
¼	cup tarragon vinegar
	Salt
	Vegetable dippers such as Belgian endive, baby romaine lettuce leaves, asparagus spears, radishes, and/or green onions

1. In a large food processor or blender combine egg product, lemon juice, mustard, and garlic; cover and process or blend until combined. With the processor or blender running, add oil in a thin, steady stream. (When necessary, stop and scrape down sides of blender.)

2. Add anchovies, parsley, tarragon, chives, and green onion; pulse until blended. Add the softened cream cheese and vinegar; pulse to combine. Season to taste with salt.

3. Serve dip with vegetable dippers. Any leftover dip may be stored, covered, in the refrigerator for up to 1 week. Makes 2¼ cups.

Each tablespoon: 69 cal., 7 g total fat (2 g sat. fat), 4 mg chol., 45 mg sodium, 1 g carbo., 0 g fiber, 1 g pro. Daily Values: 3% vit. A, 6% vit. C, 1% calcium, 1% iron.

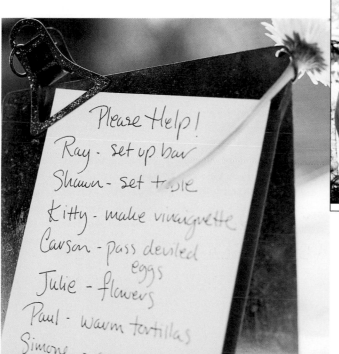

Summer gatherings

A great summer gathering is the sum of its sensations: Afternoon sun alighting on tall skewers of the freshest summer fruit, the taste of deviled eggs topped with bacon and avocado, and the laughter of familiar voices gathered around the grill.

Making wonderful moments happen for guests is simple when you understand that your life, at least your backyard life, is not a one-person show. Even if you're like Carrie Brown (*below right*)—who owns a restaurant, specialty food company, and general store—when you let guests help, the day is elevated from merely entertaining to truly enchanting others.

"I used to try to make everything perfect and flawless, but I didn't enjoy my own parties," says Carrie, whose Jimtown Store sits alongside a rural highway in the Sonoma County wine country north of San Francisco. "Then I learned to loosen up and let everyone help so we could all sit back and enjoy the chaos of the moment."

Carrie's key to successful delegation is giving people specific, but fun, assignments. Before her gatherings, she creates a to-do list for the close friends who come

to the party. When they're working for their supper, she tries to make sure they're supplied with all the tools needed for the task at hand. Carrie also posts notes on serving bowls and platters to designate which goes with each recipe.

Grilled Salmon Tacos

Make the salsa and crème fraîche one or two days ahead. Then you can devote your full attention to preparing the salmon.

PREP: 1 hour **GRILL:** 8 minutes

2 lb. fresh or frozen skinless salmon fillets	⅓ cup lime juice
1 lb. medium round red or white potatoes (2 cups)	1 tsp. kosher salt or ¾ tsp. salt
1 Tbsp. ground chipotle chile pepper	12 green onions, thinly sliced
1½ tsp. sugar	1 cup snipped fresh cilantro
1 tsp. kosher salt or ¾ tsp. salt	32 4-inch corn tortillas or twenty-four 6-inch corn tortillas, warmed
2 cups Lupe's Tomatillo Salsa (right) or purchased green salsa	1 cup Crème Fraîche (below right)
	Lime wedges

1. Thaw fish, if frozen. Peel and cube potatoes. Cook potatoes, covered, in enough boiling salted water to cover about 15 minutes or until tender. Drain and cool.

2. Rinse fish; pat dry. Measure thickness of fish in the thickest spot. In a small bowl combine chipotle pepper, sugar, and 1 teaspoon salt; rub onto both sides of fish. Place fish on greased grill rack directly over medium coals. Grill, uncovered, for 4 to 6 minutes per ½-inch thickness or until fish flakes easily when tested with a fork. Cool slightly. Break salmon into chunks.

3. In a large bowl stir together Lupe's Tomatillo Salsa, lime juice, and 1 teaspoon salt. Add the salmon, potatoes, green onions, and cilantro; stir gently.

4. Divide the salmon mixture among tortillas. Top each with a dollop of Crème Fraîche. Serve immediately with lime wedges. Makes 24 to 32 tacos.

low fat Each taco: 161 cal., 5 g total fat (2 g sat. fat), 29 mg chol., 316 mg sodium, 19 g carbo., 2 g fiber, 10 g pro. Daily Values: 12% vit. A, 28% vit. C, 8% calcium, 7% iron.

Lupe's Tomatillo Salsa

This salsa is named for one of Carrie's first employees. Canned tomatillos, though great in other dishes, are not successful in this particular recipe.

PREP: 30 minutes **ROAST:** 20 minutes

3 lb. fresh tomatillos	3 cloves garlic, minced
6 fresh serrano chile peppers	1½ tsp. kosher salt or 1 tsp. salt
2 cups fresh cilantro leaves	⅓ cup finely chopped green onions
⅓ cup finely chopped yellow or white onion	

1. Preheat oven to 425° F. Remove husks, stems, and cores from tomatillos. Cut any large tomatillos in half. Place tomatillos in a foil-lined shallow roasting pan. Remove stems and, if desired, seeds from serrano peppers*. Place peppers in roasting pan with tomatillos. Roast, uncovered, for 20 minutes or until tomatillos are soft. Drain tomatillos and cool. (Save some of the drained liquid from roasting pan to use in blender, if necessary.)

2. In a blender or food processor combine half of the tomatillos, peppers, cilantro, yellow onion, and garlic. Cover and blend or process until almost smooth. (If necessary, add a bit of the reserved cooking liquid to the blender to help blend.) Pour mixture into a medium bowl. Repeat with remaining tomatillos, peppers, cilantro, yellow onion, and garlic.

3. Stir salt and the green onions into the salsa mixture. Serve immediately or cover and chill for up to 2 days. Makes about 3¼ cups.

*NOTE: Because hot peppers contain oils that can burn your eyes, lips, and skin, when working with chile peppers, wear plastic or rubber gloves.

low fat Each ¼-cup serving: 33 cal., 1 g total fat (0 g sat. fat), 0 mg chol., 230 mg sodium, 6 g carbo., 1 g fiber, 1 g pro. Daily Values: 10% vit. A, 40% vit. C, 2% calcium, 4% iron.

Crème Fraîche

PREP: 5 minutes **STAND:** 5 hours

1 8-oz. carton dairy sour cream	1 cup whipping cream (not ultrapasteurized)

1. In a medium mixing bowl whisk together sour cream and whipping cream. Cover with plastic wrap. Let stand at room temperature for 5 to 8 hours or until mixture is thickened.

2. When thickened, cover and chill until serving time or for up to 48 hours. Stir before serving. Makes about 2 cups.

Each tablespoon serving: 41 cal., 4 g total fat (3 g sat. fat), 13 mg chol., 7 mg sodium, 1 g carbo., 0 g fiber, 0 g pro. Daily Values: 3% vit. A, 1% calcium.

"IT'S THOUGHTFUL FOOD; I'VE TAKEN
A TRIED-AND-TRUE RECIPE
AND MADE IT A LITTLE BIT SPECIAL."

CARRIE BROWN

BY RICHARD SWEARINGER. PHOTOGRAPHS: EDMUND BARR. FOOD STYLIST: ROBYN VALARIK. PRODUCER: CAROL HACKER.

Baked Bean Quintet

This crowd-pleasing recipe is perfect for potlucks and picnics. Tote it to your next summertime bring-a-dish gathering—everyone will be glad you did.

PREP: 10 minutes **BAKE:** 1 hour

1 cup chopped onion (1 large)	1 15-oz. can garbanzo beans, drained
6 slices bacon, cut up	3/4 cup catsup
1 clove garlic, minced	1/2 cup molasses
1 16-oz. can lima beans, drained	1/4 cup packed brown sugar
1 16-oz. can pork and beans in tomato sauce	1 Tbsp. prepared mustard
1 15 1/2-oz. can red kidney beans, drained	1 Tbsp. Worcestershire sauce
1 15-oz. can butter beans, drained	Cooked bacon (optional)

1. Preheat oven to 375° F. In a skillet cook onion, bacon, and garlic until bacon is crisp and onion is tender; drain. In a bowl combine onion mixture, lima beans, pork and beans, kidney beans, butter beans, garbanzo beans, catsup, molasses, brown sugar, mustard, and Worcestershire sauce.

2. Transfer bean mixture to a 3-quart casserole. Bake, covered, for 1 hour. If desired, top with additional cooked bacon. Makes 12 to 16 side-dish servings.

SLOW COOKER DIRECTIONS: Prepare bean mixture as above. Transfer to a 3 1/2- or 4-quart electric slow cooker. Cover and cook on low-heat setting for 10 to 12 hours or on high-heat setting for 4 to 5 hours.

low fat Each serving: 245 cal., 3 g total fat (1 g sat. fat), 5 mg chol., 882 mg sodium, 47 g carbo., 9 g fiber, 10 g pro. Daily Values: 5% vit. A, 13% vit. C, 10% calcium, 22% iron.

Slow-Simmered Pork Sandwiches with Roasted Tomato-Jalapeño Vinaigrette

Like coffee beans, cumin seeds retain more flavor when kept whole and ground just before use. Toasting further enhances the flavor.

PREP: 40 minutes **COOK:** 4 1/2 hours on high; 9 hours on low

1 4-lb. boneless pork shoulder roast	1 12- to 16-oz. jar pickled jalapeño chile peppers or jalapeño chile pepper slices
5 tsp. cumin seeds, toasted*	
2 Tbsp. packed brown sugar	
1 tsp. kosher salt or 3/4 tsp. salt	2/3 cup coarsely snipped fresh cilantro
1/2 tsp. cayenne pepper	1 tsp. kosher salt or 3/4 tsp. salt
1/2 tsp. ground black pepper	
1 medium onion, sliced	1/4 tsp. ground black pepper
3 cloves garlic, minced	12 hoagie buns, Mexican torta rolls, or other hard rolls, split and toasted, if desired
1 cup chicken broth	
1 12-oz. can cola	
1/4 cup cooking oil	
1 lb. roma tomatoes, cored, seeded, and chopped	2 limes, cut into wedges

1. Trim fat from meat. Remove netting, if present. If necessary, cut meat into 2 or 3 pieces that will fit into a 3 1/2- to 5-quart electric slow cooker; set aside. Use a mortar and pestle or a blender to grind cumin seeds. In a small bowl combine the cumin seeds, brown sugar, the 1 teaspoon salt, the cayenne pepper, and 1/2 teaspoon black pepper. Rub mixture onto meat.

2. In the slow cooker combine onion and garlic; add meat. Pour broth and cola over meat. Cover and cook on low-heat setting for 9 to 10 hours or on high-heat setting for 4 1/2 to 5 hours or until meat is fork tender.

3. Meanwhile, in a large skillet heat the oil over medium heat. Add tomatoes and cook, uncovered, for 4 minutes, stirring occasionally. Drain jalapeños, reserving 1/2 cup juice; set jalapeños aside. Add reserved juice to tomatoes along with cilantro, 1 teaspoon salt, and 1/4 teaspoon black pepper. Bring to boiling; reduce heat. Cook, uncovered, 3 to 4 minutes more or until slightly thickened, stirring occasionally; set aside.

4. Use a slotted spoon to transfer meat from liquid to cutting board; remove onions with a slotted spoon and discard remaining liquid. Shred meat; stir onion into shredded meat mixture.

5. To assemble, spoon meat and tomato mixture onto split buns. Serve with jalapeños and lime wedges. Makes 12 servings.

*NOTE: To toast cumin seeds, place seeds in small skillet. Cook over medium heat about 2 minutes or until fragrant, shaking pan occasionally to toast seeds evenly.

Each serving: 683 cal., 22 g total fat (6 g sat. fat), 98 mg chol., 1,354 mg sodium, 80 g carbo., 5 g fiber, 42 g pro. Daily Values: 10% vit. A, 26% vit. C, 16% calcium, 37% iron.

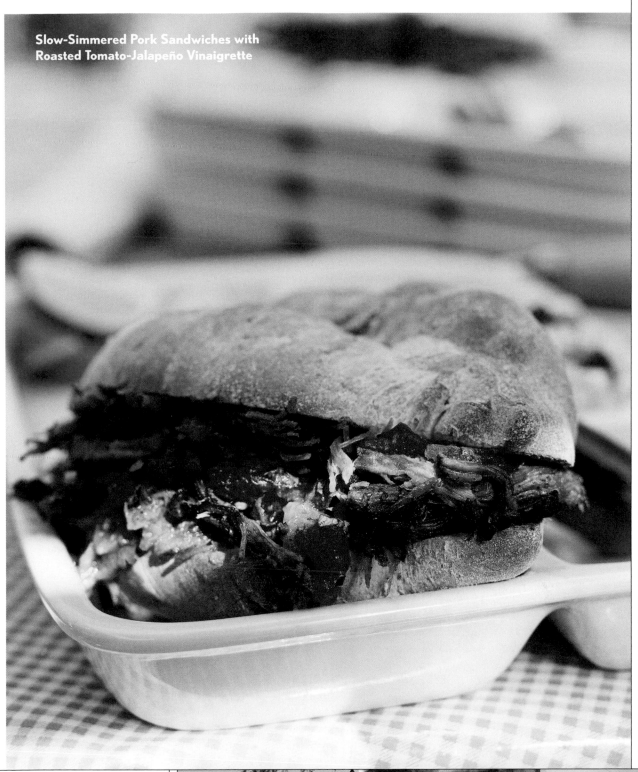

Slow-Simmered Pork Sandwiches with Roasted Tomato-Jalapeño Vinaigrette

Her friends insist that dinner in the garden is such a memorable event because of the way Carrie pays attention to the smallest details. For Carrie, "It's about the bonding and laughing and spending time together."

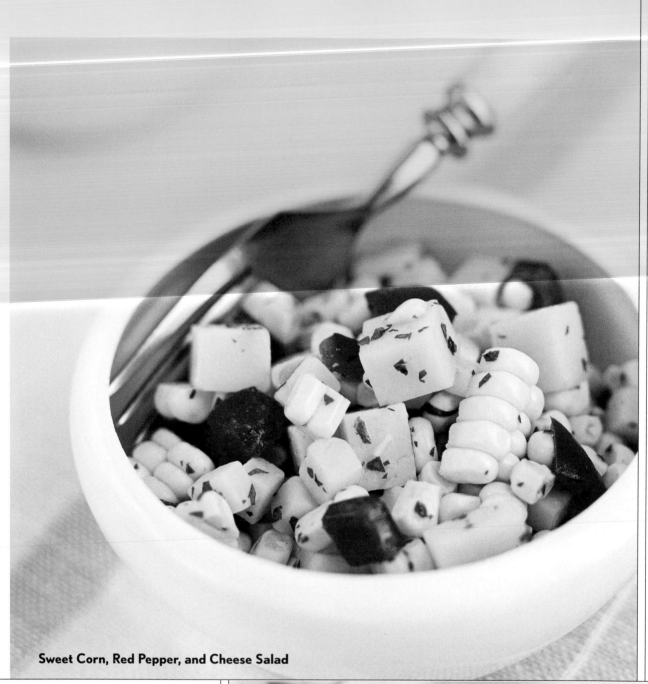

Sweet Corn, Red Pepper, and Cheese Salad

Bacon-Avocado Deviled Eggs

Bacon-Avocado Deviled Eggs

Deviled eggs are traditional favorites for outdoor summer gatherings. This innovative variation makes a great thing even better.

START TO FINISH: 45 minutes

12 eggs
5 slices thick-sliced bacon, chopped
1/2 cup mayonnaise
1 Tbsp. grainy (country) Dijon-style mustard
2 tsp. caper juice
Few dashes bottled hot pepper sauce

1/4 tsp. ground black pepper
1 ripe but firm avocado, halved, seeded, and peeled
2 tsp. lemon juice
Snipped fresh chives (optional)

1. Place eggs in a single layer in a large saucepan or 4-quart Dutch oven. Add enough cold water to just cover the eggs. Bring to a rapid boil over high heat (water will have large rapidly breaking bubbles). Remove from heat; cover. Let stand for 15 minutes; drain. Run cold water over eggs or place in ice water until cool enough to handle; drain. Peel eggs; slice in half lengthwise. Remove yolks; place in a medium bowl. Set whites aside.

2. Meanwhile, cook bacon in a small skillet over medium heat until crisp. Drain on paper towels; set aside.

3. Use a fork to mash egg yolks. Stir in mayonnaise, mustard, caper juice, hot pepper sauce, and black pepper until combined.

4. Chop the avocado into 1/2-inch pieces; toss with lemon juice. Place pieces of avocado in the hollow of each egg white. Spoon or pipe egg yolk mixture into egg white halves. Sprinkle with bacon pieces, any remaining avocado pieces, and snipped chives. Cover and chill for up to 4 hours. Makes 24 servings.

Each serving: 109 cal., 9 g total fat (2 g sat. fat), 110 mg chol., 112 mg sodium, 1 g carbo., 0 g fiber, 4 g pro. Daily Values: 4% vit. A, 1% vit. C, 1% calcium, 2% iron.

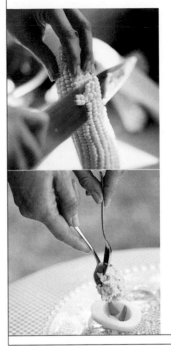

CUTTING KERNELS
To cut kernels from a fresh ear of corn, place the cob on a steady surface and saw downward with a sharp knife.

FILLING EGGS
Use one teaspoon to scoop the egg yolk mixture and another to gently push the mixture into the halved egg whites.

Sweet Corn, Red Pepper, and Cheese Salad

This recipe also works with frozen corn; cook it briefly, then chill.

START TO FINISH: 40 minutes

8 ears of sweet corn
2/3 cup finely chopped red sweet pepper
8 oz. manchego, Teleme, or Monterey Jack cheese with jalapeño peppers, cut into 1/4-inch cubes

1 recipe Sherry Vinaigrette (below)
2 Tbsp. snipped fresh flat-leaf parsley
Salt or kosher salt
Ground black pepper

1. Remove husks from ears of corn. Scrub ears with a stiff brush to remove silks; rinse. Cut kernels from cobs; scrape cobs with knife to release juices. In a large bowl combine corn and juices, sweet pepper, and cheese. Prepare Sherry Vinaigrette; add to corn mixture. Stir gently to coat; stir in parsley. Season to taste with salt and pepper. Makes 12 servings.

SHERRY VINAIGRETTE: In a medium mixing bowl combine 3 tablespoons sherry wine vinegar, 2 teaspoons Dijon-style mustard, and 1/2 teaspoon salt or kosher salt; whisk until smooth. Gradually add 2/3 cup extra-virgin olive oil, whisking constantly until dressing thickens slightly. Season to taste with ground black pepper. Cover and chill for up to 3 days. Makes about 3/4 cup.

Each serving: 233 cal., 18 g total fat (5 g sat. fat), 17 mg chol., 209 mg sodium, 12 g carbo., 2 g fiber, 7 g pro. Daily Values: 17% vit. A, 35% vit. C, 14% calcium, 3% iron.

SKEWER ART

Carrie suggests spearing the fruit so it rests toward the blunt end of the skewer. This keeps the sharp end free for poking into more fruit, as well as making the fruit on the skewer safer to eat.

Fruit Wands

There's an art to making great fruit skewers; use a few fruit varieties, but vary shapes and sizes for maximum visual and flavor impact.

START TO FINISH: 30 minutes

8 cups assorted fresh fruit, such as kiwifruit pieces, strawberry halves, watermelon chunks, and/or thin honeydew melon strips	2 cups Crème Fraîche, (page 96)
	¼ cup snipped fresh herbs, such as lemon verbena or basil
	Raw sugar

1. On eight 8- to 10-inch skewers thread some of the fruit. Place any remaining fruit in a serving bowl.

2. For dip, in a small bowl stir together Crème Fraîche and herb. Serve fruit with crème fraîche dip. Makes 8 servings.

Each serving: 242 cal., 18 g total fat (11 g sat. fat), 54 mg chol., 31 mg sodium, 21 g carbo., 2 g fiber, 2 g pro. Daily Values: 20% vit. A, 63% vit. C, 7% calcium, 3% iron.

Trilevel Brownies

Who doesn't love chocolate and brownies? This recipe boasts three sweet layers—a chewy oatmeal cookie crust, a fudgy layer, and a creamy frosting—for one solid-gold treat.

PREP: 15 minutes **BAKE:** 35 minutes

1	cup quick-cooking rolled oats	1	tsp. vanilla
½	cup all-purpose flour	¼	tsp. baking powder
½	cup packed brown sugar	½	cup chopped walnuts
¼	tsp. baking soda	1	oz. unsweetened chocolate
½	cup butter, melted	2	Tbsp. butter
1	egg	1½	cups sifted powdered sugar
¾	cup granulated sugar	½	tsp. vanilla
⅔	cup all-purpose flour		Walnut halves (optional)
¼	cup milk		
¼	cup butter, melted		
1	oz. unsweetened chocolate, melted and cooled		

1. Preheat oven to 350° F. For the bottom layer, stir together oats, the ½ cup flour, the brown sugar, and baking soda. Stir in the ½ cup melted butter. Pat mixture onto the bottom of an ungreased 11×7×1½-inch baking pan. Bake for 10 minutes.

2. Meanwhile, for the middle layer, beat egg; stir in granulated sugar, the ⅔ cup flour, the milk, the ¼ cup melted butter, the 1 ounce melted chocolate, the 1 teaspoon vanilla, and the baking powder until smooth. Fold in chopped walnuts. Spread batter evenly over baked layer in pan. Bake for 25 minutes more. Place on a wire rack while preparing top layer.

3. For the top layer, in a medium saucepan heat and stir the 1 ounce chocolate and the 2 tablespoons butter until melted. Stir in the powdered sugar and the ½ teaspoon vanilla. Stir in enough hot water (1 to 2 tablespoons) to make a mixture that is almost pourable. Spread onto brownies. If desired, garnish with walnut halves. Cool in pan on a wire rack. Cut into bars. Makes 24 brownies.

Each brownie: 199 cal., 11 g total fat (6 g sat. fat), 28 mg chol., 96 mg sodium, 25 g carbo., 1 g fiber, 2 g pro. Daily Values: 6% vit. A, 2% calcium, 4% iron.

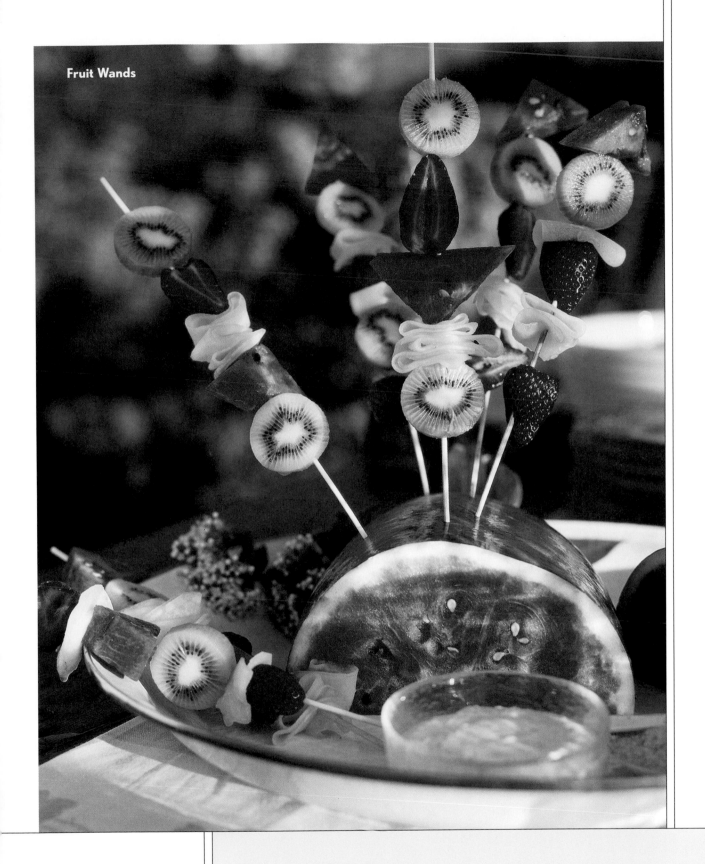

Fruit Wands

WAYS WITH WATERMELON
The reverse twist from using watermelon to hold skewers *(above)* is to hollow it into a bowl or basket. This makes a decorative vessel for foods such as salads and bite-sized fruits and veggies. Reserve some of the watermelon to shape into balls, freezing them for several hours in a single layer on a cookie sheet. The frozen fruit is delicious added to cold drinks, including teas, lemonades, and sweet sparkling wines.

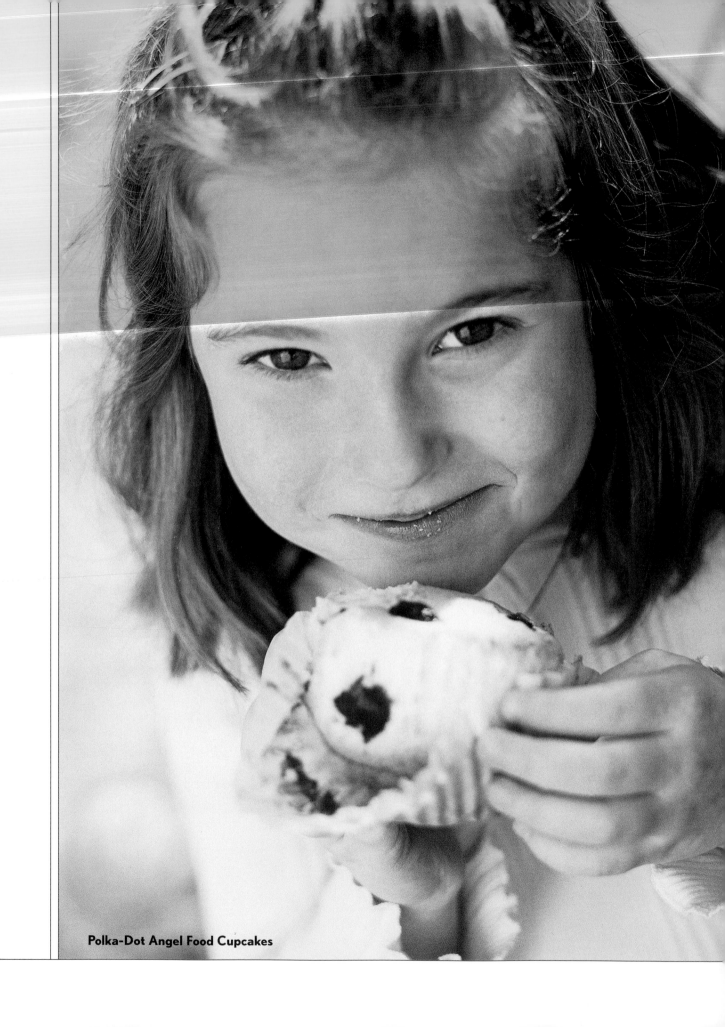

Polka-Dot Angel Food Cupcakes

Polka-Dot Angel Food Cupcakes

The berries become unexpected bursts of jamlike flavor in these light popovers or cupcakes. The popover version is pictured on the cover.

PREP: 1 hour **BAKE:** 15 minutes

1½	cups egg whites (10 to 12)	½	tsp. salt
1	cup sifted cake flour	¾	cup sugar
½	cup sugar	1	cup assorted fresh red
1½	tsp. cream of tartar		raspberries, blueberries,
1	tsp. vanilla		blackberries, and
½	tsp. almond extract		strawberries, diced

1. In a very large mixing bowl let egg whites stand at room temperature for 30 minutes. Meanwhile, sift cake flour and ½ cup sugar together 3 times; set aside. Grease 12 popover pans, if using. Line popover pans or 12 jumbo (3¼-inch) muffin cups with large paper bake cups. Preheat oven to 350° F.

2. Add cream of tartar, vanilla, almond extract, and salt to egg whites. Beat with an electric mixer on medium speed until soft peaks form (tips curl). Gradually add ¾ cup sugar, about 2 tablespoons at a time, beating until stiff peaks form (tips stand straight).

3. Sift one-fourth of the cake flour mixture over beaten egg whites; fold in gently. Repeat, folding in the remaining flour mixture by fourths.

4. Spoon half of the batter into popover or muffin pans, filling about half full. Sprinkle a few berry pieces onto each, then top with another large dollop of batter and remaining berries. Mound remaining batter over fruit pieces (the cups will be very full).

5. Bake for 15 to 18 minutes or until tops are golden and spring back when lightly touched. Cool on a wire rack in the pan. To remove, run a knife around edges. If desired, wrap with new paper bake cups and tie with ribbon. Makes 12 cupcakes.

low fat Each cupcake: 134 cal., 0 g total fat (0 g sat. fat), 0 mg chol., 143 mg sodium, 29 g carbo., 1 g fiber, 4 g pro. Daily Values: 2% vit. C, 4% iron.

SUMMER PICNIC

Bacon-Avocado Deviled Eggs *(page 101)*
Sweet Corn, Red Pepper, and Cheese Salad *(page 101)*
Slow-Simmered Pork Sandwiches with
Roasted Tomato-Jalapeño Vinaigrette *(page 98)*
Polka-Dot Angel Food Cupcakes *(above)*
Hibiscus Tea or Lavender Coolers *(page 106)*

Fudge Ribbon Pie

This pie, with its combination of rich chocolate sauce, refreshing peppermint ice cream, and airy meringue, is sure to dazzle and impress. If making a meringue sounds too fussy, replace the meringue topping with sweetened whipped cream.

PREP: 50 minutes **BAKE:** 3 minutes **FREEZE:** Several hours

1	cup sugar	1	9-inch baked pastry shell,
1	5-oz. can (⅔ cup)		cooled
	evaporated milk	1	recipe Peppermint
2	Tbsp. butter or margarine		Meringue (below)
2	oz. unsweetened	1	Tbsp. crushed peppermint
	chocolate, cut up		stick candy
1	tsp. vanilla		
2	pt. (4 cups) peppermint		
	ice cream		

1. For fudge sauce, in a small saucepan combine the 1 cup sugar, the evaporated milk, butter, and chocolate. Cook and stir over medium heat until bubbly. Reduce heat; boil gently for 4 to 5 minutes, stirring occasionally, until thickened and reduced to 1½ cups. Remove from heat; stir in vanilla. If necessary, beat until smooth with wire whisk or rotary beater. Set aside to cool.

2. In a chilled bowl stir 1 pint of the ice cream until softened. Spread into cooled pastry shell. Cover with half of the cooled fudge sauce. Freeze until nearly firm. Repeat with remaining ice cream and fudge sauce. Return to freezer.

3. Prepare Peppermint Meringue. Spread meringue onto fudge sauce layer, sealing to edge. Sprinkle with crushed candy. Freeze for several hours or overnight or until firm.

4. Preheat oven to 475° F. Bake frozen pie for 3 to 4 minutes or just until meringue is golden. Cover loosely; freeze for a few hours or overnight before serving. Makes 8 servings.

PEPPERMINT MERINGUE: In a medium mixing bowl dissolve ¾ cup sugar in ½ cup boiling water. Cool to room temperature. Add ¼ cup meringue powder. Beat on low speed until combined; beat on high speed until stiff peaks form (tips stand straight). By hand, fold 3 tablespoons crushed peppermint stick candy into the meringue.

Each serving: 564 cal., 24 g total fat (12 g sat. fat), 43 mg chol., 198 mg sodium, 83 g carbo., 2 g fiber, 6 g pro. Daily Values: 3% vit. A, 1% vit. C, 10% calcium, 7% iron.

Lavender Cooler

Look for unsprayed, organic lavender flowers in health food stores, or purchase them either online at www.matanzascreek.com or by calling 800/590-6464.

PREP: 30 minutes   **COOL:** 2 hours

3	cups sugar	Ice
3	cups water	Sprigs of Spanish lavender
1/2	cup dried lavender flowers	or other edible flowers
4	cups lemon juice	(optional)
8	cups cold water	

1. For syrup, in a medium saucepan combine sugar and the 3 cups water. Bring to boiling; reduce heat, stirring often until the sugar is dissolved.

2. Place lavender flowers in a large bowl. Pour syrup over dried flowers. Let cool to room temperature.

3. Strain the syrup through a fine sieve, pressing the flowers with the back of a wooden spoon to extract all the liquid. Cover and chill for up to 1 week.

4. To serve, in a very large pitcher or crock measure 4 cups of the syrup. Add the lemon juice and 8 cups cold water. Stir to combine. Serve over ice in tall glasses. If desired, garnish with sprigs of lavender. Makes about 20 servings.

low fat Each serving: 124 cal., 0 g total fat (0 g sat. fat), 0 mg chol., 5 mg sodium, 33 g carbo., 0 g fiber, 0 g pro. Daily Values: 37% vit. C, 1% calcium.

Watermelon Lemonade

The sweetness of watermelon along with a splash of apple juice make this version of lemonade unexpectedly delightful.

PREP: 10 minutes

2	cups cubed watermelon, seeded	1/3 cup lemon or lime juice
1/2	cup apple or white grape juice	1 to 2 Tbsp. honey

1. In a blender combine watermelon, apple juice, lemon juice, and honey. Cover and blend until smooth. Serve over ice in tall glasses. Makes 2 to 3 servings.

low fat Each serving: 120 cal., 1 g total fat (0 g sat. fat), 0 mg chol., 6 mg sodium, 30 g carbo., 1 g fiber, 1 g pro. Daily Values: 11% vit. A, 56% vit. C, 2% calcium, 3% iron.

Hibiscus Tea

Find hibiscus, also called Flor de Jamaica, in the Mexican section of supermarkets, Latin markets, and health food stores.

PREP: 10 minutes   **COOL:** 2 hours

1	medium lemon	4	cardamom pods or
1	medium orange		1/4 tsp. ground
2	cups dried hibiscus flowers		cardamom
1	cup sugar	12	cups boiling water
6	inches stick cinnamon		Ice
12	whole cloves		Lemon wedges

1. Using a vegetable peeler, remove the peel from the lemon and orange. In a large bowl combine lemon peel, orange peel, hibiscus flowers, sugar, cinnamon sticks, cloves, and cardamom pods. Add boiling water and stir. Let cool to room temperature.

2. Strain tea into a pitcher and serve. Or cover and chill for up to 24 hours. Serve over ice in tall glasses. Garnish with lemon wedges. Makes 12 servings.

low fat Each serving: 62 cal., 0 g total fat (0 g sat. fat), 0 mg chol., 7 mg sodium, 16 g carbo., 0 g fiber, 0 g pro.

Lime-Pineapple Punch

Make the syrup for this punch ahead of time. But once you add the sherbet and carbonated beverage, serve it right away.

PREP: 10 minutes   **CHILL:** 4 hours

1	cup sugar	1	pt. lime sherbet
2	cups water	1	pt. pineapple sherbet
2	tsp. finely shredded lime peel	3 1/2	cups lemon-lime carbonated beverage, chilled
1/2	cup lime juice (about 4 limes)		

1. In a medium saucepan, combine sugar and 1 cup of the water; cook and stir until sugar is dissolved. Add the remaining 1 cup water and the lime peel and juice. Cover and chill for at least 4 hours.

2. Before serving, strain syrup mixture. Pour strained mixture into a chilled punch bowl; add scoops of lime sherbet and pineapple sherbet, stirring until partially melted. Slowly pour in carbonated beverage, stirring with up-and-down motion. Serve punch immediately. Makes about 10 servings.

low fat Each serving: 240 cal., 2 g total fat (1 g sat. fat), 4 mg chol., 63 mg sodium, 57 g carbo., 0 g fiber, 1 g pro. Daily Values: 12% vit. C, 4% calcium, 1% iron.

Hibiscus Tea
Lavender Cooler

Country French Ribeyes

WHAT'S THE CUT?

LOOK FOR STANDARD INDUSTRY CUT NAMES ON MEAT LABELS. HERE ARE A FEW CLUES FOR CLARIFICATION.

It's a familiar scene: Your recipe calls for a certain cut of beef and the butcher in your new neighborhood gives you a blank stare. "Never heard of it," he says. Chances are, that cut of meat is simply known by a different name than the one you've used before. Across the country, the names of meat cuts vary from region to region.

For example, a Kansas City steak and New York strip steak are the same cut. Until recently, asking for Kansas City steak in Kansas City or a New York strip steak in New York earned you only a blank stare. Regardless of your location, a top loin steak is what you want.

Look for beef short plate in Chicago, and you'll get skirt steak. Order skirt steak in other parts of the Midwest, and the butcher-paper-wrapped package may bear the label "steak for fajitas." You'll also find skirt steak labeled as Philadelphia steak or London broil. London broil has nothing to do with London or skirt steak. It's a recipe name for marinated flank steak, so purchase flank steak when you want London broil.

Don't let Swiss steak fool you. It has no relation to bank accounts, the Alps, or Heidi and her goats. The name is said to originate in Britain, where "swissing" is a method of smoothing bolts of cloth with huge rollers. When you want Swiss steak, look for beef chuck arm steak, round steak, or steak for swissing—meaning the meat is intended to be pounded thin.

PHOTOGRAPH: MIKE DIETER. PROP STYLIST: SUE MITCHELL. FOOD STYLIST: JILL LUST.

Swiss Steak

With this version of Swiss Steak, you can choose the cooking method—range-top or oven—that best fits your schedule.

PREP: 25 minutes **COOK:** 1¼ hours

1 lb. boneless beef round steak, cut ³/₄ inch thick	1 small onion, sliced and separated into rings
2 Tbsp. all-purpose flour	½ cup sliced celery (1 stalk)
¼ tsp. salt	½ cup sliced carrot (1 medium)
¼ tsp. ground black pepper	2 cups hot cooked noodles or mashed potatoes
1 Tbsp. cooking oil	
1 14½-oz. can diced tomatoes with basil, oregano, and garlic, undrained	

1. Trim fat from meat. Cut into 4 serving-size pieces. Combine flour, salt, and pepper. Use the notched side of a meat mallet to pound the flour mixture into the meat.

2. In a large skillet brown meat on both sides in hot oil. Drain off fat. Add undrained tomatoes, onion, celery, and carrot. Bring to boiling; reduce heat. Simmer, covered, about 1¼ hours or until meat is tender. Skim off fat. Serve with noodles or mashed potatoes. Makes 4 main-dish servings.

OVEN DIRECTIONS: Prepare and brown meat in skillet as above. Transfer meat to a 2-quart casserole. In the same skillet combine undrained tomatoes, onion, celery, and carrot. Bring mixture to boiling, scraping up any browned bits. Pour over meat. Cover and bake in a 350° F oven about 1 hour or until tender. Serve as above.

low fat Each serving: 340 cal., 9 g total fat (2 g sat. fat), 82 mg chol., 459 mg sodium, 35 g carbo., 3 g fiber, 28 g pro. Daily Values: 78% vit. A, 26% vit. C, 7% calcium, 26% iron.

FATHER'S DAY DINNER

Country French Ribeyes *(right)*
Steak Fries *(right)*
Coleslaw
Macaroon Fruit Tart *(page 295)*
Iced coffee

Country French Ribeyes

Harvested abundantly in the French region of Provence, lavender is a key ingredient in the seasoning blend known as herbes de Provence. When used as a rub, as it is here, lavender imbues meats with an enticing flavor and aroma that is at once herbal and floral.

PREP: 5 minutes **GRILL:** 16 minutes

5 green onions	4 6- to 8-oz. beef ribeye steaks, cut 1 inch thick
2 tsp. dried lavender, crushed	1 Tbsp. olive oil
2 tsp. dried thyme, crushed	4 to 8 roma tomatoes
1 tsp. ground black pepper	1 recipe Steak Fries (below) (optional)
½ tsp. ground rock sea salt or coarse salt	

1. Clean and trim green onions. Finely chop 1 green onion; set remaining onions aside. In a small bowl combine chopped onion, lavender, thyme, pepper, and salt. Rub mixture onto steaks. Brush steaks with half of the olive oil. Brush tomatoes and remaining green onions with remaining olive oil.

2. Place steaks on the lightly-oiled rack of a grill directly over medium-high heat. Grill for 8 to 10 minutes. Place tomatoes and onions on grill. Turn steaks; grill 8 to 10 minutes more or until desired doneness. Grill tomatoes and onions for 8 to 10 minutes or until slightly charred, turning several times. If desired, serve steaks with Steak Fries. Makes 4 servings.

STEAK FRIES: Slice 2 medium potatoes into ¼-inch-thick wedges. In a large mixing bowl toss potatoes with 2 teaspoons olive oil. Add seasoned salt to taste; stir. Fold a 36×18-inch piece of heavy foil in half to form an 18-inch square. Arrange potatoes evenly in center of square. Bring up opposite edges of foil; seal with a double fold. Place packet on the rack of a grill directly over medium heat. Grill for 25 minutes or until potatoes are tender.

Each serving: 433 cal., 18 g total fat (5 g sat. fat), 94 mg chol., 422 mg sodium, 18 g carbo., 3 g fiber, 46 g pro. Daily Values: 19% vit. A, 5% vit. C, 48% calcium, 29% iron.

Simple Salmon Spread

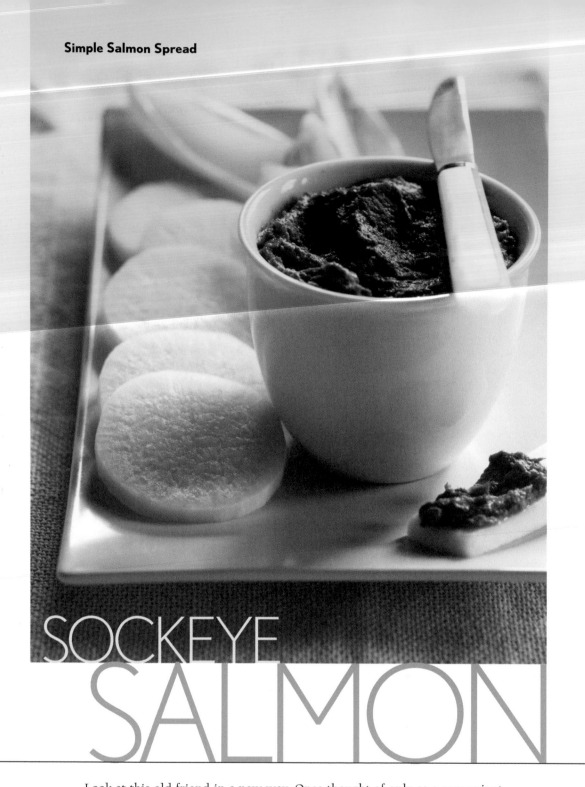

SOCKEYE SALMON

Look at this old friend in a new way. Once thought of only as a convenient food-budget stretcher, canned red sockeye salmon does an amazing Cinderella act when it's wearing the right glass slipper. For example, Simple Salmon Spread is an elegant party starter that pulls together in minutes. Cool, crunchy kohlrabi slices, endive leaves, or daikon rounds partner well with the spread's slightly grainy texture; celery is a nice option too.

Before using canned sockeye salmon, drain it well, remove the skin, and be sure to pick out the little bones—a necessary but quick job. Flake fish into large pieces before adding to your recipe. Sockeye salmon can be a little salty, so adjust the salt level in your recipe to suit your personal taste.

Simple Salmon Spread

Anchovy paste adds maximum depth of flavor to this dish. For a slightly less salty spread, however, feel free to omit it.

START TO FINISH: 20 minutes

1	14³/4-oz. can red sockeye salmon, drained, skin and bones removed	2	Tbsp. mayonnaise
		2	cloves garlic, minced
		1	tsp. capers, drained
¹/4	cup snipped oil-packed dried tomatoes, drained	1	tsp. anchovy paste (optional)
2	Tbsp. lemon juice	¹/4	tsp. ground white pepper

1. In a food processor,*combine all ingredients. Cover; process until smooth, adding additional mayonnaise, if necessary, for desired consistency. Transfer mixture to a serving dish. Cover; chill for up to 24 hours. Makes about 1³/4 cups.

*NOTE: If you don't have a food processor, combine ingredients in a medium bowl and mash with a potato masher until combined, adding additional mayonnaise, if necessary, for desired consistency.

Each serving: 67 cal., 4 g total fat (1 g sat. fat), 12 mg chol., 189 mg sodium, 1 g carbo., 0 g fiber, 6 g pro. Daily Values: 2% vit. A, 5% vit. C, 8% calcium, 2% iron.

Salmon-Sauced Mostaccioli

PREP: 15 minutes **COOK:** 15 minutes

8	oz. dried mostaccioli or rigatoni (about 3 cups)	2	tsp. snipped fresh dill or ¹/2 tsp. dried dill
1	small green or red sweet pepper, cut into bite-size strips	¹/2	cup plain low-fat yogurt
		3	Tbsp. all-purpose flour
¹/2	cup chopped onion (1 medium)	1	15¹/2-oz. can salmon, drained, broken into large chunks, and skin and bones removed
2	Tbsp. butter or margarine		
1¹/2	cups chicken broth	2	Tbsp. snipped fresh parsley

1. Cook pasta according to package directions. Drain pasta and keep it warm.

2. Meanwhile, for sauce, in a medium saucepan cook sweet pepper and onion in hot butter until tender but not brown. Stir in 1 cup of the broth and the dill. Bring to boiling; reduce heat. Stir together remaining ¹/2 cup broth, the yogurt, and flour. Add yogurt mixture to saucepan. Cook and stir until thickened and bubbly. Cook and stir for 1 minute more. Gently stir in salmon; heat through. Serve sauce over hot pasta. Sprinkle with parsley. Makes 4 servings.

Each serving: 471 cal., 13 g total fat (6 g sat. fat), 78 mg chol., 964 mg sodium, 53 g carbo., 2 g fiber, 30 g pro. Daily Values: 9% vit. A, 30% vit. C, 9% calcium, 20% iron.

DELIVER THE (CANNED) GOODS

With its firm and delicious red flesh, wild Pacific red sockeye salmon has long been a favorite variety of salmon for canning. In addition to the recipes here, try it as a flavorful substitute for canned tuna in recipes. Here are a few more quick ideas to help you start enjoying canned sockeye's incredible versatility:

- Asian Salmon Salad: Combine canned red sockeye salmon with mayonnaise, sliced green onion, sliced bok choy, crushed red pepper, unsalted roasted peanuts, and peanut sauce.
- New Salmon Cakes: Substitute canned red sockeye salmon for the crab in your favorite crab cake recipe. Cook until golden brown and heated through; serve with lemon wedges and tartar sauce.

Salmon Mousse

PREP: 30 minutes **CHILL:** 4¹/2 hours

1	14³/4- to 15¹/2-oz. can red salmon	¹/2	cup finely chopped celery
		2	hard-cooked eggs, chopped
2	envelopes unflavored gelatin	2	Tbsp. snipped fresh chives
1	tsp. sugar	¹/4	tsp. ground black pepper
1¹/4	cups mayonnaise or salad dressing	¹/2	cup whipping cream
			Lettuce leaves
¹/4	cup tomato sauce		Thin cucumber slices
2	Tbsp. lemon juice		Assorted crackers
2	tsp. Worcestershire sauce		

1. Chill a small bowl and beaters of electric mixer. Drain salmon, reserving the liquid. Bone and flake salmon; set aside. Add enough water to the reserved salmon liquid to equal 1 cup; pour into a small saucepan. Sprinkle unflavored gelatin and sugar over the salmon liquid mixture; let stand for 3 minutes to soften gelatin. Heat over medium-low heat until gelatin is dissolved, stirring constantly. Remove from heat.

2. In a large bowl combine mayonnaise, tomato sauce, lemon juice, and Worcestershire sauce; stir in gelatin mixture. Chill until partially set, about 30 minutes. Fold in salmon, celery, chopped hard-cooked eggs, chives, and pepper.

3. In chilled bowl beat cream with chilled beaters until soft peaks form; fold into gelatin mixture. Pour into a 6-cup fish-shape or ring mold. Cover and chill until firm, about 4 hours.

4. To serve, line a tray with lettuce. Unmold mousse onto tray. Serve with cucumber slices and crackers. Makes 16 servings.

Each serving: 211 cal., 20 g total fat (4 g sat. fat), 58 mg chol., 280 mg sodium, 2 g carbo., 0 g fiber, 7 g pro. Daily Values: 6% vit. A, 4% vit. C, 8% calcium, 3% iron.

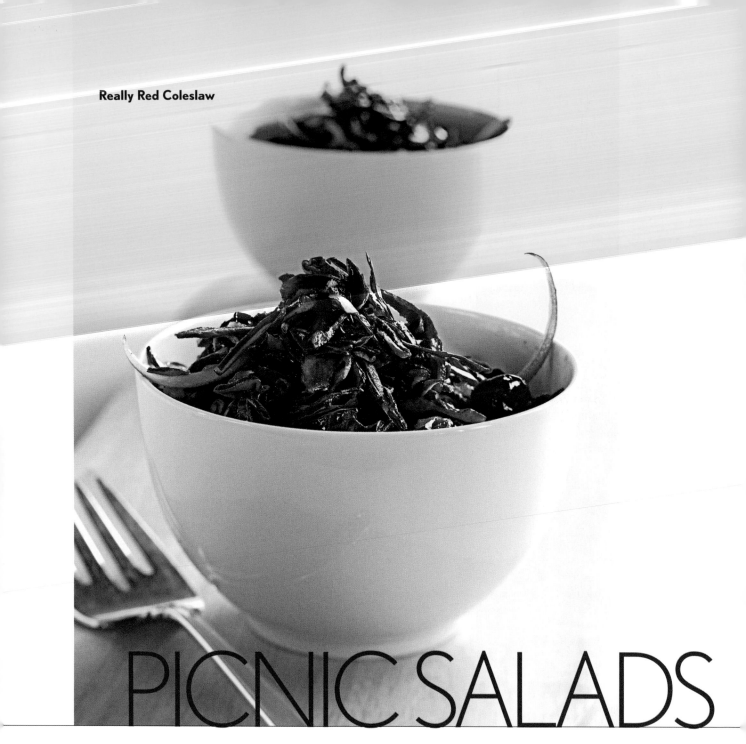

Really Red Coleslaw

PICNIC SALADS

The first promise of a warm summer day gets us right into the mood: Let's eat outside! The park, the beach, the backyard, the bike trail—they're all beckoning for an impromptu outdoor feast. Here are six essential picnic salads you can toss together in less time than it takes to plan where to go.

You won't need gourmet ingredients—the recipes call for readily available items, such as convenient bagged slaws or jarred stir-ins—but the flavors are anything but ordinary. Cabbage slaw dresses up in a single color with a blend of textures; pineapple salad revs up with a dash of heat; macaroni salad trades its mayonnaise base for pesto; and potato salad turns Thai. Best of all, you can make these salads ahead and chill until departure time if you have a premonition that the day may hold an outdoor adventure in store.

Really Red Coleslaw

Well, purple, actually, but you get the idea. Make sure you use a vinegar-and-oil-based dressing.

START TO FINISH: 15 minutes

1	10-oz. pkg. red cabbage slaw (about 6 cups)	½	cup red raspberry vinaigrette
1	medium red onion, slivered (1 cup)	1	Tbsp. seedless red raspberry preserves
½	cup dried tart red cherries		

1. In a large bowl combine slaw, red onion, and dried cherries; set aside. Combine vinaigrette and preserves; pour over slaw mixture and toss gently to coat. Serve at room temperature or chill for up to 6 hours. Makes 8 side-dish servings.

Each serving: 108 cal., 6 g total fat (1 g sat. fat), 0 mg chol., 5 mg sodium, 12 g carbo., 1 g fiber, 1 g pro. Daily Values: 1% vit. A, 36% vit. C, 2% calcium, 1% iron.

GET THERE, STAY THERE, EAT THERE

Packing and serving picnic fare in a food-safe manner is essential for a happy and healthy outing. Follow these guidelines:

- Move salads directly from the refrigerator to the cooler. To avoid a soggy lettuce salad, pack dressings and ingredients separately, then toss together at the picnic site.
- Place cooked meats and raw items for the barbecue, as well as items more likely to be used last, on the bottom of the cooler close to the cooling source.
- Pack the cooler with ice packs or blocks of ice; they last longer than ice cubes. Once the cooler is packed, avoid opening it as much as possible.
- The shadier the spot you find to set up your picnic, the better. Foods will warm up quickly when placed in the hot sun, even if they are in a cooler.
- Remove foods from coolers as close as possible to the time you plan to eat. Rather than setting out all the food at once, put out starters first, then main courses and side dishes, and desserts last. If possible, set salads and other foods in bowls of ice for serving.
- Dispose of any leftover foods on site. Food that still looks appealing but was exposed to sunshine and warm temperatures for more than one hour can be harmful.

Hot-and-Sweet Pineapple Slaw

PREP: 10 minutes **CHILL:** 1 hour

1	16-oz. pkg. shredded broccoli (broccoli slaw mix)	½	cup mayonnaise or salad dressing
2	cups fresh pineapple chunks or one 20-oz. can pineapple chunks, drained	1	to 2 Tbsp. adobo sauce from canned chipotle peppers in adobo sauce
2	cups broccoli florets	¼	tsp. salt

1. Rinse and drain shredded broccoli; dry thoroughly. In a bowl combine shredded broccoli, pineapple, and broccoli florets. In a small bowl stir together mayonnaise, adobo sauce, and salt. Add mayonnaise mixture to broccoli mixture. Toss gently to coat. Cover and chill for 1 to 4 hours. Toss before serving. Makes 10 side-dish servings.

Each serving: 112 cal., 11 g total fat (1 g sat. fat), 6 mg chol., 145 mg sodium, 7 g carbo., 2 g fiber, 2 g pro. Daily Values: 20% vit. A, 106% vit. C, 3% calcium, 4% iron.

Hot-and-Sweet Pineapple Slaw

Pesto Macaroni Salad

To add even more freshness and flavor, you stir an extra dose of basil into the salad before chilling and serving.

START TO FINISH: 30 minutes

3	cups dried elbow macaroni	1	7-oz. container purchased
5	oz. fresh green beans,		refrigerated basil pesto
	trimmed and cut into	1/2	cup fresh basil leaves, torn
	1-inch pieces (about 1 cup)	1/2	tsp. salt
1	lb. small fresh mozzarella		
	balls, drained and sliced		

1. Cook macaroni according to package directions; drain. Rinse with cold water; drain again. In a saucepan cook green beans, covered, in a small amount of boiling lightly salted water for 10 to 15 minutes or until crisp-tender; drain. Rinse with cold water; drain again.

2. In a large bowl combine macaroni, green beans, mozzarella, and pesto. Stir in basil and salt. Cover and chill for up to 2 hours before serving. Makes 14 side-dish servings.

Each serving: 249 cal., 14 g total fat (4 g sat. fat), 26 mg chol., 255 mg sodium, 20 g carbo., 1 g fiber, 11 g pro. Daily Values: 8% vit. A, 18% vit. C, 18% calcium, 5% iron.

Southwestern-Style Three-Bean Salad

PREP: 20 minutes **CHILL:** 3 hours

1	15-oz. can garbanzo	1	cup thinly sliced celery
	beans, rinsed and drained	3/4	cup chopped red onion
1	15-oz. can black beans,	1	recipe Cilantro Lime
	rinsed and drained		Dressing (below)
1	15-oz. can red kidney		
	beans, rinsed and drained		

1. In a large mixing bowl stir together garbanzo beans, black beans, kidney beans, celery, and onion.

2. Prepare Cilantro Lime Dressing; pour over bean mixture. Toss gently to coat. Cover and chill for 3 to 24 hours, stirring occasionally. Serve with a slotted spoon. Makes 8 side-dish servings.

CILANTRO LIME DRESSING: In a screw-top jar combine 1/4 cup salad oil, 1/4 cup vinegar, 1 minced garlic clove, 2 tablespoons snipped fresh cilantro, 2 tablespoons lime juice, 1 tablespoon sugar, 1/2 teaspoon chili powder, 1/2 teaspoon ground cumin, and 1/4 teaspoon salt. Cover and shake well.

low fat Each serving: 202 cal., 8 g total fat (1 g sat. fat), 0 mg chol., 562 mg sodium, 27 g carbo., 9 g fiber, 9 g pro. Daily Values: 3% vit. A, 9% vit. C, 7% calcium, 11% iron.

Thai Beef-Potato Salad

PREP: 20 minutes **CHILL:** 4 hours

2	20-oz. pkg. refrigerated	1/2	tsp. salt
	diced potatoes with onions	2/3	cup purchased Thai
	Cooking oil		peanut sauce
1/2	lb. medium-rare deli roast	1	large lime
	beef, cut into thin strips		
3/4	cup 1-inch bias-sliced		
	green onion		

1. In a very large skillet cook potatoes in hot oil according to package directions; cool slightly. In a large bowl combine potatoes, roast beef, green onion, and salt. Stir in peanut sauce.

2. Finely shred enough peel from lime to equal 1 tablespoon. Squeeze juice from lime. Add peel and 2 to 3 tablespoons lime juice to salad; stir gently. Cover; chill for 4 to 24 hours. Stir before serving. Makes 12 to 16 side-dish servings.

low fat Each serving: 157 cal., 3 g total fat (1 g sat. fat), 13 mg chol., 473 mg sodium, 24 g carbo., 3 g fiber, 9 g pro. Daily Values: 1% vit. A, 21% vit. C, 1% calcium, 5% iron.

Citrus-Avocado Salad

START TO FINISH: 30 minutes

4	medium oranges	1/4	cup pomegranate seeds
2	ruby red grapefruit	1	recipe Celery Seed
4	small ripe avocados,		Dressing (below)
	peeled and seeded	8	leaves red leaf lettuce

1. Peel and section the oranges and grapefuit, working over a bowl to catch juices; set juices aside. Reserve 24 orange sections; dice the remaining sections.

2. Slash rounded end of each avocado 3 times, cutting about three-quarters of the way to the opposite end each time. Turn flat sides up and insert an orange section in each slash. Brush avocados with reserved fruit juices. Heap diced oranges and grapefruit sections into avocados; garnish with pomegranate seeds. Prepare Celery Seed Dressing; serve over avocados on lettuce. (Chill any remaining dressing for another use.) Makes 8 side-dish servings.

CELERY SEED DRESSING: In a small mixing bowl, blender, or food processor combine 1/2 cup sugar, 1/3 cup lemon juice, 1 teaspoon celery seeds, 1 teaspoon dry mustard, 1 teaspoon paprika, and 1/2 teaspoon salt. With mixer, blender, or food processor running, slowly add 3/4 cup salad oil in a thin, steady stream. (This should take 2 to 3 minutes.) Continue mixing, blending, or processing until mixture reaches desired consistency. Makes about 1 1/4 cups.

Each serving: 335 cal., 28 g total fat (4 g sat. fat), 0 mg chol., 152 mg sodium, 23 g carbo., 4 g fiber, 2 g pro. Daily Values: 15% vit. A, 67% vit. C, 3% calcium, 5% iron.

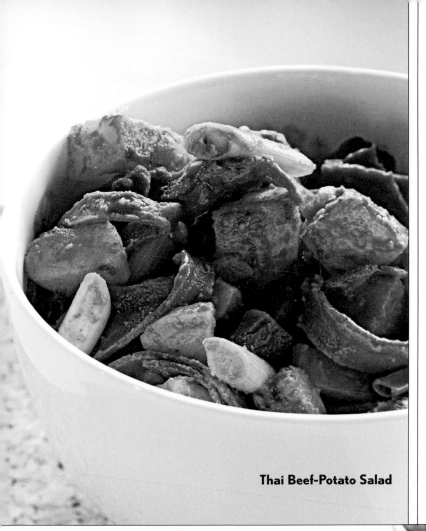

Thai Beef-Potato Salad

TAKING CARE OF FRESH GREENS

Proper washing and storing of lettuce and other greens makes a big difference in how long they remain at peak freshness and flavor. This is crucial in summer, when high temperatures can accelerate their decline.

- First, remove and discard any leaves that are discolored, bruised, or wilted. Wash the greens under cold running water by separating the leaves from each other, then rinsing them in a colander.

- Next, get rid of any excess water—wet greens make soggy salads. Salad spinners can do a good job of drying greens as long as they are filled no more than two-thirds full—overfilling can cause the spinner to bruise the leaves. You can also place wet greens on a clean kitchen towel or several layers of paper towels to dry.

- To store, layer or wrap greens in a clean, dry kitchen towel or paper towels. Seal them in a resealable plastic bag or airtight container and chill them for 30 minutes or up to several hours to crisp before serving.

Pesto Macaroni Salad

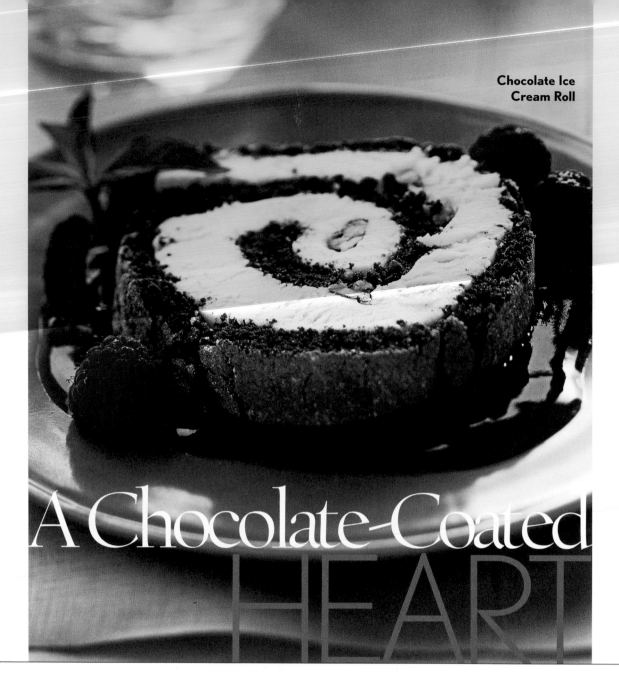

A Chocolate-Coated HEART

Chocolate is good for your heart—according to researchers at the University of California at Davis who reviewed a number of studies. Single studies conducted previously have suggested this, but it's the first time the issue has been analyzed from a broad perspective. It appears that certain compounds in chocolate called flavan-3-ols are responsible for the decreased risk of cardiovascular disease among people who regularly eat chocolate. Flavan-3-ols are antioxidants that give chocolate most of its beloved flavor. Studies suggest that chocolate has an aspirinlike effect—it thins your blood slightly, reducing the inflammation that may lead to heart attacks and strokes. No one is recommending that you throw your aspirin away, but the American Dietetic Association (ADA) says that chocolate can be a part of a heart-healthy diet. The association does say you should take your "medicine" in moderation and make sure your diet includes other antioxidant-rich foods, such as fruits, vegetables, tea, and red wine.

Chocolate Ice Cream Roll

This do-ahead dessert is spectacular enough to serve as a grand finale to your most elegant dinner. (P.S.: Kids will like it too.)

BAKE: 12 minutes **FREEZE:** 4 hours

4 egg whites	Sifted powdered sugar
1/3 cup all-purpose flour	1 qt. fat-free vanilla ice
1/4 cup unsweetened	cream, softened
cocoa powder	1/4 cup broken pecans,
1 tsp. baking powder	toasted
1/4 tsp. salt	1 recipe Raspberry Sauce
4 egg yolks	(below) (optional)
1/2 tsp. vanilla	Fresh red raspberries
1/3 cup granulated sugar	(optional)
1/2 cup granulated sugar	Fresh mint sprigs (optional)

1. Let egg whites stand at room temperature for 30 minutes. Grease and flour a 15×10×1-inch baking pan. In a large bowl stir together flour, cocoa powder, baking powder, and salt. Set aside.

2. Preheat oven to 375° F. In a small mixing bowl beat egg yolks and vanilla with an electric mixer on high speed for 5 minutes or until lemon-colored. Gradually add the 1/3 cup sugar, beating on medium speed about 5 minutes or until sugar is almost dissolved. Wash and dry beaters.

3. In a large mixing bowl beat egg whites on high speed until soft peaks form (tips curl). Add the 1/2 cup sugar, beating until stiff peaks form (tips stand straight). Fold yolk mixture into egg white mixture. Sprinkle flour mixture over egg mixture; fold in gently. Spread batter into prepared pan.

4. Bake for 12 to 15 minutes or until top springs back when touched. Loosen edges of hot cake from pan; turn out onto a clean dish towel sprinkled with powdered sugar. Starting with a narrow end, roll up cake and towel together. Cool.

5. Unroll cake. Spread ice cream onto cake to within 1 inch of edges. Sprinkle with pecans. Reroll cake without towel. Wrap and freeze for at least 4 hours.

6. Meanwhile, prepare Raspberry Sauce, if desired. To serve, drizzle Raspberry Sauce onto 10 plates. Slice cake; place slices on plates. If desired, garnish with fresh raspberries and mint. Makes 10 servings.

RASPBERRY SAUCE: In a small saucepan combine 2/3 cup seedless red raspberry spreadable fruit, 1 tablespoon lemon juice, and 1/4 teaspoon almond extract; heat and stir until spreadable fruit is melted. Cool slightly.

low fat Each serving: 214 cal., 4 g total fat (1 g sat. fat), 85 mg chol., 211 mg sodium, 37 g carbo., 0 g fiber, 7 g pro. Daily Values: 5% vit. A, 18% calcium, 4% iron.

CHOCOLATE TASTING TIPS

While all chocolate contains some heart-healthy compounds, dark chocolate has the most (with fewer calories than lighter varieties). No matter which kind you choose, the ADA offers these hints:

- Chocolate tastes best on an empty stomach. The delicate flavors of chocolate are easily overwhelmed by competing flavors.
- Serve chocolate at room temperature (66° to 77° F). If too hot, chocolate melts and separates. If too cold, the flavors deaden.
- Finally, let the chocolate linger in your mouth. Like wine, chocolate has a host of primary and secondary flavors. You'll eat less chocolate and it enjoy more if you slow down to savor all the nuances.

Chocolate-Cream Cheese Cupcakes

PREP: 15 minutes **BAKE:** 25 minutes **COOL:** 30 minutes

1/2 of an 8-oz. package fat-free	1 tsp. baking powder
cream cheese, softened	1/4 tsp. baking soda
1 1/3 cups sugar	1/8 tsp. salt
1/4 cup refrigerated or frozen	1 cup water
egg product, thawed	1/3 cup cooking oil
1/3 cup miniature semisweet	1 Tbsp. vinegar
chocolate pieces	1 tsp. vanilla
1 1/2 cups all-purpose flour	1/2 cup low-fat granola
1/4 cup unsweetened cocoa powder	

1. Line 18 muffin cups with paper bake cups; set aside.

2. In a small mixing bowl beat cream cheese with an electric mixer on medium speed until smooth. Add 1/3 cup of the sugar and the egg product. Beat on medium speed for 1 minute or until smooth. Stir in the semisweet chocolate pieces; set aside.

3. Preheat oven to 350° F. In a large mixing bowl stir together remaining 1 cup sugar, the flour, cocoa powder, baking powder, baking soda, and salt. Add water, oil, vinegar, and vanilla. Beat with an electric mixer on medium speed for 2 minutes, scraping sides of bowl occasionally. Spoon batter into the prepared muffin cups, filling each half full. Spoon about 1 tablespoon of the cream cheese mixture over each. Sprinkle with granola.

4. Bake for 25 to 30 minutes or until tops spring back when touched. Cool cupcakes in pan on a wire rack for 10 minutes. Remove cupcakes from pan; cool thoroughly on the wire rack. Makes 18 cupcakes.

low fat Each serving: 162 cal., 5 g total fat (1 g sat. fat), 1 mg chol., 69 mg sodium, 27 g carbo., 1 g fiber, 3 g pro. Daily Values: 1% vit. A, 5% calcium, 5% iron.

July

ENTERTAIN FRIENDS AND FAMILY WITH
SIZZLING-HOT IDEAS ALL SUMMER LONG.

Celebrate Summer in a Big Way

celebrate summer

in a big way

FAMILY REUNIONS. BACKYARD BARBECUES. BLOCK PARTIES. PICNICS IN THE PARK. HERE'S HOW TO STAGE THE SEASON'S TASTIEST OUTDOOR BASHES.

Corn-on-the-Cob Salad

PREP: 40 minutes **GRILL:** 20 minutes **CHILL:** 2 hours

8 fresh ears of corn	1 medium sweet onion, such
1 recipe Herb Vinaigrette	as Vidalia or Walla Walla,
(below)	chopped
1 lb. fresh or frozen shelled	1 to 2 fresh jalapeño chile
baby lima beans	peppers,* seeded and
1 medium red, yellow, or	chopped
orange sweet pepper,	
chopped	

1. Remove husks and silk from corn. Break or cut each ear of corn in half (leave some whole, if desired); set aside.

2. Prepare Herb Vinaigrette; brush some onto corn. Grill corn on the rack of an uncovered gas grill on medium or a charcoal grill directly over medium coals about 20 minutes or until tender, turning often. Let cool. Remove kernels from 4 grilled corn halves; set aside. Brush remaining corn with some of the remaining vinaigrette. Cover ears of corn and chill.

3. Meanwhile, in a medium saucepan cook lima beans in a small amount of lightly salted boiling water for 10 to 15 minutes or until beans are crisp-tender; drain. Rinse with cold water; drain again.

4. In a large bowl combine lima beans, corn kernels, sweet pepper, onion, and jalapeño pepper. Add remaining vinaigrette; toss to coat. Cover and chill for 2 to 24 hours. To serve, spoon lima bean mixture into a serving container. Top with remaining ears of corn. Makes 12 side-dish servings.

HERB VINAIGRETTE: In a small bowl whisk together ½ cup olive oil, ½ cup cider vinegar, 2 tablespoons snipped fresh oregano, ¼ teaspoon salt, and ⅛ teaspoon ground black pepper.

*NOTE: Because hot chile peppers, such as jalapeños, contain volatile oils that can burn your skin and eyes, avoid direct contact with chiles as much as possible. When working with chile peppers, wear plastic or rubber gloves. If your bare hands do touch the chile peppers, wash your hands well with soap and water.

Each serving: 190 cal., 10 g total fat (1 g sat. fat), 0 mg chol., 76 mg sodium, 23 g carbo., 4 g fiber, 5 g pro. Daily Values: 5% vit. A, 59% vit. C, 2% calcium, 7% iron.

Potluck for a crowd

You might be tempted to take the easy way out when you're preparing a potluck dish for a crowd. Well, so are we. Let's face it: Necessity is the mother of shortcuts, especially when it's summertime. With our cut-to-the-chase techniques and big-batch recipes, you'll be able to put together incredible dishes and still have plenty of hammock time left before the party.

When everyone brings a dish to pass and Mother Nature contributes a generous portion of sunshine, the food is bound to taste good. We've infused the typical tote-along classics with fresh flourishes bold enough to stand up to the fireworks to come. Success relies on an easy three-step strategy: Plan ahead. Depend on good-to-the-last-crumb recipes. And keep everything simple.

When it comes to presentation, think hassle-free and practical. Go ahead and use foil pans or toss-away plastic containers. Big punch bowls make supersize serving vessels. Grab inexpensive white painter's dropcloths from the hardware store to cover tables. Have everyone bring a vintage linen or favorite place mat to add pizzazz. Be sure to have plenty of heavy-duty paper plates that won't buckle and spill when they're piled high.

Whether you're hosting the picnic or simply bringing a dish, do as much as you can ahead of time. As you plan and shop, bear in mind that repetition makes for an awesome display. A platter full of red berries or a big tray piled with mounds of carrots can be dazzling. Get vivid. It's the season for flaunting garden-fresh bursts of color.

Magically transform any basic buffet table into a vivid summer show-off with a massive watermelon split down the center. When melon shopping, go ahead and thump away if you have aspirations to be a drummer, but professional watermelon pickers say it's better to check the bottom of the melon to determine whether it is ripe. The underside should be pale green to light yellow, or just beginning to turn white.

Watermelon Salad with Watercress

Chunky Mustard Potato Salad

Purchased precooked potato wedges give this salad a quick start. For an even faster version, substitute a 9-ounce jar of mustard pickle relish for the pickles, mustard, and roasted red pepper. This recipe can easily be doubled to serve 24, but be sure to start with a Dutch oven for cooking the bigger batch of potatoes.

PREP: 35 minutes **CHILL:** 2 + 4 hours

2	20-oz. pkg. refrigerated new potato wedges	½	cup sliced green onions
¼	tsp. salt	⅓	cup chopped radishes
½	cup coarsely chopped dill pickles	4	hard-cooked eggs, peeled and coarsely chopped
¼	cup Dijon-style mustard	½	tsp. salt
¼	cup chopped, roasted red sweet pepper	¼	tsp. ground black pepper
1	cup chopped celery (2 stalks)	¾	cup mayonnaise or salad dressing

1. Place potatoes in a large saucepan. Add enough water to cover the potatoes and the ¼ teaspoon salt. Bring to boiling; reduce heat. Cover and simmer for 5 minutes. Drain well; cool for 10 minutes.

2. In a very large serving bowl combine warm potatoes, pickles, mustard, and roasted pepper; stir gently. Cover and chill for 2 hours. Add celery, green onions, radishes, eggs, the ½ teaspoon salt, and black pepper. Add mayonnaise; mix gently. Cover and chill for 4 to 24 hours. Makes 12 side-dish servings.

Each serving: 194 cal., 13 g total fat (2 g sat. fat), 76 mg chol., 521 mg sodium, 13 g carbo., 3 g fiber, 5 g pro. Daily Values: 3% vit. A, 22% vit. C, 2% calcium, 4% iron.

Watermelon Salad with Watercress

In this fruit salad, the peppery bite of watercress and onion is quickly mellowed by the sweet, cool watermelon and a refreshing hint of mint. Half of a large watermelon will disappear quickly if you put it in front of about 12 guests. If you're expecting double that number, use both halves of the melon and double the remaining ingredients. You'll have plenty to serve a crowd of 24.

PREP: 45 minutes **CHILL:** up to 6 hours

1	13- to 14-lb. oval watermelon	¼	cup snipped fresh mint
4	cups snipped fresh watercress	2	Tbsp. olive oil flavored with red pepper or plain olive oil
1	medium red onion, cut into thin wedges	¼	tsp. sea salt or salt
		¼	tsp. ground black pepper

1. Cut watermelon in half horizontally. Reserve half for another use. With remaining half, use a small paring knife or grapefruit knife to carefully cut around the fruit, just inside the rind. Cut fruit in the melon crosswise into 1-inch-thick slices (leaving the rind intact). Cut underneath each slice and remove from the shell. Pile slices into the shell. Cover and chill up to 6 hours.

2. Just before serving, in a large bowl combine watercress, onion, mint, olive oil, salt, and pepper; toss to coat. Sprinkle mixture over watermelon slices. Makes 12 side-dish servings.

low fat Each serving: 64 cal., 3 g total fat (0 g sat. fat), 0 mg chol., 41 mg sodium, 10 g carbo., 1 g fiber, 1 g pro. Daily Values: 20% vit. A, 29% vit. C, 3% calcium, 2% iron.

FOURTH OF JULY PICNIC

Watermelon Salad with Watercress *(left)*
Chunky Mustard Potato Salad *(above)*
Oven-Fried Buttermilk Chicken *(page 128)*
Biscuits with red, white, and blue sprinkles
Sweet Layers of Red, White, and Blue *(page 130)*
Madeline's Lemonade *(page 136)*

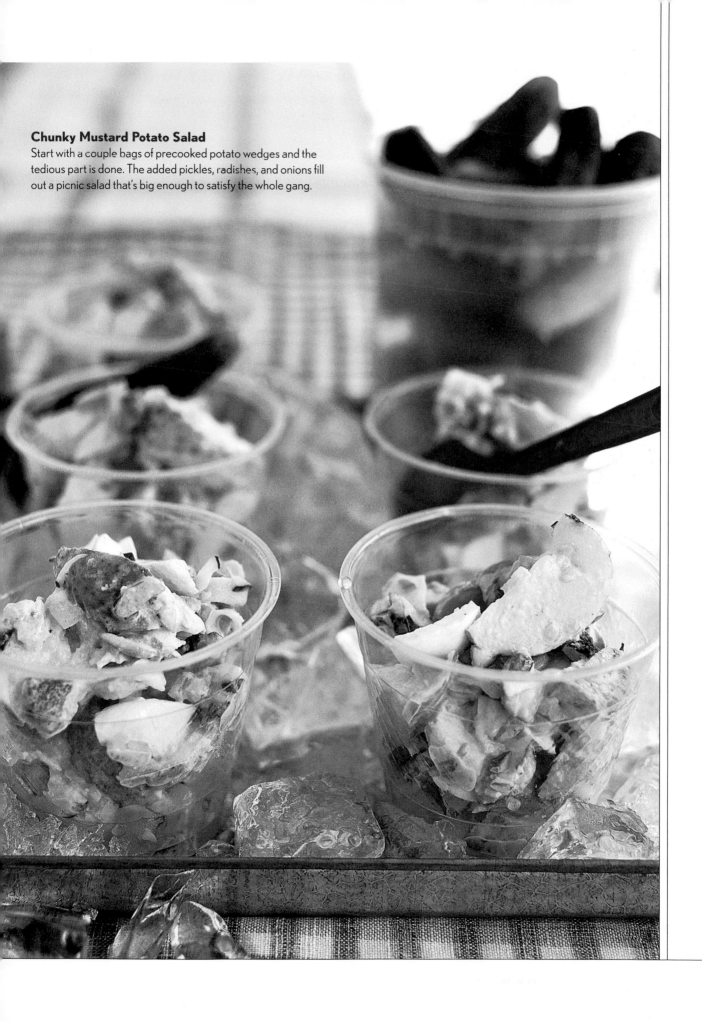

Chunky Mustard Potato Salad
Start with a couple bags of precooked potato wedges and the tedious part is done. The added pickles, radishes, and onions fill out a picnic salad that's big enough to satisfy the whole gang.

Veggies with a Splash

Veggies with a Splash

Three pounds of veggies will feed about 12 people. Serving 24? Just double everything. If your guest list grows to three dozen, prepare a 3-pound platter of carrots, a 3-pound platter of green beans, and a 3-pound platter of pea pods. Steamed asparagus is a good option too.

PREP: 25 minutes **CHILL:** 4 hours

3 lb. baby maroon carrots (Beta Sweet), baby carrots with tops, carrot sticks, Chinese long beans or whole green beans, and/or pea pods, washed and trimmed	2 Tbsp. snipped fresh dill
	2 Tbsp. snipped fresh garlic chives or chives
	Salt
	Ground black pepper
	Coarse sea salt
1/2 cup olive oil	Black or red radishes, thinly
1/3 cup lime juice	sliced (optional)

1. If using baby maroon carrots, wash and cut off all but about 1 1/2 inches of the green top. In a Dutch oven or large saucepan bring a small amount of salted water to boiling. Add baby carrots, carrot sticks, and/or green beans; cook, covered, about 5 minutes or until crisp-tender. Cook pea pods, covered, for 2 to 4 minutes or until crisp-tender. Drain. Immediately transfer vegetables to a large bowl of ice water to stop cooking; drain. Cover and chill for 4 to 24 hours.

2. For vinaigrette, in a screw-top jar combine olive oil, lime juice, dill, and chives. Season to taste with salt and pepper. Cover and shake well.

3. Just before serving, toss vegetables with half of the vinaigrette. Arrange vegetables on a tray or platter and drizzle with remaining vinaigrette. Sprinkle with coarse sea salt. If desired, serve with thinly sliced radishes. Makes 12 side-dish servings.

Each serving: 122 cal., 9 g total fat (1 g sat. fat), 0 mg chol., 186 mg sodium, 9 g carbo., 3 g fiber, 2 g pro. Daily Values: 195% vit. A, 46% vit. C, 4% calcium, 7% iron.

KEEPING VEGETABLES FRESH

Picking the prettiest produce from your garden, the farmers' market, or the grocery store is a big part of presentation. However, you've got to treat your tender gems right at home to keep them beautiful.

- Wash greens in cold water, then dry in a salad spinner or pat with paper towels. Store in an airtight container wrapped in moist paper towels in the refrigerator.
- Trim ends of fresh herbs and asparagus. Store unwashed stalks in a container of water or wrapped in moist paper towels. Keep in an airtight container in the refrigerator. Wash and trim before using.
- Store carrots, green beans, pea pods, zucchini, and peppers unwashed in resealable bags in the refrigerator. Wash and trim before using.

Strawberry-Spinach Salad

For this potluck favorite, you can easily double, triple, or quadruple the ingredients to serve the number of people you need. Just be sure to pack the pecans and dressing separately from the spinach mixture then toss it all together at your picnic. That way, the greens stay crisp and fresh and the nuts are nice and crunchy

START TO FINISH: 30 minutes

1 lb. asparagus spears	8 cups fresh baby spinach or assorted salad greens
1/3 cup bottled poppy seed salad dressing or Italian salad dressing	2 cups sliced fresh strawberries and/or blueberries
1 tsp. finely shredded orange peel	3/4 to 1 lb. cooked turkey, cut into 1/2-inch cubes
1 Tbsp. orange juice	1/4 cup pecan halves, toasted

1. Snap off and discard woody bases from asparagus. If desired, scrape off scales. Cut into 1-inch pieces. Cook asparagus, covered, in a small amount of boiling lightly salted water for 3 to 5 minutes or until crisp-tender. Drain asparagus. Rinse with cold water. Let stand in cold water until cool; drain.

2. Meanwhile, for dressing, in a small mixing bowl stir together poppy seed dressing, orange peel, and orange juice; set aside.

3. In a salad bowl combine asparagus, spinach, berries, and turkey. Top with pecans. Serve with dressing. Makes 4 to 6 main-dish servings.

Each serving: 329 cal., 19 g total fat (3 g sat. fat), 65 mg chol., 299 mg sodium, 10 g carbo., 9 g fiber, 30 g pro. Daily Values: 71% vit. A, 25% vit. C, 10% calcium, 37% iron.

Zucchini Pilaf

A little goat cheese and a lot of zucchini emphasize summer in this double-rice dish. The wild rice mixture comes in a box, making it a quick-start side dish. Even better, the entire dish can be made a day ahead of time, allowing you more time for other preparations or perhaps even a little time to play.

Zucchini Pilaf

Fresh summer color comes to this warm rice side dish from vivid tomatoes and your pick of green zucchini or sunny yellow summer squash. This pilaf is easily made the day before your gathering. Just reheat it before serving.

PREP: 20 minutes **COOK:** 25 minutes **BAKE:** 35 minutes

1 cup chopped onion	1 lb. medium zucchini or
3 cloves garlic, minced	yellow summer squash,
3 Tbsp. olive oil	quartered lengthwise
4½ cups water	and sliced ½ inch thick
2 6-oz. pkg. long grain	(cut some thin strips of
and wild rice mix or	peel for garnish, if desired)
rice pilaf mix	2 tsp. snipped fresh
8 oz. semisoft goat cheese,	rosemary
cubed	¼ tsp. salt
3 to 4 medium assorted	⅛ tsp. ground black pepper
fresh summer tomatoes	
(red, yellow, and/or	
orange), seeded and	
coarsely chopped	

1. In a large saucepan cook onion and garlic in 2 tablespoons of the hot olive oil until tender. Add water, bring to boiling. Stir in rice mix (including seasoning packet). Cover; reduce heat to low. Simmer about 25 minutes or until most of the water is absorbed. Add cheese; stir until melted and combined.

2. Preheat oven to 350° F. Transfer rice mixture to a large bowl. Stir in tomatoes, zucchini, rosemary, salt, and pepper. Transfer to a greased 3-quart rectangular baking dish or a 13×9×2-inch foil pan. If desired, top with strips of zucchini peel. Bake, covered, for 35 to 45 minutes or until heated through. Drizzle with remaining 1 tablespoon olive oil. Makes 12 side-dish servings.

MAKE-AHEAD DIRECTIONS: Prepare as directed, except cover and chill for up to 24 hours before baking. Bake, covered, in a 350° F oven for 50 to 60 minutes or until heated through.

Each serving: 212 cal., 9 g total fat (4 g sat. fat), 15 mg chol., 542 mg sodium, 26 g carbo., 2 g fiber, 7 g pro. Daily Values: 13% vit. A, 18% vit. C, 8% calcium, 7% iron.

GET THE LOOK

The mix-and-match look is part of the ambience of a great potluck. To make the setting even better, tie it all together with the help of white tablecloths and vintage linens and napkins.

■ Tell everyone to use disposable cookware and toss-away foil pans for the food they're toting. But have them bring their favorite summer linens or big napkins.

■ Start with plain white tablecloths as your base. Use the linens to emphasize each dish—as stand-out mats beneath each item or as wraparound color for the cookware and pans.

Farm-Style Green Beans

This recipe was published in a 1976 *Better Homes and Gardens®* magazine story that featured specialties from the tables of Wisconsin dairy farmers. Try it when fresh green beans and homegrown tomatoes are in season and you'll really understand why it ranks as one of the best ways ever to prepare green beans.

PREP: 20 minutes **COOK:** 10 minutes

4 thick slices bacon,	½ tsp. salt
cut up	1 lb. green beans, washed,
2 medium onions,	stemmed, and cut up
sliced	(4 cups)
3 medium tomatoes,	
peeled, seeded, and	
chopped (2 cups)	

1. In a large skillet cook bacon until crisp. Remove bacon, reserving 3 tablespoons of the drippings. Drain bacon and set aside. Cook the onions in the reserved drippings over medium heat until onions are tender. Add the tomatoes and salt; cook, uncovered, about 5 minutes more or until most of the liquid is absorbed.

2. Meanwhile, in a medium saucepan cook the beans in small amount of boiling salted water for 10 to 15 minutes or until crisp-tender; drain. Transfer beans to a serving bowl. Top beans with tomato mixture and bacon pieces. Makes 8 side-dish servings.

Each serving: 86 cal., 5 g total fat (2 g sat. fat), 6 mg chol., 217 mg sodium, 8 g carbo., 3 g fiber, 3 g pro. Daily Values: 13% vit. A, 29% vit. C, 3% calcium, 5% iron.

Poor Boy Filets

In the late 1970s and early 1980s, as men became more interested in cooking, *Better Homes and Gardens*® magazine ran a monthly feature entitled "He Cooks," with recipes sent in from men all over the country. The bachelor cook who concocted this recipe said, "My guests love the filets, and they're a great way to dress up ground beef." These days, the topic of men in the kitchen doesn't merit any special mention because so many men love to cook.

PREP: 30 minutes **GRILL:** 20 minutes

10	slices bacon	3	Tbsp. finely chopped
1	lb. lean ground beef		pimiento-stuffed olives
1/4	tsp. lemon-pepper	2	Tbsp. finely chopped onion
	seasoning	2	Tbsp. finely chopped
1/8	tsp. salt		green sweet pepper
1/4	cup grated Parmesan		Halved cherry tomatoes
	cheese		(optional)
1	4-oz. can mushroom		
	stems and pieces, drained		
	and chopped		

1. In a very large skillet partially cook bacon just until light brown, but still soft. Drain on paper towels. Set aside.

2. Pat ground beef on waxed paper to a 12×7½-inch rectangle that is ¼ inch thick. Sprinkle with lemon-pepper seasoning and salt. Top with Parmesan cheese. Combine mushrooms, olives, onion, and sweet pepper; sprinkle evenly over meat. Lightly press into meat.

3. Carefully roll meat into a spiral, starting from a short side. Cut into 1½-inch-thick slices. Wrap the edge of each slice with 2 strips of partially cooked bacon, overlapping as needed and securing ends with wooden picks.

4. Grill meat on the rack of uncovered gas grill on medium or a charcoal grill directly over medium coals for 10 minutes. Turn meat over and grill about 10 minutes more or until meat is done (instant-read thermometer registers 160° F). Serve on a platter. If desired, garnish with cherry tomatoes. Makes 5 servings.

Each serving: 273 cal., 18 g total fat (7 g sat. fat), 74 mg chol., 673 mg sodium, 2 g carbo., 1 g fiber, 24 g pro. Daily Values: 3% vit. A, 10% vit. C, 7% calcium, 12% iron.

Oven-Fried Buttermilk Chicken

It's easy to add "wow" to oven-fried chicken by creating two different crushed-cracker coatings. A deep brown coating with rye crackers adds great flavor. A second batch coated with pepper-flavored water crackers yields a light brown color. Two tones. Two fantastic flavors. It's delicious cold, too, if you want to make it the night before.

PREP: 20 minutes **MARINATE:** 4 hours **BAKE:** 45 minutes

5	to 6 lb. meaty chicken	1	8-oz. pkg. crisp rye
	pieces (small bone-in		crackers
	breast halves, thighs, and	2	Tbsp. Greek seasoning
	drumsticks), skinned,		blend
	if desired	1/2	cup butter, melted
2	cups buttermilk	3	eggs
1½	tsp. salt	2	Tbsp. water

1. Place chicken pieces in a plastic bag set in a bowl. (If breast halves are large, cut in half before marinating.) For marinade, stir together buttermilk and salt. Pour over chicken; seal bag. Chill for 4 to 24 hours, turning bag occasionally.

2. Meanwhile, place half of the crackers and half of the Greek seasoning blend in a blender or food processor. Cover and blend or process until crackers are crushed.* Repeat with remaining crackers and Greek seasoning blend. In a shallow dish toss together crushed crackers and melted butter. Set aside.

3. Preheat oven to 400° F. In another shallow dish beat eggs; stir in water. Drain chicken pieces, discarding marinade. Dip chicken pieces, one at a time, into egg mixture; roll in cracker mixture to coat. Arrange chicken in 2 lightly greased 13×9×2-inch foil baking pans, making sure pieces do not touch.

4. Bake, uncovered, for 45 to 50 minutes or until chicken pieces are tender and no longer pink (170° F for breast pieces and 180° F for thighs or drumsticks). Serve warm or cover and chill for up to 24 hours. Makes 12 servings.

Each serving: 388 cal., 20 g total fat (8 g sat. fat), 162 mg chol., 476 mg sodium, 18 g carbo., 5 g fiber, 33 g pro. Daily Values: 8% vit. A, 5% calcium, 10% iron.

PEPPER FRIED CHICKEN: You can substitute two 4¼-ounce packages water crackers with cracked pepper for the crisp rye crackers and the Greek seasoning. Continue as directed above.

***NOTE:** If you like, you can crush the crackers in a resealable plastic bag with a rolling pin.

Each serving: 344 cal., 17 g total fat (7 g sat. fat), 153 mg chol., 612 mg sodium, 17 g carbo., 1 g fiber, 30 g pro. Daily Values: 8% vit. A, 1% vit. C, 7% calcium, 7% iron.

Oven-Fried Buttermilk Chicken
A long soaking in buttermilk guarantees moist chicken. This version gets a crunchy cracker coating too. While it bakes, you have time to grab a book and your lawn chair.

Sweet Layers of Red, White, and Blue

This patriotic dessert includes berries, an herb-flavored whipped cream, and purchased small meringue cookies.

PREP: 20 minutes **CHILL:** 24 hours

1 recipe Rosemary-Lemon Cream (below)	6 cups fresh red raspberries and/or strawberries, halved
1 8-oz. carton dairy sour cream	
1/3 cup sifted powdered sugar	1 5.1-oz. container bite-size vanilla meringue cookies
6 cups fresh blueberries	Fresh herbs (optional)

1. Prepare Rosemary-Lemon Cream; strain to remove herbs and lemon peel. Discard herbs and peel.

2. In a large mixing bowl combine strained whipping cream, sour cream, and powdered sugar. Beat with an electric mixer on medium speed until soft peaks form (tips curl). Serve immediately or cover and chill for up to 24 hours. (The cream may thicken upon chilling. Stir before serving.)

3. To serve, alternate layers of berries with layers of meringue cookies and whipped cream in twelve 16-ounce glasses or bowls. (The cream helps soften the crunch of the cookies, so keep this in mind when layering.) If desired, garnish with fresh herbs. Makes 12 servings.

ROSEMARY-LEMON CREAM: In a 2-cup glass measuring cup combine 1 1/3 cups whipping cream, five 4-inch sprigs of fresh rosemary (stems removed), and one 2×1-inch piece of lemon peel. (If desired, 1/4 cup torn basil leaves may be substituted for the rosemary.) Cover with plastic wrap; chill for 24 hours.

Each serving: 232 cal., 14 g total fat (9 g sat. fat), 45 mg chol., 28 mg sodium, 25 g carbo., 5 g fiber, 3 g pro. Daily Values: 12% vit. A, 81% vit. C, 6% calcium, 3% iron.

Peaches and Ice Cream Sandwich Bars

Purchased ice cream sandwiches form the base for this frozen dessert. You can change the toppings at whim. For instance, eliminate the sorbet, mound with whipped cream, and cap it off with a massive pile of whatever fresh fruit calls to you from the produce stand.

PREP: 25 minutes **FREEZE:** 4 hours **STAND:** 10 minutes

10 to 14 rectangular ice cream sandwiches, unwrapped	1 8-oz. carton dairy sour cream
	1 cup whipping cream
2 pt. peach or mango sorbet, softened	3/4 cup sifted powdered sugar
	2 cups fresh blueberries or red raspberries

1. Place ice cream sandwiches in the bottom of a 13×9×2-inch baking pan, cutting to fit. Spread sorbet onto top of ice cream sandwiches. Freeze about 15 minutes or until sorbet is firm.

2. Meanwhile, in medium bowl combine sour cream, whipping cream, and powdered sugar. Beat with an electric mixer on medium speed until soft peaks form (tips curl). Spread onto sorbet.

3. Cover and freeze for 4 to 24 hours or until firm. Let stand at room temperature for 10 minutes before serving. Sprinkle berries over whipped cream mixture. Makes 12 servings.

Each serving: 354 cal., 16 g total fat (10 g sat. fat), 52 mg chol., 49 mg sodium, 51 g carbo., 1 g fiber, 3 g pro. Daily Values: 15% vit. A, 10% vit. C, 9% calcium, 2% iron.

Butter Pecan Ice Cream

Our taste panel's response to this rich treasure was unanimous—you just can't buy ice cream like this, not even as a gourmet brand.

PREP: 20 minutes **FREEZE:** per freezer's directions **RIPEN:** 4 hours

1 cup chopped pecans	2 cups packed brown sugar
1/2 cup sugar	1 Tbsp. vanilla
2 Tbsp. butter	4 cups whipping cream
4 cups half-and-half or light cream	

1. In heavy 8-inch skillet combine nuts, sugar, and butter; heat over medium heat, stirring constantly, for 6 to 8 minutes or until sugar melts and turns a rich brown color. Quickly spread on buttered foil; separate into clusters. Cool; break into small chunks.

2. In a large bowl combine half-and-half, brown sugar, and vanilla; stir until sugar is dissolved. Stir in whipping cream.

3. Freeze in a 4- to 5-quart ice cream freezer according to manufacturer's directions. Stir in pecan mixture. Ripen for 4 hours. Makes 16 servings.

Each serving: 354 cal., 16 g total fat (10 g sat. fat), 52 mg chol., 49 mg sodium, 51 g carbo., 1 g fiber, 3 g pro. Daily Values: 15% vit. A, 10% vit. C, 9% calcium, 2% iron.

Peaches and Ice Cream Sandwich Bars

ICE CREAM DELIGHTS

A potluck is bound to end happily ever after when you serve ice cream—homemade or otherwise. Dress up plain ice cream with one of these easy-does-it fix-ups.

- Roll scoops of ice cream in miniature semisweet chocolate pieces or grated semisweet chocolate and freeze until dessert time.
- Fold crushed peppermint candies or crushed toffee into thawed frozen whipped dessert topping and spoon it over chocolate ice cream.
- Top sliced cantaloupe or strawberries with scoops of your favorite sherbet or ice cream and sprinkle with toasted coconut.
- Mix equal parts of apricot or peach nectar with lemon-lime or grapefruit carbonated beverage. Float vanilla ice cream or fruit-flavored sherbet on top.

Sweet Layers of Red, White, and Blue

Tuna Salad Niçoise

TAKE Fish TO HEART

SEAFOOD IS GOOD FOR YOU, BUT CONCERNS ABOUT MERCURY IN FISH MEAN YOU MUST PICK WISELY.

When it comes to your heart, a few servings of fish go a long, long way. But government warnings about high methylmercury levels in some fish have people worried about adding more fish to their diet. Although rare in the United States, too much methylmercury in a diet can cause nerve damage and blood pressure problems. It can also harm an unborn child's developing nervous system.

According to the U.S. Department of Agriculture, most fish are safe to eat because they contain methylmercury only in trace amounts. The species of concern are larger fish that feed on other fish. Fish lovers should dine only once a week on swordfish, shark, tilefish, and king mackerel, which contain the highest levels of mercury. Young children and women who are pregnant, planning to become pregnant, or who are breastfeeding should avoid these fish altogether. Those women and young children also should limit their intake of lower-mercury seafood to 12 ounces per week. Tuna steaks also can contain high levels of mercury, but not as high as those fish listed above.

Seafood lower in methylmercury and considered safe to eat include clams, cod, crab, flounder, haddock, halibut, herring, lobster, mahi mahi, oysters, scallops, shrimp, canned tuna and other canned fish, whitefish, and farm-raised fish.

Don't avoid fish because of the mercury issue. Medical experts still highly recommend making fish a regular part of your diet (two 3-ounce servings per week) because the oil in fish (omega-3 fatty acids) has heart-healthy benefits: lowering blood pressure, reducing fat levels in blood, and helping to prevent sudden cardiac death.

BY MARTHA MILLER. ILLUSTRATION: TOM GARRETT. PHOTOGRAPHS: GREG SCHEIDEMANN [N] HAUS FOTO AND MIKE DIETER.
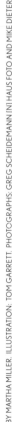

Tuna Salad Niçoise

PREP: 45 minutes **MARINATE:** 4 hours

1½	cups cut fresh green beans	1	medium green sweet pepper, cut into strips
8	oz. whole tiny new potatoes (4 to 6)	1	cup cherry tomatoes, halved
1	recipe Caper Vinaigrette (below)	¾	cup pitted ripe olives
1	9¼-oz. can chunk white tuna (water pack), drained and broken into chunks, or 12 oz. cooked tuna	4	cups torn romaine and/or Bibb or Boston lettuce
		½	of a 2-oz. can anchovy fillets, drained and halved

1. In a medium covered saucepan cook beans in lightly salted boiling water for 10 minutes. Add potatoes; cook about 15 minutes more or until tender. Drain; rinse with cold water. Drain again.

2. Prepare Caper Vinaigrette. Place tuna chunks in a small bowl; top with ⅔ cup vinaigrette. Quarter potatoes. In a medium bowl combine potatoes, beans, green pepper, tomatoes, olives, and ⅔ cup vinaigrette. Cover each bowl; chill for 4 hours.

3. To serve, line 4 plates with lettuce. Using a slotted spoon, top with tuna and bean mixture. Top with anchovies; pass remaining vinaigrette. Makes 4 main-dish servings.

CAPER VINAIGRETTE: In a screw-top jar combine 1 cup olive oil or salad oil, ½ cup white wine vinegar or white vinegar, 1 tablespoon dry mustard, 1 tablespoon drained and chopped capers, 2 minced garlic cloves, 1 tablespoon snipped fresh basil or 1 teaspoon crushed dried basil, and 1 tablespoon snipped fresh oregano or 1 teaspoon crushed dried oregano. Cover and shake well to mix.

Each serving: 404 cal., 23 g total fat (3 g sat. fat), 55 mg chol., 551 mg sodium, 19 g carbo., 5 g fiber, 31 g pro. Daily Values: 37% vit. A, 94% vit. C, 11% calcium, 21% iron.

THE TUNA CHOICE: CANNED OR FRESH?

Believe it or not, canned is better. The tuna used for canning are typically younger than the tuna sold in the fresh and frozen market and have not accumulated high levels of mercury in their bodies.

- Also, canned tuna is often composed of smaller species of tuna, such as albacore and skipjack, both of which have lower levels of mercury. The Food and Drug Administration recommends that tuna lovers eat white albacore tuna because it's from smaller fish and contains minimal traces of mercury.

- Be sure to buy water-pack tuna rather than the type packed in oil. The oil used to preserve canned tuna extracts all the good fatty acids, says longtime fish oil researcher Alexander Leaf, M.D., professor emeritus of clinical medicine at Harvard Medical School.

Lime Seafood Salad

START TO FINISH: 30 minutes

1	lb. sea scallops, skinless salmon fillet, whitefish fillet, or mahi mahi fillet	1	Tbsp. soy sauce
		½	tsp. grated fresh ginger
		¼	tsp. cayenne pepper
2	Tbsp. all-purpose flour	4	cups sliced bok choy or Chinese cabbage
½	tsp. ground black pepper		
2	Tbsp. butter or margarine	½	cup coarsely shredded carrot
¼	cup orange marmalade		
2	Tbsp. lime juice	1	lime, cut into wedges

1. If using scallops, in a plastic bag combine flour and black pepper. Add scallops; toss to coat. If using fish, cut into 4 serving-size portions; sprinkle with black pepper (omit flour).

2. In a large skillet heat butter. Add scallops or fish. Cook scallops about 2 minutes per side or until golden brown. (Cook fish pieces 4 to 6 minutes per side or until the fish flakes easily when tested with a fork.) Use a slotted spatula to remove fish from skillet, reserving drippings in skillet.

3. Add orange marmalade, lime juice, soy sauce, ginger, and cayenne pepper to skillet; heat through. Remove from heat. Add bok choy and carrot to skillet. Toss to coat. Serve with scallops and lime wedges. Makes 4 main-dish servings.

low fat Each serving: 250 cal., 7 g total fat (4 g sat. fat), 54 mg chol., 864 mg sodium, 25 g carbo., 3 g fiber, 23 g pro. Daily Values: 180% vit. A, 88% vit. C, 20% calcium, 14% iron.

Lime Seafood Salad

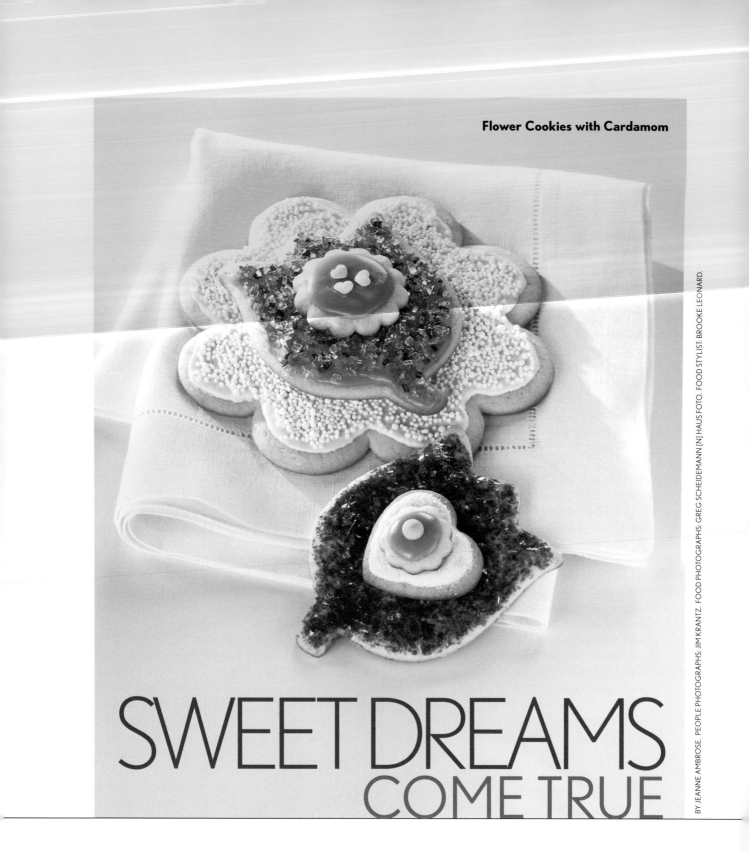

Flower Cookies with Cardamom

BY JEANNE AMBROSE. PEOPLE PHOTOGRAPHS: JIM KRANTZ. FOOD PHOTOGRAPHS: GREG SCHEIDEMANN [N] HAUS FOTO. FOOD STYLIST: BROOKE LEONARD.

SWEET DREAMS
COME TRUE

MADELINE CALLAHAN'S CREATIVITY IN THE KITCHEN
HAS TURNED HER INTO A FOOD MOGUL.

Flower Cookies with Cardamom

Ground cardamom loses much of its flavor if it is stored for a long time. Make sure your supply smells fresh before you begin baking.

PREP: 1 hour **CHILL:** 2 hours **BAKE:** 5 minutes per batch
STAND: 1 hour

1	cup butter, softened	1½	tsp. vanilla
1½	cups granulated sugar	3	cups all-purpose flour
¾	tsp. ground cardamom	1	recipe Powdered Sugar
½	tsp. baking powder		Frosting (below)
½	tsp. salt		Colored sprinkles or
2	eggs		colored sugar (optional)
¼	cup milk		

1. In a large bowl beat butter with an electric mixer on medium to high speed for 30 seconds. Add granulated sugar, cardamom, baking powder, and salt. Beat until combined. Add eggs, milk, and vanilla. Beat until combined. Beat in as much of the flour as you can with the mixer. Stir in any remaining flour. Divide dough in half. Cover and chill about 2 hours or until easy to handle.

2. Preheat oven to 425° F. On a lightly floured surface roll half of the dough to an ⅛-inch thickness. Cut cookie dough using 1¾-, 2½-, and 4-inch flower-shape cookie cutters. (By rerolling the dough you should get 12 to 15 cutouts of each size from each dough half.) Place cutouts 1 inch apart on ungreased cookie sheets. Bake about 5 minutes or until edges just start to brown. Remove and cool cookies on a wire rack.

3. Spread cookies with Powdered Sugar Frosting.* While still moist, stack cookies together, placing a 2½-inch cookie in the center of a 4-inch cookie and a 1¾-inch cookie in the center of the 2½-inch cookie. If desired, add sprinkles or colored sugar. Allow cookies to stand for 1 to 2 hours to set before serving. Makes 24 to 30 stacked cookies.

POWDERED SUGAR FROSTING: In a large mixing bowl stir together 6 cups powdered sugar, ⅓ cup milk, and 1 tablespoon vanilla. Add additional milk, 1 tablespoon at a time, until frosting is of a spreading consistency. Tint as desired with food coloring.

***NOTE:** Store unfrosted cookies in the freezer for up to 3 months.

low fat Each cookie: 280 cal., 9 g total fat (5 g sat. fat), 40 mg chol., 148 mg sodium, 49 g carbo., 0 g fiber, 2 g protein. Daily Values: 7% vit. A, 2% calcium, 4% iron.

Uniquely *together*

It seems every time 14-year-old Madeline Callahan steps into the kitchen, her creative taste buds kick into high gear. Her first attempt at baking, however, wasn't exactly success. The Illinois teen decided to bake a cake when she was 7 years old. Without measuring, Madeline stirred together lots of yeast, plus flour, sugar, butter, and eggs. She poured the mixture into a pan, popped it in the oven, and watched it rise and overflow. "We decorated it with sprinkles, but it still tasted pretty gross," Madeline says. That failure didn't keep the self-confident girl from experimenting. After tasting a biscuit flavored with cardamom, "I thought, 'What is that mysterious taste?'" Madeline says. "It intrigued me." So she added cardamom to a sugar cookie recipe and loved it.

Although her family's interest has helped to spark Madeline's love of cooking, her mother, Anne, says she comes by her culinary flair naturally. "Madeline is extremely creative and always has been," says Anne. Her greatest idea (so far) came at a party her family hosted. "My parents were getting ready for the adults, and I thought, 'There's nothing for the kids to drink,'" Madeline says. Looking for inspiration, Madeline spied bowls of limes and lemons. So she squeezed, stirred,

and tasted. Still not satisfied with the pale color of the finished product, she pulled some fresh raspberries from the fridge and tossed them into the pitcher. Madeline's Lemonade (*page 136*) was such a hit, a family friend—a buyer for Crate&Barrel— snapped it up. Madeline's Lemonade is now featured in Crate&Barrel stores.

Madeline's Lemonade

Madeline's Lemonade

In a 2-quart pitcher combine the juice from 6 large lemons (1½ cups juice) and 2 large limes (⅓ cup juice). Add 6 cups water and 1 cup sugar; stir to dissolve sugar. Add 1 cup fresh red raspberries; cover and chill overnight. Serve over ice. Garnish with lemon and lime slices. Makes 8 or 9 servings.

Grilled Cheese Sandwich with Sautéed Onions and Mushrooms

To make 4 sandwiches, slice a large onion. In a skillet cook onion slices in 2 tablespoons butter over medium heat about 10 minutes or until onion is soft and golden brown, stirring occasionally. Stir in about 1 cup sliced fresh mushrooms. Cook and stir for 2 minutes more. Remove from heat. Sprinkle with sea salt and about 1 teaspoon berry-balsamic vinegar. Place slices of desired cheese onto 4 slices sourdough bread. Top each with some of the onion-mushroom mixture and another slice of sourdough bread. Butter bread and cook on a griddle or in a skillet over medium heat for 2 to 3 minutes per side or until the cheese is melted.

Grilled Cheese Sandwich with Sautéed Onions and Mushrooms

Super-Quick Ice Cream Sandwiches

Super-Quick Ice Cream Sandwiches

Stir 1/2 cup chopped malted milk balls into a pint of softened strawberry ice cream. Spoon ice cream onto the flat side of 6 soft cookies (such as chocolate, oatmeal, or chocolate chip). Spread about 1 tablespoon fudge ice cream topping onto flat side of each of 6 additional cookies. Place cookies, fudge sides down, on ice cream. Wrap and freeze at least 6 hours or until firm. Let frozen sandwiches stand about 10 minutes before eating.

August

MIDSUMMER'S THE PERFECT TIME TO THROW A
GARDEN PARTY. HERE'S HOW TO DO IT WITH STYLE.

Gathering Herbs & Friends

STEP INTO THIS MAINE GARDEN
AND EAT YOUR WAY TO DESSERT.

gathering
herbs&friends

Figs with Herbed Goat Cheese

Fig fanciers tend to be a selfish lot. Once you taste fresh figs, you'll understand why. The season is short, making them a precious commodity. Their soft skin means they should be handled with care, and their delicate nature and sweet flavor make them all the more desired. Fresh figs need little embellishment, but pairing them with goat cheese and herbs makes a tasty exclamation point.

START TO FINISH: 15 minutes

3 oz. soft goat cheese (chèvre)	Salt
1½ tsp. snipped fresh chives	Ground black pepper
1½ tsp. snipped fresh parsley	6 fresh figs or apricots
½ tsp. snipped fresh rosemary	Fresh rosemary sprigs (optional)

1. In a small bowl combine goat cheese, chives, parsley, snipped rosemary, salt, and pepper.

2. Cut the figs in half. If using apricots, cut in half; remove and discard pits. Top fig halves with herbed cheese. Cover and chill for up to 1 hour before serving. If desired, top with rosemary sprigs just before serving. Makes 6 appetizer servings.

Each serving: 75 cal., 3 g total fat (2 g sat. fat), 7 mg chol., 150 mg sodium, 10 g carbo., 2 g fiber, 3 g pro. Daily Values: 5% vit. A, 3% vit. C, 4% calcium, 3% iron.

Figs with Herbed Goat Cheese

BY JEANNE AMBROSE. PHOTOGRAPHS: QUENTIN BACON. FOOD STYLIST: WILLIAM SMITH.

A passion for herbs

Jonathan King's passion for herbs began as a love affair with rosemary. It grew to encompass herbs in all forms, which is evident in nearly everything he does. The fragrant bounty of summer thrives on the grounds surrounding his picturesque home not far from the southern coast of Maine. The homegrown herbs star in his impromptu outdoor dinners. His basil patch alone fills a 12×12-foot waist-high raised bed. If he's fixing a salad, he steps outside the back door and snips from the beds of lemon thyme, garlic chives, parsley, and mint to add to the mix of lettuces he grows from spring to fall.

Jonathan's interest in gardening began as a high school student and eventually evolved into a business. Jonathan and Jim Stott run Stonewall Kitchen, a specialty food company in York, Maine, known for bottling up the bounty in fresh ways. "It's amazing to me that we started by putting herbs in a few bottles of vinegar and now we're producing 50,000 jars a day," he says.

Jonathan loves to entertain, much to the delight of friends, family, and coworkers. Spontaneous meals are common at his home in the summer. When he's cooking, friends often

gather around the kitchen island. "If you're standing at the island, you'd better be prepared to pitch in, because I'll put you to work," Jonathan says. "I love cooking with family and friends. The food always seems to taste better that way."

Summer Tomato Salad

Maine Vichyssoise with Chive Oil

When making this creamy-smooth soup, it's important to pick the proper potatoes for the best results. Starchy potatoes—such as russets, a favorite baking potato—work better than waxy potatoes, which have skin that's smooth and thin. Waxy potatoes tend to get a little gummy when mashed or puréed in a blender.

PREP: 30 minutes   **COOK:** 30 minutes
COOL: 20 minutes **CHILL:** 8 hours

4	medium leeks	1/8	tsp. ground black pepper
1	Tbsp. olive oil	1/3	cup milk
1 1/2	lb. Maine potatoes, Yukon Gold potatoes, or russet potatoes, peeled and cut into 2-inch pieces (about 5 medium potatoes)	3	Tbsp. finely snipped fresh chives
		2	Tbsp. finely snipped fresh thyme
		1	recipe Chive Oil (below) Fresh chives
4	cups chicken broth		
1/4	tsp. salt		

1. Trim leeks, separating the dark green stems from the white leek. Discard green section. Cut the white part of the leek in half lengthwise and clean out the dirt between the layers. Cut the leek into 2-inch-long pieces.

2. In a Dutch oven heat the olive oil over medium-low heat. Add leeks. Cook, covered, for 10 minutes, stirring occasionally. Stir in potato pieces; cook 2 minutes. Increase the heat to high. Add the broth, salt, and pepper. Bring to boiling; reduce heat to medium-low. Simmer, covered, about 15 minutes or until the potatoes are tender. Remove from heat. Let cool slightly.

3. Place the mixture in batches in a food processor or blender. Cover and process or blend until smooth. Place in a large bowl; stir in the milk and snipped herbs. Cover and chill at least 8 hours or until cold.

4. About 20 minutes before serving, prepare Chive Oil. Serve vichyssoise in small glasses or bowls. Drizzle each serving with 2 teaspoons Chive Oil. Top with chives. Makes 6 appetizer servings.

CHIVE OIL: In a small saucepan combine 1/4 cup very finely snipped fresh chives and 1/4 cup olive oil. Place over low heat for 5 minutes, stirring occasionally. Remove from heat. Add 1/8 teaspoon coarse sea salt and a dash ground black pepper; let cool for 20 minutes. (Use chive oil immediately. Discard any remaining.) Makes about 1/4 cup.

Each serving: 232 cal., 13 g total fat (2 g sat. fat), 1 mg chol., 821 mg sodium, 25 g carbo., 3 g fiber, 5 g pro. Daily Values: 5% vit. A, 36% vit. C, 6% calcium, 12% iron.

Summer Tomato Salad

This tarragon-touched salad offers a tasting of different colors and types of tomatoes. Let the selection at your farmer's market or your garden be your guide.

START TO FINISH: 30 minutes

1	recipe Tarragon-Dijon Vinaigrette (below)	1	cup red or yellow cherry tomatoes, halved if desired
3	cups mesclun salad greens		
2	medium red tomatoes, cut into wedges or sliced	1	small red onion, cut into thin slices
2	medium yellow or heirloom green tomatoes, cut into 8 wedges each	1/4	tsp. coarse salt
		1/4	tsp. ground black pepper

1. Prepare Tarragon-Dijon Vinaigrette; set aside.

2. Divide the greens among 6 individual salad plates. Arrange the tomatoes on and around the greens. Top each serving with onion slices. Sprinkle with salt and pepper. Drizzle with desired amount of dressing. Store any remaining dressing, covered, in the refrigerator for up to 1 week. Makes 6 side-dish servings.

TARRAGON-DIJON VINAIGRETTE: In a small bowl whisk together 1/2 cup olive oil, 1/4 cup red or white wine vinegar, 1 tablespoon finely snipped fresh tarragon, 1 tablespoon finely snipped fresh chives, and 1/4 teaspoon Dijon-style mustard.

Each serving: 192 cal., 19 g total fat (3 g sat. fat), 0 mg chol., 109 mg sodium, 7 g carbo., 2 g fiber, 2 g pro. Daily Values: 14% vit. A, 37% vit. C, 3% calcium, 5% iron.

"I'M A CRAZED GARDENER.
OUR WHOLE MENU IS
SPUR-OF-THE-MOMENT,
BASED ON WHAT'S READY
IN THE GARDEN."
JONATHAN KING

Maine Vichyssoise with Chive Oil

Rosemary Lamb Chops

Orzo and
Corn Off
the Cob

Rosemary Lamb Chops

Rosemary thrives in rocky sunny spots, much like the islands of Greece. There, lamb and rosemary are an inseparable pair.

PREP: 35 minutes **MARINATE:** 2 hours **GRILL:** 12 minutes

6	lamb chops, cut about 1 inch thick (about 1¾ lb. total)	1	Tbsp. balsamic vinegar
¾	cup dry red wine	½	tsp. ground black pepper
3	Tbsp. finely snipped fresh rosemary	¼	tsp. salt
2	cloves garlic, finely chopped	1	Tbsp. butter
			Fresh rosemary sprigs (optional)

1. Trim fat from lamb chops. Place chops in a resealable plastic bag set in a shallow dish. Add red wine, 2 tablespoons of the snipped rosemary, the garlic, balsamic vinegar, the ½ teaspoon pepper, and the ¼ teaspoon salt. Seal the bag. Marinate in the refrigerator for 2 to 48 hours, turning bag occasionally.

2. Drain the chops, reserving the marinade. Grill chops on the rack of an uncovered gas grill on medium or a charcoal grill directly over medium coals until desired doneness, turning once halfway through grilling. Allow 12 to 14 minutes for medium-rare (instant-read thermometer registers 145° F) or 15 to 17 minutes for medium doneness (instant-read thermometer registers 160° F). Season to taste with additional salt and pepper.

3. Meanwhile, strain reserved marinade into a small saucepan; discard solids. Simmer, uncovered, over medium heat about 5 minutes or until reduced to ⅓ cup. Add butter and the remaining 1 tablespoon snipped rosemary; cook for 1 minute. Serve sauce with the chops. If desired, top with rosemary sprigs. Makes 6 servings.

Each serving: 134 cal., 7 g total fat (3 g sat. fat), 43 mg chol., 154 mg sodium, 1 g carbo., 0 g fiber, 11 g pro. Daily Values: 2% vit. A, 1% calcium, 6% iron.

Orzo and Corn Off the Cob

Fresh corn and orzo can be cooked together in the same pot. Orzo is a quick-cooking pasta that looks like large grains of rice. Feel free to substitute other small types of pasta, such as acini de pepe.

PREP: 30 minutes **COOK:** 8 minutes

4	fresh ears of corn	¼	cup finely snipped fresh basil
1¼	cups orzo (rosamarina)		
1	cup kalamata olives, pitted and halved	¼	cup finely snipped fresh parsley
1	medium red sweet pepper, chopped (¾ cup)	¼	cup olive oil
¼	cup thinly sliced green onions	2	Tbsp. white wine vinegar
		¼	tsp. salt
		¼	tsp. ground black pepper

1. Cut corn kernels off cob (you should have about 2 cups). Set aside. Bring a large pot of lightly salted water to boiling. Add the orzo and cook, stirring occasionally, for 8 to 9 minutes or until just tender, adding corn for the last 3 minutes of cooking. Drain well; place in a large serving bowl.

2. Add olives, sweet pepper, and onions; toss well. Add basil, parsley, oil, vinegar, salt, and black pepper. Toss gently to combine. Serve at room temperature. Makes 6 to 8 side-dish servings.

Each serving: 308 cal., 13 g total fat (1 g sat. fat), 0 mg chol., 361 mg sodium, 42 g carbo., 4 g fiber, 7 g pro. Daily Values: 30% vit. A, 75% vit. C, 2% calcium, 12% iron.

JONATHAN'S GARDEN DINNER

Maine Vichyssoise with Chive Oil *(page 142)*
Rosemary Lamb Chops *(above left)*
Orzo and Corn Off the Cob *(above)*
Peach Crostada with Herb-Scented Ice Cream *(page 152)*
Double-Mint Brandy Cooler *(page 152)*

Grilled Beef Tenderloin with Mediterranean Relish

This favorite calls on two rediscovered old-world ingredients—kalamata olives and balsamic vinegar—for a new-world take on grilled beef tenderloin.

PREP: 25 minutes **GRILL:** 10 + 25 minutes **STAND:** 15 minutes

2	tsp. dried oregano, crushed	1	sweet onion, such as Walla Walla or Vidalia, cut into 1/2-inch-thick slices
2	tsp. cracked black pepper	2	Tbsp. olive oil
1 1/2	tsp. finely shredded lemon peel	2	plum tomatoes, chopped
3	cloves garlic, minced	2	Tbsp. chopped, pitted kalamata olives
1	3- to 4-lb. center-cut beef tenderloin	2	Tbsp. snipped fresh basil
2	Japanese eggplants, halved lengthwise	1	Tbsp. balsamic vinegar
2	red or yellow sweet peppers, halved lengthwise and seeded	1/4	to 1/2 tsp. salt
		1/8	tsp. ground black pepper

1. In a small bowl combine oregano, cracked pepper, lemon peel, and 2 cloves of the garlic. Use your fingers to rub the mixture onto all sides of the meat.

2. For a charcoal grill, arrange hot coals around a drip pan. Test for medium-hot heat above the pan. Place meat on grill rack over drip pan. For a gas grill, place meat adjacent to heat source. Brush eggplants, sweet peppers, and onion slices with olive oil. Arrange vegetables on edges of grill rack directly over coals. Cover and grill for 10 to 12 minutes or until vegetables are tender, turning once. Remove vegetables from grill; set aside. Cover grill and continue grilling meat for 25 to 30 minutes more or until medium-rare doneness (instant-read thermometer registers 135° F). Cover meat; let stand for 15 minutes before slicing.

3. Meanwhile, for relish, coarsely chop grilled vegetables. In a medium bowl combine grilled vegetables, tomatoes, olives, basil, the remaining garlic clove, the vinegar, salt, and the ground black pepper. Serve the beef with relish. Makes 10 servings.

Each serving: 240 cal., 12 g total fat (4 g sat. fat), 77 mg chol., 133 mg sodium, 6 g carbo., 2 g fiber, 27 g pro. Daily Values: 12% vit. A, 49% vit. C, 1% calcium, 25% iron.

Chicken with Lemon Thyme Pesto

This recipe will make twice as much pesto as you need for the chicken. Save the rest to toss with pasta for a light dinner or to drizzle over sliced summer tomatoes.

PREP: 1 hour **GRILL:** 50 minutes

3 1/2	lb. meaty chicken pieces (breast halves, thighs, and drumsticks)	1 1/3	cups lemon thyme*
		1/2	cup salted pistachio nuts
		1/2	cup olive oil
	Salt	1/4	tsp. ground black pepper
	Ground black pepper		Lemon wedges (optional)

1. If desired, skin chicken. Season with salt and pepper.

2. In a food processor or blender combine lemon thyme and pistachio nuts; cover and process or blend with several on/off turns until finely chopped. With processor or blender running, gradually drizzle in oil, stopping to scrape down sides as necessary. Stir in pepper to taste. Set aside half to brush on chicken. Reserve remaining pesto for another use.

3. For a charcoal grill, arrange medium-hot coals around a drip pan. Test for medium heat above pan. Place chicken, bone side down, on grill rack over drip pan. For gas grill, place chicken adjacent to heat source. Cover and grill for 50 to 60 minutes or until chicken is no longer pink (instant-read thermometer registers 170° F for breasts or 180° F for thighs and drumsticks), turning chicken and brushing with pesto during the last 5 minutes of grilling. If desired, serve chicken with lemon wedges. Makes 6 servings.

*NOTE: If you don't have lemon thyme, use 1 1/3 cups fresh thyme plus 2 teaspoons finely shredded lemon peel.

Each serving: 414 cal., 26 g total fat (6 g sat. fat), 121 mg chol., 225 mg sodium, 3 g carbo., 1 g fiber, 40 g pro. Daily Values: 5% vit. A, 12% vit. C, 4% calcium, 15% iron.

JONATHAN'S GARDEN LUNCH

Figs with Herbed Goat Cheese *(page 141)*
Chicken with Lemon Thyme Pesto *(above)*
Summer Tomato Salad *(page 142)*
Watermelon-Berry Sorbet *(page 149)*
Lavender Cooler *(page 106)*

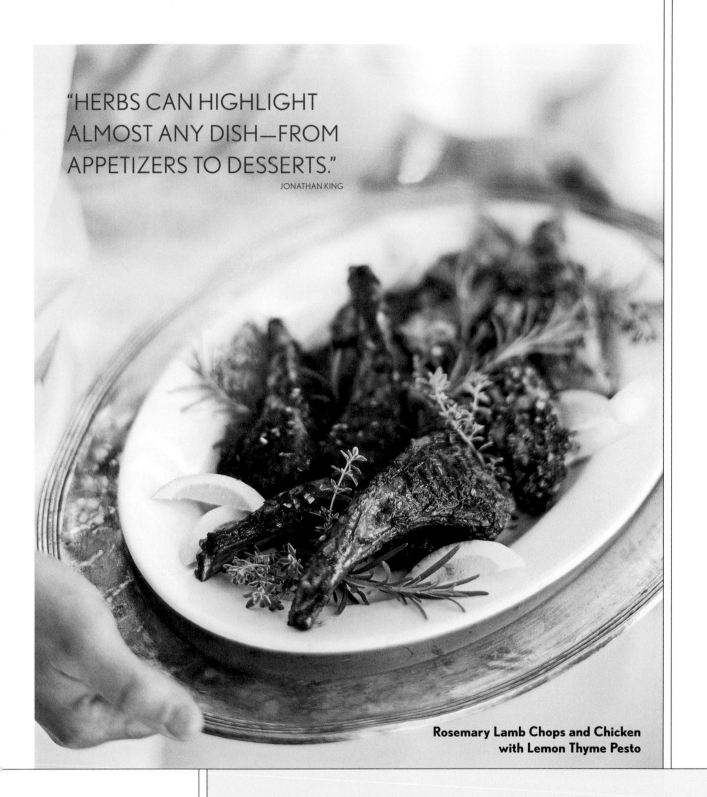

"HERBS CAN HIGHLIGHT ALMOST ANY DISH—FROM APPETIZERS TO DESSERTS."
JONATHAN KING

Rosemary Lamb Chops and Chicken with Lemon Thyme Pesto

PRESERVING FRESH HERBS

Because fresh herbs are highly perishable, it's important to take a few minutes to store your precious supply properly. To keep fresh herbs at their peak in the refrigerator, cut off ends of the stems and place the herbs in a container with about 2 inches of water. Cover the leaves loosely with a plastic bag or plastic wrap and refrigerate for up to several days.

To dry fresh herbs, hang them in bunches, upside down by the stems, in a dry, warm spot out of direct sunlight. Be sure air circulates freely around the bunches. Dry the herbs until the leaves are brittle. This can take anywhere from a few days to a week, depending on the thickness of the leaves. Then remove the leaves from the stems and store the leaves in a tightly covered container.

HERBAL ACCENTS

This bouquet garni *(right)* has an American accent. Jonathan ties fresh thyme, garlic chives, rosemary, and fennel blossoms with a name tag and uses them as a place marker. During dinner, the mini bouquets are combined in a vase for an instant centerpiece *(pages 140 and 144)*. "You can literally create a bouquet garni with whatever herbs suit your taste," Jonathan says. "Dill, tarragon, chervil, and parsley make a light combination for poaching fish."

Watermelon-Berry Sorbet

Watermelon-Berry Sorbet

Your berry choice determines the color of this icy refresher. Using all blueberries with the watermelon will give you a purply-blue sorbet. Skip the blues and focus on raspberries and strawberries and you'll get a vivid red hue.

PREP: 25 minutes **FREEZE:** $1^{1}/_{2}$ + 1 hour

1 cup water	Snipped fresh lemon balm or
$1/2$ cup sugar	snipped fresh mint
2 cups seeded watermelon	Fresh lemon balm sprigs or
cubes	fresh mint sprigs (optional)
2 cups fresh berries	Fresh red raspberries and/or
(red raspberries,	blueberries (optional)
strawberries, and/or	
blueberries)	

1. In a medium saucepan combine the water and sugar; bring to boiling, stirring frequently. Boil gently, uncovered, for 2 minutes. Remove from heat; cool slightly.

2. Place the watermelon and the 2 cups berries in a blender or large food processor; cover and blend or process for 30 seconds. Add the warm syrup and blend until almost smooth. Transfer the mixture to a 3-quart rectangular baking dish or a 13×9×2-inch baking pan. Place in freezer, uncovered, about $1^{1}/_{2}$ hours or until almost solid.

3. Remove sorbet from freezer. Using a fork, break up the frozen fruit into a somewhat smooth mixture. Stir in snipped lemon balm. Freeze for 1 hour more.* Break up the ice with a fork and serve in shallow bowls. If desired, top with lemon balm sprigs and a few blueberries and/or raspberries. Makes 6 to 8 servings.

*NOTE: If the mixture is frozen longer than the final hour, let it stand at room temperature for 20 minutes before breaking it up and serving.

low fat Each serving: 98 cal., 0 g total fat (0 g sat. fat), 0 mg chol., 2 mg sodium, 24 g carbo., 3 g fiber, 1 g pro. Daily Values: 5% vit. A, 25% vit. C, 1% calcium, 2% iron.

Lemon-Berry Cobbler-Puff

The golden soufflélike topping on this fresh-tasting dessert just melts in your mouth.

PREP: 30 minutes **BAKE:** 30 minutes **COOL:** 30 minutes

3 egg whites	2 Tbsp. lemon juice
4 cups sliced fresh	3 egg yolks
strawberries	$1/3$ cup dairy sour cream
2 cups fresh red raspberries	1 Tbsp. all-purpose flour
$1/4$ cup granulated sugar	$1/4$ cup granulated sugar
2 Tbsp. cornstarch	Sifted powdered sugar
1 Tbsp. snipped fresh basil	(optional)
$1^{1}/_{2}$ tsp. finely shredded lemon	
peel	

1. Let egg whites stand at room temperature for 30 minutes. Preheat oven to 350° F. Lightly grease a 2-quart square baking dish; set aside.

2. In a medium saucepan combine strawberries, raspberries, $1/4$ cup sugar, the cornstarch, basil, $1/2$ teaspoon of the lemon peel, and 1 tablespoon of the lemon juice. Bring to boiling, stirring constantly; remove from heat. Set aside.

3. In a small mixing bowl beat egg yolks until thick and lemon colored. Beat in sour cream, the remaining lemon peel, the remaining lemon juice, and the flour.

4. In a large mixing bowl beat egg whites until soft peaks form (tips curl). Gradually add remaining $1/4$ cup sugar, beating until stiff peaks form (tips stand straight). Fold in egg yolk mixture.

5. Transfer fruit mixture to prepared baking dish; spoon egg mixture on top.

6. Bake for 30 minutes (fruit mixture will bubble in the corners). Cool for 30 to 40 minutes. If desired, sprinkle with sifted powdered sugar. Serve warm. Makes 8 servings.

low fat Each serving: 144 cal., 4 g total fat (2 g sat. fat), 83 mg chol., 29 mg sodium, 25 g carbo., 3 g fiber, 4 g pro. Daily Values: 5% vit. A, 85% vit. C, 4% calcium, 4% iron.

Peach Crostada

You'll taste the essence of summer in this dessert. Super-fresh peaches need little embellishment beyond piling them on top of a slab of pastry, tucking in the sides, and baking.

PREP: 1 hour **CHILL:** 1 hour **BAKE:** 35 minutes

1	recipe Butter Pastry (below)	½ tsp. vanilla
6	ripe medium peaches (about 2 lb.)	1 Tbsp. packed brown sugar
¼	cup packed brown sugar	¼ cup orange blossom honey *
1	Tbsp. all-purpose flour	1 recipe Herb-Scented Ice Cream (right) (optional)

Peach Crostada with Herb-Scented Ice Cream

1. Prepare Butter Pastry; chill until needed. To peel peaches, bring a medium saucepan of water to boiling. Add peaches, one at a time; heat for 20 seconds. Remove from boiling water and immediately place peaches in a bowl of ice water. Peel, pit, and slice peaches (should have about 6 cups).

2. For filling, in a large bowl combine peach slices, the ¼ cup brown sugar, the 1 tablespoon flour, and the vanilla; toss gently to coat. Set aside.

3. Preheat oven to 425° F. On a lightly floured surface, roll pastry from center to edges into a 16×12-inch oval. (If chilled pastry is too firm, let stand at room temperature for 10 to 15 minutes before rolling.) Transfer to a very large ungreased baking sheet. Mound the peach filling in the center of the dough, leaving an outside border of 2 inches. Drape the edges of dough over the filling. (The dough won't cover the filling completely.) Sprinkle the filling with the 1 tablespoon brown sugar.

4. Bake for 35 to 40 minutes or until the filling is bubbly. Cover loosely with foil if necessary to prevent overbrowning. Remove from oven and drizzle fruit with honey. Cool on a wire rack. Serve warm or at room temperature with Herb-Scented Ice Cream, if desired. Makes 8 servings.

BUTTER PASTRY: In a medium bowl combine 2 cups all-purpose flour and ¼ teaspoon salt. Cut ¾ cup cold butter into cubes. Using a pastry blender, cut butter into flour mixture until pieces are pea-size. Sprinkle 6 to 7 tablespoons cold water, 1 tablespoon at a time, over flour-butter mixture, tossing with a fork until all of the dough is moistened. Gently knead the dough just until a ball forms. If necessary, wrap pastry in plastic wrap; chill for 1 to 24 hours.

*NOTE: If you don't have orange blossom honey, use ¼ cup honey combined with ¼ teaspoon finely shredded orange peel.

Each serving (without ice cream): 386 cal., 19 g total fat (11 g sat. fat), 50 mg chol., 263 mg sodium, 52 g carbo., 3 g fiber, 5 g pro. Daily Values: 24% vit. A, 11% vit. C, 2% calcium, 10% iron.

Herb-Scented Ice Cream

This is one of those experiment-at-will recipes. Snip whatever fresh herb beckons to be sampled and stir it into softened ice cream.

PREP: 10 minutes **FREEZE:** 4 hours

1	pt. vanilla ice cream	Fresh herb sprigs (optional)
2	Tbsp. coarse sugar	
4	tsp. snipped fresh lemon thyme, cinnamon basil, pineapple sage, or lemon verbena	

1. In a chilled medium bowl stir ice cream just enough to soften, using a wooden spoon to press ice cream against side of bowl. Quickly stir in coarse sugar and herbs. Cover and freeze about 4 hours or until firm. Store, covered, for up to 1 week. Serve alone or with Peach Crostada. If desired, garnish with small herb sprigs. Makes 6 servings.

Each serving: 104 cal., 5 g total fat (3 g sat. fat), 19 mg chol., 35 mg sodium, 15 g carbo., 0 g fiber, 2 g pro. Daily Values: 4% vit. A, 2% vit. C, 6% calcium, 1% iron.

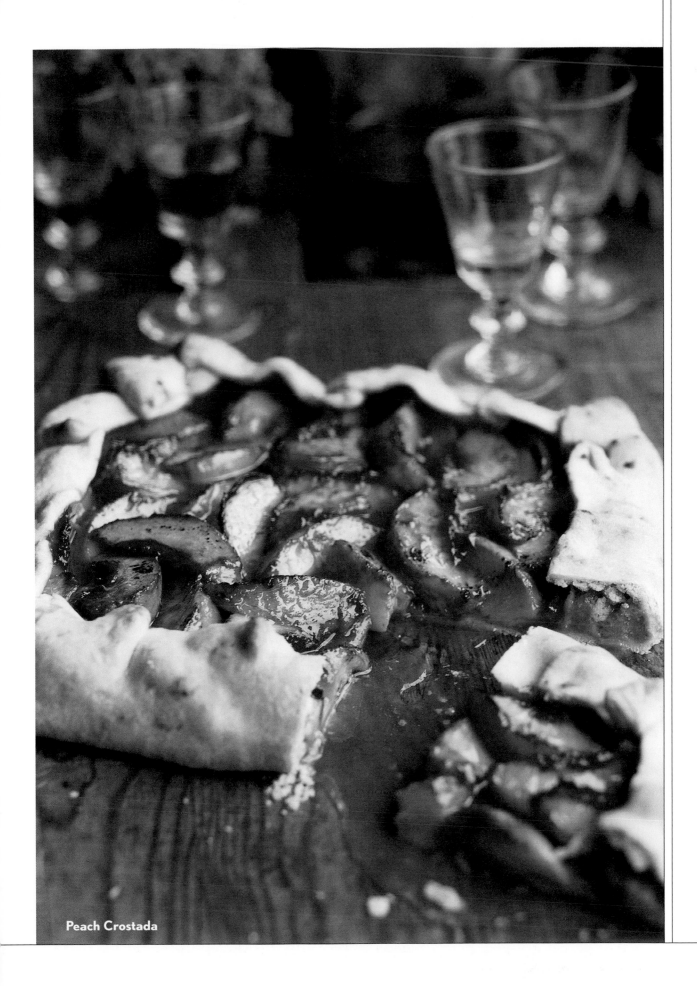

Peach Crostada

Herbed Leek Tart

PREP: 15 minutes **BAKE:** 7 + 8 minutes **STAND:** 5 minutes

1	10-oz. pkg. refrigerated pizza dough	3	Tbsp. creamy Dijon-style mustard blend
6	medium leeks, thinly sliced	1	cup shredded Gruyère or Swiss cheese (4 oz.)
3	cloves garlic, minced	1/4	cup pine nuts or chopped almonds, toasted
2	Tbsp. olive oil		
1	Tbsp. snipped fresh savory, marjoram, and/or thyme		

1. Preheat oven to 425° F. Grease a baking sheet. Unroll pizza dough onto prepared baking sheet; press dough to form a 12×9-inch rectangle. Bake for 7 minutes.

2. Meanwhile, in a large skillet cook leeks and garlic in olive oil about 5 minutes or until tender. Remove from heat. Stir in snipped herb(s). Spread mustard blend onto prebaked crust. Top with leek mixture, cheese, and nuts.

3. Bake about 8 minutes more or until cheese is bubbly. Let stand for 5 minutes before serving. Cut into 24 squares. Makes 24 appetizer servings.

Each serving: 53 cal., 3 g total fat (0 g sat. fat), 0 mg chol., 66 mg sodium, 6 g carbo., 0 g fiber, 1 g pro. Daily Values: 2% vit. C, 1% calcium, 3% iron.

Toasted Almonds with Rosemary and Cayenne

START TO FINISH: 15 minutes

8	oz. unblanched almonds or pecan halves (about 2 cups)	1½	tsp. packed brown sugar
1½	tsp. butter	1/4	to ½ tsp. salt
1	Tbsp. finely snipped fresh rosemary	1/4	tsp. cayenne pepper

1. Preheat oven to 350° F. Spread almonds in a single layer on a baking sheet. Bake about 10 minutes or until almonds are lightly toasted and fragrant.

2. Meanwhile, in a medium saucepan melt butter over medium heat until sizzling. Remove from heat. Stir in rosemary, brown sugar, salt, and cayenne. Add almonds to butter mixture; toss gently to coat. Cool slightly before serving. If desired, seal cooled nuts in an airtight container and store for up to 1 month in refrigerator or up to 3 months in freezer. Makes 16 servings.

Each serving: 80 cal., 7 g total fat (1 g sat. fat), 1 mg chol., 37 mg sodium, 3 g carbo., 1 g fiber, 4 g pro. Daily Values: 4% calcium, 5% iron.

Double-Mint Brandy Cooler

Modeled after a Southern specialty traditionally made with bourbon, sugar syrup, mint, and fine-as-snow ice, this version uses brandy and gets a little bubbly with a splash of club soda. You can substitute bourbon, if you prefer.

START TO FINISH: 5 minutes

10	large fresh mint leaves	1/4	cup carbonated water or club soda*
2	tsp. sugar		Fresh mint sprigs
	Crushed ice		
1/4	cup brandy*		

1. For each drink, place mint leaves in a tall cocktail glass. Add sugar. With an iced-tea spoon or bar spoon, press sugar into leaves to release mint oils. Fill the glass half full with crushed ice.

2. Add brandy and carbonated water. Stir gently to dissolve sugar. Top with fresh mint sprigs. Makes 1 serving.

*NOTE: For a nonalcoholic version, substitute ½ cup lemonade for the brandy and the carbonated water.

Each serving: 160 cal., 0 g total fat (0 g sat. fat), 0 mg chol., 13 mg sodium, 8 g carbo., 0 g fiber, 0 g pro.

Dill Dip

Take a cool and creamy dip to show off the flavors of favorite herbs. Serve this with garden-fresh vegetables or crackers

START TO FINISH: 10 minutes

1	8-oz. pkg. cream cheese, softened	2	Tbsp. snipped fresh dill or 2 tsp. dried dill weed
1	8-oz. carton dairy sour cream	1/2	tsp. seasoned salt or salt
2	Tbsp. finely chopped green onion		Milk (optional)
		4	small fresh dill sprigs

1. In a medium mixing bowl beat cream chese, sour cream, green onion, snipped dill, and seasoned salt with an electric mixer on low speed until fluffy. Cover and chill for up to 24 hours. If the dip thickens during chilling, stir in 1 to 2 tablespoons milk. If desired, garnish with dill sprigs. Makes about 2 cups.

Each tablespoon: 40 cal., 4 g total fat (2 g sat. fat), 11 mg chol., 49 mg sodium, 1 g carbo., 0 g fiber, 1 g pro. Daily Values: 3% vit. A, 1% calcium, 1% iron.

CREAMY BLUE CHEESE DIP: Prepare dip as above, except omit dill and seasoned salt or salt. Stir ½ cup crumbled blue cheese (2 ounces) and 1/3 cup finely chopped walnuts into the beaten cream cheese mixture. Makes about 2 cups.

Each tablespoon: 55 cal., 5 g total fat (3 g sat. fat), 12 mg chol., 50 mg sodium, 1 g carbo., 0 g fiber, 1 g pro. Daily Values: 3% vit. A, 2% calcium, 1% iron.

Double-Mint Brandy Cooler

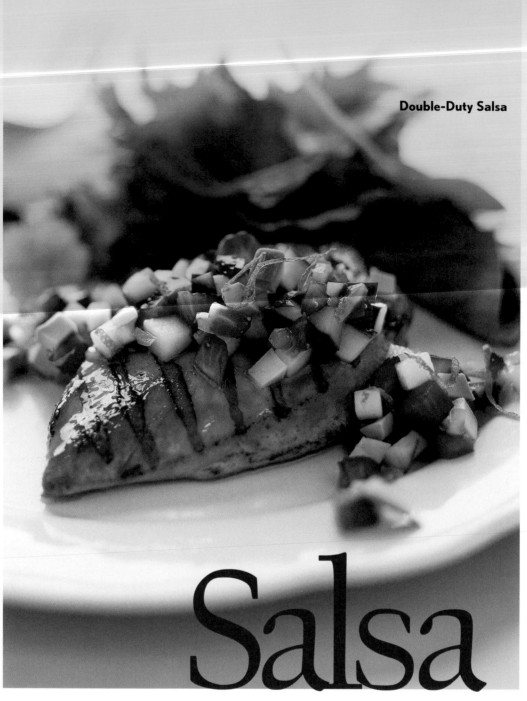

Double-Duty Salsa

Salsa
GOES FRUITY

Summer is the time for glorious fresh fruits, and there's no better way to enjoy them than in sensational salsas. Here are two exciting fruit medleys to add zip to your warm-weather meals. Double-Duty Salsa starts with fresh strawberries and adds a touch of the tropics, a sweet hint of honey, and the zing of black pepper. This sweet salsa's quite different from the traditional chopped tomato-onion mixture. However, you can go from sweet to savory by switching to the suggested alternative ingredients for a sassy jalapeño-black pepper salsa that adds zest to grilled pork, ham, or turkey. And, when the weather's almost too hot to eat, beat the heat with refreshing Mango Sorbet with Gingered Fruit Salsa. The smooth, luscious sorbet makes the perfect base for a lively ginger-and-mint-accented berry salsa topper.

BY JEANNE AMBROSE. PHOTOGRAPHS: COLLEEN DUFFLEY. FOOD STYLIST: BROOKE LEONARD.

Double-Duty Salsa

PREP: 15 minutes **CHILL:** 2 hours

- 1 pt. fresh strawberries, hulled and coarsely chopped
- 1 cup coarsely chopped fresh pineapple or avocado
- ½ cup coarsely chopped fresh mango or peach, or seeded cucumber
- 1 tsp. finely shredded lime peel
- 2 Tbsp. lime juice
- 2 Tbsp. honey
- ½ tsp. grated fresh ginger or 1 to 2 Tbsp. seeded and finely chopped jalapeño pepper (see note, page 121)
- ¼ tsp. cracked black pepper

1. For sweet salsa, combine strawberries, pineapple, mango or peach, lime peel, lime juice, honey, fresh ginger, and cracked black pepper.

2. For savory salsa, combine strawberries, avocado, cucumber, lime peel, lime juice, honey, jalapeño pepper, and cracked black pepper.

3. Cover and chill for 2 to 24 hours. Makes about 3 cups.

low fat Each serving sweet salsa (¼ cup): 28 cal., 0 g total fat (0 g sat. fat), 0 mg chol., 1 mg sodium, 7 g carbo., 1 g fiber, and 0 g pro. Daily Values: 3% vit. A, 34% vit. C, 1% calcium, and 1% iron.

low fat Each serving savory salsa (¼ cup): 23 cal., 1 g total fat (0 g sat. fat), 0 mg chol., 1 mg sodium, 5 g carbo., 1 g fiber, and 0 g pro. Daily Values: 30% vit. C, 1% calcium, 1% iron.

Mango Sorbet with Ginger Fruit Salsa

STRAWBERRY SAVVY

To make sure the strawberries in your salsas are top-notch, look for plump, fresh-looking berries with bright green caps and a rich red color. Select only fully ripe berries because strawberries do not ripen after picking. Size is not a good indicator of quality, so the largest berries aren't necessarily the most flavorful. Avoid bruised, wet, or mushy berries. To keep the berries at their best once you get them home, don't wash or hull them until you're ready to use them. Store berries loosely covered in a single layer in the refrigerator and use them within a day or two.

Mango Sorbet with Ginger Fruit Salsa

PREP: 30 minutes **FREEZE:** 8 hours

- 3 cups chopped fresh mango (about 3 large)
- 1 8¼-oz. can crushed pineapple (syrup pack)
- 2 large bananas, sliced (about 2 cups)
- ¼ cup frozen orange juice concentrate, thawed
- 1 Tbsp. finely chopped crystallized ginger
- 1 recipe Ginger Fruit Salsa (below)
- Fresh mint leaves (optional)

1. For sorbet, in a bowl combine mango, undrained pineapple, bananas, and orange juice concentrate. In food processor or blender place 2 cups mixture at a time; cover and process or blend until smooth. Pour all of the mixture into a freezer container; stir in ginger. Cover and freeze about 8 hours or until firm.

2. Meanwhile, prepare Ginger Fruit Salsa; cover and chill for up to 1 hour.

3. Break frozen mango mixture into small chunks. (If necessary, let mixture stand at room temperature for 30 minutes to soften before breaking into chunks.) Place small portions at a time into food processor.* Cover and process until fluffy. If desired, return to freezer container and freeze. Or serve immediately in dessert dishes topped with salsa. If desired, garnish with mint leaves. Makes 10 servings.

*MIXER METHOD: Break up mango mixture and place all of the mixture in a chilled very large mixing bowl. Beat until fluffy. Proceed as above.

GINGER FRUIT SALSA: In a small bowl combine 1 cup chopped mango, 1 cup chopped fresh strawberries, ½ cup fresh blueberries, 1 tablespoon crystallized ginger, and 1 tablespoon snipped fresh mint.

low fat Each serving: 113 cal., 0 g total fat (0 g sat. fat), 0 mg chol., 3 mg sodium, 29 g carbo., 3 g fiber, and 1 g pro. Daily Values: 53% vit. A, 70% vit. C, 2% calcium, 3% iron.

September

1

AS THE DAYS GROW EVER SHORTER, WE SAVOR SUMMER'S
LAST GLOW AND STOW AWAY THE FRUITS OF HER SEASON.

Perfect Pears

Perfect Pears

THE REWARDS OF FALL'S ESSENTIAL FRUIT

LOCK UP THE FLAVORS OF FALL BY CANNING, FREEZING, AND DRYING GOLDEN PEARS, READY FOR FABULOUS FALL DINNERS AND DESSERTS.

Spiced Canned Pears (page 168)

Creamy Pear Soup

Can your own pears for this rosemary-scented soup or purchase pears canned in a light syrup. Our recipe for home-canned pears on page 168 calls for a lighter syrup to suit today's tastes.

PREP: 25 minutes **COOK:** 25 minutes

2 cups water	1/4 cup Riesling or other
1/2 tsp. salt	sweet white wine
1 fresh rosemary sprig	1/4 cup whipping cream
1/2 of a large celery root	Fresh Parmesan cheese
(8 oz.), peeled and	shards (optional)
chopped, or 1 1/2 cups	Cracked black pepper
chopped celery	(optional)
1 qt. Spiced Canned Pears	
(page 168) or one 29-oz.	
can pear halves in light	
syrup	

1. In a large saucepan bring water, salt, and rosemary sprig to boiling. Add celery root. Return to boiling; reduce heat. Simmer, covered, about 20 minutes or until tender.

2. Meanwhile, place undrained pears in a blender (or half of the pears at a time in a food processor). Cover and blend or process until smooth (you should have about 3 1/2 cups).

3. Remove rosemary from hot mixture. Stir in pureed pears, wine, and cream; heat through. Ladle into 6 bowls. If desired, top with Parmesan and pepper. Makes 6 appetizer servings.

low fat Each serving: 222 cal., 6 g total fat (3 g sat. fat), 17 mg chol., 308 mg sodium, 42 g carbo., 3 g fiber, 3 g pro. Daily Values: 4% vit. A, 8% vit. C, 9% calcium, 3% iron.

Creamy Pear Soup

A flavor favorite

It's that abundance of flavor that makes people buy pears by the bushel to put up for later—a perfect cook's ally. More than any other fruit, the pear benefits from being preserved. Consider plump halves suspended in thick glass jars; slices simmered into long-lasting chutneys; slivers dried to make intense, chewy fruit leather; and sweet, ice-fast wedges in a deep-freeze slumber.

"In the middle of a dreary winter, there's nothing like opening up a jar of fruit you've canned that summer," says Sydney Blaine, a pear farmer in Mount Hood, Oregon.

Unlike many other fruits, the pear's affinity for preservation comes from the complexity of its flavor and the role that cooking plays in bringing out its best aspects—whether on the stove in preparation for canning or freezing, or the low and slow heat during drying.

"They're perfumy and really unctuous and juicy," says Cathy Whims, a Portland cooking teacher and chef who often incorporates pears into her classes. "It's not a one-hit taste. And their aroma is so amazing. It's flowery, kind of sweet in a way. They have an earthy quality to them, similar to grapes. And cooking intensifies the flavors I really like."

Pears not only taste "unctuous" in our collection of recipes, but also lend themselves to improvisation. For example, you can toss dried pears into a salad. Cut up canned pears and skewer them with chicken for a unique kabob. Or, for one of the best tricks around, throw slightly thawed frozen pears into the blender, where they become sorbet. From cheesy appetizer to chocolatey dessert, with dried, canned, and frozen pears, here you'll find a winter's worth of delectable ideas based on the golden fruit of fall.

THE MEAT OF THE MOMENT—LAMB—GETS
FAMILY-FRIENDLY WITH A JAR OF HOME-CANNED
PEARS FOR THIS 30-MINUTE MAIN DISH.

**Spiced Pears
and Lamb Chops**

BY RICHARD SWEARINGER. PHOTOGRAPHS: ALISON MIKSCH. FOOD STYLIST: MICHAEL PEDERSON. PROP STYLIST: BARB FRITZ.

N.Y. Steak with Pear Brandy-Black Pepper Sauce

Pear brandy is available at fine wine and liquor shops. Brandy made with Oregon pears can be found at www.clearcreekdistillery.com.

START TO FINISH: 30 minutes

½	cup snipped Oven-Dried Pears (page 166) or purchased dried pears	4	beef tenderloin steaks or beef top loin steaks, cut 1 inch thick (1 to 1½ lb. total)
⅓	cup Poire Williams brandy, pear brandy, or pear nectar	3	Tbsp. butter or margarine
4	tsp. all-purpose flour	¼	cup finely chopped shallots or green onions
1	tsp. cracked black pepper	¼	cup reduced-sodium beef broth
½	tsp. salt		

1. In a small bowl stir together pears and brandy or nectar. Cover; let stand for 15 minutes.

2. Meanwhile, in a shallow dish stir together flour, pepper, and salt. Dip steaks into flour mixture to coat. In a large skillet cook steaks in 2 tablespoons of the hot butter over medium heat to desired doneness, turning once. For tenderloin steaks, allow 10 to 13 minutes for medium rare (145° F) to medium (160° F). For top loin steaks, allow 12 to 15 minutes for medium rare to medium. Transfer steaks to a platter, reserving the drippings in the skillet. Cover and keep warm.

3. For sauce, in the same skillet cook shallots in the drippings over medium heat for 1 minute. Remove from heat. Let stand for 1 minute. Carefully stir in dried pear mixture and beef broth. Bring to boiling. Boil gently, uncovered, over medium heat about 3 minutes or until mixture is slightly thickened, stirring occasionally. Whisk in remaining 1 tablespoon butter. To serve, spoon sauce over steaks. Makes 4 servings.

Each serving: 322 cal., 17 g total fat (8 g sat. fat), 81 mg chol., 465 mg sodium, 6 g carbo., 0 g fiber, 24 g pro. Daily Values: 9% vit. A, 2% vit. C, 2% calcium, 19% iron.

A PEAR-FECT FALL DINNER

Creamy Pear Soup (page 159)
N.Y. Steak with Pear Brandy-Black Pepper Sauce (above)
French fries
Steamed broccoli
Dried Pear-Chocolate Caramel Pie (page 170)
Pinot Noir or other dry red wine
Coffee or tea

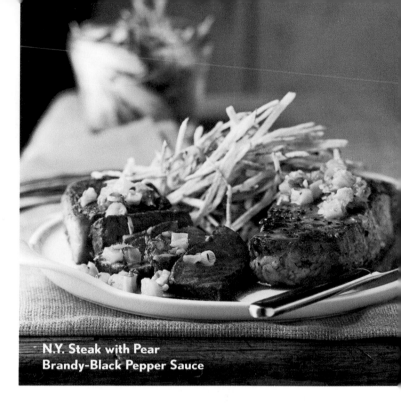

N.Y. Steak with Pear Brandy-Black Pepper Sauce

Spiced Pears and Lamb Chops

Simmer pears and pear nectar for a few minutes to concentrate the fruity flavor and thicken the sauce naturally.

PREP: 15 minutes **COOK:** 16 minutes

8	lamb rib or loin chops, cut 1 inch thick	1	tsp. ground cumin
	Salt	½	tsp. celery seeds
	Ground black pepper	2	Tbsp. butter or margarine
2	tsp. olive oil	½	cup pear nectar
2	large onions, sliced (2 cups)	1	qt. Spiced Canned Pears (page 168) or two 16-oz. cans pear halves, drained
1	tsp. paprika	2	cups torn radicchio leaves

1. Trim fat from chops. Sprinkle with salt and pepper. In a large skillet cook chops in hot oil over medium heat for 9 to 11 minutes for medium (160° F), turning once. Transfer chops to a platter; cover and keep warm. Drain fat from skillet.

2. For sauce, in the same large skillet cook onions, paprika, cumin, and celery seeds in hot butter about 5 minutes or until tender, stirring occasionally. Add pear nectar and drained pears. Bring to boiling. Boil gently, uncovered, about 2 minutes or until sauce is slightly thickened.

3. To serve, arrange chops on radicchio leaves. Spoon pear sauce over chops. Makes 4 servings.

low fat Each serving: 518 cal., 18 g total fat (7 g sat. fat), 80 mg chol., 209 mg sodium, 72 g carbo., 6 g fiber, 22 g pro. Daily Values: 12% vit. A, 19% vit. C, 7% calcium, 15% iron.

Pears and Brie in Phyllo

Serve this pear-filled cheese spread with assorted crackers or sliced French bread. Ooh-la-la!

PREP: 35 minutes **BAKE:** 40 minutes

1 small pear, finely chopped (½ cup)	1 recipe Sugar-Coated Walnuts (below)
2 Tbsp. snipped dried tart cherries	1 8-oz. round Brie cheese
½ tsp. snipped fresh rosemary	4 sheets frozen phyllo dough (9x14-inch rectangles), thawed
3 Tbsp. butter, melted	

1. For filling, in a small saucepan cook pear, cherries, and rosemary in 1 tablespoon hot butter about 3 minutes or until pear is just tender; remove from heat. Cool slightly. Prepare Sugar-Coated Walnuts; set aside.

2. Preheat oven to 400° F. Split Brie round in half horizontally, making 2 rounds. Top a cut side with pear filling and half of the Sugar-Coated Walnuts. Top with the other Brie half, cut side down (Brie will be full).

3. Lightly brush a sheet of phyllo with some of the melted butter. Top with 3 more sheets, brushing each sheet with butter.

4. Place the Brie round in center of phyllo stack. Bring phyllo up and around Brie to enclose, pleating phyllo as necessary. Invert onto a greased 15×10×1-inch baking pan; brush with butter.

5. Bake about 15 minutes or until golden. Transfer to a platter. Top with remaining Sugar-Coated Walnuts. Serve warm. Makes 20 appetizer servings.

SUGAR-COATED WALNUTS: In a small skillet melt 1 tablespoon butter over medium heat. Add ½ cup broken walnuts and 1 table-spoon sugar (sugar will not dissolve). Cook and stir over medium heat about 5 minutes or until walnuts are toasted and sugar is brown. Pour mixture onto a piece of foil; let cool. Coarsely crush the nut mixture. Makes about ½ cup.

Each serving: 91 cal., 8 g total fat (4 g sat. fat), 18 mg chol., 105 mg sodium, 3 g carbo., 0 g fiber, 3 g pro. Daily Values: 3% vit. A, 3% calcium, 1% iron.

Pear Roquefort Tart

Serve this knife-and-fork appetizer to start off a harvest feast.

PREP: 40 minutes **BAKE:** 12 minutes

1 recipe Walnut Tart Pastry (below)	3 small fresh pears, peeled, cored, and sliced; or 1 pt. Spiced Canned Pears (fennel-flavored) (page 168), drained and sliced; or one 15-oz. can pear slices, drained
½ of an 8-oz. pkg. cream cheese, softened	
2 oz. Roquefort or blue cheese, crumbled (½ cup)	
¾ cup Pear Butter (page 166)	¼ cup bite-size strips prosciutto
2 Tbsp. butter	

1. Prepare, bake, and cool Tart Pastry. Meanwhile, in a medium mixing bowl beat cream cheese and blue cheese with an electric mixer on low to medium speed until smooth.

2. Spread cheese mixture onto bottom of the pastry. Top with Pear Butter.

3. In a large skillet melt butter over medium-high heat; add pear slices. Cook until tender and heated through, allowing 5 minutes for fresh pears or 2 minutes for canned pears, turning gently occasionally. Cool slightly in pan for 5 minutes.

4. Arrange pear slices on cheese mixture in crust-lined pan. Top with prosciutto. If desired, cover and chill in the refrigerator up to 4 hours. To serve, cut into squares. Makes 9 servings.

WALNUT TART PASTRY: Preheat oven to 425° F. In a medium bowl stir together 1¼ cups all-purpose flour, ¼ cup chopped walnuts, 2 tablespoons sugar, 1 teaspoon cracked black pepper, and 1 teaspoon snipped fresh thyme. Using a pastry blender, cut ½ cup butter into flour mixture until pieces are pea-size. In a small bowl stir together 2 beaten egg yolks and 1 tablespoon ice water; gradually stir into flour mixture. Using your fingers, gently knead the dough just until a ball forms. Pat onto bottom and halfway up the sides of a 9-inch square baking pan. Prick generously with a fork. Bake for 12 to 14 minutes or until golden. Cool on a wire rack.

Each serving: 348 cal., 24 g total fat (13 g sat. fat), 103 mg chol., 307 mg sodium, 30 g carbo., 2 g fiber, 6 g pro. Daily Values: 17% vit. A, 6% vit. C, 7% calcium, 8% iron.

Pear Roquefort Tart

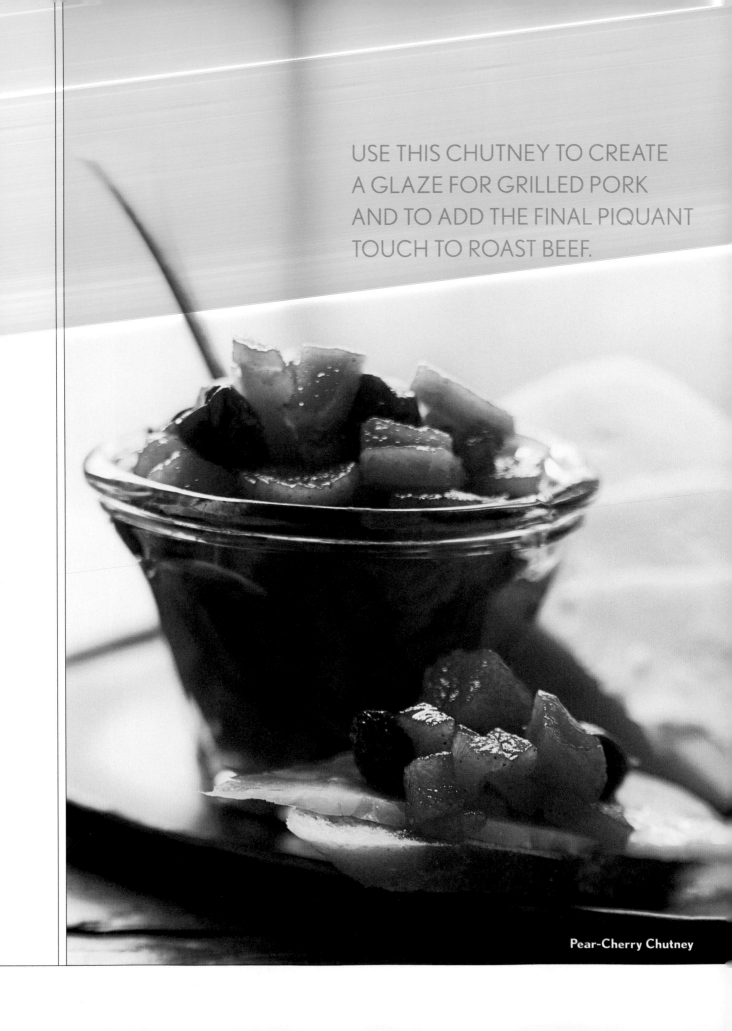

USE THIS CHUTNEY TO CREATE
A GLAZE FOR GRILLED PORK
AND TO ADD THE FINAL PIQUANT
TOUCH TO ROAST BEEF.

Pear-Cherry Chutney

Pear-Cherry Chutney

For an easy and pretty appetizer, spoon this sweet-tart combo over cheese and serve it with French bread.

PREP: 20 minutes **COOK:** 10 minutes

½ cup sugar	½ tsp. ground cinnamon
1 cup dried tart red cherries	½ tsp. ground allspice
2 tsp. finely shredded lemon peel	5 cups chopped, peeled firm fresh pears
⅓ cup lemon juice	

1. In a large saucepan combine sugar, dried cherries, lemon peel, lemon juice, cinnamon, and allspice. Bring to boiling; reduce heat. Simmer, uncovered, for 5 minutes, stirring occasionally. Stir in pears; return to boiling. Simmer, uncovered, for 5 minutes or until pears are just tender. Let cool.

2. Transfer chutney to a storage container. Cover and chill in the refrigerator for up to 2 weeks. Or place in a freezer container; cover and freeze up to 6 months. Use a slotted spoon to serve chutney as a topper for cheese or as a condiment with beef, pork, or lamb. Makes 4½ cups chutney (18 servings).

low fat Each ¼-cup serving: 71 cal., 0 g total fat (0 g sat. fat), 0 mg chol., 0 mg sodium, 18 g carbo., 1 g fiber, 0 g pro. Daily Values: 7% vit. C, 1% calcium, 1% iron.

PICKING PEARS

Thanks to imports and advances in storage, most pear varieties are available year-round. Choose from the kinds listed below.

BOSC: Best for cooking as well as for canning, freezing, and drying is the swan-necked, sandy-skinned Bosc, which many experts consider to be their favorite all-around pear. It holds its shape and flavor well under a variety of cooking, preserving, and baking conditions. The charm of the Bosc—available August through April—is its flowery aroma and spicy, clovelike flavor.

BARTLETT: Equally versatile in the minds of many cooks are the Bartletts, both red and yellow. Available July through December—and canned year-round—they are a little more tender and slightly sweeter than Boscs, with a floral, hint-of-jasmine character.

SECKEL: Maroon-blushed or all-maroon Seckels have been dubbed honey or sugar pears for their lusciously juicy, syrupy quality. These September-to-May pears are less practical for preserving because of their small size, but they are beauties when canned whole. And, for anyone with a little patience, they make outstanding preserves.

ANJOU, COMICE, FORELLE, AND ASIAN: The Anjou (October to June), the Comice (September to March), and the tiny Forelle (September to February) are better appreciated fresh. Both green and red Anjous have all the best of the honey-wine-butter character of pears. Asian pears, which combine the crunchiness of apple with the flavor of pear, are also best fresh.

(below, left to right) Yellow Anjou, Red Anjou, Forelle, Comice, Bosc, Red Bartlett, Seckel, Maroon Seckel

Pear Scones

The texture of these scones will vary with the form of pears you use. Fresh and canned pears will make moister scones; for drier scones, use the dried-pear option.

PREP: 25 minutes **BAKE:** 14 minutes

2	cups all-purpose flour	1½	tsp. vanilla
⅓	cup granulated sugar	1	cup chopped, peeled fresh
1½	tsp. baking powder		pears; canned pears,
½	tsp. baking soda		patted dry; or 1 cup finely
6	Tbsp. butter, chilled		chopped Oven-Dried
⅓	cup buttermilk		Pears* (right)
1	egg		Coarse sugar (optional)

1. Preheat oven to 400° F. In a large bowl combine flour, granulated sugar, baking powder, and baking soda. Using a pastry blender, cut in butter until mixture resembles coarse crumbs. Make a well in center of flour mixture; set aside.

2. In a bowl stir together buttermilk, egg, and vanilla. Add buttermilk mixture to flour mixture. Stir just until combined (mixture may appear dry). Stir in pears. Form dough into a ball.

3. Turn dough out onto a well floured surface (lightly floured if using dried pears). Knead by folding and gently pressing dough for 8 to 10 strokes or until dough holds together and is no longer sticky. Pat or lightly roll dough to 1-inch thickness. Cut with a floured 2- to 2½-inch biscuit cutter. Gather any remaining dough; pat to 1-inch thickness and cut additional scones (handle dough gently; don't overwork).

4. Arrange scones on an ungreased baking sheet. If desired, sprinkle with coarse sugar. Bake for 14 to 18 minutes or until golden. Serve warm. Makes 10 to 12 scones.

*NOTE: If using dried pears, increase the buttermilk to ½ cup.

Each serving: 205 cal., 8 g total fat (5 g sat. fat), 41 mg chol., 197 mg sodium, 29 g carbo., 1 g fiber, 3 g pro. Daily Values: 6% vit. A, 2% vit. C, 6% calcium, 7% iron.

PEAR-FECT FALL PICNIC

Pear Roquefort Tart *(page 162)*
Pear Scones *(above)*
Pear Butter *(right)*
Spiced Canned Pears *(page 168)*
Pear or apple cider

Oven-Dried Pears

PREP: 20 minutes **BAKE:** 3½ hours

2	lb. ripe but firm fresh pears, such as Bartlett, Anjou, and Bosc, peeled and cored

1. Preheat oven to 200° F. Line 2 large baking sheets with parchment paper or nonstick foil. Cut pears into ¼-inch-thick slices. Arrange in a single layer on baking sheets (see photo, *above*). Bake about 3½ hours or until pears are dry but still slightly chewy, turning pear slices every hour.

2. Let pear slices cool completely. Transfer pear slices to an airtight container. Cover and store in the freezer for up to 6 months. Pears may develop a sugary appearance during storage. Makes 5 to 6 ounces pear slices (about 1½ cups).

low fat Each ounce: 98 cal., 1 g total fat (0 g sat. fat), 0 mg chol., 0 mg sodium, 25 g carbo., 4 g fiber, 1 g pro. Daily Values: 1% vit. A, 8% vit. C, 2% calcium, 2% iron.

Pear Butter

In addition to being a key element in Pear Roquefort Tart, this butter is delicious when spread onto scones or toast or when stirred into plain yogurt or salad dressing.

PREP: 40 minutes **COOK:** 1¾ hours

4	lb. fresh cooking pears, such as Bosc or Bartlett (about 9 pears)	1½	cups sugar
		1	Tbsp. finely shredded orange peel
2½	cups water	¼	cup orange juice

1. Quarter and core pears. In a 6- to 8-quart Dutch oven combine pears and the water. Bring to boiling; reduce heat. Simmer, covered, for 30 minutes, stirring occasionally. Press mixture through a food mill, discarding solids (you should have about 6 cups sieved mixture). Return to Dutch oven.

2. Stir in sugar, orange peel, and orange juice. Bring to boiling; reduce heat. Simmer, uncovered, over medium-low heat for 1¼ hours or until very thick. As the mixture thickens, reduce heat to low, if necessary, stirring often.

3. Ladle hot pear butter into hot, sterilized half-pint canning jars, leaving ¼-inch headspace. Wipe jar rims; adjust lids. Process in a boiling-water canner for 5 minutes (start timing when water returns to boil). Remove jars; cool on racks. Makes 4 half-pints.

low fat Each tablespoon: 38 cal., 0 g total fat, 0 mg chol., 0 mg sodium, 10 g carbo., 1 g fiber, 0 g pro. Daily Values: 3% vit. C.

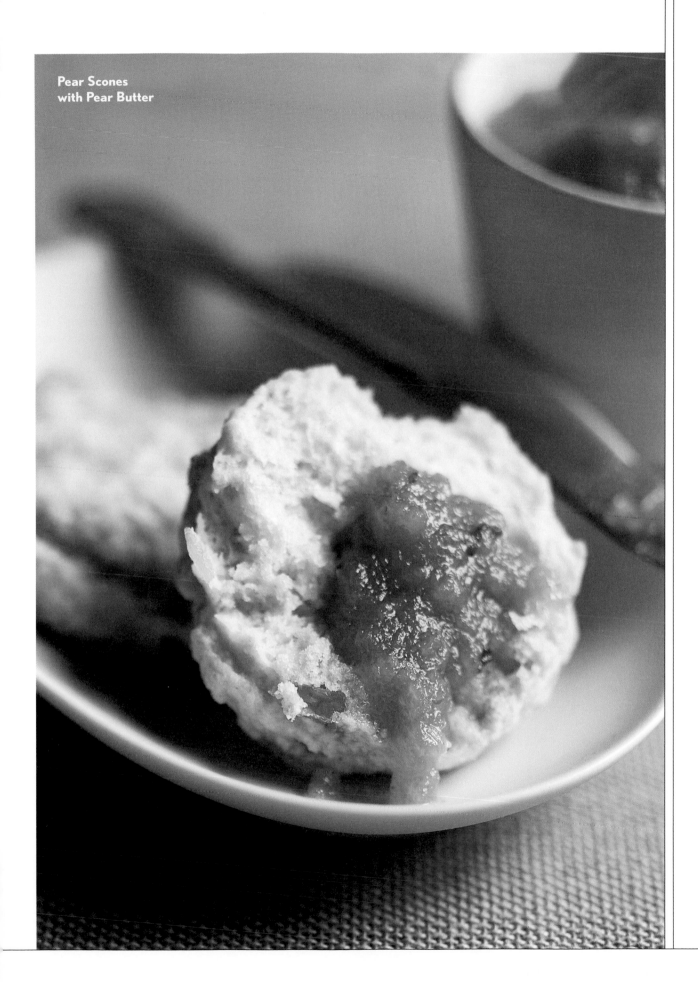

Pear Scones
with Pear Butter

Freezing Pears

Find ascorbic acid in the spice section or canning supplies section of your supermarket.

PREP: 50 minutes **COOK:** 2 minutes **COOL:** 30 minutes

4 tsp. ascorbic acid color-keeper	4 cups water
1/3 cup water	1 cup sugar
4 lb. fresh pears, such as Bartlett, Bosc, or Seckel	

1. In a large bowl combine ascorbic acid color-keeper and the 1/3 cup water. Peel, core, and cut pears into 1/4-inch-thick slices, adding pears to color-keeper solution as they are sliced. Gently toss the mixture occasionally to prevent fruit from discoloring.

2. In a Dutch oven or kettle bring the 4 cups water to boiling. Add sugar and stir until dissolved. Return sugar-water mixture to boiling. Add pear mixture. Cook for 2 minutes. Drain pears, reserving syrup; cool.

3. Pack pears into resealable freezer bags or clean pint canning jars or freezer containers. Add cooled syrup, completely covering the pears. For wide-top jars or containers, leave a 1/2-inch headspace; for narrow-top containers, leave a 3/4-inch headspace (see photo, *right*). Seal, label, and freeze. Use pears within 8 months. Makes 3 pints (12 servings).

low fat Each 1/2-cup serving: 44 cal., 1 g total fat (0 g sat. fat), 0 mg chol., 3 mg sodium, 37 g carbo., 3 g fiber, 1 g pro. Daily Values: 8% vit. C, 2% calcium, 2% iron.

Spiced Canned Pears

When selecting pears for canning, look for fruit that is ripe and still firm to the touch. Avoid pears that are overripe, because canning will make them too soft.

START TO FINISH: 2 1/2 hours

5 lb. fresh Bartlett or Bosc pears	2 cups sugar
Ascorbic acid color-keeper	Whole cloves, stick cinnamon, or fennel seeds (optional)
8 cups water	

1. Fill an 18- to 20-quart boiling-water canner (with rack) half full of water; cover and heat over high heat until boiling. Heat additional water in another kettle. Wash jars in hot, soapy water. Rinse thoroughly. Prepare screw bands and new flat metal lids with a built-in sealing compound according to manufacturer's directions.

2. Peel, halve, and core pears. Treat with color-keeper solution according to package directions. In a 6- to 8-quart large kettle or Dutch oven combine water and sugar; bring to boiling. Add pear halves. Return to boiling; simmer in syrup for 5 minutes.

3. When the water in the canner is boiling, fill each jar and place it on rack in canner. To fill jars, use a slotted spoon to transfer pear halves to jars. Pack pears tightly in jars to avoid excess air space between pears, leaving about 1/2-inch headspace at the top of the jar. (If you are using medium-sized pears, you should be able to get 8 to 10 pear halves in a quart jar.)

4. Add desired spices or seeds to each jar. For cloves, add 1/4 teaspoon whole cloves per jar. For cinnamon, add one 3-inch stick of cinnamon per quart jar (if canning pints, use one 1 1/2-inch stick per jar). For fennel seeds, add 1 teaspoon per jar.

5. Add syrup to jars using a funnel and small ladle or 1-cup liquid measuring cup (see photo 1, *opposite*). Use a small spatula to release air bubbles and pack pears (photo 2, *opposite*). Adjust liquid to create 1/2-inch headspace (see photo 3, *opposite*). Wipe jar rims with a clean, damp cloth. Place prepared lids on jars; add screw bands and tighten. Place jars on rack in canner using a jar lifter (photo 4, *opposite*).

6. After the last jar has been added to canner, add enough additional boiling water to put tops of jars 1 inch below the waterline. Cover; heat to a brisk, rolling boil. Keep water boiling gently during canning. If canning quarts, boil for 25 minutes; for pints, boil for 20 minutes. Using a jar lifter, remove jars from canner and place on a wire rack to cool.

7. When jars are completely cool (12 to 24 hours), press the center of each lid to check the seal. If the dip in the lid holds, the jar is sealed. If the lid bounces up and down, the jar isn't sealed. (The contents of unsealed jars can be refrigerated and used within 2 to 3 days.) Store canned pears in a cool, dry place for up to 1 year. Makes 3 quarts (4 or 5 servings per quart).

low fat Each serving: 226 cal., 1 g total fat (0 g sat. fat), 0 mg chol., 5 mg sodium, 58 g carbo., 4 g fiber, 1 g pro. Daily Values: 1% vit. A, 8% vit. C, 2% calcium, 3% iron.

Spiced Canned Pears

The steps necessary to can your own pears, ranging from filling and removing bubbles (see photos 1 and 2, *right*) to measuring headspace and cooking pears in a large kettle called a "canner" (see photos 3 and 4, *right*), ensure both food safety and the maximum flavor.

PIECRUST POINTER

To transfer the pastry for baking, drape it over the rolling pin and unroll pastry into the pie plate.

Caramel Sauce

Serve this silky sauce warm or cool with Dried Pear-Chocolate Caramel Pie or spoon it over ice cream or cake.

START TO FINISH: 20 minutes

3/4 cup packed brown sugar	2 Tbsp. pear brandy
1/4 cup water	(optional)
1 tsp. lemon juice	1/2 tsp. vanilla
1/3 cup whipping cream	
1 Tbsp. butter	

1. In a heavy small saucepan combine brown sugar, water, and lemon juice. Cook and stir over medium heat until bubbly. Cook and stir about 10 minutes more or until thickened.

2. Carefully stir in cream and butter. Cook and stir until butter is melted. Remove from heat. Stir in pear brandy, if desired, and vanilla. Serve warm or cool. Cover and chill any leftovers in the refrigerator for up to 3 days. Makes 1 cup sauce (8 servings).

Each 2-tablespoon serving: 132 cal., 5 g total fat (3 g sat. fat), 18 mg chol., 28 mg sodium, 22 g carbo., 0 g fiber, 0 g pro. Daily Values: 4% vit. A, 1% vit. C, 3% calcium, 2% iron.

Dried Pear-Chocolate Caramel Pie

You can make your own pastry or use a folded, refrigerated piecrust from the supermarket.

PREP: 45 minutes **BAKE:** 52 minutes
COOK: 15 minutes **COOL:** 4 hours

1 recipe Pastry for Single-Crust Pie (below)	1/4 tsp. ground nutmeg
4 cups Oven-Dried Pears (page 166) or five 3-oz. pkg. dried pears, sliced into 1/4-inch-thick slices	1 Tbsp. butter
	1 recipe Almond Crumb Topping (below)
2 12-oz. cans pear nectar (3 cups)	1 recipe Caramel Sauce (left) or 3/4 cup prepared caramel ice cream topping
2 Tbsp. honey	1 oz. bittersweet chocolate, chopped
1/2 tsp. ground cinnamon	

1. Preheat oven to 450° F. Prepare Pastry for Single-Crust Pie. Roll pastry to a 12-inch circle. Transfer pastry to a 9-inch pie plate (see photo, *left*). Trim pastry to 1/2 inch beyond edge of pie plate. Fold under extra pastry. Flute edges high. Do not prick. Line pastry with a double thickness of foil. Bake for 8 minutes. Remove foil. Bake 4 to 5 minutes more or until set and dry. Remove crust from oven; reduce oven temperature to 375° F.

2. Meanwhile, for filling, in a large saucepan combine dried pears and nectar. Bring to boiling; reduce heat. Simmer, covered, for 5 minutes. Stir in honey, cinnamon, and nutmeg. Simmer, uncovered, for 10 minutes (juices will be thick).

3. Add pear filling to pastry shell, spreading evenly. Dot with butter. Prepare Almond Crumb Topping; sprinkle onto pie.

4. Bake for 40 to 45 minutes or until topping is light brown. If needed, cover edge of pie with foil the last 5 to 10 minutes of baking time to prevent overbrowning. Cool on a wire rack for 20 minutes. Drizzle with 1/4 cup of the Caramel Sauce; sprinkle with chocolate. Cool completely. Serve with remaining Caramel Sauce. Makes 8 servings.

PASTRY FOR SINGLE-CRUST PIE: In a medium bowl stir together 1 1/4 cups all-purpose flour and 1/4 teaspoon salt. Using a pastry blender, cut in 1/3 cup shortening until pieces are pea-size. Using a total of 4 to 5 tablespoons cold water, sprinkle 1 tablespoon water over part of the mixture; gently toss with a fork. Push moistened dough to side of bowl. Repeat until all is moistened. Form dough into a ball.

ALMOND CRUMB TOPPING: In a bowl combine 1/2 cup all-purpose flour, 1/4 cup granulated sugar, 1/4 cup packed brown sugar, and 1/4 teaspoon salt. Using a pastry blender or 2 knives, cut in 1/3 cup cold butter until mixture resembles coarse crumbs. Stir in 3/4 cup coarsely chopped almonds.

Each serving: 628 cal., 31 g total fat (12 g sat. fat), 43 mg chol., 278 mg sodium, 86 g carbo., 5 g fiber, 6 g pro. Daily Values: 11% vit. A, 5% vit. C, 8% calcium, 16% iron.

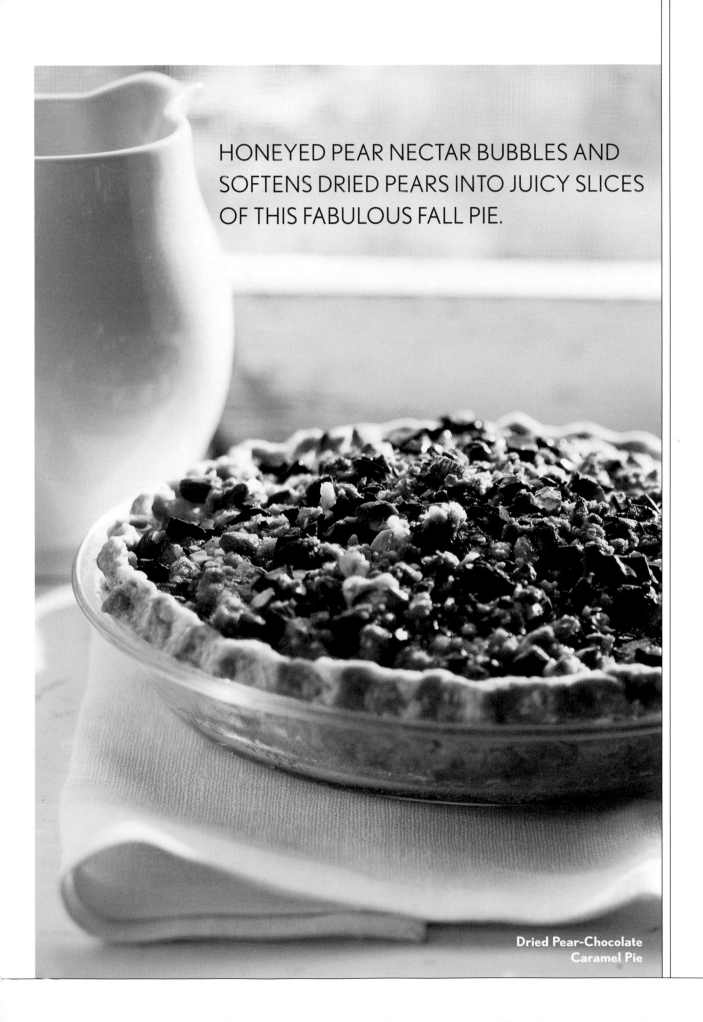

HONEYED PEAR NECTAR BUBBLES AND SOFTENS DRIED PEARS INTO JUICY SLICES OF THIS FABULOUS FALL PIE.

Dried Pear-Chocolate Caramel Pie

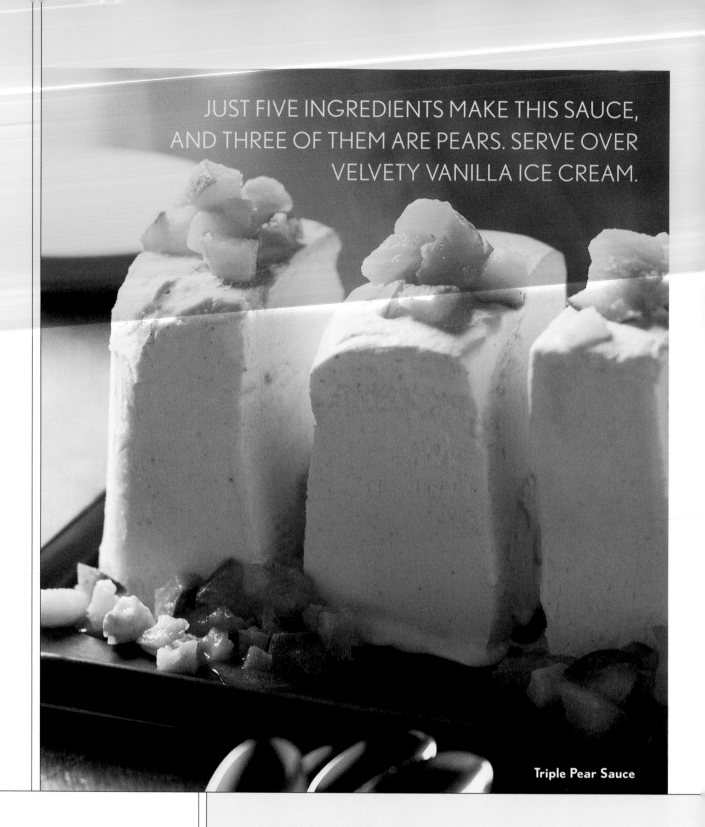

JUST FIVE INGREDIENTS MAKE THIS SAUCE, AND THREE OF THEM ARE PEARS. SERVE OVER VELVETY VANILLA ICE CREAM.

Triple Pear Sauce

A WORD ABOUT RIPENESS

Growers pick their pears when the fruit on the trees is mature (full in size and shape) but still unripe. Because of the packing and storing procedures, the pears are often still not quite ripe when you buy them at the supermarket. If that's the case, follow these easy steps and you'll have juicy, drip-down-your-arms pears every time!

- To ripen pears at home, place the fruit, stems up, in a brown paper bag and close the bag.
- Check the fruit daily for ripeness; usually two or three days will do the trick.
- A pear is ripe when the skin is yellow or pink and yields to gentle pressure.
- Once pears are ripe, store them in your refrigerator to keep them as fresh as possible.

Triple Pear Sauce

Try this sauce over slices of vanilla ice cream or pound cake and top with toasted, chopped hazelnuts.

PREP: 20 minutes **COOK:** 11 minutes

1 pt. or ½ qt. Spiced Canned Pears (page 168) or one 15-oz. can pear halves in light or extra light syrup
2 cups snipped Oven-Dried Pears (page 166)
½ cup butter or margarine
½ cup sugar
2 cups fresh Seckel, Forelle, or Bartlett pears, cored and cut into small chunks

1. Drain pears, reserving ¾ cup syrup. Cut canned pears into large chunks; set aside.

2. In a large nonstick skillet bring the reserved syrup and the dried pears to boiling; reduce heat. Simmer, uncovered, until the liquid is evaporated. Remove pears from the skillet; set aside.

3. In the same skillet melt butter over medium heat. Add sugar; cook and stir for 1 to 2 minutes until sugar is almost dissolved. Decrease heat to medium-low. Stir in cooked and canned pears. Cook, covered, for 5 minutes, stirring frequently.

4. Add fresh pears. Cover and cook for 5 minutes more, stirring frequently. Cool slightly. Serve warm. Cover and chill any remaining sauce for up to 2 days; heat slightly before serving. Makes 8 (½-cup) servings.

Each serving: 252 cal., 13 g total fat (8 g sat. fat), 33 mg chol., 125 mg sodium, 37 g carbo., 3 g fiber, 1 g pro. Daily Values: 10% vit. A, 6% vit. C, 2% calcium, 2% iron.

PEAR-FECT SUNDAY SUPPER

Spiced Pears and Lamb Chops *(page 161)*
Raddichio leaves or steamed red cabbage
Mashed potatoes
Rye rolls
Triple Pear Sauce *(above)* over vanilla ice cream
Iced tea or water

Pear-Pecan Cake with Caramel Topping

You can serve this potluck favorite plain as a coffee cake or top it with whipped cream for a real old-fashioned dessert.

PREP: 20 minutes **BAKE:** 50 minutes **COOL:** 2 hours

3 cups all-purpose flour
1 tsp. baking soda
½ tsp. salt
3 eggs
2 cups sugar
1 cup cooking oil
2 tsp. vanilla
3 medium pears, cored, peeled, and finely chopped (3 cups)
1 cup toasted, chopped pecans
1 recipe Caramel Topping (below)
Whipped cream (optional)

1. Preheat oven to 350° F. Lightly grease a 13×9×2-inch baking pan; set aside. In a medium bowl stir together flour, baking soda, and salt; set aside.

2. In a large bowl beat eggs; stir in sugar, oil, and vanilla. Add flour mixture to oil mixture; stir until combined. Stir in pears and pecans (batter will be thick).

3. Spread batter in prepared pan. Bake about 50 minutes or until golden brown and a toothpick inserted near the center comes out clean. Cool in pan on a wire rack.

4. Prepare Caramel Topping; spoon warm topping over cooled cake. Allow topping to cool. Cut into squares to serve. If desired, serve with whipped cream. Makes 20 servings.

CARAMEL TOPPING: In a medium saucepan melt ½ cup butter over medium heat. Stir in 1 cup packed brown sugar and ¼ cup evaporated milk. Bring to boiling over medium-high heat. Reduce heat to medium. Boil, uncovered, for 3 minutes, stirring constantly. Remove from heat.

Each serving with topping: 389 cal., 21 g total fat (5 g sat. fat), 46 mg chol., 189 mg sodium, 49 g carbo., 2 g fiber, 4 g pro. Daily Values: 5% vit. A, 2% vit. C, 3% calcium, 8% iron.

a bit of garlic guidance

GARLIC CAN BE MELLOW OR ASSERTIVE. IT ALL DEPENDS ON HOW YOU HANDLE IT.

Garlic lovers can easily understand why ancient Egyptians worshiped the herb, Confucius wrote ballads to it, and early Vikings toted it with them on voyages. Its pronounced flavor, which mellows sweetly with cooking, adds a taste sensation to nearly any dish.

Whether you're after a sweetly subtle note or a bold and tasty blast, you can control garlic's flavor with a few kitchen tricks. It boils down to timing and cutting. Garlic that is cooked for a long time generally is mild and creamy. Hence, if you toss a whole clove or thick slices of garlic into a long-simmering casserole or soup, you'll get a gentle hint of garlic.

On the other hand, if you wait until just before serving to crush or finely chop fresh garlic before stirring it into your pot, you'll get a much more potent effect. The finer that garlic is minced, the bigger the flavor.

That pesky papery covering you find on garlic will easily slip off if you soak the individual cloves in plain water about an hour before using. Or if you're in a hurry, just drop the cloves into boiling water for 30 seconds, rinse under cold water, and drain. The papery skins pop right off.

Cheesy Garlic Rolls

BY JEANNE AMBROSE. PHOTOGRAPHS: GREG SCHEIDEMANN/(N)HAUS FOTO. FOOD STYLIST: CHARLES WORTHINGTON.

GROW YOUR OWN GARLIC

You can reap at least 10 times what you sow if you plant your own garlic. Here's how:

- Order garlic bulbs in in the fall if you live in the North or spring in the South. To order, check a local nursery or try: Johnny's Selected Seeds, 207/437-4301, or Seed Savers Exchange, 563/382-5990.
- Plant garlic in the North at least one month before the soil freezes, usually about mid-September to mid-October. In the South, you can plant in February or March.
- Break open bulbs, separate cloves, and peel away papery layers of skin immediately before planting.
- Plant cloves, pointy tips up, 4 to 6 inches apart and 2 to 4 inches deep (the colder your winters, the deeper you plant).
- As green growth appears, trim off any flower buds that bloom.

Cheesy Garlic Rolls

This bread recipe was inspired by an appetizer created by Jim Powell, chef/owner of Gibson's Restaurant in Grand Rapids, Michigan.

PREP: 25 minutes **BAKE:** 8 minutes
COOK: 25 minutes **COOL:** 20 minutes

1/3 cup peeled garlic cloves (24 cloves, 2 to 3 bulbs)	2 oz. fontina cheese, shredded (1/2 cup)
2/3 cup chicken broth	Olive oil
1/2 cup dry white wine	
1/2 of a 12-oz. pkg. (6 rolls) Hawaiian sweet rolls or dinner rolls	

1. In a heavy small saucepan combine garlic, broth, and wine. Bring to boiling; reduce heat. Simmer, uncovered, over medium heat about 25 minutes or until garlic is tender and 1/3 cup of the liquid remains. Set aside to cool.

2. Preheat oven to 325° F. Place rolls (do not separate) in a greased 8×8×2-inch baking pan. Cut an "X" about 1/2 inch deep in the top of each roll; spread open slightly. Spoon garlic cloves and cheese into openings, pressing gently into rolls. Drizzle with broth mixture; brush with olive oil.

3. Bake for 8 to 10 minutes until heated through and cheese is melted. Serve warm. Makes 6 appetizer servings.

Each serving: 181 cal., 7 g total fat (3 g sat. fat), 21 mg chol., 275 mg sodium, 19 g carbo., 0 g dietary fiber, 6 g protein. Daily Values: 2% vit. A, 6% vit. C, 8% calcium, 2% iron.

Spicy Garlic Chicken Pizza

PREP: 20 minutes **CHILL:** 30 minutes **BAKE:** 12 + 2 minutes

12 oz. skinless, boneless chicken breast halves	1 Tbsp. cornstarch
1/2 cup sliced green onions	1 16-oz. Italian bread shell (Boboli)
2 cloves garlic, minced	2 oz. Monterey Jack cheese, shredded (1/2 cup)
2 Tbsp. rice vinegar	
2 Tbsp. reduced-sodium soy sauce	2 oz. mozzarella cheese, shredded (1/2 cup)
2 Tbsp. olive oil	2 Tbsp. pine nuts or sliced almonds
1/2 tsp. crushed red pepper	
1/4 tsp. ground black pepper	

1. Cut chicken into 1/2-inch pieces. In a large mixing bowl combine half of the green onions, the garlic, vinegar, soy sauce, 1 tablespoon of the oil, the red pepper, and black pepper. Add chicken pieces; stir to coat. Cover and chill for 30 minutes.

2. Preheat oven to 400° F. Drain chicken, reserving liquid. In a large skillet heat 1 tablespoon of the oil; add chicken mixture. Cook and stir about 3 minutes or until chicken is no longer pink. Stir cornstarch into reserved liquid. Add to chicken mixture in skillet. Cook and stir until thickened and bubbly.

3. Place bread shell on baking sheet. Spread with chicken mixture; sprinkle with cheeses. Bake, uncovered, for 12 minutes. Top with remaining green onions and the nuts. Bake for 2 minutes more. To serve, cut into 6 wedges. Makes 6 servings.

Each serving: 392 cal., 16 g total fat (4 g sat. fat), 50 mg chol., 729 mg sodium, 36 g carbo., 2 g dietary fiber, 28 g protein. Daily Values: 5% vit. A, 5% vit. C, 23% calcium, 14% iron.

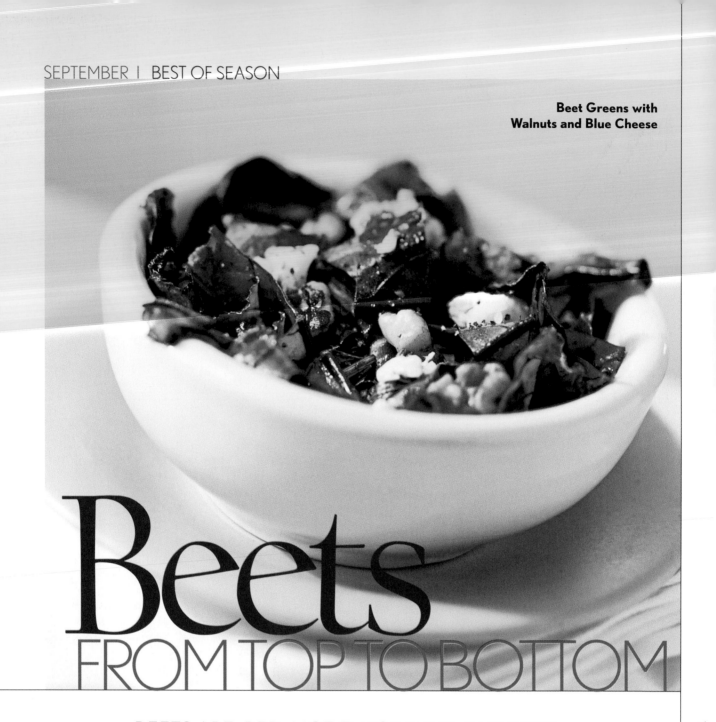

**Beet Greens with
Walnuts and Blue Cheese**

Beets
FROM TOP TO BOTTOM

BEETS ARE RED-HOT THESE DAYS, BUT BEET GREENS MAY BE THE RUBY ROOT'S BEST-KEPT SECRET. SIMILAR IN FLAVOR TO CHARD AND SPINACH, BEET GREENS ARE SCRUMPTIOUS WHETHER ENJOYED RAW IN SALADS OR LIGHTLY COOKED AS A NUTRITIOUS SIDE DISH.

PHOTOGRAPH: SCOTT LITTLE. FOOD STYLIST: CHARLES WORHTINGTON.

Beet Greens with Walnuts and Blue Cheese

PREP: 10 minutes **COOK:** 3 minutes

8 oz. beet greens*	1 Tbsp. crumbled blue
2 tsp. cooking oil	cheese
2 Tbsp. chopped walnuts	1/4 tsp. ground black pepper

1. Thoroughly clean greens. Drain well. Cut into 1-inch strips.

2. In a large skillet heat oil over medium-high heat. Add walnuts. Cook and stir for 2 minutes. Add beet greens; cook and stir, uncovered, for 1 minute or until just wilted.

3. Spoon into 4 bowls. Top each serving with crumbled blue cheese and pepper. Makes 4 side-dish servings.

*NOTE: You can also make this recipe with spinach or chard. Just clean the leaves well under cold running water, drain, and use as directed above.

Each serving: 55 cal., 5 g total fat (1 g sat. fat), 0 mg chol., 109 mg sodium, 3 g carbo., 2 g fiber, 2 g pro. Daily Values: 66% vit. A, 17% vit. C, 7% calcium.

Roasted Vegetables over Salad Greens

PREP: 20 minutes **COOK:** 40 minutes

8 oz. baby beets or	1/2 tsp. salt
3 medium beets	1/2 tsp. ground black pepper
12 oz. whole tiny new	2 Tbsp. balsamic vinegar
potatoes, halved	1 Tbsp. snipped fresh chives
4 oz. pearl onions, peeled	1 Tbsp. water
1/4 cup olive oil	6 cups torn Boston or Bibb
6 cloves garlic, minced	lettuce
1 Tbsp. snipped fresh	
rosemary or basil	

1. Preheat oven to 375° F. Scrub beets; trim off stem and root ends. (If using medium beets, peel and cut into 1-inch pieces.) Place beets, potatoes, and onions in a 13×9×2-inch baking pan.

2. In a small bowl combine 2 tablespoons of the olive oil, the garlic, rosemary, salt, and pepper. Drizzle over vegetables in pan; toss to coat. Cover; roast for 30 minutes. Uncover; roast for 10 to 20 minutes more or until vegetables are tender. Cool to room temperature; drain, reserving pan drippings.

3. For dressing, in a screw-top jar combine reserved pan drippings, the remaining 2 tablespoons oil, balsamic vinegar, chives, and water. Cover and shake well.

4. Divide lettuce among 6 salad plates. Top lettuce with roasted vegetable mixture; drizzle with dressing. Serve immediately. Makes 6 side-dish servings.

Each serving: 172 cal., 9 g total fat (1 g sat. fat), 0 mg chol., 245 mg sodium, 20 g carbo., 3 g fiber, 3 g pro. Daily Values: 30% vit. C, 4% calcium, 7% iron.

Borsch-Style Casserole

To anyone of Polish descent, beets mean borsch—a red beet soup. In this Test Kitchen favorite, beet soup takes on a heartier tone, beefed up into a main-dish stew. Top each serving with a dollop of sour cream and serve with black bread and frosty mugs of beer.

PREP: 30 minutes **BAKE:** 3 1/2 hours

2 lb. beef short ribs, cut up	1 1/2 tsp. sugar
1 Tbsp. cooking oil	1 1/2 tsp. vinegar
2 stalks celery, sliced	1 medium beet, cut into
(1 cup)	strips (1 cup)
1 medium onion, sliced	2 carrots, sliced (1 cup)
(1/2 cup)	1 turnip, cut into strips
1/2 of 6-oz. can (1/3 cup)	(3/4 cup)
tomato paste	1 small head cabbage,
1 tsp. salt	cut into 4 wedges
1/8 tsp. ground black pepper	Dairy sour cream (optional)

1. Preheat oven to 350°F. Trim fat from ribs. In 4-quart Dutch oven brown ribs in hot oil. Drain off fat. Add celery and onion. In a large bowl combine 3 cups water, the tomato paste, salt, and pepper; pour over vegetables and meat in pan. Cover and bake for 2 1/2 hours.

2. Skim off fat. Combine 1/2 cup water, the sugar, and vinegar; add to meat mixture. Add beet strips, carrot slices, and turnip strips; place cabbage wedges on top of vegetable and meat mixture, pushing cabbage wedges into the liquid. Cover and bake for 1 hour.

3. To serve, spoon stew into bowls. Season to taste with salt and pepper. If desired, top each serving with sour cream. Makes 4 main-dish servings.

Each serving: 272 cal., 11 g total fat (4 g sat. fat), 43 mg chol., 759 mg sodium, 21 g carbo., 6 g fiber, 23 g pro. Daily Values: 157% vit. A, 63% vit. C, 9% calcium, 18% iron.

jewels of Mt. Rainier

THESE PLUMP, SWEET FRUITS GO FAST ONCE THEY HIT THE STORES, SO YOU MAY WANT TO BUY AND FREEZE EXTRAS.

Rainier cherries sparkle gold and blush like the rays of a Northwestern sunset. As these cherries have grown more popular, their season has stretched beyond the summer months. Once available only in July, you can now find Rainiers as late as October.

Still, these fruits go quickly once they hit the stores, so you may want to buy and freeze extras. Wash them, then pat them dry with paper towels. Pit them, if you like, and freeze them, tightly covered, for up to six months.

Rainier Cherry Tart

Almond-Cherry Trifles

This simple dessert showcases cherries in triplicate: juicy cherry preserves, cherry liqueur, and golden Rainier cherries.

START TO FINISH: 20 minutes

1	8-oz. carton plain low-fat yogurt	1	cup halved and pitted fresh Rainier or other sweet cherries
¼	cup cherry preserves		
2	Tbsp. cherry liqueur or maraschino cherry juice	¼	cup sliced almonds, toasted
½	of a 10-oz. frozen pound cake, thawed		

1. In a small bowl stir together yogurt, 2 tablespoons of the cherry preserves, and cherry liqueur. Set aside.

2. Slice the cake in half lengthwise. Spread the cut sides of each cake half with the remaining cherry preserves. Cut each half into ½-inch cubes. Place half of the cake cubes in 4 parfait glasses or dessert dishes. Top with half of the cherries, then half of the yogurt mixture. Sprinkle with half of the nuts. Repeat layering with the remaining ingredients.

3. Cover and chill for up to 2 hours. Makes 4 servings.

Each serving: 298 cal., 10 g total fat (5 g sat. fat), 43 mg chol., 177 mg sodium, 44 g carbo., 2 g fiber, 6 g pro. Daily Values: 6% vit. A, 8% vit. C, 13% calcium, 5% iron.

Rainier Cherry Tart

PREP: 45 minutes **BAKE:** 15 minutes

1	recipe Almond Tart Shell (below)	1	Tbsp. cherry-flavored liqueur or cherry cider
½	cup dairy sour cream*	3½	cups fresh Rainier cherries or other sweet cherries, pitted
¼	of an 8-oz. tub cream cheese*		
3	Tbsp. sifted powdered sugar	½	cup apple jelly

1. Prepare Almond Tart Shell. For filling, in a medium bowl combine sour cream, cream cheese, powdered sugar, and liqueur or cider; beat with an electric mixer on low speed until smooth. Cover and chill for up to 60 minutes.

2. To assemble, spread filling evenly onto the bottom of Almond Tart Shell. Arrange cherries on top.

3. In a small saucepan heat apple jelly over low heat just until melted. Cool slightly; drizzle onto cherries. To serve, remove sides of tart pan. Cut into wedges; serve immediately. Makes 8 servings.

ALMOND TART SHELL: Preheat oven to 400° F. In a medium bowl stir together ¾ cup all-purpose flour, ¼ cup finely chopped almonds, and 3 tablespoons granulated sugar. Using a pastry blender, cut in ⅓ cup butter until the mixture resembles coarse crumbs. Sprinkle with 2 tablespoons water, working in with a fork until moistened. Form dough into a ball. Press dough evenly onto the bottom and up the sides of a 9-inch tart pan with removable bottom. Bake for 15 minutes or until light brown. Cool in pan on a wire rack.

*NOTE: For a lighter tart (269 calories, 30 mg cholesterol, 13 g total fat, 6 g saturated fat): Substitute sour cream and cream cheese with equal amounts of light dairy sour cream and light cream cheese.

Each serving: 295 cal., 16 g total fat (8 g sat. fat), 34 mg chol., 113 mg sodium, 36 g carbo., 2 g fiber, 4 g pro. Daily Values: 13% vit. A, 9% vit. C, 3% calcium, 7% iron.

October

WITH PUMPKINS ON THE DOORSTEP AND A CHILL IN THE AIR,
FALL HAS US YEARNING FOR STEAMING BOWLS OF GOODNESS.

The Magic of Soup

COOK UP A POT OF SOUP TO RESTORE, INVIGORATE, NURTURE, AND EVEN INSPIRE. THESE HEARTY SOUPS MINGLE THE ESSENCE OF BOTH FLAVOR AND SOUL, NOURISHING OUR BODIES AND OUR HEARTS.

THE MAGIC OF
SOUP

Potato-Carrot Soup

Potato-Carrot Soup

If fresh figs aren't available for topping this soup, rehydrate dried figs by covering them with boiling water. Let them stand for 10 minutes, then drain and cool. Halve the figs and sauté in a little olive oil.

PREP: 15 minutes   **COOK:** 20 minutes

2 medium garlic bulbs (about 16 cloves)	⅓ cup whipping cream
4 14-oz. cans reduced-sodium chicken broth	Salt
	Ground black pepper
3 medium potatoes, peeled and cut into ½-inch pieces (about 1 lb.)	1 recipe Roasted Fresh Figs (below) (optional)
3 medium carrots, peeled and chopped (1½ cups)	Snipped fresh chives (optional)

1. Separate garlic bulbs into cloves; peel. In a large saucepan combine garlic, broth, potatoes, and carrots. Bring to boiling; reduce heat. Simmer, covered, for 20 to 25 minutes or until vegetables are tender. Cool slightly.

2. In a blender or food processor puree soup, a third at a time, until smooth. Return all of the soup to saucepan. Stir in whipping cream. Season to taste with salt and pepper. Cook and stir until heated through.

3. To serve, spoon into 6 bowls. If desired, garnish with Roasted Fresh Figs and chives. Makes 6 side-dish servings.

ROASTED FRESH FIGS: Preheat oven to 425° F. Halve 6 fresh figs lengthwise. Place fig halves, cut sides up, on a baking sheet lined with parchment or foil. Brush figs with 1 tablespoon olive oil. Bake, uncovered, about 15 minutes or until fig halves are softened and heated through.

Each serving: 163 cal., 7 g total fat (4 g sat. fat), 18 mg chol., 1,172 mg sodium, 21 g carbo., 2 g fiber, 5 g pro. Daily Values: 158% vit. A, 26% vit. C, 4% calcium, 5% iron.

SOUP SUPPER BUFFET

Potato-Carrot Soup *(above)*
Smoked Sausage-Lentil Soup *(page 197)*
Beef and Cabbage Soup *(page 194)*
Assorted crackers and breads
Mixed green salad
Strawberry-Lemon Bars *(page 297)*
Iced tea

Autumn warmth

Soups fill the house with their warmth and aroma as they simmer on the stove, fulfilling a promise greater than just satisfying hunger. With soups, we feel comforted, our spirits revive, a bad day gets better.

Jana Kolpen, cook, painter, and author of the enchantingly illustrated fable and cookbook, *The Secrets of Pistoulet,* knows well the journey from hearth to heart. This month, she contributes a collection of everyday autumn soup recipes that are a graceful blend of cherished standards juxtaposed with clean, honest flavor. Jana has an understanding of the meaning behind ingredients—some are based in folklore, some in mythology. Her instinctual ability to combine them infuses her soups with a soulfulness that says as much about food's vitality as it does about our appetites.

"Soups are the humblest of fares; most are not very complicated. Cooking soup combines ritual, compassion, and fresh ingredients to give back what the harvest has given to us," Jana says. You could almost suspect Jana of spell-casting; in truth, it's her bubbling passion that makes her philosophy so believable.

For example, Jana's Potato-Carrot Soup is heady with garlic, which the ancient Egyptians and Greeks saw as a godlike food. Carrots and potatoes soften its powerful flavor. The soup is satisfying and surprising— roasted end-of-season figs crown it with a touch of sweetness. This soup offers a boost of energy that's especially helpful when you're tired.

For all of us, Jana's soups carry a message that goes beyond their expressive flavors. The spirit of the cook manifests itself in every dish, from simple Tuesday night suppers to holiday dinners or a batch of cookies named for a favorite aunt. We relish the reaction to our cooking as much as we enjoy its taste. The empty bowl and the heartfelt "thank you" give back the love we put in. That is the magic of soup.

SO MANY SOUPS, SO LITTLE TIME

"I love simple foods; there is something pure and honest about them," author Jana Kolpen says. "I just love having people over and watching them enjoy themselves. That's the essence of cooking."

Jana's insight into soups is the result of her stay at the small French farm Pistoulet, which she chronicles in her first book, *The Secrets of Pistoulet*. While visiting there, she started cooking with her hosts—making a variety of soups because the oven didn't work—and watched the effects the soups had on other visitors to the farm. "Guests would arrive worn and withered, and leave refreshed."

Today, Jana prepares her soups for company at her New York City apartment, where she is working on her third book. Most recently, she has designed a full line of dinnerware and serving pieces based on *The Secrets of Pistoulet* and featuring her hand-painted designs.

If you'd like to discover firsthand other secrets and recipes from

Pistoulet, you can order the 72-page hardcover book. AF81250, $17.95. TO ORDER: Visit our Web site at www.bhgcatalog.com or call 800/881-4066. Please specify item number. Shipping, handling, and tax, if applicable, will be added to the price shown.

Beet Soup

Jana learned to cook at her Russian-born grandmother's New Jersey farm kitchen, and the rustic beets in her Beet Soup resonate with a grandmother's compassion and caretaking. The flavor of the beets is delivered by preparing them three ways: pureed to give a velvety texture, chopped for a chunky contrast, and roasted for strong, earthy flavor. The recipe is as uncomplicated as the purest emotion. You can add a spoonful of sour cream or crème fraîche to each bowl of soup at serving time.

PREP: 15 minutes **COOK:** 35 + 25 minutes

1³⁄₄ lb. small beets	2 14-oz. cans chicken broth
1 to 2 cloves garlic, minced	Salt
1 Tbsp. olive oil	Ground black pepper
1 large russet potato, peeled, diced (1¹⁄₂ cups)	1 recipe Roasted Baby Beets (below) (optional)

1. Cut off all but 1 inch of beet stems and roots; wash. Do not peel. In a large covered saucepan cook beets, covered, in boiling salted water for 35 to 45 minutes or until tender. Drain and cool slightly. Slip skins off beets; dice.

2. In the same saucepan cook garlic in olive oil over medium heat for 1 minute. Add potato; cook and stir for 5 minutes. Add beets and broth; bring to boiling. Simmer, covered, for 20 minutes.

3. Transfer half of the mixture to a blender or food processor (process in batches if using a small food processor). Cover and blend or process until smooth. Return pureed mixture to the saucepan; heat through. Add salt and pepper to taste.

4. To serve, spoon soup into 6 bowls. If desired, add half of a Roasted Baby Beet to each. Makes 6 side-dish servings.

ROASTED BABY BEETS: Preheat oven to 425° F. Wash 3 baby beets and trim tops. Fold a 24×18-inch piece of heavy-duty foil in half. Place beets in center of foil; drizzle with 1 to 2 tablespoons olive oil. Fold foil up and around beets; seal with a double fold, leaving space for steam to build. Place packet on a baking sheet; roast for 35 to 40 minutes or until beets are tender. Cool slightly; cut beets in half.

low fat Each serving: 124 cal., 4 g total fat (1 g sat. fat), 0 mg chol., 700 mg sodium, 20 g carbo., 3 g fiber, and 4 g pro. Daily Values: 1% vit. A, 16% vit. C, 2% calcium, 7% iron.

Beet Soup

It takes just five ingredients to capture the old-world feeling of this warming soup.

BY STEPHEN EXEL. PHOTOGRAPHS: SHIMON AND TAMMAR. FOOD STYLIST: WILLIAM SMITH. PROP STYLIST: BARB FRITZ.

Potato-Onion Soup

This approach to potato soup—plain and simple—takes its flavor from a bit of crumbled bacon and humble onions.

START TO FINISH: 25 minutes

6 slices bacon	3 medium onions, cut into
5 cups sliced red potatoes	thin wedges (1½ cups)
3 cups water	2 cups milk
1 Tbsp. instant chicken	¼ tsp. ground black
bouillon granules	pepper

1. In a large skillet cook bacon over medium heat until crisp. Remove bacon, reserving 1 tablespoon drippings in skillet. Drain bacon on paper towels. Crumble bacon; set aside.

2. In a large saucepan combine potatoes, water, and chicken bouillon granules. Bring to boiling; reduce heat. Simmer, covered, about 15 minutes or until potatoes are very tender.

3. Meanwhile, cook onions in reserved bacon drippings over medium-low heat for 8 to 10 minutes or until tender and golden brown. Remove from skillet; set aside.

4. Do not drain potatoes. Use a potato masher to mash potatoes slightly. Stir in bacon, onions, milk, and pepper; heat through. If desired, season to taste with additional pepper. To serve, spoon into 6 bowls. Makes 6 side-dish servings.

low fat Each serving: 201 cal., 6 g total fat (3 g sat. fat), 14 mg chol., 600 mg sodium, 27 g carbo., 3 g fiber, 8 g pro. Daily Values: 34% vit. C, 12% calcium, 7% iron.

ITALIAN DINNER

Tomato-Basil Soup *(above right)*
Green Lasagna *(page 277)*
Steamed carrots
Garlic breadsticks
Italian Cheesecake *(page 299)*
Red wine or sparkling water
Espresso

Tomato-Basil Soup

When tomatoes first arrived in France, they were called "pommes d'amour," or "love apples." So Jana is sure her tomato soup will inspire passion. "The rich tomato taste is enhanced by basil, which brings out friendliness, and a touch of cream, which makes anyone happy," she asserts. "Armagnac is a special brandy whose long aging gives the soup depth and is said to arouse age-old passions." If you prefer, let everyone add the cheese, cream, Armagnac, and chopped tomato-basil mixture to taste.

PREP: 30 minutes **COOK:** about 40 minutes

3½ lb. ripe beefsteak or	¼ tsp. cracked black pepper
globe tomatoes	6 oz. Gruyère or
2 Tbsp. unsalted butter	Emmentaler cheese,
2 cloves garlic, minced	grated
2 to 3 small onions, diced	½ cup whipping cream
1½ cups loosely packed	1 Tbsp. Armagnac or
fresh basil leaves	brandy (optional)
1½ tsp. sea salt or kosher salt	

1. Set aside 1 tomato. Peel remaining tomatoes by dipping into boiling water for 30 seconds or until skins start to split. Dip into cold water; when cool enough to handle, remove skins and core tomatoes. Coarsely chop; set aside.

2. In a 4-quart Dutch oven melt butter over high heat. Add garlic; cook for 30 seconds. Add onions; cook for 4 to 5 minutes or until tender. Add chopped tomatoes; bring to boiling. Simmer, covered, for 30 minutes, stirring occasionally.

3. Puree tomato mixture in batches in food processor or food mill (discard tomato seeds and onion pulp if using food mill). Return liquid to pan.

4. Meanwhile, finely chop basil; reserve ¼ cup. Stir basil, salt, and pepper into tomato mixture. Heat through. Add cheese, whipping cream, and Armagnac, if desired. Heat and stir until cheese is just melted (natural or unprocessed cheese may give soup a slightly grainy texture).

5. To serve, spoon soup into 6 bowls. Chop remaining tomato; combine with reserved basil. Sprinkle tomato mixture onto each serving. Makes 6 side-dish servings.

Each serving: 284 cal., 22 g total fat (13 g sat. fat), 70 mg chol., 26 mg sodium, 14 g carbo., 3 g fiber, 12 g pro. Daily Values: 53% vit. A, 71% vit. C, 33% calcium, 9% iron.

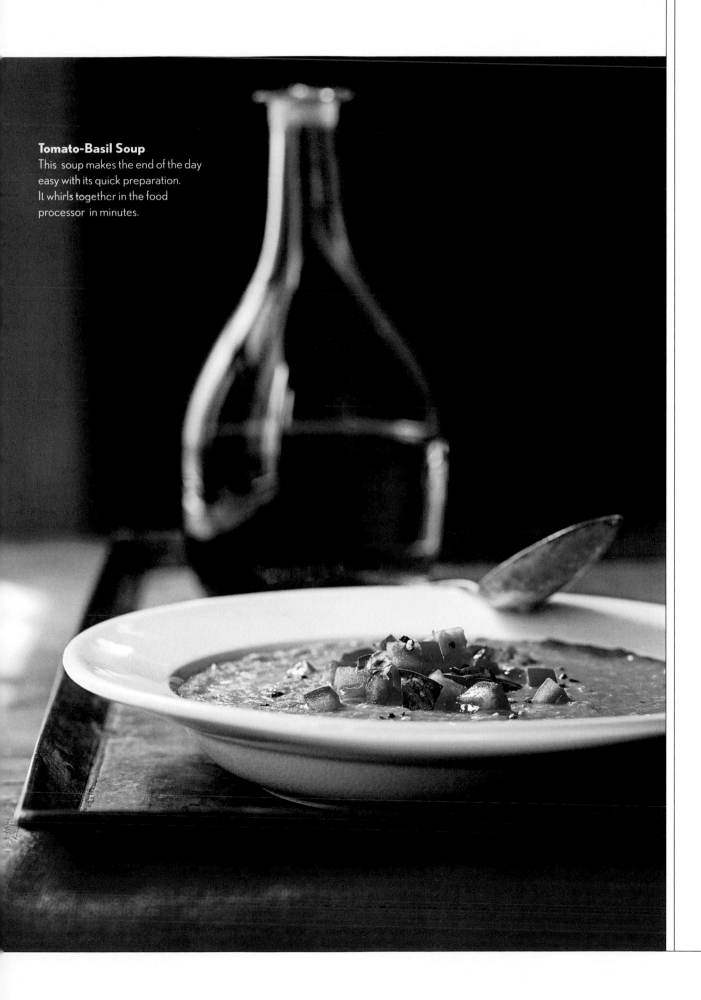

Tomato-Basil Soup
This soup makes the end of the day
easy with its quick preparation.
It whirls together in the food
processor in minutes.

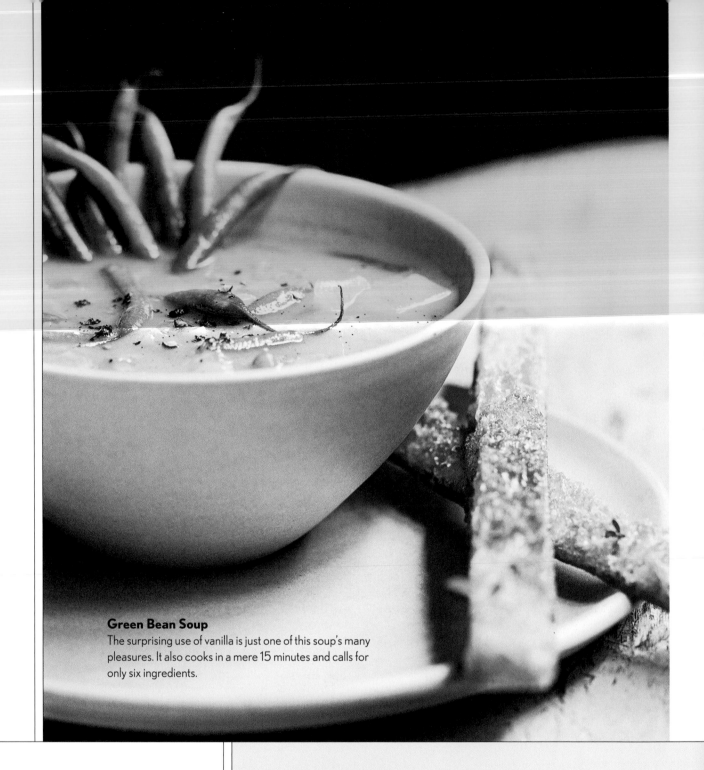

Green Bean Soup
The surprising use of vanilla is just one of this soup's many pleasures. It also cooks in a mere 15 minutes and calls for only six ingredients.

COLOR YOUR SOUP

What makes a soup exciting at first glance may not be what's in it, but what's on it. For an attention grabber, float a colorful ingredient on top, such as the green beans above, the tomatoes on page 187 or the beets on page 185. Try some of the ideas below and think of complementary or contrasting colors for your soups.

- Brighten with orange: Curl long shreds of orange peel, carrot, or cheddar cheese on top. Or chop it finely. And if you have 'em, pieces of orange peppers or tomatoes work well.
- Shine with yellow: Strips or pieces of lemon, yellow squash, or yellow pepper lift soup. And remember corn kernels, slices of pear, golden caviar, or yellow edible flowers.
- Splash with red: Beets, radishes, apples, tomatoes, red peppers, red caviar, and pomegranates all have their own shade of red. Chop, shred, julienne, or slice for the right look.
- Go with green: One of the easiest colors to add to soup, green means a sprig of herb, capers, snipped chives or green onion, or snippets of green pepper, zucchini, or lime.

Green Bean Soup

Haricots vert are tiny French green beans, but you can substitute regular-size green beans if you like.

PREP: 25 minutes **COOK:** 15 minutes

2	14-oz. cans vegetable broth	1	lb. haricots vert or green beans, cut into bite-size pieces (3 to 3½ cups)
1	medium onion, chopped (½ cup)	8	oz. whole haricots vert (optional)
½	of a vanilla bean*, split lengthwise	1	recipe Herb Sourdough Breadsticks (below) (optional)
3	Tbsp. butter, softened		
3	Tbsp. all-purpose flour		

1. In a large saucepan combine broth, onion, and vanilla bean. Bring to boiling; reduce heat. Cover and simmer about 10 minutes or until onion is tender. Discard vanilla bean.

2. In a small bowl stir together butter and flour. Whisk into broth mixture. Cook and stir until slightly thickened and bubbly.

3. Add beans; return to boiling. Reduce heat; cover and simmer for 5 to 7 minutes or until beans are crisp-tender. Meanwhile, if desired, place whole haricots vert in a steamer basket. Cover and steam over boiling water about 5 minutes or until tender; drain.

4. To serve, ladle soup into 6 to 8 bowls. If desired, add steamed whole haricots vert; serve with Herbed Sourdough Breadsticks. Makes 6 to 8 side-dish servings.

HERB SOURDOUGH BREADSTICKS: Preheat oven to 375° F. Cut half of a 12-inch sourdough baguette lengthwise into ½-inch-thick slices. Cut into 1-inch-wide sticks. Brush cut surfaces with 2 tablespoons olive oil; sprinkle with 1 teaspoon snipped fresh thyme. Place on a baking sheet. Bake about 16 minutes or until golden brown.

*NOTE: Store the unused half of the vanilla bean in the refrigerator, wrapped in plastic wrap, in an airtight jar for up to 6 months.

Each serving: 94 cal., 7 g total fat (4 g sat. fat), 16 mg chol., 607 mg sodium, 11 g carbo., 3 g fiber, 2 g pro. Daily Values: 13% vit. A, 15% vit. C, 3% calcium, 6% iron.

Root Vegetable and Bean Soup

Underappreciated for decades, the simple technique of roasting has come back into fashion. We love the way roasting adds a caramel color and flavor to fruits and vegetables. Here root vegetables (also making a culinary comeback) get the royal roasting treatment in this utterly satisfying vegetarian soup.

START TO FINISH: 40 minutes

2	medium parsnips, peeled and cut into ½-inch pieces (1½ cups)	1	Tbsp. olive oil
1	medium potato, cut into ½-inch pieces (1 cup)	½	tsp. sea salt or kosher salt
1	small rutabaga, peeled and cut into ½-inch pieces (1 cup)	3	cups vegetable or chicken broth
2	medium carrots, sliced ½ inch thick	1	15-oz. can small red beans, garbanzo beans, or great northern beans, rinsed and drained
1	medium onion, cut into 8 wedges	2	tsp. snipped fresh thyme

1. Preheat oven to 450° F. In a large roasting pan combine parsnips, potato, rutabaga, carrots, and onion with oil; sprinkle with salt and toss. Spread in a single layer in the pan. Roast for 15 to 20 minutes or until the vegetables start to brown.

2. In a large saucepan bring broth and beans to boiling; add roasted vegetables. Return to boiling; reduce heat. Simmer, covered, about 5 minutes or until vegetables are tender. Stir in thyme. (For a thicker consistency, mash vegetables and beans slightly.) Makes 4 side-dish servings.

low fat Each serving: 274 cal., 5 g total fat (1 g sat. fat), 0 mg chol., 1,338 mg sodium, 58 g carbo., 13 g fiber, 11 g pro. Daily Values: 150% vit. A, 44% vit. C, 8% calcium, 22% iron.

Cauliflower-Crab Chowder

Creamy seafood chowder reaches beyond the usual potatoes to cauliflower, cream cheese, and a splash of sherry.

START TO FINISH: 35 minutes

2	cups frozen cauliflower	2	Tbsp. chopped pimiento
1/2	cup water		or roasted red sweet
3	Tbsp. butter		pepper
3	Tbsp. all-purpose flour	1	Tbsp. snipped fresh
1	14-oz. can vegetable or		chives
	chicken broth	1/4	tsp. salt
1 1/4	cups milk	1	6-oz. pkg. frozen
1	3-oz. pkg. cream cheese,		crabmeat, thawed
	cubed		and drained
2	Tbsp. snipped fresh	1/4	cup dry white wine or dry
	parsley		sherry

1. In a medium saucepan combine cauliflower and water. Bring to boiling; reduce heat. Simmer, covered, about 4 minutes or just until crisp-tender. Do not drain. Cut up large pieces of cauliflower; set aside.

2. Meanwhile, in a large saucepan melt butter. Stir in flour. Add broth and milk. Cook and stir until slightly thickened and bubbly.

3. Stir in undrained cauliflower, cream cheese, parsley, pimiento, chives, and salt. Stir over low heat until cheese is melted. Stir in crab; heat through. Stir in wine. To serve, spoon into 6 soup bowls. Makes 6 appetizer servings.

Each serving: 189 cal., 13 g total fat (8 g sat. fat), 64 mg chol., 589 mg sodium, 9 g carbo., 1 g fiber, 10 g pro. Daily Values: 15% vit. A, 42% vit. C, 12% calcium, 6% iron.

SEAFARER'S SUPPER

Seafood-Melon Cocktail *(page 259)*
Cauliflower-Crab Chowder *(above)*
Dill-buttered rolls
Minty Summer Shortcake *(page 294)*
Sparkling water

Hearty Pumpkin Soup

The spices in this pumpkin soup all supposedly have healing qualities—cumin, especially, is thought to bring on peace of mind.

START TO FINISH: 50 minutes

2	Tbsp. butter	7	cups chicken broth
2	tsp. ground cumin	1/2	cup long grain white rice
3/4	tsp. ground turmeric	4	cups coarsely chopped
1/2	tsp. ground cinnamon		green cabbage
2	leeks, chopped (2/3 cup)		Kosher salt or salt
2 1/2	lb. pie pumpkin or acorn		Ground black pepper
	squash, peeled and cut	1	Tbsp. snipped fresh
	into 1- to 1 1/2-inch pieces		tarragon
	(about 9 cups)		

1. In a 5 1/2- to 6-quart stockpot melt butter over medium heat. Add cumin, turmeric, and cinnamon; cook and stir for 1 minute. Add leeks; cook 2 minutes, stirring to coat. Add pumpkin and broth. Bring to boiling; reduce heat. Simmer, covered, for 10 minutes.

2. Add uncooked rice. Simmer, covered, for 10 minutes more. Add cabbage; simmer, covered, for 5 to 10 minutes more or until rice and squash are tender. Season to taste with salt and pepper. Just before serving, add tarragon. To serve, spoon into 10 to 12 bowls. Makes 10 to 12 side-dish or 6 main-dish servings.

low fat Each side-dish serving: 120 cal., 4 g total fat (2 g sat. fat), 7 mg chol., 760 mg sodium, 18 g carbo., 2 g fiber, 4 g pro. Daily Values: 65% vit. A, 30% vit. C, 5% calcium, 8% iron.

Cheesy Chicken-Corn Chowder

PREP: 15 minutes **COOK:** 15 minutes **COOL:** 15 minutes

2	small skinless, boneless	1	cup frozen whole kernel
	chicken breast halves		corn
	(about 8 oz. total)	1/2	cup milk
1/4	cup chopped onion	2	oz. American cheese or
1/4	cup chopped celery		cheddar cheese,
1	10 3/4-oz. can condensed		shredded (1/2 cup)
	cream of chicken soup	2	Tbsp. chopped pimiento

1. In a medium saucepan combine chicken, onion, celery, and 1 cup water. Bring to boiling; reduce heat. Simmer, covered, for 15 to 20 minutes or until chicken is no longer pink.

2. Remove chicken, reserving cooking liquid. When cool, chop chicken; return to pan. Stir in reserved cooking liquid, soup, corn, milk, cheese, and pimiento. Bring just to boiling, stirring until cheese is melted. To serve, spoon into 4 bowls. Makes 4 main-dish servings.

Each serving: 251 cal., 11 g total fat (5 g sat. fat), 54 mg chol., 868 mg sodium, 18 g carbo., 1 g fiber, 21 g pro. Daily Values: 9% vit. A, 16% vit. C, 14% calcium, 5% iron.

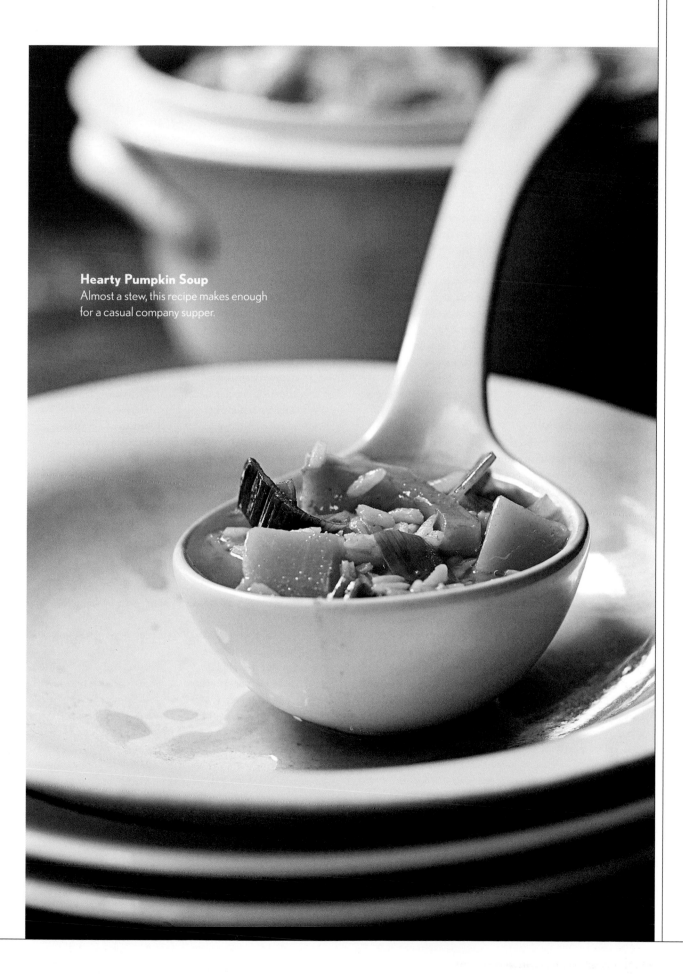

Hearty Pumpkin Soup
Almost a stew, this recipe makes enough
for a casual company supper.

Cassoulet-Style Stew

STAND: 1 hour **PREP:** 50 minutes **COOK:** 1¾ hours

8	oz. dry navy beans	⅔	cup dry black-eyed peas, rinsed and drained
1	meaty lamb shank (1 to 1½ pounds)	½	cup dry red wine or beef broth
1	Tbsp. olive oil or cooking oil	1¼	tsp. salt
1	cup chopped celery (including leaves)	1	Tbsp. snipped fresh thyme or 1 tsp. dried thyme, crushed
1	medium potato, peeled and coarsely chopped	2	tsp. snipped fresh rosemary or ½ tsp. dried rosemary, crushed
½	cup coarsely chopped peeled carrot	¼	tsp. ground black pepper
½	cup coarsely chopped peeled parsnip	1	14½-oz. can diced tomatoes, drained
2	cloves garlic, minced		Fresh rosemary or thyme sprigs (optional)
1½	cups sliced fresh mushrooms		

1. Rinse beans. In a Dutch oven combine beans and 3 cups water. Bring to boiling; reduce heat. Simmer, uncovered, for 2 minutes. Remove from heat. Cover; let stand for 1 hour. (Or place beans in water in a Dutch oven. Cover and let stand in a cool place for 6 to 8 hours or overnight.) Drain beans; rinse. Set aside.

2. In a 4- to 5-quart Dutch oven or kettle brown lamb shank in hot oil over medium-high heat. Add celery, potato, carrot, parsnip, and garlic. Cook over medium-high heat for 5 minutes, stirring frequently. Add 3½ cups water, mushrooms, black-eyed peas, wine, salt, dried thyme (if using), dried rosemary (if using), pepper, and beans. Bring to boiling; reduce heat. Simmer, covered, about 1½ hours or until beans and peas are tender.

3. Remove shank; let cool. Remove meat from shank; chop meat. Stir meat, tomatoes, fresh thyme (if using), and fresh rosemary (if using) into bean mixture. Return to boiling; reduce heat. Simmer, covered, for 15 minutes more.

4. To serve, spoon stew into 6 bowls. If desired, garnish with fresh rosemary or thyme sprigs. Makes 6 main-dish servings.

MAKE-AHEAD DIRECTIONS: Prepare stew as directed. Let cool for 30 minutes. Place stew in freezer containers; freeze for up to 3 months. To serve, place frozen stew in a saucepan. Heat, covered, over medium-low heat about 45 minutes or until heated through, stirring occasionally to break apart mixture.

low fat Each serving: 295 cal., 7 g total fat (2 g sat. fat), 25 mg chol., 662 mg sodium, 39 g carbo., 12 g fiber, 18 g pro. Daily Values: 55% vit. A, 29% vit. C, 13% calcium, 21% iron.

Vegetable-Orzo Soup

Homemade pistou, a basil-based condiment similar to pesto, garnishes this soup. Basil is known as the herb of friendliness, opening you up to the world around you. Use pistou in other friendly ways: Stir it into pasta, spoon it over vegetables, or serve it on top of a baked potato.

STAND: 1 hour **PREP:** 15 minutes **COOK:** 1½ hours

½	cup dry cannellini (white kidney) beans	1	medium zucchini, chopped
½	recipe Bouquet Garni (page 194)	2	medium tomatoes
1	medium onion, chopped (½ cup)	2	sprigs fresh thyme
3	cloves garlic, minced	½	tsp. salt
1	Tbsp. extra-virgin olive oil	⅓	cup dried orzo or any small pasta
3	cups chicken broth	1	recipe Pistou (below)
8	oz. green beans, halved		Grated Parmigiano-Reggiano cheese (optional)
½	of a fennel bulb, chopped (about ⅔ cup)		

1. Rinse beans; drain. In a large saucepan combine beans and 2 cups water. Bring to boiling; reduce heat. Simmer, uncovered, for 2 minutes. Remove from heat. Cover; let stand for 1 hour. (Or place beans in water in the saucepan. Cover; soak overnight in a cool place.) Drain beans; rinse. Set aside.

2. Prepare Bouquet Garni; set aside. In a 4-quart Dutch oven cook onion and garlic in the 1 tablespoon olive oil until tender. Add soaked beans and 2 cups water. Add Bouquet Garni; bring to boiling. Reduce heat; simmer, covered, for 55 minutes. Remove Bouquet Garni; discard.

3. Add chicken broth, green beans, fennel, zucchini, tomatoes, thyme, and salt. Bring to boiling; reduce heat. Simmer, covered, for 20 minutes. Add pasta; simmer, covered, for 10 minutes more. Discard thyme sprigs.

4. To serve, spoon soup into 4 or 5 bowls. Top with Pistou and cheese, if desired. Makes 4 or 5 main-dish servings.

PISTOU: In a food processor or blender combine 2 cups firmly packed basil; 6 cloves garlic, halved; 2 tablespoons grated Parmigiano-Reggiano cheese; and 2 tablespoons olive oil. Cover and process or blend until finely chopped. Thin to desired consistency with an additional 1 to 2 tablespoons olive oil.

Each serving: 400 cal., 20 g total fat (5 g sat. fat), 12 mg chol., 1,350 mg sodium, 39 g carbo., 14 g fiber, 18 g pro. Daily Values: 35% vit. A, 52% vit. C, 33% calcium, 24% iron.

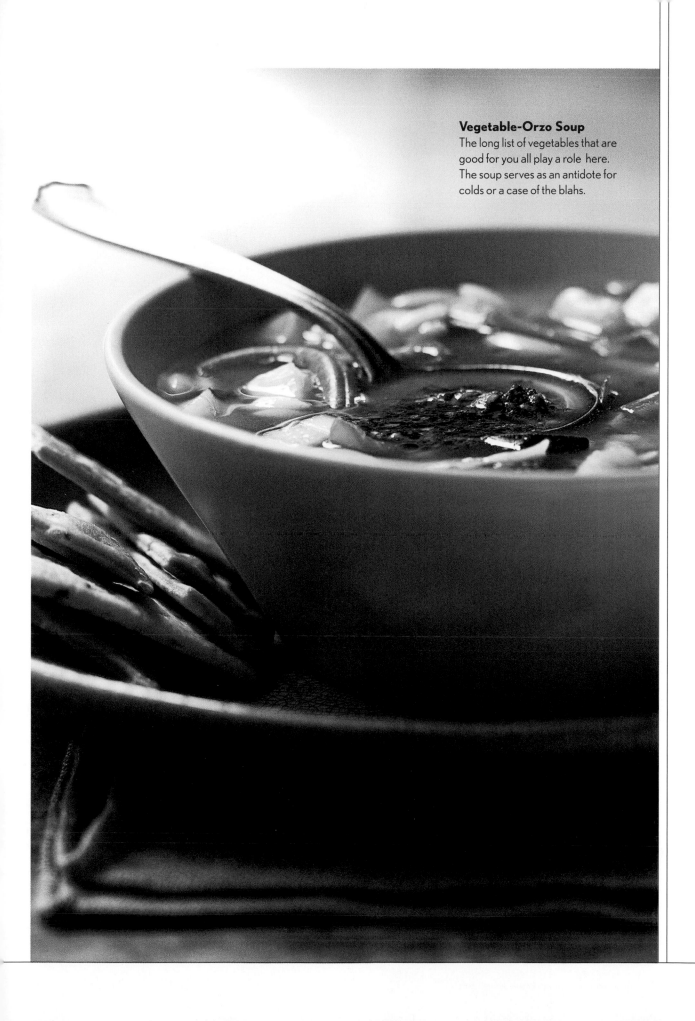

Vegetable-Orzo Soup
The long list of vegetables that are good for you all play a role here. The soup serves as an antidote for colds or a case of the blahs.

Beef and Cabbage Soup

A dash of thyme from the bouquet garni supposedly imparts courage to those who eat this hearty soup. A bouquet garni is a useful cook's bag of tricks. It's a variety of herbs and spices wrapped in cheesecloth and simmered to flavor soups and stews.

PREP: 50 minutes **COOK:** 2 hours

Beef and Cabbage Soup
A long simmer on the stove makes this a great Sunday soup. Serve a stack of thick slices of crusty bread, rubbed with garlic and olive oil, to sop up the last bits.

1 recipe Bouquet Garni (below)	2 medium turnips, peeled and quartered (12 oz. total)
1 lb. slab bacon or prosciutto, diced	1 15- to 19-oz. can navy or cannellini (white kidney) beans
1½ to 2 lb. beef shank cross cuts	4 cloves garlic, minced
6 cups water	4 cups coarsely chopped green cabbage
1½ lb. new potatoes, quartered	Kosher salt or salt
2 medium yellow onions, coarsely chopped (1 cup)	8 slices French bread, toasted and rubbed with olive oil and garlic
4 medium carrots, peeled and quartered crosswise	

1. Prepare Bouquet Garni; set aside. In a 10- to 12-quart stockpot or Dutch oven, cook bacon or prosciutto until crisp, stirring frequently. Remove with a slotted spoon. Drain on paper towels, reserving 2 tablespoons drippings in stockpot. (If using prosciutto, add oil to equal 2 tablespoons.)

2. Brown beef shanks on both sides in reserved drippings. Add water, potatoes, onions, carrots, turnips, undrained beans, garlic, and Bouquet Garni. Bring to boiling; reduce heat. Simmer, covered, for 1½ hours. Add cabbage. Simmer, covered, about 30 minutes more or until meat is tender.

3. Discard Bouquet Garni. Remove beef shanks; cool slightly. Remove meat from bones. Using 2 forks, shred meat; return to soup. Skim fat from soup. Stir in cooked bacon or prosciutto. Heat through. Season to taste with salt.

4. To serve, place a slice of bread in 8 bowls. Spoon soup over bread. Makes 8 main-dish servings.

BOUQUET GARNI: Cut a 10-inch square of 100-percent-cotton cheesecloth. Place 8 sprigs fresh parsley, 2 bay leaves, 12 lightly crushed whole black peppercorns, and 4 or 5 sprigs each of fresh thyme and marjoram on center of cheesecloth. Draw up corners of square to create a bag; tie with clean kitchen string.

Each serving: 548 cal., 23 g total fat (10 g sat. fat), 45 mg chol., 925 mg sodium, 48 g carbo., 8 g fiber, 26 g pro. Daily Values: 155% vit. A, 52% vit. C, 11% calcium, 27% iron.

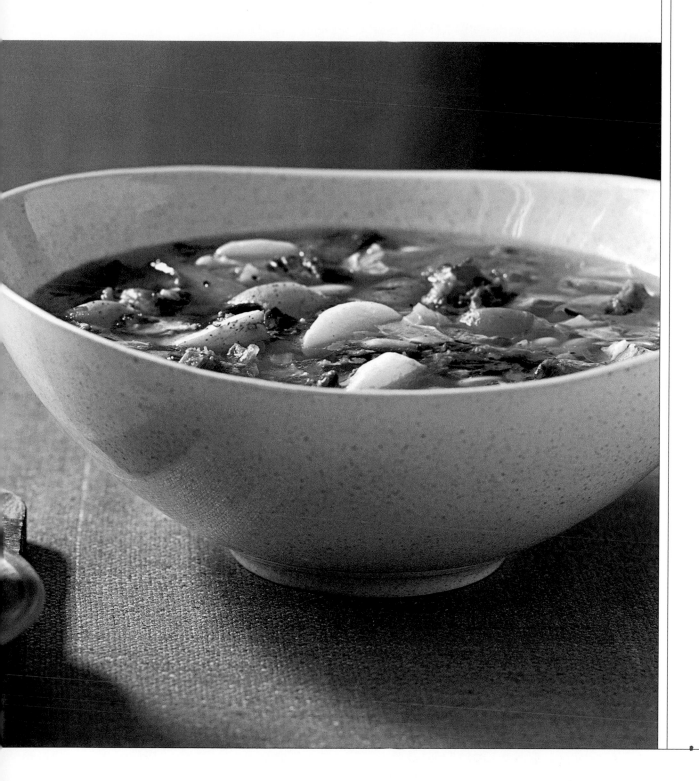

FLAVORED TOASTS FOR SOUP

A toasted slice of French bread or crostini just seems to go with soup, especially when it's flavored. To make your own crostini, cut French bread into 1/2-inch-thick slices. Lightly brush both sides of each slice with olive oil. Arrange the slices on an ungreased baking sheet. If you like, brush on a little garlic, pesto, or olive paste. Or sprinkle with snipped herbs, cracked pepper, or shredded Parmesan cheese. Bake in a 425° F oven for 5 to 7 minutes or until crisp and light brown. Serve warm or cool.

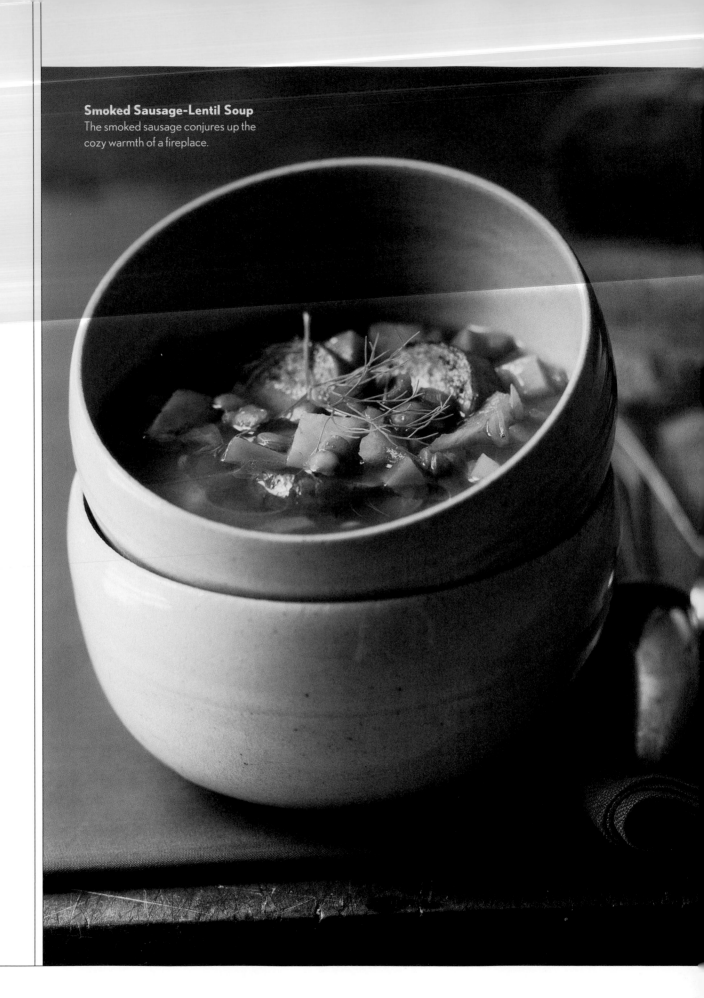

Smoked Sausage-Lentil Soup
The smoked sausage conjures up the
cozy warmth of a fireplace.

Smoked Sausage-Lentil Soup

Lentils are considered to be a symbol of good fortune. In fact, Italians eat lentils at New Year's to bring luck. In addition to lentils, you'll find sausage, carrots, onion, garlic, and anise-like fennel in this lucky soup. Snip the delicate fennel fronds to add a last-minute garnish.

PREP: 20 minutes **COOK:** 25 minutes

1	small fennel bulb, fronds reserved	1¼	cups green lentils, rinsed and drained
4	cloves garlic, minced	2	tsp. kosher salt or sea salt
1	Tbsp. olive oil	¼	tsp. ground black pepper
1	medium onion, chopped (¼ cup)	6	oz. cooked smoked sausage links, cut into
2	medium carrots, chopped		¼-inch-thick pieces
6	cups water	3	Tbsp. red wine vinegar

1. Chop enough of the fennel bulb to measure 1 cup.

2. In a Dutch oven cook garlic in hot oil over medium heat for 1 minute. Add onion; cook until golden brown. Add fennel and carrots; cook until tender, stirring occasionally. Add water, lentils, salt, and pepper; bring to boiling. Reduce heat; simmer, uncovered, for 25 to 30 minutes or until lentils are tender.

3. Meanwhile, in a large skillet brown sausage on all sides. Using a slotted spoon, remove sausage from skillet. Add sausage to soup; stir in red wine vinegar.

4. To serve, spoon soup into 5 or 6 bowls. Top with fennel fronds. Makes 5 to 6 main-dish servings.

Each serving: 347 cal., 14 g total fat (4 g sat. fat), 23 mg chol., 1,314 mg sodium, 34 g carbo., 20 g fiber, 22 g pro. Daily Values: 137% vit. A, 14% vit. C, 6% calcium, 24% iron.

Ham and Bean Stew

PREP: 10 minutes **COOK:** 6 to 8 hours (low), 3 to 4 hours (high)

1	28-oz. can diced tomatoes, undrained	1	cup chopped onion
2½	cups diced cooked ham	¼	cup water
1	15-oz. can navy beans, rinsed and drained	¼	tsp. ground black pepper
1	14¾-oz. can cream-style corn		Dash bottled hot pepper sauce

1. In a 3½- or 4-quart electric slow cooker combine undrained tomatoes, ham, beans, corn, onion, water, black pepper, and hot pepper sauce. Cover; cook on low-heat setting for 6 to 8 hours or on high-heat setting for 3 to 4 hours. To serve, spoon into 5 bowls. Makes 5 main-dish servings.

low fat Each serving: 368 cal., 8 g total fat (3 g sat. fat), 50 mg chol., 2,190 mg sodium, 45 g carbo., 7 g fiber, 29 g pro. Daily Values: 2% vit. A, 43% vit. C, 12% calcium, 22% iron.

Hearty Hodgepodge

A hodgepodge of four different flavorful meats makes this stick-to-your-ribs simmered supper something to remember. Because the bacon, sausage, beef, and ham are so full of flavor, you need little else in the way of seasoning.

PREP: 20 minutes **BAKE:** 1½ hours + 30 + 15 minutes

6	slices bacon	3	cups cubed potatoes (4 medium)
1	medium onion, thinly sliced	1	clove garlic, minced
1	lb. beef shank cross cuts	1	4-oz. link cooked, smoked Polish sausage, thinly sliced
¾	lb. meaty ham bone		
6	cups water	8	French bread slices, toasted and buttered (optional)
½	tsp. salt		
2	15-oz. cans chickpeas (garbanzo beans), drained		

1. In a 4- to 6-quart Dutch oven cook bacon until crisp; drain, reserving 2 tablespoons drippings in pan. Add sliced onion to reserved drippings. Cook and stir until onion is tender. Crumble bacon and chill.

2. Add beef shanks, ham hock, water, and salt to pan. Heat to boiling; reduce heat. Cover and simmer about 1½ hours or until beef is tender.

3. Carefully remove meat from beef shanks and ham hock and cut up; discard bones. Carefully skim fat from broth. Return the cut-up meat to soup; add chickpeas, potatoes, and garlic. Return to boiling; reduce heat. Simmer, covered, for 30 minutes more.

4. Add sausage; simmer, covered, for 15 minutes more. Stir in bacon. To serve, spoon into 8 bowls. If desired, serve with toasted French bread. Makes 8 main-dish servings.

Each serving: 390 cal., 16 g total fat (6 g sat. fat), 40 mg chol., 1,008 mg sodium, 40 g carbo., 6 g fiber, 22 g pro. Daily Values: 1% vit. A, 15% vit. C, 8% calcium, 20% iron.

BROWNED BUTTER

WHAT'S SIMPLER THAN A SAUCE BASED ON BUTTER? NOT MUCH.

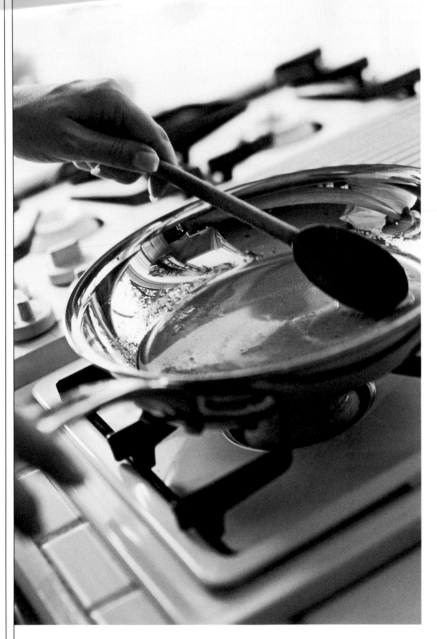

If you think making a sauce is too fussy, too confusing, or too much trouble, there's one you've overlooked: browned butter sauce. Melt a stick of butter, and you're nearly there.

Browned butter is melted butter with a toasted attitude. The taste is bigger and earthier, and the aroma more enticing—much the way a toasted nut compares to a raw one.

Chefs like to make browned butter sauce with butter they've clarified, a process which removes the milk solids from melted butter. You can be more relaxed, though. Instead of clarifying the butter, just pour it through a fine mesh sieve to get a clearer sauce.

To make a simple browned butter sauce for potatoes, steak, or pasta (far right), melt $^1/_2$ cup butter in a medium skillet over medium-low heat. Continue cooking about 10 minutes, stirring the butter, and lifting and swirling the pan occasionally, until the butter is golden brown. Strain the butter through a fine mesh sieve over a bowl. Stir in 2 tablespoons lemon juice and 2 tablespoons snipped fresh parsley. The result is a clear winner.

BY KEN HAEDRICH. PHOTOGRAPHS: COLLEEN DUFFLEY. FOOD STYLIST: BROOKE LEONARD.

Pumpkin Ravioli with Browned Butter
START TO FINISH: 75 minutes

1 recipe Pasta Dough (below)	1/4 tsp. ground cinnamon
1 cup canned pumpkin	1/8 tsp. ground black pepper
1/4 cup butter, melted	Dash ground nutmeg
1/3 cup finely shredded Parmesan cheese	1 egg, slightly beaten
	1/3 cup butter
1/4 tsp. salt	4 fresh sage leaves
	Fresh sage leaves (optional)

1. Prepare Pasta Dough. For filling, in a small bowl stir together pumpkin, the 1/4 cup melted butter, Parmesan, salt, cinnamon, pepper, and nutmeg; set aside.

2. Use a sharp knife to cut pasta into 2- to 2 1/2-inch-wide strips. Leaving a 1/2-inch margin on edges, place 1 slightly rounded teaspoon of filling at 1 1/2-inch intervals on 1 strip of dough.

3. Using a pastry brush, brush dough around mounds of filling with egg. Lay a second strip of dough atop the first. Press pasta around each mound of filling so the dough sticks together. With a fluted pastry wheel or a sharp knife, cut the pasta between the mounds of filling to separate into squares. (To prevent the filled ravioli from tearing or sticking until you are ready to cook them, lay them on a lightly floured surface without touching.)

4. In a Dutch oven cook the ravioli, half at a time, in boiling salted water for 2 minutes or until tender. Use a slotted spoon to transfer to a colander-lined bowl; drain well.

5. Melt the 1/3 cup butter in a large skillet over medium-low heat. Continue cooking about 10 minutes or until butter is golden brown, stirring butter and lifting and swirling the pan occasionally. Add the 4 sage leaves. Cook and stir for 1 minute. Remove from heat.

6. To serve, arrange the ravioli on 6 plates. Top with sage butter. If desired, garnish with additional fresh sage leaves. Serve warm. Makes 6 servings.

PASTA DOUGH: In a large bowl stir together 2 cups all-purpose flour and 1/2 teaspoon salt. Make a well in the center of the flour mixture. In a small bowl combine 2 eggs, 1/3 cup water, and 1 teaspoon olive oil. Add to flour mixture; stir to combine. Sprinkle a clean kneading surface with 1/3 cup all-purpose flour. Turn dough out onto floured surface. Knead until dough is smooth and elastic (8 to 10 minutes total). Cover; let the dough rest for 10 minutes. Divide dough into 4 equal portions. On a lightly floured surface roll each portion into a 12-inch square (about 1/16 inch thick). Let stand, uncovered, about 20 minutes. Or, if using a pasta machine, pass each portion through the machine according to manufacturer's directions until dough is 1/16 inch thick.

Each serving: 509 cal., 31 g total fat (18 g sat. fat), 178 mg chol., 1,014 mg sodium, 39 g carbo., 2 g fiber, 19 g pro. Daily Values: 201% vit. A, 3% vit. C, 40% calcium, 19% iron.

BUTTER 'EM UP
Try these simple ideas for browned butter or make some traditional ravioli with your own pasta at left.

POTATOES: Spooning browned butter into mashed potatoes is a Pennsylvania Dutch tradition. But don't stop with potatoes. Steamed vegetables taste bolder with a browned butter drizzle.

STEAK: A spoonful of browned butter sauce over steak does double duty: It enhances any topper, such as a quick mushroom sauté, plus gives the steak a shiny, moist glaze.

PASTA: Toss browned butter with hot pasta as an alternative to sauce or olive oil. Take full advantage of the nutty flavor by keeping the accompaniments simple.

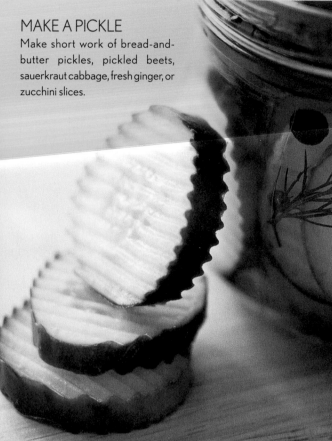

MAKE A PICKLE
Make short work of bread-and-butter pickles, pickled beets, sauerkraut cabbage, fresh ginger, or zucchini slices.

SHRED A SALAD
Create a sassy, colorful slaw with cabbages, peppers, carrots, fennel, and radishes.

SAVVY SLICING
THE MANDOLINE CUTS A JAZZY TUNE IN THE KITCHEN REPERTOIRE. PLAY IT SAFE, THOUGH.

For the record, the mandoline is a precision cutting tool with a precise job description: cutting thin, uniform, or decorative slices from potatoes, cucumbers, cabbages, lettuces, carrots, and the like. It won't replace your knives, but it's a useful supplement to your other cutting tools.

When purchasing a mandoline, it's a good idea to spend a few extra dollars for one with all the bells and whistles. Check for stability, a comfortable angle for slicing, and blades that are easy to change or adjust for thickness. Blades should give you the cuts you want, such as a ripple cut or wafer-thin slices. Make sure there is a finger guard or food carriage for safety.

The mandoline is a quick and creative tool that brings a level of artistry to a dish's final presentation. But you need a little practice before using it becomes second nature, so pay special attention to the safety tips, *right*.

BY KEN HAEDRICH. PHOTOGRAPHS: COLLEEN DUFFLEY. FOOD STYLIST: BROOKE LEONARD.

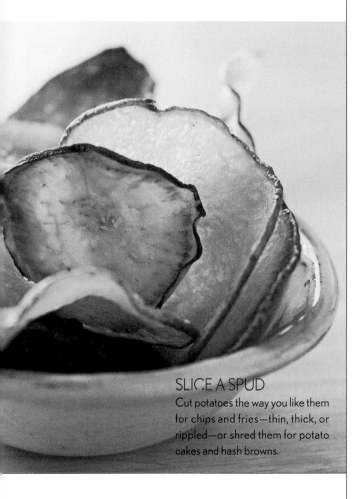

SLICE A SPUD

Cut potatoes the way you like them for chips and fries—thin, thick, or rippled—or shred them for potato cakes and hash browns.

SAFETY TIPS

- Place the mandoline on a damp tea towel to prevent it from sliding around. If a table clamp comes with your model, use it.
- Dry your hands thoroughly before using your mandoline so you won't slip and cut yourself.
- Let the mandoline do the work. The blades are sharp; slide foods over them—don't push.
- Use the finger guard at all times.
- Preslice the bottom side of the food first to create a flat surface for cutting.
- Always cut away from you, not toward.
- When the finger guard starts to stick or the food becomes difficult to move over the blades, stop slicing. Reserve the remainder of the vegetable or fruit you're cutting for another use.
- Take care to avoid exposed blades when cleaning.
- Keep the mandoline away from children!

Artichoke and Basil Hero

Practice slicing cheese and firm tomatoes for this hearty sandwich. You'll find the mandoline makes quick work of slicing all sorts of sandwich fixings.

START TO FINISH: 30 minutes

1 cup fresh basil (leaves only)	1 16-oz. loaf unsliced French bread
1/4 cup olive oil or salad oil	1 14-oz. can artichoke hearts, drained and sliced
2 Tbsp. grated Parmesan cheese	4 oz. sliced provolone cheese
1 Tbsp. capers, drained	1 medium tomato, thinly sliced
1 Tbsp. white wine vinegar	2 cups torn fresh spinach
2 tsp. Dijon-style mustard	
1 clove garlic, quartered	

1. In a blender or food processor combine basil, oil, Parmesan cheese, capers, vinegar, mustard, and garlic. Cover; blend or process until nearly smooth. Set aside.

2. Cut bread in half lengthwise. Hollow out each half, leaving a 1/2- to 1-inch-thick shell. (Save bread crumbs for another use.)

3. Spread basil mixture onto cut side of each bread half. On bottom half, layer artichoke hearts, provolone cheese, tomato, and spinach. Cover with top half of bread. To serve, cut sandwich crosswise into 6 slices. Makes 6 servings.

Each serving: 396 cal., 17 g total fat (5 g sat. fat), 14 mg chol., 887 mg sodium, 46 g carbo., 4 g fiber, 15 g pro. Daily Values: 18% vit. C, 24% calcium, 23% iron.

EASY SUBSTITUTES

DON'T DESPAIR WHEN YOU RUN OUT OF A KEY RECIPE INGREDIENT AND THE PANTRY HOLDS ONLY ITS DISTANT COUSIN. THIS HANDY CHART WILL HELP YOU REPLACE THE MISSING ITEM.

AIOLI (1/2 CUP): Mix 1/2 cup mayonnaise and 1 large garlic clove, minced.

APPLE CIDER (2 TBSP.): Combine 2 tablespoons apple juice and 1/4 teaspoon cider vinegar.

BAKING POWDER (1 TSP.): Combine 1/2 teaspoon cream of tartar with 1/4 teaspoon baking soda.

BALSAMIC VINEGAR (1 TBSP.): Combine 1 tablespoon cider vinegar or red wine vinegar and 1/2 teaspoon sugar.

CAKE FLOUR (1 CUP): Omit 2 tablespoons from 1 cup all-purpose flour.

CAPERS (1 TBSP.): Use 1 tablespoon chopped green olives.

CHILI OIL (1 TBSP.): Whisk a few drops of hot pepper sauce and/or red pepper flakes into 1 tablespoon olive oil or vegetable oil.

CHIVES: Substitute an equal amount of snipped green onion tops.

CILANTRO: For fresh, substitute an equal amount of fresh parsley. For dried, substitute equal parts dried parsley and dried coriander.

CRÉME FRAICHE (1 CUP): Combine 1/2 cup whipping cream and 1/2 cup sour cream. Let stand at room temperature for 30 minutes. Chill for longer storage. (Note: Do not use ultra-pasteurized whipping cream.)

EGGS (LARGE): If your egg size is different than large, try this:
Jumbo: For 1 or 2 eggs, substitute 1 jumbo egg for each egg called for. For 3 or more, use the number called for minus 1.
Extra large: Up to 4 eggs, substitute 1 for 1. For 5 or more, use the number called for minus 1.
Medium: Up to 3 eggs, substitute 1 for 1. For 4 or more, use the number called for plus one.

FRESH GARLIC (1 CLOVE): Use 1/2 teaspoon bottled minced garlic or 1/8 teaspoon garlic powder.

FRESH GINGERROOT (1 TSP.): Use 1/4 teaspoon ground ginger.

HERBES DE PROVENCE: Mix together at least 5 of the following dried spices in a mortar and pestle: basil, fennel seeds, lavender, marjoram, rosemary, sage, savory, or thyme.

MADIERA (1 TBSP.): Stir together 1 tablespoon red wine and 1/2 teaspoon sugar.

MOLASSES (1 CUP): Substitute 1 cup of honey.

PRESERVED LEMON SLICES: Brush lemon slices with olive oil; sprinkle liberally with kosher salt. Cover with paper towel and let stand for 10 to 30 minutes.

SAFFRON: Substitute an equal amount of turmeric.

SESAME SEEDS (1 TBSP.): Substitute 1 tablespoon finely chopped blanched almonds.

SOUR CREAM: Use an equal amount of plain low-fat yogurt.

STAR ANISE: Substitute an equal amount of Chinese five-spice powder or ground anise seeds.

TAMARI (2 TEASPOONS): Substitute 1 tablespoon soy sauce.

TOMATO PASTE (1/2 CUP): Cook 1 cup tomato sauce, uncovered, until reduced to 1/2 cup.

VANILLA EXTRACT: Substitute an equal amount of almond extract plus a pinch of cream of tartar.

Moussaka

Check out the ingredient list for this Greek classic before you start cooking. If you don't have exactly what you need, there are some smart substitutions you can make, using the list opposite.

PREP: 40 minutes **BAKE:** 35 minutes **STAND:** 10 minutes

2	1-lb. eggplants, peeled and cut into 1/2-inch-thick slices	3/4	tsp. salt
1/4	cup cooking oil	1/4	tsp. dried oregano, crushed
2	lb. ground lamb or ground beef	1/4	tsp. ground cinnamon
1	large onion, chopped (1 cup)	1	beaten egg
1	clove garlic, minced	1/4	cup butter or margarine
1	8-oz. can tomato sauce	1/4	cup all-purpose flour
3/4	cup dry red wine	1/2	tsp. salt
2	Tbsp. snipped fresh parsley		Dash ground black pepper
		2	cups milk
		3	eggs
		1/4	cup grated Parmesan cheese

1. Preheat oven to 325° F. Brush both sides of eggplant slices with the oil. In a large skillet brown eggplant slices over medium heat about 2 minutes per side. Drain; set aside.

2. In the same skillet cook ground lamb, half at a time, until meat is brown, cooking onion and garlic with the second half of meat. Drain off fat. Stir in tomato sauce, wine, parsley, the 3/4 teaspoon salt, oregano, and cinnamon. Heat to boiling; reduce heat. Simmer, uncovered, for 10 minutes or until most of the liquid is absorbed. Cool mixture slightly. Stir 1/2 cup of the meat mixture into the 1 beaten egg. Stir egg mixture into meat mixture in skillet.

3. Meanwhile, in a medium saucepan melt butter. Stir in flour, the 1/2 teaspoon salt, and pepper. Add milk all at once. Cook and stir until thickened and bubbly. Cook and stir for 1 minute more. In a medium bowl beat the 3 eggs. Gradually stir the thickened milk mixture into the beaten eggs.

4. In a 3-quart rectangular baking dish arrange half of the eggplant slices. Spread meat mixture over eggplant slices; top with remaining eggplant slices. Pour hot egg mixture over all. Top with Parmesan cheese; sprinkle with additional cinnamon. Bake, uncovered, for 35 to 40 minutes or until edges are bubbly. Let stand for 10 minutes. To serve, cut into squares. If desired, sprinkle with additional parsley. Makes 8 to 10 servings.

Each serving: 536 cal., 39 g total fat (16 g sat. fat), 207 mg chol., 764 mg sodium, 16 g carbo., 3 g fiber, 27 g pro. Daliy Values: 19% vit. A, 14% vit. C, 16% calcium, 17% iron.

Banana Split Cake

Hopefully, you have all of the ingredients for this soda-fountain-inspired pound cake right on your shelf. But if not, the list opposite will help you pinch-hit your way to a home run.

PREP: 30 minutes **BAKE:** 55 minutes **STAND:** 30 minutes

1	cup butter	1/2	cup milk
4	eggs	1	tsp. vanilla
3	cups all-purpose flour	1/2	cup strawberry preserves
2	tsp. baking powder		Few drops red food coloring
1	tsp. salt	1/2	cup presweetened cocoa powder (not low calorie)
1/4	tsp. baking soda		
1 1/2	cups sugar	1	12-oz. jar chocolate fudge ice cream topping
1	large banana, mashed (1/2 cup)		Vanilla ice cream (optional)
1/2	cup dairy sour cream		

1. Let butter and eggs stand at room temperature for 30 minutes. Preheat oven to 350° F. Meanwhile, grease and flour a 10-inch fluted tube pan. In a medium bowl stir together flour, baking powder, salt, and baking soda. Set aside.

2. In a large bowl beat butter with an electric mixer on low to medium speed for 30 seconds. Add sugar; beat until fluffy. Add eggs, 1 at a time, beating well after each addition. In a small bowl, combine banana, sour cream, milk, and vanilla. Alternately add flour mixture and banana mixture to butter mixture, beating on low speed after each addition just until combined.

3. Stir 1/2 cup strawberry preserves and red food coloring into 1 cup of the batter. Stir cocoa powder into another 1 cup of the batter. Spoon half the remaining plain batter into prepared pan. Spoon strawberry batter over plain batter. Top with remaining plain, then chocolate batter.

4. Bake for 55 to 65 minutes or until a wooden toothpick inserted near center comes out clean. Cool in pan on a wire rack for 10 minutes; remove from pan. Cool on wire rack.

5. Before serving, in a small saucepan heat chocolate fudge ice cream topping until warm; drizzle onto cake. If desired, serve cake with ice cream; top with additional chocolate fudge topping. Makes 12 servings.

Each serving: 561 cal., 24 g total fat (14 g sat. fat), 121 mg chol., 635 mg sodium, 79 g carbo., 2 g fiber, 8 g pro. Daliy Values: 16% vit. A, 3% vit. C, 11% calcium, 10% iron..

BY JEANNE AMBROSE. PHOTOGRAPHS: GREG SCHEIDEMANN/N)HAUS FOTO. FOOD STYLIST: CHARLES WORTHINGTON.

SWEET AND SIMPLE

HERE'S HOW TO WOW A CELEBRATION CROWD IN THREE EASY STEPS. TAKE THE CAKE. FROST. EMBELLISH.

(Purchased cake and frosting from a can makes the project even simpler.)

SAY IT WITH A SUNFLOWER

Chocolate chips mimic sunflower seeds when arranged in a circle and surrounded by edible chrysanthemum petals and mint leaves. Be sure to use only edible flowers and herbs that have been grown organically (not those from a florist). Sunflower blossoms also are edible. So if you've still got some of the sunny flowers nodding on their stalks in your garden, borrow some of their petals. Let your guests know that mums and sunflower petals have a slightly bitter taste.

LOLLIPOP CAROUSEL

This brilliantly colored merry-go-round of a cake is gussied up in minutes. Use scissors to trim the sticks so the candies peek out above the edge of the cake. Remove the wrappers. Guide the lollipops in place by holding the top of the candy with your fingertips (plastic gloves, please) and pressing each lollipop into place.

SWEET LEAVES OF THE SEASON

Make melt-in-your-mouth leaves out of thinly rolled chocolate. Or stencil leaf patterns on top of the cake.

STENCILED LEAVES: Place leaf-shape cookie cutters on frosting; sprinkle sifted cocoa powder or colored decorative sugar inside. Remove cutters to reveal the pattern.

CHOCOLATE LEAVES: In a small saucepan melt 6 ounces semisweet chocolate over low heat, stirring often; cool slightly. Stir in 3 tablespoons light-colored corn syrup (do not overmix). Transfer to a large sheet of waxed paper. Cover; let stand at room temperature for 6 to 24 hours or until dry. (The mixture stiffens after standing, but kneading makes it pliable again.) Gently knead for 10 to 15 strokes or until smooth and pliable. If too soft, chill in the refrigerator about 15 minutes or until easy to handle. To make leaves, shape half of the chocolate mixture into a ball. Flatten slightly; place between 2 sheets of waxed paper dusted lightly with powdered sugar. Roll to 1/8-inch thickness. Use 2-inch leaf-shape cookie cutters to cut chocolate. Repeat with remaining half. Dust leaves with cocoa powder or colored decorative sugar. Store unused chocolate in a sealed plastic bag at room temperature for 3 to 4 weeks. Makes about thirty-six 2-inch leaves.

Best-Ever Chocolate Cake
PREP: 30 minutes **BAKE:** 30 minutes **COOL:** 1 hour

3/4 cup butter, softened	1/2 tsp. salt
3 eggs	2 cups sugar
2 cups all-purpose flour	2 tsp. vanilla
3/4 cup unsweetened cocoa powder	1 1/2 cups milk
1 tsp. baking soda	1 recipe Chocolate-Sour Cream Frosting (below)
3/4 tsp. baking powder	

1. Let butter and eggs stand at room temperature for 30 minutes. Lightly grease bottoms of three 8x1 1/2- or 9x1 1/2-inch round cake pans. Line bottoms of pans with waxed paper. Grease and lightly flour bottoms and sides of pans. Set pans aside.

2. Preheat oven to 350° F. In a mixing bowl stir together flour, cocoa powder, baking soda, baking powder, and salt; set aside.

3. In a large mixing bowl beat butter with an electric mixer on medium to high speed for 30 seconds. Gradually add sugar, about 1/2 cup at a time, beating on medium speed for 3 to 4 minutes or until combined. Scrape side of bowl; continue beating on medium speed for 2 minutes. Add eggs, 1 at a time, beating after each addition (about 1 minute total). Beat in vanilla.

4. Alternately add flour mixture and milk to beaten mixture, beating on low speed after each addition just until combined. Beat on medium to high speed for 20 seconds more. Spread batter evenly in the prepared pans.

5. Bake for 30 to 35 minutes or until a wooden toothpick inserted in the centers comes out clean.

6. Cool cake layers in pans for 10 minutes. Remove from pans. Peel off waxed paper. Cool on a wire rack.

7. Prepare Chocolate-Sour Cream Frosting. Frost cake with frosting. Decorate cake as desired. Cut cake into wedges to serve. Cover and store any leftover cake in the refrigerator. Makes 12 to 16 servings.

CHOCOLATE-SOUR CREAM FROSTING: In a large saucepan melt one 12-ounce package semisweet chocolate pieces and 1/2 cup butter over low heat, stirring frequently. Cool for 5 minutes. Stir in one 8-ounce carton dairy sour cream. Gradually add 4 1/2 cups sifted powdered sugar, beating until smooth.

Each serving: 760 cal., 36 g total fat (20 g sat. fat), 118 mg chol., 475 mg sodium, 99 g carbo., 5 g fiber, 7 g pro. Daily Values: 21% vit. A, 14% calcium.

November

HOME IS WHERE THE HEART IS–ESPECIALLY WHEN
IT'S TIME FOR THE FAMILY FEAST OF THE YEAR.

Homecoming Feast

homecoming FEAST

grandpa

IT'S THAT TIME OF YEAR WHEN YOUR FAVORITE
PEOPLE—AND FOOD—COME TOGETHER
AGAIN. HERE'S HOW TO MAKE IT ALL HAPPEN.

Pomegranate Starter

Served in individual cups, this warm, sweet starter soup is a three-ingredient sensation. Look for pomegranate juice in the refrigerated produce section of grocery stores, health food stores, or online at www.pomwonderful.com.

PREP: 15 minutes **STAND:** 10 minutes

3½ cups pomegranate juice
     or red grape juice
  1 2-inch strip tangerine peel

½ tsp. coriander seeds,
    lightly crushed, or ¼ tsp.
    ground coriander

1. In a medium saucepan heat pomegranate juice just until simmering; remove from heat. Add tangerine peel and coriander; let stand, covered, for 10 minutes.

2. Strain juice through a fine-mesh sieve. Discard the solids. To serve, ladle juice into small heatproof cups. Makes 10 to 12 servings (about 3 ounces each).

low fat Each serving: 53 cal., 0 g total fat, 0 mg chol., 4 mg sodium, 13 g carbo., 0 g fiber, 0 g pro. Daily Values: 16% vit. C, 2% iron.

Pomegranate Starter

A Time to Remember

From the sweet squeeze of a toddler's little arms around your neck to the comfy hold-tight hugs of your favorite uncle, when everyone comes home again, it's an experience to savor. No matter what event you're celebrating—a gathering of old college chums, Grandpa's 80th birthday, or the annual Thanksgiving dinner—your home is about to become a sanctuary for loved ones. Plan for good cheer and great food that will make this a homecoming to remember for years to come.

Be sure to serve foods that stir up warm memories—a few tried-and-true favorites and traditional family fare. The pièce de résistance? A turkey, of course, whetting appetites with the savory smells of the season as it roasts. Set out wines, glasses, and a cork puller, and let people help themselves. For the younger set, have a stash of soft drinks chilled. If the weather's nippy, a warm mulled cider simmering in a slow cooker is yummy.

Encourage those who want to help to step up to the stove and strut their stuffing. Put kids to work mashing potatoes—don't forget the extra aprons! Leave time to step back and bask in the warmth of your family's familiar routine of working as a crew: chopping and teasing, mashing and laughing, stirring and noshing. Better yet, capture those moments on film. (A teenager and a digital camera are incredible together.)

Forgotten anything? It's OK. You're with family and friends. Just have fun!

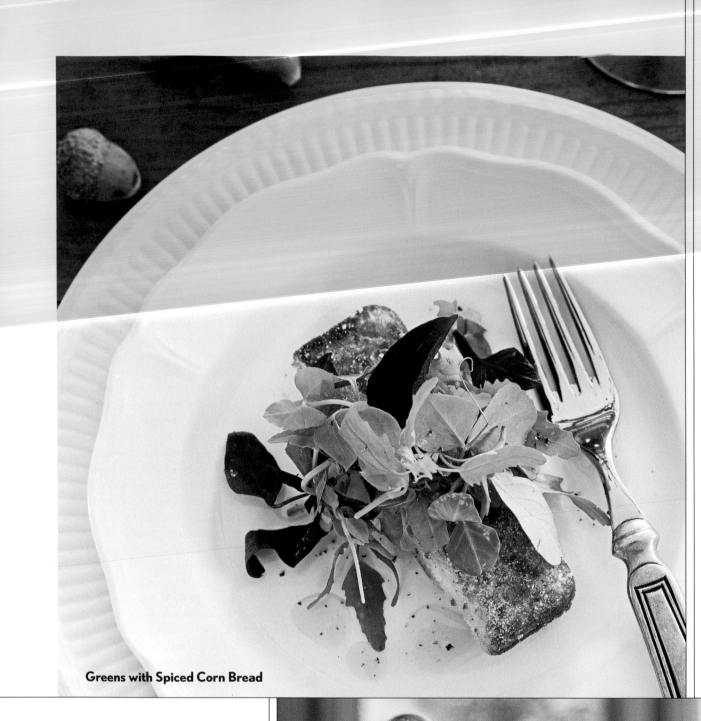

Greens with Spiced Corn Bread

Roasted Beet and Goat Cheese Salad

If you find fresh beets with the greens still attached, go ahead and include them as part of the mixed greens to add color.

PREP: 30 minutes   **ROAST:** 40 minutes

1 lb. red baby beets or small beets, rinsed and trimmed	10 cups baby salad greens (mesclun) or other mild salad greens
1 Tbsp. olive oil	1 8-oz. tube semisoft goat cheese (chèvre or Montrachet), cut into 1/2-inch rounds
1/3 cup olive oil	
1/4 cup white wine vinegar	
2 tsp. Dijon-style mustard	
1/4 tsp. salt	
1/8 tsp. ground black pepper	
2 Tbsp. finely chopped shallots	

1. Preheat oven to 425° F. If using small beets, halve or quarter. Place beets in a single layer in a shallow baking pan. Drizzle with the 1 tablespoon olive oil; toss to coat. Season with salt and pepper; toss again. Cover with foil; roast for 25 minutes. Uncover; roast about 15 minutes more or until fork-tender. Cool; peel the small beets if using. (Baby beets do not need to be peeled.) Cut beets into 1/2-inch cubes. Place cubes in a medium bowl; set aside.

2. Meanwhile, for dressing, in a screw-top jar combine the 1/3 cup olive oil, the white wine vinegar, Dijon-style mustard, salt, and pepper. Cover; shake well.

3. Add shallots to beets; drizzle with 1 tablespoon of the dressing. Toss to coat; set aside. Place the greens in a very large bowl; drizzle with remaining dressing and toss to coat.

4. Divide salad greens among 8 salad plates. Top each serving with a slice of cheese and some beet mixture. Makes 8 servings.

MAKE-AHEAD TIP: Roast beets and make dressing up to 24 hours in advance. Cover and store in the refrigerator.

Each serving: 237 cal., 19 g total fat (7 g sat. fat), 22 mg chol., 350 mg sodium, 8 g carbo., 2 g fiber, 8 g pro. Daily Values: 21% vit. A, 11% vit. C, 12% calcium, 8% iron.

Greens with Spiced Corn Bread

Packaged corn muffin mix turns into oversized croutons for a fantastic flavor accent to a mix of salad greens. The croutons are dusted with sugar and spices.

PREP: 20 minutes   **BAKE:** 20 minutes   **COOL:** 10 minutes

1 recipe Buttermilk Corn Bread (below) or purchased corn bread	3 Tbsp. lemon juice
	1/2 tsp. coarse salt or 1/4 tsp. salt
6 cups arugula, baby red lettuce, and/or baby mixed salad greens	1/4 tsp. ground black pepper
	2 Tbsp. butter or margarine
	1 Tbsp. sugar
1/4 cup olive oil	1/4 tsp. pumpkin pie spice

1. Prepare Buttermilk Corn Bread, if using. Wash greens; pat dry. For dressing, in a screw-top jar combine olive oil, lemon juice, salt, and pepper. Cover; shake well.

2. Cut corn bread in half crosswise to form two 5×4 1/2-inch rectangles. In a large skillet melt 1 tablespoon of the butter over medium heat. Add one of the corn bread rectangles; cook until browned on top and bottom, turning once. Remove. Repeat with remaining 1 tablespoon butter and other corn bread rectangle.

3. In a small bowl stir together sugar and pumpkin pie spice; sprinkle onto corn bread rectangles. Cut each corn bread rectangle into six 5×3/4-inch croutons. (You will have 12 rectangular croutons total.)

4. To serve, shake dressing and toss with greens. Place a corn bread crouton on each of 12 salad plates. Top with greens. Makes 12 servings.

BUTTERMILK CORN BREAD: Preheat oven to 400° F. Prepare one 8 1/2-ounce package corn muffin mix according to package directions, except add 1 egg and substitute 1/3 cup buttermilk for the liquid. Pour batter into a greased 9×5×3-inch loaf pan. Bake about 20 minutes or until a wooden toothpick inserted into the center comes out clean. Cool in pan on a wire rack for 10 minutes. Remove from pan. Cool on a wire rack. (Loaf will only be about 2 inches thick.)

MAKE-AHEAD TIP: Prepare and bake corn bread up to 24 hours in advance. Store tightly wrapped at room temperature. Just before serving, proceed with step 2.

Each serving: 155 cal., 9 g total fat (2 g sat. fat), 23 mg chol., 225 mg sodium, 16 g carbo., 0 g fiber, 2 g pro. Daily Values: 7% vit. A, 6% vit. C, 2% calcium, 4% iron.

BY JEANNE AMBROSE. PHOTOGRAPHS: EDMUND BARR. FOOD STYLIST: WILLIAM SMITH. PRODUCERS: RICHARD KOLLATH AND ED MCCANN. PROP STYLIST: CAROLYN BARTEL.

Brown Bread Squash Stuffing *(page 214)*

Buttery Cider-Glazed Turkey

Two all-American standards, turkey and apples, combine to provide a double dose of incredible taste. Try Golden Delicious, Gravenstein, Granny Smith, Winesap, Rhode Island Greening, or Braeburn apples. Use the apple-tinged drippings to make a gravy like none you've ever tasted.

PREP: 45 minutes **ROAST:** 3¼ hours **STAND:** 15 minutes

1 12- to 14-lb. turkey	2 Tbsp. lemon juice
Kosher salt or salt	1 recipe Cider Glaze (right)
Ground black pepper	Fresh fruit, such as grapes,
4 large cloves garlic, peeled	berries, and apples
and halved	(optional)
1 small onion, peeled and	Fresh herb sprigs, such as
cut into wedges	flat-leaf parsley or
1 medium baking apple,	variegated sage (optional)
cored and cut into wedges	⅓ cup all-purpose flour
2 Tbsp. butter, melted	Chicken broth
6 medium baking apples,	
cored and cut into eighths	

1. Preheat oven to 325° F. Rinse turkey; pat dry with paper towels. Season inside cavity with salt and pepper. Rub 1 of the halved garlic cloves inside cavity. Place garlic cloves, onion, and 1 apple into the cavity.

2. Pull neck skin to back; fasten with skewer. If a band of skin crosses the tail, tuck drumsticks under band. If there isn't a band, tie drumsticks securely to tail with 100-percent-cotton string. Twist wing tips under back. Brush turkey with the 2 tablespoons melted butter. Season with additional salt and pepper.

3. Place bird, breast side up, on a rack in a shallow roasting pan. Insert an oven-safe meat thermometer into the center of an inside thigh muscle without letting thermometer touch bone. Cover bird loosely with foil. Roast for 2½ to 3½ hours or until thermometer registers 160° F. (Cut band of skin or string between drumsticks after 2½ hours.)

4. Toss apple wedges with lemon juice. Place apple wedges around turkey. Cover apple wedges with foil. Roast turkey and apples for 30 minutes more.

5. Meanwhile, prepare Cider Glaze. Remove foil from turkey; baste turkey and drizzle apples with Cider Glaze. Continue roasting, uncovered, until meat thermometer registers 180° F, basting bird and drizzling cider mixture onto apples every 10 minutes.

6. Remove turkey from oven; discard cavity ingredients. Transfer roasted bird to a large platter. Surround with roasted apples. Cover with foil; let stand for 15 to 20 minutes before carving turkey. If desired, garnish platter with fresh fruit and herbs.

7. Meanwhile, for gravy, pour pan drippings into a large measuring cup. Scrape browned bits from the pan into the cup. Skim and reserve fat from drippings. Pour ¼ cup of the fat into a medium saucepan (discard remaining fat). Stir in flour. Add enough broth to remaining drippings to measure 2½ cups total liquid; add broth mixture all at once to flour mixture. Cook and stir over medium heat until thickened and bubbly. Cook and stir for 1 minute more. Season to taste with salt and pepper. Makes 16 to 18 servings.

CIDER GLAZE: In a small saucepan bring 2 cups apple cider and five 3-inch cinnamon sticks to boiling. Reduce heat and boil steadily about 30 minutes or until cider is reduced to ⅔ cup. Add ⅓ cup butter, ⅓ cup brown sugar, and 1 teaspoon dried thyme, crushed. Heat and stir until brown sugar is dissolved. Remove and discard cinnamon sticks.

Each serving: 544 cal., 26 g total fat (9 g sat. fat), 196 mg chol., 359 mg sodium, 18 g carbo., 2 g fiber, 55 g pro. Daily Values: 5% vit. A, 6% vit. C, 7% calcium, 23% iron.

Buttery Cider-Glazed Turkey

THE SPREAD IS READY
Make the golden turkey the centerpiece of your buffet or dining room table. This year, carve a cider-glazed version decorated with roasted apples and eye-catching fresh fruits and herbs.

Brown Bread Squash Stuffing

Remember brown bread in a can? The super-moist, molasses-flavored bread adds a nostalgic twist to this baked stuffing. Pictured on page 212.

PREP: 35 minutes **BAKE:** 45 minutes

7 cups honey wheat bread cut into ½-inch cubes (7 to 9 slices)	1 large red onion, cut into thin wedges
1 16-oz. can brown bread with raisins, cut into ½-inch cubes (5 cups)	2¼ to 2¾ cups chicken broth
	¼ cup snipped fresh sage or 2 tsp. dried sage, crushed
6 Tbsp. butter or margarine	2 Tbsp. snipped fresh flat-leaf parsley
4 cups peeled and seeded winter squash, such as butternut or acorn squash, cut into ¾-inch cubes,	1 tsp. ground nutmeg
	½ tsp. salt
	½ tsp. ground black pepper
1½ cups sliced celery with tops	Fresh sage sprigs (optional)

1. Preheat oven to 325° F. Spread wheat bread cubes and brown bread cubes in 2 shallow baking pans. Melt 4 tablespoons of the butter and drizzle evenly over bread cubes; toss to coat. Bake, uncovered, for 15 to 20 minutes or until lightly toasted, stirring once. Transfer to a very large mixing bowl.

2. In a very large skillet melt remaining 2 tablespoons butter over medium heat. Add squash. Cook, uncovered, 5 minutes, stirring occasionally. Add celery and onion; cover and cook 10 minutes more. Stir in ¼ cup of the chicken broth. Cover and cook 5 minutes more or until squash is just tender, stirring occasionally. Remove from heat. Stir in snipped or dried sage, parsley, nutmeg, salt, and pepper.

3. Add squash mixture to bread in bowl. Add 2 cups of the remaining broth; toss lightly to coat. Add enough of the remaining broth to make a stuffing of desired moistness.

4. Grease a 3-quart casserole. Transfer stuffing mixture to casserole. Bake, covered, for 30 minutes. Uncover; bake for 15 to 20 minutes more or until stuffing is heated through. If desired, garnish with fresh sage sprigs. Makes 10 to 12 servings.

MAKE-AHEAD TIP: You can toast bread cubes up to 2 days in advance and keep them dry in an airtight container.

Each serving: 261 cal., 9 g total fat (5 g sat. fat), 20 mg chol., 823 mg sodium, 41 g carbo., 3 g fiber, 6 g pro. Daily Values: 90% vit. A, 21% vit. C, 6% calcium, 7% iron.

Rosemary Roasted Vegetables

The flavors jump to the foreground of this fresh spin on the classic green bean casserole. Brussels sprouts add welcome variety.

PREP: 30 minutes **ROAST:** 20 minutes

12 oz. fresh whole green beans	8 slices pancetta or bacon, partially cooked, drained, and cut up
1 lb. fresh brussels sprouts	
1 bunch green onions (6), trimmed and cut up	2 Tbsp. olive oil
	Salt
12 fresh rosemary sprigs	Ground black pepper
	1 lemon, halved

1. Preheat oven to 425° F. Wash beans and brussels sprouts; drain. Halve large brussels sprouts. In a covered large saucepan cook brussels sprouts in a small amount of boiling lightly salted water for 3 minutes. Add beans; cook for 5 minutes more.

2. Drain; place brussels sprouts and beans in a shallow roasting pan. Add green onions and rosemary sprigs; toss to combine. Top with partially cooked pancetta or bacon.

3. Drizzle vegetable mixture with olive oil. Sprinkle with salt and pepper. Roast, uncovered, about 20 minutes or until vegetables are crisp-tender and pancetta is crisp. Transfer to a platter. Squeeze lemon juice over vegetables. Makes 12 servings.

MAKE-AHEAD TIP: One day in advance, clean vegetables. Cut brussels sprouts in half. Place brussels sprouts, beans, and onions in separate sealed food-storage bags in the refrigerator.

Each serving: 143 cal., 10 g total fat (4 g sat. fat), 10 mg chol., 275 mg sodium, 6 g carbo., 3 g fiber, 4 g pro. Daily Values: 10% vit. A, 51% vit. C, 3% calcium, 6% iron.

THANKSGIVING DINNER

Pomegranate Starter *(page 209)*
Greens with Spiced Corn Bread *(page 211)*
or Roasted Beet and Goat Cheese Salad *(page 211)*
Buttery Cider-Glazed Turkey *(page 212)*
Brown Bread Squash Stuffing *(left)*
Rosemary Roasted Vegetables *(above)*
Mashed Potatoes with Caramelized Onions *(page 217)*
Harvest Breadsticks *(page 217)*
Maple-Pumpkin Cheesecake *(page 218)*
or Deep-Dish Cranberry Pie *(page 218)*

A Bounty of Sides
You can't do without the green beans. Stuffing. Billowy rolls and cranberry sauce. The homier, the better. Present these favorites with an easy added touch of flavor that will appeal to even the most cautious guests. Rosemary Roasted Vegetables tops off the beans with pancetta or bacon and brussels sprouts.

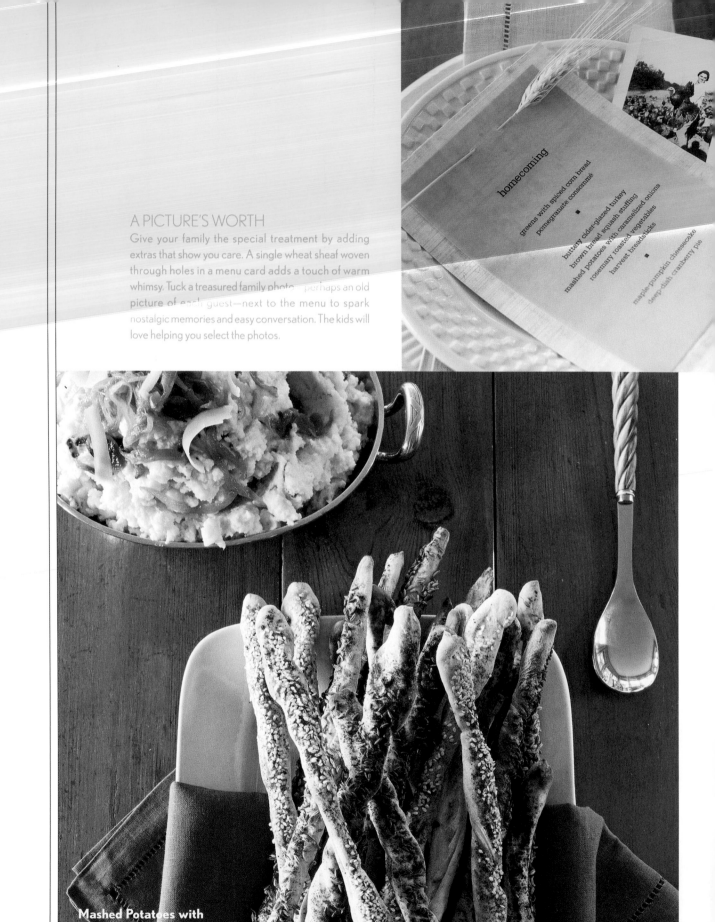

A PICTURE'S WORTH

Give your family the special treatment by adding extras that show you care. A single wheat sheaf woven through holes in a menu card adds a touch of warm whimsy. Tuck a treasured family photo—perhaps an old picture of each guest—next to the menu to spark nostalgic memories and easy conversation. The kids will love helping you select the photos.

homecoming

greens with spiced corn bread
pomegranate consommé

•

buttery cider-glazed turkey
brown bread squash stuffing
mashed potatoes with caramelized onions
rosemary roasted vegetables
harvest breadsticks

•

maple-pumpkin cheesecake
deep-dish cranberry pie

**Mashed Potatoes with
Caramelized Onions and
Harvest Breadsticks**

Harvest Breadsticks

Choose from a variety of toppings to flavor these extra-long breadsticks. Bundle them together on a long tray or stand them upright in a clean glass vase.

PREP: 45 minutes **RISE:** 50 minutes **BAKE:** 15 minutes per batch

1¼ cups water	2 pkg. active dry yeast
2 small russet (baking) potatoes, peeled and cubed (1⅓ cups)	1 egg white
	1 Tbsp. water
1 cup buttermilk	Desired toppings, such as
2 Tbsp. sugar	sesame seeds, fennel
2 Tbsp. butter or margarine	seeds, cumin seeds,
2 tsp. salt	and/or crushed red
6 to 6½ cups all-purpose flour	peppercorns

1. In a small saucepan bring water and cubed potatoes to boiling. Simmer, covered, about 15 minutes or until potatoes are tender; do not drain. Mash potatoes in the water. Measure potato mixture. If necessary, add additional water to make 1⅔ cups total.

2. Return potato mixture to saucepan. Add buttermilk, sugar, butter, and salt. Heat or cool as necessary until warm (120° F to 130° F), stirring constantly.

3. In a large mixing bowl combine 2 cups of the flour and the yeast. Add the potato mixture. Beat with an electric mixer on low to medium speed for 30 seconds, scraping the side of the bowl constantly. Beat on high speed for 3 minutes. Using a wooden spoon, stir in as much of the remaining flour as you can.

4. Turn dough out onto a lightly floured surface. Knead in enough of the remaining flour to make a moderately stiff dough that is smooth and elastic (6 to 8 minutes total). Shape dough into a ball. Place in a lightly greased bowl; turn once to grease the surface. Cover; let rise in warm place until double in size (30 to 45 minutes). Lightly grease baking sheets; set aside.

5. Punch dough down. Turn dough out onto a lightly floured surface; divide dough in half. Cover and let rest for 10 minutes. Roll one portion into a 15×8-inch rectangle. Cut into twenty 8×¾-inch pieces. Stretch and roll each piece to form a 15-inch-long breadstick. Place ¾ to 1 inch apart on prepared baking sheets. Repeat with remaining dough.

6. Preheat oven to 375° F. Cover and let breadsticks rise for 20 minutes. Stir together egg white and the water; brush onto breadsticks. Sprinkle with desired toppings. Bake about 15 minutes or until light brown. Transfer to wire racks. Serve warm or at room temperature. Makes 40 breadsticks.

MAKE-AHEAD TIP: To freeze these breadsticks or any yeast bread, place completely cooled breads in a freezer bag; freeze for up to 3 months. Thaw the wrapped bread at room temperature for 2 hours.

low fat Each breadstick: 87 cal., 1 g total fat (0 g sat. fat), 2 mg chol., 131 mg sodium, 17 g carbo., 1 g fiber, 3 g pro. Daily Values: 1% vit. C, 1% calcium, 6% iron.

Mashed Potatoes with Caramelized Onions

The essential comfort food—mashed potatoes—forms the base of this dish. But by the time you top the mashed potatoes with sautéed onions and thin shards of white cheddar cheese, you won't need to add gravy. Melty cheese plays a big role in the appeal of this dish, so don't delay in getting the cheddar on the hot potatoes. And yes, orange cheddar can be substituted for the white.

START TO FINISH: 40 minutes

3 lb. russet (baking) potatoes, peeled and quartered	2 Tbsp. snipped fresh sage or 1 tsp. dried sage, crushed
1 tsp. salt	¼ tsp. ground black pepper
2 Tbsp. olive oil	½ to ¾ cup half-and-half, light cream, or milk
2 large yellow onions, peeled and cut into thin wedges (about 2 cups)	1 oz. aged white cheddar cheese, shaved into thin shards
¼ cup butter or margarine, softened	

1. In a covered large saucepan cook potatoes and ½ teaspoon of the salt in enough boiling water to cover for 20 to 25 minutes or until tender; drain.

2. Meanwhile, for caramelized onions, in a large skillet heat oil. Stir in the onion wedges. Cook, uncovered, over medium heat about 20 minutes or until onions are tender, stirring frequently. (If necessary, reduce heat to medium-low to prevent overbrowning before onions are tender.) Increase heat to medium-high and cook about 5 minutes more or until onions are golden brown, stirring frequently.

3. Mash drained potatoes with a potato masher. Add butter, sage, the remaining ½ teaspoon salt, and the pepper. Gradually beat in enough half-and-half to make mixture light and fluffy.

4. Mound potatoes in a serving dish. Top with caramelized onions and cheese shards; serve immediately. Makes 10 to 12 servings.

Each serving: 187 cal., 10 g total fat (5 g sat. fat), 21 mg chol., 309 mg sodium, 20 g carbo., 3 g fiber, 4 g pro. Daily Values: 5% vit. A, 29% vit. C, 5% calcium, 6% iron.

Maple-Pumpkin Cheesecake

Inspired by chef Joanne Bondy's individual pumpkin cheesecakes served at Ciudad Restaurant in Dallas, this full-size version is beautiful when embellished with glittering fruit. This time of year, look for currants, champagne grapes, raspberries, or other small fruit. It's also elegant served with just a drizzle of caramel sauce.

PREP: 35 minutes **BAKE:** 1 hour

COOL: 1³/₄ hours **CHILL:** 4 hours

1½	cups finely crushed graham crackers (about 20 squares)	1	Tbsp. whipping cream
1⅓	cups maple sugar or granulated sugar	1½	tsp. vanilla
		³/₄	tsp. ground allspice
½	cup butter (1 stick), melted	3	eggs, slightly beaten
3	8-oz. pkg. cream cheese, softened	½	cup caramel ice cream topping
1	cup canned pumpkin		Fresh currants and/or small fruit (optional)

1. Preheat oven to 325° F. For crust, in a medium bowl combine crushed graham crackers, ⅓ cup of the maple sugar, and the melted butter. Press crumb mixture onto the bottom and about 2 inches up the side of an ungreased 9-inch springform pan. Bake for 8 minutes. Remove from oven; cool on a wire rack.

2. For filling, in a medium mixing bowl beat cream cheese, the remaining 1 cup maple sugar, the pumpkin, cream, vanilla, and allspice with an electric mixer on medium speed until combined. Add eggs; beat on low speed just until combined.

3. Preheat oven to 325° F. Spoon filling into crust-lined pan. Place pan in a shallow baking pan. Bake about 1 hour or until center appears nearly set when gently shaken.

4. Cool in springform pan on a wire rack for 15 minutes. Using a thin-bladed knife or narrow spatula, loosen crust from side of pan; cool for 30 minutes more. Remove side of pan; cool for 1 hour. Cover and chill for 4 to 24 hours.

5. Just before serving, spoon caramel ice cream topping over cheesecake. If desired, garnish with fresh currants and/or small fruit. Makes 12 servings.

MAKE-AHEAD TIP: To store, before adding caramel ice cream topping, cover cheesecake with plastic wrap and refrigerate for up to 2 days. (Or carefully transfer cheesecake to a freezerproof plate or platter. Place cheesecake in a freezer bag or airtight container. Freeze for up to 1 month. Thaw frozen cheesecake in the refrigerator for 24 hours.) Continue with step 5.

Each serving: 475 cal., 31 g total fat (18 g sat. fat), 139 mg chol., 362 mg sodium, 44 g carbo., 1 g fiber, 7 g pro. Daily Values: 114% vit. A, 7% vit. C, 9% calcium, 11% iron.

Deep-Dish Cranberry Pie

We took traditional cranberry pie to the oooh-ahhh level by adding lots more filling and capping it with a pastry that drapes low over the edge of the bowl.

PREP: 40 minutes **BAKE:** 1¼ hours

¼	cup brandy or water	3	Tbsp. all-purpose flour
2³/₄	cups dried tart cherries	2	tsp. finely shredded lemon peel
1	recipe Deep-Dish Pastry (below)		Milk
1	12-oz. pkg. fresh cranberries (3½ cups)		Coarse sugar
1½	cups granulated sugar	1	recipe Honey Cream Sauce (below)

1. In a small saucepan combine ³/₄ cup water and the brandy or additional water. Heat until mixture starts to boil; add cherries. Remove from heat. Cover; let stand for 20 minutes.

2. Meanwhile, prepare Deep-Dish Pastry. Preheat oven to 375° F. On a lightly floured surface, roll out half of the pastry to a 13-inch circle if using a 1½-quart oven-safe bowl or an 18×14-inch oval or rectangle if using a 2-quart oval or rectangular casserole. Gently fit pastry onto bottom and up side of the bowl or casserole, letting excess pastry extend beyond edge of dish; fold pastry into pleats as needed to fit dish. Set aside.

3. In a large bowl stir together cranberries, undrained cherry mixture, granulated sugar, flour, and lemon peel. Turn into pastry-lined dish. Roll out remaining half of pastry to a 10-inch circle or a 14×10-inch oval or rectangle. Use a cookie cutter or knife to cut a design or circle in the center of the circle, oval, or rectangle. Place pastry over filling, allowing it to hang over the edge of the dish. Pinch top and bottom pastry together to seal. Brush with milk; sprinkle with coarse sugar. Place dish on a baking sheet.

4. Cover edge of pie with foil. Bake for 55 minutes; remove foil and bake for 20 to 25 minutes more or until juices bubble and pastry is light brown. Cool on a wire rack.

5. Serve pie with Honey Cream Sauce. Break off and serve pastry overhang with pie. Makes 10 servings.

DEEP-DISH PASTRY: In a large bowl combine 2¼ cups all-purpose flour and ³/₄ teaspoon salt. Cut in ²/₃ cup shortening until pieces are pea-size. Sprinkle 1 tablespoon cold water over part of flour mixture; gently toss with a fork. Push moistened dough to side of bowl. Repeat, using 1 tablespoon water at a time (8 to 10 tablespoons cold water total), until all of the flour is moistened. Divide dough in half.

HONEY CREAM SAUCE: Stir together one 8-ounce carton dairy sour cream and 3 tablespoons wildflower or orange blossom honey; stir in 1 to 2 tablespoons half-and-half, light cream, or milk to make desired consistency. Cover and chill until serving time.

Each serving: 551 cal., 19 g total fat (7 g sat. fat), 11 mg chol., 190 mg sodium, 88 g carbo., 4 g fiber, 5 g pro. Daily Values: 4% vit. A, 9% vit. C, 4% calcium, 8% iron.

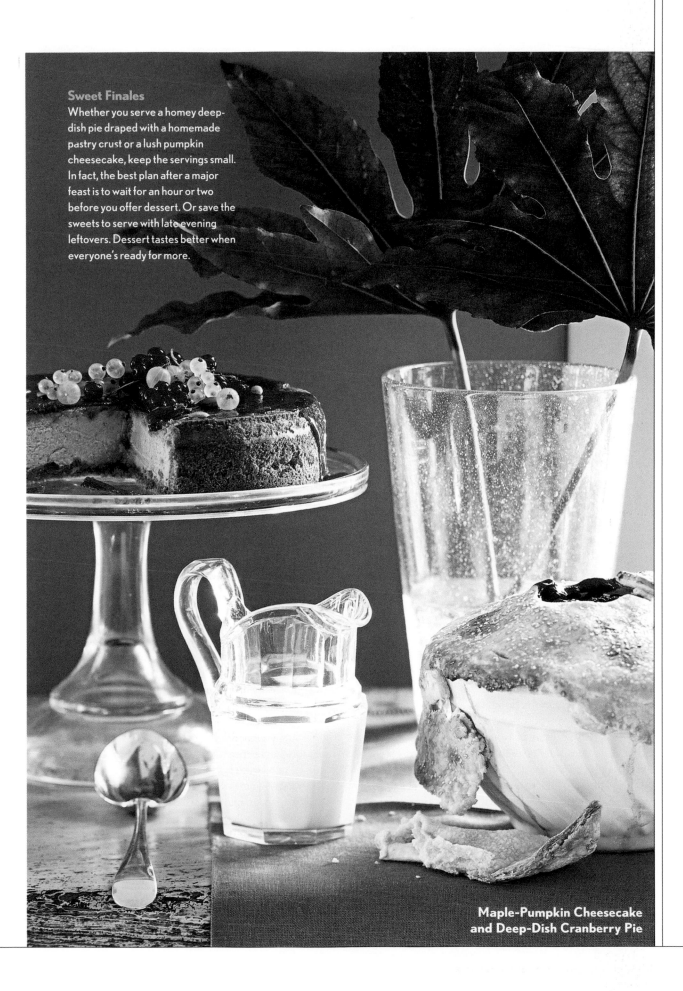

Sweet Finales

Whether you serve a homey deep-dish pie draped with a homemade pastry crust or a lush pumpkin cheesecake, keep the servings small. In fact, the best plan after a major feast is to wait for an hour or two before you offer dessert. Or save the sweets to serve with late-evening leftovers. Dessert tastes better when everyone's ready for more.

Maple-Pumpkin Cheesecake and Deep-Dish Cranberry Pie

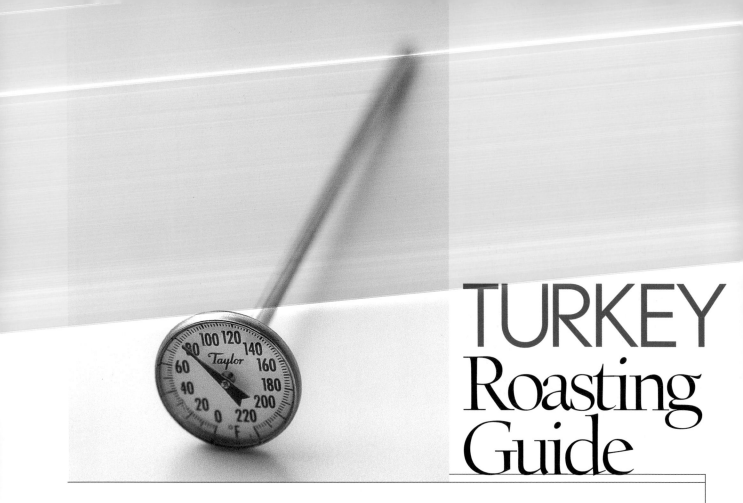

TURKEY Roasting Guide

HOW MUCH TO BUY

To make sure you have plenty of turkey, purchase 1 to 1½ pounds of bird per person. For each pound of bird you put into the oven, you'll get just under a half pound of meat. Fresh or frozen birds are about equal in quality. Fresh turkeys take up space for less time in the fridge; frozen turkeys must spend up to a week thawing.

For a fresh turkey, check the sell-by date. The unopened turkey will taste best and be safe to use up to 1 or 2 days after the date on the wrapper. If you're buying a frozen bird, look for one that is clean, undamaged, and free of ice crystals.

BEFORE YOU START

If you're serious about making a perfect turkey, invest in a meat thermometer. Turkey gets dry when it's overcooked, and for $10 to $20, you can be sure of serving a savory turkey. Meat thermometers are available both as instant-read and conventional. The main difference: conventionals stay in the bird; the smaller instant-reads can't be left in the oven.

Another key to success is to allow plenty of time. On average, it takes about an hour to stuff and prepare a turkey for roasting. The depth of your roasting time may affect the roasting time. A depth of more than 3 inches can increase the roasting time by up to an hour.

THAWING

A sticking point for many cooks is allowing enough time to thaw the bird. For a whole frozen turkey, leave the bird in its wrapping and place it on a tray or platter in the refrigerator for 2 to 5 days. Plan on 24 hours for every 5 pounds and don't count the day you'll be cooking as part of the thawing time. For instance, a 15-pound bird should start thawing Sunday night to be ready for Thanksgiving. Thawed birds will keep for 2 days in the refrigerator.

The bird is ready for roasting if the giblets can be removed easily and there are no ice crystals in the body cavities. If the center is still frozen, the bird will cook unevenly.

If your turkey is not completely thawed on the day you plan to roast it, place the bird in a clean sink full of cold water and change the water every 30 minutes. This method works really well, so don't be tempted to thaw at room temperature, in the microwave, or in warm water; these methods can cause bacteria to grow.

After thawing, remove the giblets and neck. If you wish, rinse the bird. In either case, pat dry with paper towels.

STUFFING

Prepare the stuffing just before you put the bird in the oven. Measure out the amount of stuffing that will go into the bird, allowing ¾ cup per pound of bird. (That's 11 cups for a 15-pound bird.) Spoon some stuffing loosely into the neck cavity. Pull the neck skin over stuffing; fasten to the turkey's back with a short skewer.

BY RICHARD SWEARINGER. ILLUSTRATOR: JACKIE PARSONS.

The drumsticks are usually held in place by a band of skin, or a plastic or metal clamp. Unhook the legs and loosely spoon the stuffing into the body cavity; don't pack it or the stuffing may not be fully cooked and safe to eat by the time the turkey is done. Spoon any remaining stuffing into a greased casserole; cover and chill until you're ready to bake it (about an hour before the turkey is scheduled to come out of the oven).

After stuffing, tuck the drumsticks under the band of skin that crosses the tail or reset them into the leg clamp. If there isn't a band or if you've removed the clamp, tie the drumsticks to the tail using kitchen string. Twist the wing tips under the back—this gives the turkey a nice stable base.

If you don't have an accurate thermometer, cook the stuffing in a covered casserole alongside the turkey, rather than inside the bird.

ROAST AND SERVE

Place your oven rack in its lowest position; preheat the oven to 325° F. Place turkey, breast side up, on a rack in a shallow pan. To promote browning, brush with cooking oil or melted butter. Push an oven-safe meat thermometer into the center of an inside thigh muscle without touching bone. Cover turkey loosely with foil, pressing it over the drumsticks and neck. Roast, using our timing chart (below) as a guide. Since most turkeys are self-basting, basting is not necessary, but it will add flavor.

When the bird has been in the oven for two-thirds of the time shown on the chart, cut the string between the drumsticks. Remove the foil for the last 30 to 45 minutes of roasting. The meat thermometer (or instant-read thermometer) in the thigh should register 180° F and the stuffing should be at least 165° F.

When the turkey is done, the drumsticks should move very easily in their sockets and their thickest parts should feel soft when pressed. In addition, juices from the thigh should run clear when pierced deeply with a long-tined fork. Remove from the oven and cover loosely with foil. Let stand for 20 minutes. Release legs from leg clamp, if present. To avoid burns or splatters, do not remove clamp until bird has cooled slightly. Remove stuffing before carving.

Pear-Pecan Stuffing

Pears, toasted pecans, and nutmeg create a festive holiday twist on old-fashioned stuffing. It's equally delicious when baked inside the bird or in a casserole.

PREP: 30 minutes **BAKE:** 40 minutes (in casserole)

1 lb. firm-textured white sandwich bread
2 Tbsp. butter
1 cup chopped onion
2 large ripe, yet firm, Barlett pears, cored, peeled, and chopped
1/2 cup water
1/4 cup butter
1 cup coarsely chopped pecans, toasted
2 Tbsp. snipped fresh flat-leaf parsley
1/4 tsp. ground nutmeg
1/8 tsp. salt
Dash ground black pepper

1. Preheat oven to 350° F. Spread bread slices on baking sheets. Place baking sheets in the preheated oven about 20 minutes or until bread is dry.

2. In a large skillet melt the 2 tablespoons butter over medium heat. Add onion and pear; cook about 4 minutes or until tender. Set aside.

3. Break the dried bread into small pieces; place in a very large bowl. In a small saucepan combine the water and the 1/4 cup butter; bring to boiling. Add to bread; toss just until moistened.

4. Stir in pear mixture, pecans, parsley, nutmeg, salt, and pepper. Add just enough additional water (about 1/4 cup) to make desired moistness. Stuff turkey and roast according to directions at left. (Or transfer stuffing to a greased 2-quart casserole and bake, covered, in a 350° F oven about 40 minutes or until heated through.) Makes 12 to 14 servings.

Each serving: 243 cal., 15 g total fat (4 g sat. fat), 16 mg chol., 291 mg sodium, 26 g carbo., 2 g fiber, 4 g pro. Daily Values: 5% vit. A, 5% vit. C, 5% calcium, 8% iron.

STUFFED TURKEY ROASTING TIMES

READY-TO-COOK TURKEY WEIGHT	OVEN TEMPERATURE	ROASTING TIME
8 to 12 lb.	325° F	3 to 3 3/4 hours
12 to 14 lb.	325° F	3 1/4 to 4 1/2 hours
14 to 18 lb.	325° F	4 to 5 hours
18 to 20 lb.	325° F	4 1/2 to 5 1/4 hours
20 to 24 lb.	325° F	4 3/4 to 5 3/4 hours

FOR UNSTUFFED TURKEYS OF THE SAME WEIGHT, REDUCE THE TOTAL ROASTING TIME BY 15 TO 45 MINUTES. THE TURKEY IS DONE WHEN THE THIGH TEMPERATURE REACHES 180° F AND THE STUFFING IS 165° F.

LEFTOVERS
go right

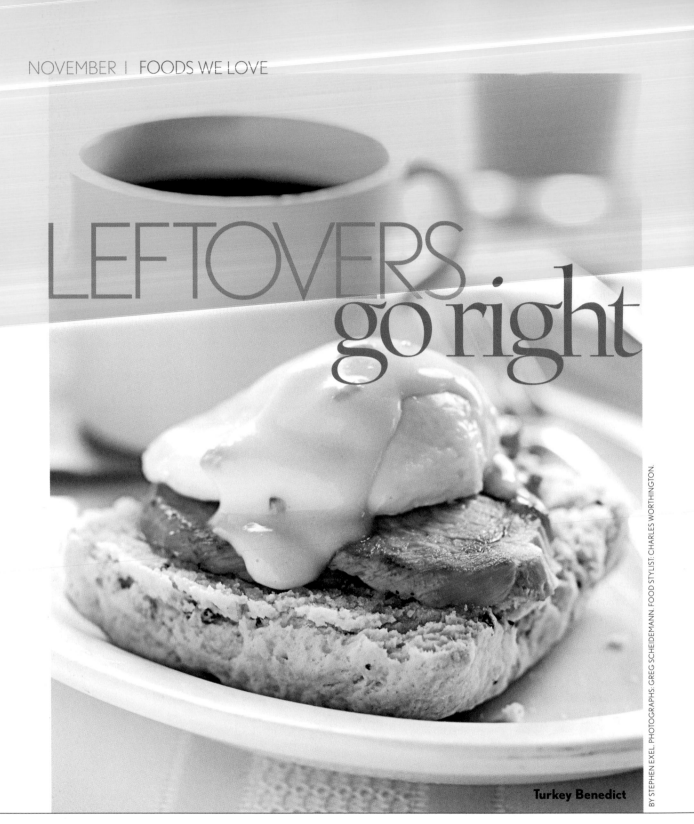

Turkey Benedict

BY STEPHEN EXEL. PHOTOGRAPHS: GREG SCHEIDEMANN. FOOD STYLIST: CHARLES WORTHINGTON.

CHEF-BROTHERS KENT AND KEVIN RATHBUN TRADE SIBLING
RIVALRY FOR KITCHEN COOPERATION WHEN THEY DIG
INTO LEFTOVERS FOR A POST-HOLIDAY SUNDAY BRUNCH.

Turkey Benedict

START TO FINISH: 1 hour

1³/₄ cups all-purpose flour	¼ cup buttermilk
2 Tbsp. snipped fresh parsley	¼ tsp. bottled minced
1 Tbsp. sugar	roasted garlic
1 Tbsp. baking powder	1 recipe Spicy Hollandaise
³/₄ tsp. kosher salt	Sauce (below)
or ½ tsp. salt	8 to 10 oz. roasted turkey
⅓ cup cold butter	breast slices
½ cup half-and-half or light	8 eggs
cream	

1. For biscuits, preheat oven to 400° F. In a bowl stir together flour, parsley, sugar, baking powder, and salt. Cut in butter until mixture resembles coarse crumbs. Add half-and-half, buttermilk, and garlic. Use a fork to gently mix until a slightly sticky dough forms. Do not overmix. Turn out onto a floured surface. Knead a few times until nearly smooth. Roll or pat dough to a 6-inch square. Cut into 4 squares. Place on an ungreased cookie sheet. Bake for 18 to 20 minutes or until brown on tops; set aside.

2. Meanwhile, prepare Spicy Hollandaise Sauce; keep warm.

3. Heat a griddle or large skillet over medium-high heat. Add turkey; cook about 4 minutes or until brown, turning once.

4. Half fill a large saucepan with water. Bring to boiling; reduce heat to just simmering. Break 1 egg into custard cup. Carefully slide egg into the simmering water, holding the lip of the cup as close to the water as possible. Repeat with 3 more eggs, allowing each egg an equal amount of space. Simmer, uncovered, for 3 to 5 minutes or until yolks and whites are set. Using a slotted spoon, transfer eggs to an oven-safe shallow dish. Cover; keep warm in a 300° F oven. Repeat with remaining eggs.

5. To assemble, split biscuits; arrange on a platter. Top each half with turkey, a poached egg, and about 1 tablespoon sauce. Serve with remaining sauce. Makes 8 servings.

SPICY HOLLANDAISE SAUCE: In top of a double boiler whisk together 2 egg yolks, 2 tablespoons water, and 2 tablespoons lemon juice. Place over simmering water (the bottom of the pan should not touch the water) and whisk until the mixture thickens and doubles in volume (1½ to 2 minutes) and an instant-read thermometer inserted into the mixture registers 160° F (you may need to tilt the pan to get an accurate reading). Gradually add 1 cup cut-up and softened butter, whisking constantly after each addition until butter is melted. Remove double boiler from heat. Stir in 1 seeded and chopped serrano chile pepper (see note, page 121). Keep sauce warm over water.

Each serving: 535 cal., 41 g total fat (23 g sat. fat), 384 mg chol., 832 mg sodium, 23 g carbo., 1 g fiber, 19 g pro. Daily Values: 35% vit. A, 6% vit. C, 16% calcium, 15% iron.

Final feast

Everyone pitches in to prepare Thanksgiving dinner when the Rathbun clan gathers for the holiday. But come Sunday morning, brothers Kent and Kevin are on their own to prepare the final feast of the weekend, Sunday brunch. Even though the brothers—both professional chefs—serve haute cuisine daily, like most Americans, they've got leftovers to use—and they enjoy the challenge.

Kent Rathbun is chef/owner of Abacus restaurant in Dallas; Kevin is soon to open Rathbun's in Atlanta. The brothers grew up in Kansas City. Traditionally, the family alternates between the three cities for Thanksgiving. On Sunday morning, Kent gets up first and starts cooking bacon so the aroma will get Kevin out of bed. After a cup of coffee, the two start opening up containers of leftover turkey, stuffing, gravy, and sweet potatoes.

"We get creative on the fly. We usually set out to do something that makes sense, like a strata, and just let it go. It doesn't always look great, but it always tastes great," Kent says.

Kevin joins in, "There's a very big mutual respect between us when we cook. We recognize the other may have a better idea. We bounce ideas as well as jokes."

When you're adapting an existing recipe to use up leftovers, or just making something up, the brothers

stress confidence as a key ingredient.

By the time brunch gets on the table, Kevin and Kent have cleaned out the fridge. Do too many cooks spoil the broth in the Rathbun household? "Not if they're both good cooks," Kent jokes.

Portobello and Lemon Thyme Bread Pudding

"THERE'S A VERY BIG MUTUAL RESPECT
BETWEEN US WHEN WE COOK."
Kevin Rathbun

Portobello and Lemon Thyme Bread Pudding

You can use any leftover bread from making the stuffing instead of the baguette. Just make sure you have 7 cups of bread total.

PREP: 45 minutes **BAKE:** 35 minutes **STAND:** 10 minutes

	Nonstick cooking spray	3	Tbsp. snipped fresh lemon thyme*
7	cups 1-inch cubes French-style baguette or other firm-textured bread (about 12 oz.)	10	oz. Gruyère cheese, shredded (2½ cups)
		1	cup cubed cooked turkey
4	4-oz. portobello mushrooms	6	eggs
3	Tbsp. butter	1	14-oz. can chicken broth
6	cloves garlic, minced	1½	cups whipping cream
6	shallots, finely chopped	2	tsp. cracked black pepper
		½	tsp. kosher salt or salt

1. Preheat oven to 350° F. Lightly coat eight 10-ounce ramekins or custard cups with nonstick cooking spray; set aside. Place bread cubes in a very large bowl; set aside.

2. Remove stems and gills from mushrooms; discard. Chop mushrooms (you should have about 5 cups). In a large skillet heat butter until melted. Add mushrooms, garlic, and shallots; cook about 3 minutes or until tender. Add lemon thyme. Cook and stir for 1 minute more.

3. Add mushroom mixture to bread cubes; toss to combine. Add 2 cups of the cheese and the turkey; toss to combine.

4. In a large bowl whisk together eggs, broth, cream, pepper, and salt. Add to bread mixture; fold gently to combine.

5. Divide bread mixture evenly among the prepared cups (cups will be full). Sprinkle remaining ½ cup cheese over the tops. Place cups in a foil-lined 15×10×1-inch baking pan or shallow roasting pan.

6. Bake, uncovered, for 35 to 40 minutes or until puffed and set. Let stand for 10 minutes before serving (top will deflate slightly). Makes 8 servings.

***NOTE:** If you cannot find lemon thyme, substitute 2 tablespoons snipped fresh thyme and 1 teaspoon finely shredded lemon peel.

Each serving: 585 cal., 40 g total fat (22 g sat. fat), 285 mg chol., 833 mg sodium, 30 g carbo., 2 g fiber, 28 g pro. Daily Values: 36% vit. A, 7% vit. C, 46% calcium, 16% iron.

LOWER FAT BREAD PUDDING: Prepare Portobello and Lemon Thyme Bread Pudding as above, except use only 8 ounces Gruyère cheese; substitute half-and-half for the whipping cream.

Each serving: 460 cal., 26 g total fat (13 g sat. fat), 233 mg chol., 811 mg sodium, 31 g carbo., 2 g fiber, 26 g pro. Daily Values: 25% vit. A, 7% vit. C, 41% calcium, 16% iron.

THANKS FOR THE LEFTOVERS

The brothers pinned down two recipes for leftover turkey—Turkey Benedict (page 223) and Portobello and Lemon Thyme Bread Pudding (left). Then, they shared a few spontaneous thoughts on what to do with some common Thanksgiving leftovers.

OVERALL: "Take a risk. Start small. Add a little of something at a time," Kent suggests. "Once your dish is in the oven," Kevin adds, "check it along the way. Make sure it's not too wet or dry. Leftover gravy can go a long or little way, depending on how you use it."

CRANBERRY SAUCE: Kent and Kevin suggest boiling it down to make cranberry syrup or tossing the sauce into waffle, scone, or pancake batter.

FRESH OR FROZEN CRANBERRIES: For an easy cranberry dessert, Kent suggests pureeing 1 cup frozen cranberries in a blender with ½ cup sugar, and ¼ cup orange juice. "Spoon it onto scoops of vanilla ice cream or yogurt and top with chocolate shaved from a bar with a vegetable peeler," he says.

Kevin offers a cranberry chutney by combining 1 cup lightly cooked cranberries with a peeled, chopped orange, 2 tablespoons brown sugar, and a dash of balsamic or sherry vinegar. "Serve it with ham or scones," he recommends.

GRAVY: The brothers wax ecstatic about the wonders of gravy. "Put it into soup. It's a great base for any kind you can think of. And speaking of soups, pumpkin soup made with leftover canned pumpkin is a brilliant idea, or turkey and dumpling soup made from the leftover turkey."

CANDIED SWEET POTATOES: Use them in sweet potato pie or in bread pudding. Or take them Mexican by mashing them, adding Monterey Jack cheese and diced fresh jalapeño chile pepper, and serving them in flour tortillas.

GREEN BEAN CASSEROLE: Use the casserole as the base for a filling for turkey potpie. Or mix the casserole with bread crumbs, form patties, and sauté them until crisp. Use the patties alone or top them with poached eggs. Top them off with some leftover cranberry sauce seasoned with a diced chile pepper.

read it and eat

COME ALONG AS FRIENDS GET TOGETHER TO DEVOUR A BOOK AND SHARE A MEAL INSPIRED BY THE PLOT.

A great book, great friends, great food, and a chance to ditch the guys, even if for just one evening—all in the name of fun and a little intellectual stimulation. The requisites? Each friend must bring the book and a dish or a bottle of wine to Kate Manchester's house in East Hampton, NY.

The book club members gather 'round the kitchen island, nosh on huge pimiento-stuffed olives and fresh veggies dunked in a thick homemade dip, and dish out their thoughts about the novel of the night. Nibble a little, dish a little, nibble some more, dish some more—it's all about fun.

"I try to get everybody to sit in the living room, but the girls prefer standing around the kitchen island, nibbling, drinking, and talking. I think it's the Big Girl Drinks, also known as martinis," laughs Kate.

Pastrami Panini

Marinated cucumbers and onions add crunch to the hearty sandwiches.

PREP: 40 minutes   **CHILL:** 1 hour   **COOK:** 6 minutes

1 medium cucumber, thinly sliced	2 tsp. prepared horseradish (optional)
1 medium red onion, thinly sliced	8 slices hearty wheat or rye bread
¼ cup vinegar	6 oz. thinly sliced pastrami
1 Tbsp. sugar	4 oz. Swiss cheese slices
½ tsp. salt	Olive oil
3 to 4 Tbsp. honey mustard	Bottled Thousand Island salad dressing (optional)

1. In a medium bowl stir together the cucumber, onion, vinegar, sugar, and salt. Cover and chill until serving time or up to 24 hours. Drain before using.

2. In a small bowl stir together honey mustard and, if desired, horseradish. To assemble sandwiches, spread one side of each bread slice with the mustard mixture. Top half of the bread slices, mustard sides up, with pastrami, cheese, and some of the drained cucumber mixture. Top with remaining bread slices. Brush outsides of sandwiches lightly with olive oil.

3. Heat a nonstick griddle or large skillet over medium heat. Wrap a brick completely in foil. Place a sandwich on griddle or in skillet and top with the foil-wrapped brick. Grill weighted sandwich about 3 minutes on each side or until golden brown and cheese is melted. Repeat for remaining sandwiches. (Or place sandwich on a covered indoor grill or panini grill. Close lid; grill 4 to 5 minutes or until golden brown and cheese is melted.) If desired, serve with Thousand Island salad dressing. Makes 4 sandwiches.

Each serving: 559 cal., 29 g total fat (11 g sat. fat), 66 mg chol., 1,423 mg sodium, 54 g carbo., 7 g fiber, 23 g pro. Daily Values: 8% vit. A, 10% vit. C, 33% calcium, 19% iron.

10 GREAT BOOKS FOR FOOD LOVERS

Death by Darjeeling, by Laura Childs
Fried Green Tomatoes at the Whistle Stop Cafe, by Fannie Flagg
Heartburn, by Nora Ephron
Like Water for Chocolate, by Laura Esquivel
Stuffed, by Patricia Volk
Tender at the Bone, by Ruth Reichl
The Art of Eating, by M. F. K. Fisher
The Soul of a Chef, by Michael Ruhlman
Under the Tuscan Sun, by Frances Mayes

BOOK CLUB BASICS

GOT THE E-INVITE: "There's no easier way!" says Kate who e-mails the invitations, including a menu based on food inspired by the group's current book. Sometimes, she even sends along recipes to keep the emphasis on simplicity. There's no need to throw anyone into a hissy fit. "It can't become homework; we're all too busy," says Kate, adding that the gathering is held every six or so weeks after work, midweek. "My whole schtick is to get people back in the kitchen sharing food together," says Kate.

ATTACK OF THE BOOK BEES: The girls break into groups of two or three, and the laughter and the pitch get louder and louder. "It seems like everybody talks at once. When we actually start talking about the book, watch out! We chatter our way through chapter after chapter It's a free-for-all. Everybody talks at once about their favorite parts. It's so intellectually stimulating," says Kate.

BOOK REVIEW NOTES: Rated "a very good read" by the group, *Stuffed,* by Patricia Volk, was a hit. The book is a memoir that chronicles the author's family, who introduced pastrami to America and gave birth to the first New York deli. "I thought it was hysterical—the way the family equated food with love, food with everything, and I could totally relate to all her diets over the years. It felt fun to be an observer in somebody else's crazy life with their crazy relatives," says Kate.

GETTING DISHY ABOUT THE MENU: In this case, the book inspired Kate to focus on pastrami, crudités, and chocolate cake. But every book is different. "When I'm deciding on recipes to suggest, I try to keep things pretty mainstream. If there are too many ingredients or steps, the group gets totally turned off," says Kate.

Who better to throw the party than Kate Manchester? Books are her passion; food is her forte. She's also a cookbook author and personal chef.

Everyone brings the book, a dish or a bottle of wine to Kate's house and comes ready to engage in wherever the conversation goes.

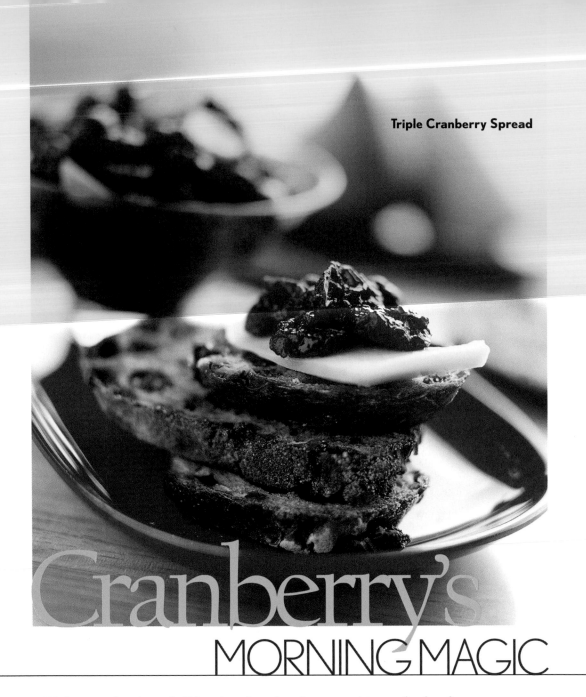

Triple Cranberry Spread

Cranberry's
MORNING MAGIC

We love cranberries at holiday time, for a lot of reasons. As one of only a few edible fruits native to the United States, their roots are deep in American cuisine. They freeze like champions, so it's easy to keep a supply on hand. And they graciously bestow their sweet-sour tang on appetizers, main dishes, and desserts. Cranberries long been favored at holiday time because they add a daring dash of color to the comfy browns of the buffet table. But, as much as we love them for dinner, cranberries make great eye openers in the morning too. Even better for holiday time, these two breakfast treats that can be made the night before.

The first is a toast topper that takes less than a half hour to stir together. It's a mix of three forms of cranberries—fresh, dried, and juice—and it's perfect for spooning onto toasted holiday breads, stollen, scones, and biscuits to get you through those early morning hours.

The second is a good-morning drink you can have waiting for guests as they drift downstairs, one by one. What a great way to toast the new day!

BY RICHARD SWEARINGER. RECIPES: JEANNE AMBROSE. PHOTOGRAPHS: COLLEEN DUFFLEY. FOOD STYLIST: BROOKE LEONARD.

Triple Cranberry Spread

Prepare this tart cranberry spread several days ahead for a stress-free holiday morning. It tastes tangy and juicy when served on hearty raisin bread with a shard of provolone cheese.

PREP: 10 minutes **COOK:** 15 minutes **CHILL:** 4 hours

²/₃	cup cranberry juice	1	tsp. finely shredded lime
½	cup sugar		peel
1½	cups fresh cranberries	½	cup dried cranberries
	(6 oz.)		Dash ground allspice
1	lime, peeled and sectioned		

1. In a medium saucepan combine cranberry juice and sugar. Bring to boiling; reduce heat. Simmer, uncovered, stirring occasionally, until sugar is dissolved.

2. Add fresh cranberries, lime sections, dried cranberries, and allspice. Return to boiling; reduce heat. Simmer, uncovered, about 15 minutes or until mixture is thickened (it will thicken more upon chilling).

3. Remove from heat; stir in lime peel. Cover and chill at least 4 hours or up to 3 days. Makes 1½ cups.

low fat Each tablespoon: 31 cal., 0 g total fat, 0 mg chol., 1 mg sodium, 8 g carbo., 1 g fiber, 0 g pro. Daily Values: 7% vit. C.

CRANBERRY COOKING TIPS

■ Fresh cranberries are available in stores between October and December. Because their season is so short, it's a good idea to stock up. You can store them in their original bags, frozen, for up to a year.

■ Count on a 12-ounce bag containing about 3 cups whole berries.

■ Before cooking, discard any soft berries or stems. Rinse the remaining berries in cold water.

■ If you're using frozen cranberries, don't thaw them before using. Sort and rinse, then use just as you would fresh cranberries.

■ Cranberries can be time-consuming to chop on a cutting board, because they tend to roll. Instead, try chopping them in small batches in either the blender or food processor—short pulses only or you'll turn them to paste.

■ Give muffins that unmistakable cranberry tang: For a recipe that makes a dozen muffins, take a cup of fresh cranberries, chop coarsely, and toss in a bowl with 3 tablespoons sugar. Add this sugar-cranberry mixture to your favorite muffin recipe. Fill the muffin cups slightly fuller than normal and you should be able to get the entire recipe into 12 muffin cups.

■ Holiday math: You'll need 24 cranberries to make a foot of Christmas tree garland. That means about 10 feet per 12-ounce bag.

Mulled Cranberry Drink

Mulled Cranberry Drink

START TO FINISH: 20 minutes

5	cups cranberry juice	1	tsp. cardamom pods or
1½	cups fresh cranberries		¼ tsp. ground cardamom
	(6 oz.)	½	tsp. whole black pepper,
⅓	cup honey		cracked
¼	cup crystallized ginger,	1	vanilla bean, split
	chopped		

1. In a large saucepan stir together all ingredients. Heat over medium heat until mixture boils and cranberry skins pop. Remove from heat. Cover and let stand for 5 minutes.

2. Strain and discard solids. Serve warm. Makes 8 to 10 servings (about 4 ounces each).

TEST KITCHEN TIP: Cover and chill any leftovers. Reheat or, if desired, serve iced.

low fat Each serving: 156 cal., 0 g total fat, 0 mg chol., 5 mg sodium, 40 g carbo., 1 g fiber, 0 g pro. Daily Values: 98% vit. C, 1% calcium, 3% iron.

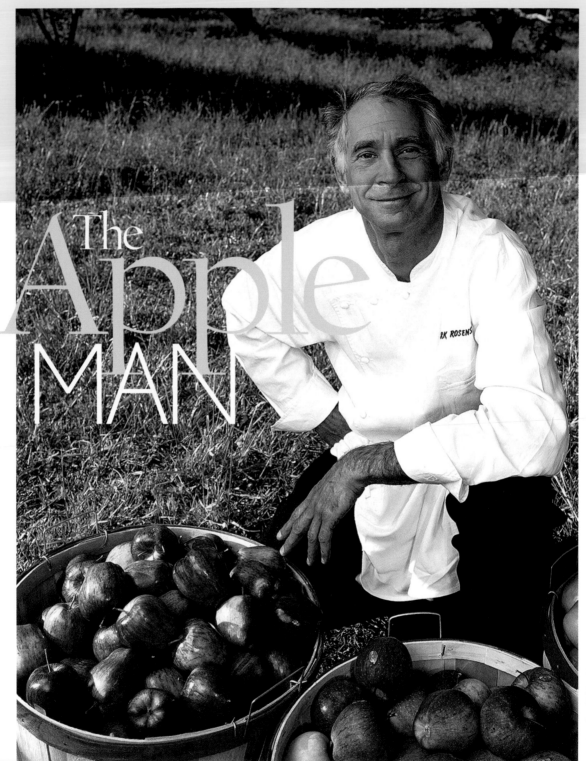

The Apple MAN

BY JEANNE AMBROSE. PORTRAIT: MILTON MORRIS. FOOD PHOTOGRAPHS: GREG SCHEIDEMANN. FOOD STYLIST: BROOKE LEONARD.

AN APPLE OBSESSION KEPT MARK ROSENSTEIN IN HIS KITCHEN FOR MONTHS IN SEARCH OF LIQUID GOLD.

Chunky Apple-Sage Sauce

Create an appetizer by serving the chunky applesauce on biscuits or toasted pita wedges that have been topped with smoked ham, cheddar cheese, and fresh sage leaves.

PREP: 15 minutes **COOK:** 10 minutes

4	medium Rome Beauty or Jonathan apples, cored and chopped (about 3 cups)
¼	cup finely chopped onion
3	Tbsp. snipped fresh sage
2	Tbsp. butter, cut up, or olive oil
2	Tbsp. lemon juice

1. In a medium saucepan combine apples, onion, sage, butter or olive oil, and lemon juice. Cook, covered, over medium heat for 10 minutes or until apples are softened, stirring occasionally.

2. If desired, mash slightly with a potato masher or fork. Let cool slightly. Serve warm or cover and chill for up to 24 hours. Let stand at room temperature for 20 minutes before serving. Makes 2½ cups.

Each ¼-cup serving: 57 cal., 3 g total fat (2 g sat. fat), 7 mg chol., 26 mg sodium, 9 g carbo., 2 g fiber, 0 g pro. Daily Values: 3% vit. A, 9% vit. C, 1% calcium, 1% iron.

Chunky Apple-Sage Sauce

Apple euphoria

There's a deep honey-brown syrup in Mark Rosenstein's kitchen that he cherishes. One taste and you'll know that it is, indeed, a treasure. The owner and chef of The Market Place restaurant in Asheville, North Carolina, has captured the essence of apples in a drizzly syrup that he uses whenever he wants to uniquely enhance a food he is preparing.

Mark created his prized syrup and many of his other delicious ideas at a time when he was at the height of his apple euphoria. It all began with an effort to include regional foods in his cooking.

"I started wondering if there was a cuisine in this neck of the woods where I live. But there wasn't really a western North Carolina cuisine," Mark says.

So he sought to find foods that epitomized the region. "We've got a lot of trout and apples around here, so I decided to start messing around with apples," he says.

His goal was to find something that would thicken and add rich flavor to vegetable stock. And he found it by gently simmering apple cider until it reduced to the consistency of maple syrup.

With a hint of cinnamon and cloves, the syrup is an incredible treat on ice cream or waffles, or drizzled over scones. Adding herbs or chile peppers gives the syrup a spicy-sweet kiss that enhances pork or seafood.

His concentration on apples resulted in enough recipes and information to fill his cookbook, *In Praise of Apples.* And he works apples and other seasonal produce into his menus. Part of his philosophy is to support local growers, something that began at his first restaurant 31 years ago. He continues to use fresh, organic local produce whenever possible. And he's still the apple man.

Apple Cider Syrup

Use fresh apple cider, not apple juice, when creating this reduction syrup. Start with 3 cups of apple cider, or double it as we did to get a bigger batch.

CINNAMON APPLE SYRUP: In a small stainless-steel or enamel saucepan bring 3 cups apple cider, a stick of cinnamon, and 2 whole cloves to boiling. Reduce heat; simmer over medium heat for 1 to 1¼ hours or until cider is thickened and reduced to ⅓ cup. Strain.

APPLE-AND-HERB SYRUP: In a small stainless-steel or enamel saucepan bring 3 cups apple cider, two 2-inch sprigs fresh thyme, one 2-inch sprig fresh rosemary, and one 2-inch sprig fresh marjoram to boiling. Reduce heat; simmer over medium heat for 1 to 1¼ hours or until cider is thickened and is reduced to ⅓ cup. Strain.

SPICY APPLE SYRUP: In a small stainless-steel or enamel saucepan bring 3 cups apple cider and 1 fresh serrano chile pepper, cut in half, to boiling. Reduce heat; simmer over medium heat for 1 to 1¼ hours or until cider is thickened and is reduced to ⅓ cup. Strain.

Each tablespoon: 70 cal., 0 g total fat, 0 mg chol., 4 mg sodium, 17 g carbo., 0 g fiber, 0 g pro. Daily Values: 2% vit. C, 1% calcium, 3% iron.

Apple Dumplings
PREP: 50 minutes **BAKE:** 40 minutes

1³⁄₄ cups water	¹⁄₄ tsp. salt
1¹⁄₄ cups sugar	²⁄₃ cup shortening
¹⁄₂ tsp. ground cinnamon	6 to 8 Tbsp. cold water
¹⁄₂ tsp. ground nutmeg	6 small cooking apples
Several drops red food	(about 1¹⁄₂ lb.), such as
coloring (optional)	Granny Smith, Rome
2 Tbsp. butter	Beauty, Braeburn, or Gala
2¹⁄₄ cups all-purpose flour	

1. For syrup, in a medium saucepan combine the 1³⁄₄ cups water, 1 cup of the sugar, ¹⁄₄ teaspoon of the cinnamon, ¹⁄₄ teaspoon of the nutmeg, and, if desired, the food coloring. Heat to boiling; reduce heat. Simmer, uncovered, about 10 minutes or until mixture is reduced to 1¹⁄₂ cups. Remove saucepan from heat; stir in butter.

2. Meanwhile, for pastry, stir together flour and salt. Cut in shortening until pieces are pea-size. Add the 6 to 8 tablespoons water, a little at a time, mixing until flour mixture is moistened. Form dough into a ball. On a lightly floured surface, roll dough into an 18×12-inch rectangle; cut into six 6-inch squares.

3. Preheat oven to 375° F. Peel and core apples. Place an apple on each pastry square. Combine the remaining ¹⁄₄ cup sugar, ¹⁄₄ teaspoon cinnamon, and ¹⁄₄ teaspoon nutmeg; sprinkle onto fruit. Moisten edges of pastry with water; fold corners to center over fruit. Pinch pastry corners together to seal. Place in a 13×9×2-inch baking pan. Pour syrup into pan around dumplings.

4. Bake, uncovered, for 40 to 45 minutes or until fruit is tender and pastry is golden. To serve, spoon syrup from baking pan over dumplings. Makes 6 servings.

Each serving: 611 cal., 26 g total fat (8 g sat. fat), 11 mg chol., 142 mg sodium, 90 g carbo., 3 g fiber, 5 g pro. Daily Values: 4% vit. A, 7% vit. C, 3% calcium, 15% iron.

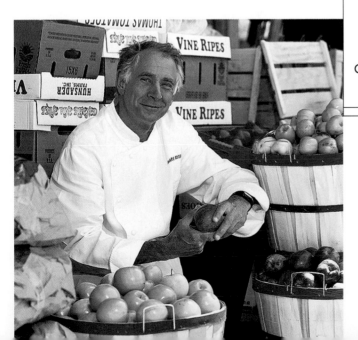

THE APPEAL'S IN THE PEEL

Most of an apple's fiber and those good-for-you antioxidants are found in the peel, so leave it on if at all possible. Do wash the fruit well before eating it. Try Mark's top picks for starters.

BRAEBURN: A spicy-sweet variety that balances well with tart Granny Smiths in a pie or cobbler.

CAMEO: Subtle red stripes make this an apple to admire as much as to eat. It's a crisp and sweet-tart apple.

GINGER GOLD: Get this one while you can. Available through November, Ginger Gold is snappy-crisp and excellent for eating out of hand.

HONEY CRISP: Its name gives a hint of its flavor. Try it in salads.

Braeburn

Cameo

Ginger Gold

Honey Crisp

December

DURING THIS SEASON OF GOOD CHEER, GATHER FOR OUTDOOR FUN AND RELAX WITH COZY DOWN-HOME MEALS.

Come for a Sledding Supper

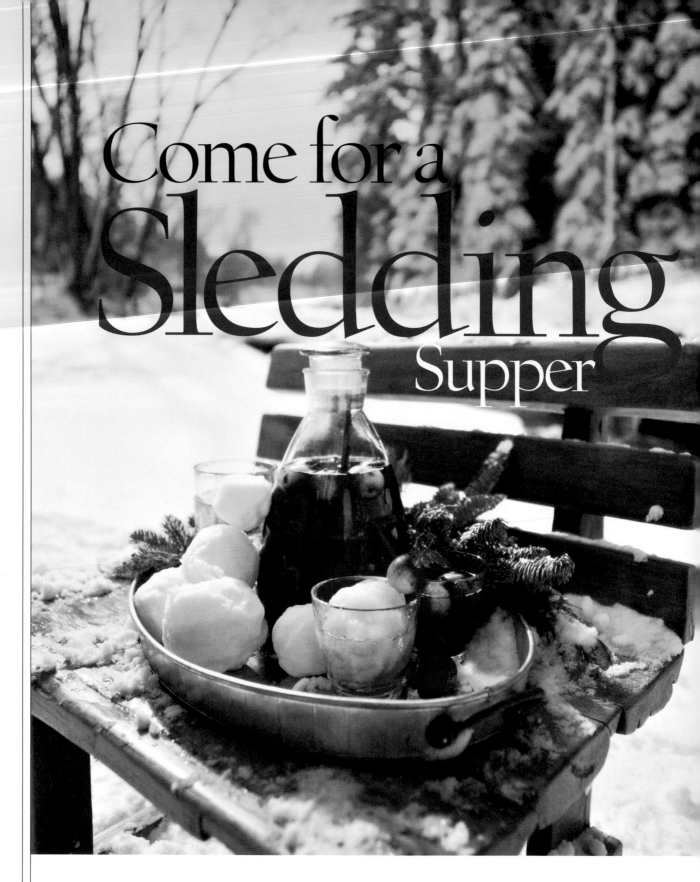

Come for a Sledding Supper

HOST A WINTER WONDERLAND SLEDDING PARTY, FOLLOWED
BY SNUG, WARM-YOU-UP ROCKY MOUNTAIN FARE.

Fire and Ice Nut Mix

This grab-a-gloveful snack balances the heat of peppery cashews with sweet and sugary maple-toasted pecans.

Prep: 15 minutes **Bake:** 45 minutes

1½	lb. lightly salted cashews (4½ cups)	3	Tbsp. honey
¾	tsp. cayenne pepper	¾	cup pure maple syrup
3	Tbsp. kecap manis (Indonesian sauce) or soy sauce	4	tsp. butter, melted
		1½	lb. pecan halves (6 cups)

1. Preheat oven to 350° F. For cashews, line two 15×10×1-inch baking pans with foil. Grease foil; set aside. In a food processor or blender place 1½ cups of the cashews. Cover and process or blend until finely ground. Stir together ground cashews and cayenne pepper; set aside.

2. In a large bowl combine kecap manis and honey. Add remaining whole cashews; toss to coat. Stir in ground cashew mixture. Spread in the prepared pans. Bake for 15 to 20 minutes (25 to 30 minutes if using soy sauce) or until golden, stirring once.

3. For pecans, line the two 15×10×1-inch baking pans with clean foil. Grease foil; set aside. In a large bowl combine maple syrup and butter. Add pecans; toss to coat. Spread pecans in prepared pans. Bake for 20 minutes, stirring twice.

4. Cool both types of nuts completely. Break into chunks. To serve, in a bowl combine both types of nuts. Store in an airtight container at room temperature. Makes 13 cups.

Each ¼-cup serving: 188 cal., 16 g total fat (2 g sat. fat), 1 mg chol., 82 mg sodium, 9 g carbo., 2 g fiber, 4 g pro. Daily Values: 1% vit. A, 1% calcium, 7% iron.

Fire and Ice Nut Mix

Winter warming

Skiing takes a powder when Charles and Aimee Dale hear the weather forecast is predicting snow. Instead, they decide sledding is just the ticket. Hills soon pile high with fluffy white stuff near their Colorado home, and an opportunity to share the afternoon and supper with friends is too much to resist for the Dales and their two children, Lily and Lucien. All it takes is a few telephone calls to quickly fill the sled run.

Out come mittens and hats, mufflers and ski pants, toboggans and sleds. Then it's red noses and squeals of delight all the way to the very bottom of the hill.

"We live in a place that's world-renowned for skiing, but Lily and Lucien are too young for that, so sledding's a great alternative," Charles says. Charles is chef/owner of two popular restaurants in nearby Aspen—Rustique and Range. Both are known for their sophisticated, unfussy approach to French country and Western cooking, respectively. At home though, Charles and Aimee bring the down-home, casual side of cooking to their kitchen. "We want people to remember the hominess and coziness, the family feeling of good cheer," Aimee says.

Aimee and Charles' agenda for parties goes like this: Plan

ahead, shop ahead, make ahead. They also build their menus around the kind of foods that kids will gobble up and adults will enjoy as well. "There's a handful of things the kids like. We tend to stick to classics or the tried-and-true. The holidays are about traditions anyway, so it's an easy road for us," Aimee says.

Cheese Fondue

For old-fashioned disposable tableware, take Charles' lead and find some clean twigs to spear and dunk the chunks of bread.
PREP: 30 minutes **STAND:** 30 minutes

12	oz. Emmentaler or Swiss cheese, shredded (3 cups)	1	Tbsp. Kirsch (optional) Dash ground black pepper
12	oz. Beaufort or Gruyère cheese, shredded (3 cups)		Dash ground nutmeg
4	tsp. cornstarch	1	or 2 loaves country bread or Two-Tone Bread (right), torn into 1-inch chunks
1	clove garlic, halved		
1³⁄4	cups dry white wine, such as Sauvignon Blanc		

1. Let shredded cheeses stand at room temperature for 30 minutes. Toss cheeses with cornstarch; set aside.

2. Rub the inside of a 4-quart Dutch oven with the halved garlic clove. Discard garlic. In Dutch oven heat wine over medium heat until small bubbles rise to the surface. Just before wine boils, reduce heat to low and stir in the cheeses, a little at a time, stirring constantly and making sure cheeses are melted before adding more. Heat and stir until the mixture bubbles gently.

3. Stir in Kirsch, if using, pepper, and nutmeg. If desired, transfer to fondue pot. Keep mixture bubbling gently over a burner. (If mixture becomes too thick, gradually stir in a little additional wine.) Serve with chunks of country bread threaded onto long skewers or clean small tree twigs. Makes 10 servings.

Each serving: 421 cal., 22 g total fat (13 g sat. fat), 68 mg chol., 467 mg sodium, 25 g carbo., 1 g fiber, 24 g pro. Daily Values: 14% vit. A, 70% calcium, 9% iron.

OUTDOOR SLEDDING PARTY

Fire and Ice Nut Mix (page 237)
Cheese Fondue (above) with bread cubes and vegetables
Lamb and Black Bean Quesadillas (page 241)
Oatmeal Jam Bars (page 244)
Hot Apple Cider with Calvados (page 244)

Two-Tone Bread

Cut up this swirled bread for white or sweet dark chunks to dunk into the fondue.
PREP: 1 hour **RISE:** 1³⁄4 hours **BAKE:** 30 minutes

5	to 5¹⁄2 cups all-purpose flour	¹⁄3	cup shortening
2	pkg. active dry yeast	1	Tbsp. salt
3	cups milk	3	Tbsp. molasses
¹⁄3	cup sugar	2¹⁄2	cups whole wheat flour

1. In a large mixing bowl stir together 3¹⁄4 cups of the all-purpose flour and the yeast; set aside. In a medium saucepan heat and stir milk, sugar, shortening, and salt just until warm (120° F to 130° F) and shortening almost melts. Add milk mixture to flour mixture. Beat with an electric mixer on low to medium speed for 30 seconds, scraping the side of the bowl constantly. Beat on high speed for 3 minutes. Remove 2¹⁄2 cups of the batter.

2. To the 2¹⁄2 cups batter, use a wooden spoon to stir in as much of the remaining all-purpose flour as you can. Turn dough out onto a lightly floured surface. Knead in enough of the remaining all-purpose flour to make a moderately stiff dough that is smooth and elastic (6 to 8 minutes total). Shape into a ball. Place in a lightly greased bowl; turn once to grease surface. Cover; set aside.

3. To remaining batter, use a wooden spoon to stir in molasses; stir in whole wheat flour and as much of the remaining all-purpose flour as you can. Turn dough out onto a lightly floured surface. Knead in enough of the remaining all-purpose flour to make a moderately stiff dough that is smooth and elastic (6 to 8 minutes total). Shape dough into a ball. Place in another lightly greased bowl; turn once to grease surface. Cover.

4. Let both doughs rise in a warm place until double (1 to 1¹⁄4 hours). Punch doughs down. Turn out onto a lightly floured surface; divide each dough portion in half. Cover; let rest for 10 minutes.

5. Meanwhile, lightly grease two 9×5×3-inch loaf pans; set aside. Roll out half of the light dough and half of the dark dough, each to a 12×8-inch rectangle. Place dark dough on top of light dough. Starting from a short side, roll up tightly and shape into a loaf; seal seams. Repeat with remaining doughs to make a second loaf. Place in prepared loaf pans. Cover and let rise in a warm place until nearly double (45 to 60 minutes).

6. Preheat oven to 375° F. Bake for 30 to 35 minutes or until bread sounds hollow when lightly tapped. If necessary, cover loosely with foil the last 10 minutes to prevent overbrowning. Immediately remove loaves from pans. Cool on wire racks. Makes 2 loaves (32 servings).

low fat Each serving: 150 cal., 3 g total fat (1 g sat. fat), 2 mg chol., 231 mg sodium, 27 g carbo., 2 g fiber, 4 g pro. Daily Values: 1% vit. A, 1% vit. C, 4% calcium, 9% iron.

BY STEPHEN EXEL. PHOTOGRAPHS: COLLEEN DUFFLEY. FOOD STYLIST: BROOKE LEONARD.

Cheese Fondue

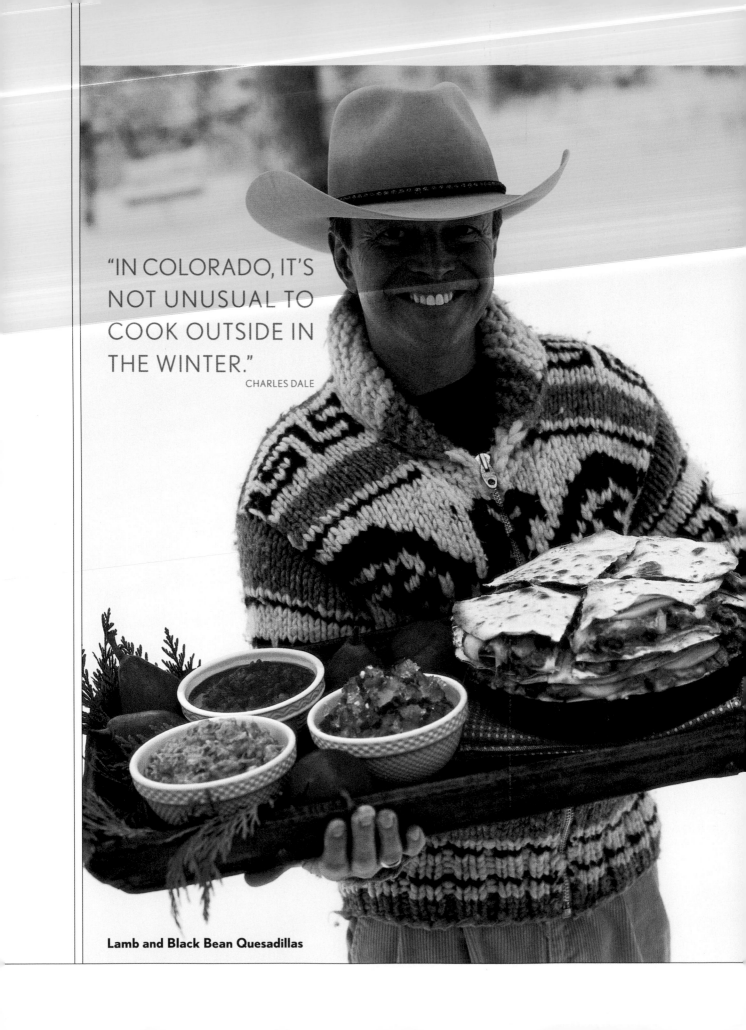

"IN COLORADO, IT'S NOT UNUSUAL TO COOK OUTSIDE IN THE WINTER."

CHARLES DALE

Lamb and Black Bean Quesadillas

Lamb and Black Bean Quesadillas

The Dales slow-cook the lamb filling the day before the party so they can enjoy the fun along with family and friends.

PREP: 35 minutes **COOK:** 4½ or 9 hours **GRILL:** 2 minutes

1 recipe Lamb-Black Bean Filling (below)	1 Tbsp. olive oil (optional)
1 medium mango, sliced	1 recipe Jalapeño Pepper Apple Jelly (right)
10 8-inch flour tortillas	Purchased avocado dip (guacamole)
8 oz. Fontina cheese, shredded (2 cups)	Bottled salsa

1. Prepare Lamb-Black Bean Filling. For quesadillas, divide filling and mango slices among 5 of the tortillas; sprinkle with cheese. Top with remaining 5 tortillas.

2. Place quesadillas on the rack of an uncovered grill directly over medium heat. Grill about 2 minutes or until tortillas are light brown and cheese is melted, carefully turning once. (Or in a 12-inch skillet or griddle cook quesadillas, one at a time, in hot oil over medium heat for 2 to 3 minutes or until tortilla is light brown and cheese is melted, carefully turning once. Remove the quesadilla from the skillet; place on a baking sheet. Keep warm in a 300° F oven while cooking remaining quesadillas, adding additional oil as needed.)

3. To serve, quarter quesadillas. Serve with Jalapeño Pepper Apple Jelly, avocado dip, and salsa. Makes 10 servings.

LAMB-BLACK BEAN FILLING: Trim fat from 2½ pounds lamb shoulder or 2 pounds boneless lamb leg; cut meat into bite-size strips. In a 3½- or 4-quart slow cooker stir together meat strips; one 15-ounce can black beans, rinsed and drained; one 12-ounce can mango nectar; 1½ cups water; 2 small red sweet peppers and/or Anaheim peppers, sliced; 1 small onion, sliced; ⅓ cup dry white wine; 8 cloves garlic, peeled; 1 teaspoon salt; and ½ teaspoon ground cumin. Cover and cook on low-heat setting for 9 to 10 hours or on high-heat setting for 4½ to 5 hours; drain. Stir 2 tablespoons tomato paste into lamb mixture.

LAMB AND BLACK BEAN BURRITOS: Fill the flour tortillas with lamb filling, mango slices, cheese, jalapeño jelly, and snipped fresh cilantro; roll up tortillas. Serve with avocado dip and salsa.

Each serving with toppings: 588 cal., 31 g total fat (14 g sat. fat), 104 mg chol., 796 mg sodium, 47 g carbo., 4 g fiber, 31 g pro. Daily Values: 47% vit. A, 77% vit. C, 21% calcium, 21% iron.

Jalapeño Pepper Apple Jelly

This simple jelly is perfect with the quesadillas, but it's also yummy spooned over cream cheese on bagels or crackers.

PREP: 10 minutes **CHILL:** 1 hour

1 small fresh jalapeño chile pepper, seeded and finely chopped*	1 tsp. butter
	1 10-oz. jar apple jelly
1 small fresh red chile pepper, seeded and finely chopped*	2 Tbsp. snipped fresh cilantro
	Fresh cilantro leaves

1. In a small saucepan cook and stir chile peppers in hot butter over medium heat about 1 minute or until tender. Remove from heat; cool. Stir in apple jelly and snipped cilantro, leaving clumps of apple jelly.

2. Transfer jelly to a small jar or serving dish. Cover and chill for at least 1 hour. Sprinkle with cilantro leaves. Makes 1 cup.

*NOTE: Because hot chile peppers, such as jalapeños, contain volatile oils that can burn your skin and eyes, avoid direct contact with chiles as much as possible. When working with chile peppers, wear plastic or rubber gloves. If your bare hands do touch the chile peppers, wash your hands well with soap and water.

low fat Each tablespoon: 54 cal., 0 g total fat, 1 mg chol., 8 mg sodium, 13 g carbo., 0 g fiber, 0 g pro. Daily Values: 7% vit. A, 13% vit. C, 1% iron.

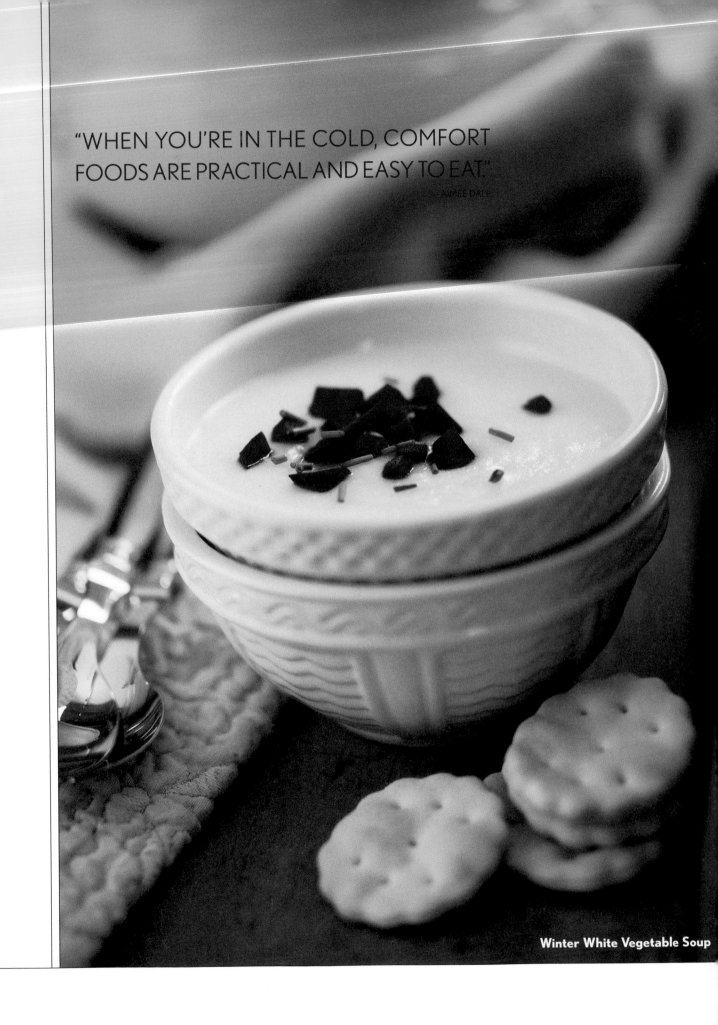

"WHEN YOU'RE IN THE COLD, COMFORT FOODS ARE PRACTICAL AND EASY TO EAT."
—AIMEE DALE

Winter White Vegetable Soup

Winter White Vegetable Soup

Chopped roasted beet and snipped chives give this creamy soup a celebratory touch of color.

PREP: 45 minutes **ROAST:** 1 hour

1 medium beet, trimmed (about 8 oz.)	1 large fennel bulb, sliced (discard leafy top) (2 cups)
1 medium onion, chopped	2 medium parsnips, peeled and coarsely chopped (1 cup)
1 Tbsp. butter	
1 small head cauliflower, coarsely chopped (4 cups)	
2 medium turnips, peeled and cut into 1-inch pieces (3 cups)	2 cloves garlic, halved
	1/4 tsp. salt
	4 cups water
1 medium celeriac, peeled and cut into 1-inch pieces (3 cups)	1 1/2 cups milk
	Milk
	1 Tbsp. snipped fresh chives (optional)
2 medium potatoes, peeled and cut into 1-inch pieces (2 cups)	

1. Preheat oven to 400° F. Wrap beet in foil. Roast about 1 hour or just until tender. Cool. Peel and chop or grate; set aside.

2. Meanwhile, in a 4- to 5-quart Dutch oven cook onion in hot butter over medium heat about 5 minutes or until tender, stirring occasionally. Add cauliflower, turnips, celeriac, potatoes, fennel, parsnips, garlic, and salt; stir in water. Bring to boiling; reduce heat. Simmer, covered, for 25 to 30 minutes or until vegetables are very tender. Remove from heat. Stir in the 1 1/2 cups milk. Let cool slightly, about 30 minutes.

3. Transfer soup mixture in batches to a blender or food processor; cover and blend or process until smooth. Return all soup to Dutch oven. Add enough additional milk to reach desired consistency. Heat through. Ladle into 10 soup bowls. Sprinkle with beet and, if desired, snipped chives. Makes 10 servings.

MAKE-AHEAD TIP: Roast, peel, and chop or grate beet up to 24 hours in advance. Store tightly wrapped in the refrigerator. Prepare soup through step 2. After cooling slightly, blend or process as in step 3. Do not return to Dutch oven. Transfer mixture to a storage container and chill for up to 24 hours. To serve, return mixture to Dutch oven and stir in enough additional milk to reach desired consistency. Heat through and serve as directed.

low fat Each serving: 119 cal., 2 g total fat (1 g sat. fat), 6 mg chol., 199 mg sodium, 22 g carbo., 9 g fiber, 4 g pro. Daily Values: 3% vit. A, 57% vit. C, 11% calcium, 6% iron.

Citrus Salad with Honey Balsamic Vinaigrette

To tote this refreshing salad to the sledding spot, pack the dressing separately from the fruit. Toss it before serving.

PREP: 25 minutes **CHILL:** 30 minutes

1 recipe Honey Balsamic Vinaigrette (below)	1 1/2 cups red and/or green seedless grapes
3 medium pink grapefruits	3 Tbsp. pomegranate seeds (optional)
3 medium oranges	1 head red leaf lettuce

1. Prepare Honey Balsamic Vinaigrette; cover and chill until serving time.

2. Peel and section grapefruits and oranges, working over a large bowl to catch juices; set juices aside. Add grapes and pomegranate seeds, if using. Cover and chill until serving time.

3. Before serving, toss citrus mixture with Honey Balsamic Vinaigrette. Serve in a lettuce-lined bowl. Makes 12 servings.

HONEY BALSAMIC VINAIGRETTE: In a blender or food processor combine 1/3 cup salad oil, 1/3 cup orange juice, 1/4 cup balsamic vinegar, 4 teaspoons honey, and 1/4 teaspoon cracked black pepper. Cover; blend until combined. Chill for at least 30 minutes.

Each serving: 140 cal., 7 g total fat (1 g sat. fat), 0 mg chol., 5 mg sodium, 21 g carbo., 2 g fiber, 1 g pro. Daily Values: 76% vit. C.

Oatmeal Jam Bars

These ready-to-go cream cheese bars reward sledders with their berry-good flavor and a boost of energy.

PREP: 15 minutes **BAKE:** 35 minutes

1⅓	cups all-purpose flour	2	3-oz. pkg. cream cheese, softened
¼	tsp. baking soda		
¼	tsp. salt	¼	cup butter, softened
¾	cup quick-cooking rolled oats	¾	cup blackberry or red raspberry jam
⅓	cup packed brown sugar	1	tsp. lemon juice
1	tsp. finely shredded lemon peel		

1. Grease a 9×9×2-inch baking pan; set aside. In a medium bowl stir together flour, baking soda, and salt. Stir in oats, brown sugar, and lemon peel; set aside.

2. Preheat oven to 350° F. In a large mixing bowl beat cream cheese and butter with an electric mixer on medium to high speed for 30 seconds. Add the flour mixture; beat on low speed until mixture is crumbly. Reserve 1 cup of the crumb mixture. Pat remaining crumb mixture onto the bottom of prepared pan. Bake for 20 minutes.

3. Meanwhile, in a small bowl stir together jam and lemon juice. Spread onto baked crust. Sprinkle with the reserved crumb mixture. Bake about 15 minutes more or until light brown. Cool in pan on a wire rack. Cut into bars. Makes 36 bars.

low fat Each bar: 78 cal., 3 g total fat (2 g sat. fat), 9 mg chol., 56 mg sodium, 11 g carbo., 0 g fiber, 1 g pro. Daily Values: 2% vit. A, 1% vit. C, 1% calcium, 2% iron.

OUTDOOR SLEDDING PARTY TOO

Fire and Ice Nut Mix *(page 237)*
Winter White Vegetable Soup *(page 243)*
Citrus Salad with Honey Balsamic Vinaigrette *(page 243)*
Giant Ginger Cookies or Mitten Cookies *(page 254)*
Minted Hot Chocolate *(right)*

Hot Apple Cider with Calvados

Sips of hot cider laced with apple brandy keep grown-ups warm while they're not slipping and sliding down the hill.

PREP: 15 minutes **COOK:** 20 minutes

1	gallon apple cider	1	cup Calvados or other apple brandy
1	cup strong brewed tea		
4	cinnamon sticks		Crushed ice (optional)
			Crabapples (optional)

1. In a 5- to 6-quart Dutch oven combine apple cider, tea, and the 4 cinnamon sticks. Bring just to simmering (do not boil). Simmer, uncovered, for 20 minutes. Remove cinnamon sticks. Stir in Calvados.

2. Serve hot cider in mugs over ice, if desired. If desired, garnish each serving with a crabapple. Makes 16 to 20 servings.

low fat Each serving: 167 cal., 0 g total fat, 0 mg chol., 21 mg sodium, 28 g carbo., 0 g fiber, 0 g pro. Daily Values: 4% vit. C, 2% calcium, 4% iron.

Minted Hot Chocolate

Mugs of this hot chocolate flavored with fresh mint warm up frosty little fingers and bright red cheeks.

PREP: 15 minutes **COOK:** 35 minutes **STAND:** 15 minutes

6	sprigs fresh mint	¾	cup sugar
1	vanilla bean, split in half lengthwise, or 1 tsp. vanilla extract	9	oz. bittersweet chocolate, chopped
12	cups milk		Peppermint sticks (optional)

1. Using 100-percent-cotton string, tie together mint sprigs and, if using, vanilla bean. In a 4-quart Dutch oven combine mint bundle, milk, and sugar. Heat just to boiling (watch carefully as milk may foam), stirring occasionally. Remove from heat. Let stand for 15 minutes.

2. Remove mint bundle and discard. Whisk chocolate into milk. Heat and stir just until mixture returns to boiling and chocolate is melted. Remove from heat. If using, stir in vanilla extract.

3. Serve in mugs. If desired, garnish each serving with a peppermint stick. Makes 12 servings.

Each serving: 272 cal., 12 g total fat (7 g sat. fat), 20 mg chol., 124 mg sodium, 36 g carbo., 2 g fiber, 9 g pro. Daily Values: 10% vit. A, 4% vit. C, 31% calcium, 5% iron.

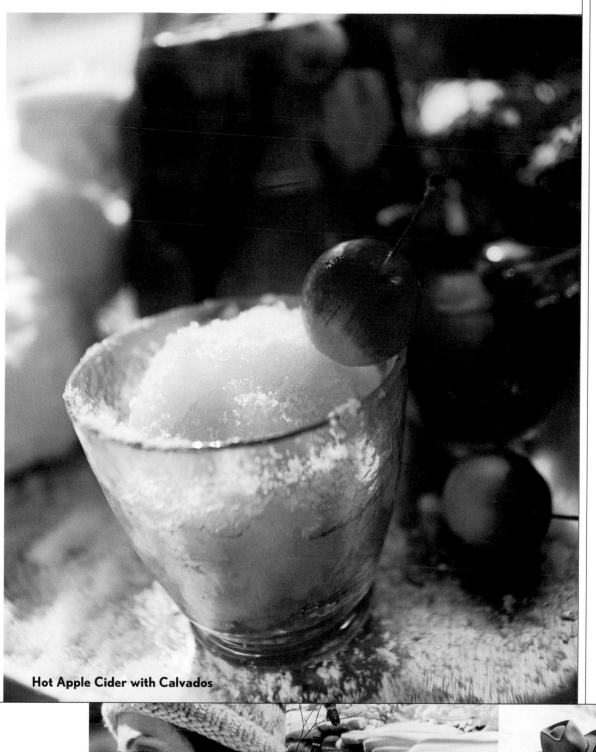

Hot Apple Cider with Calvados

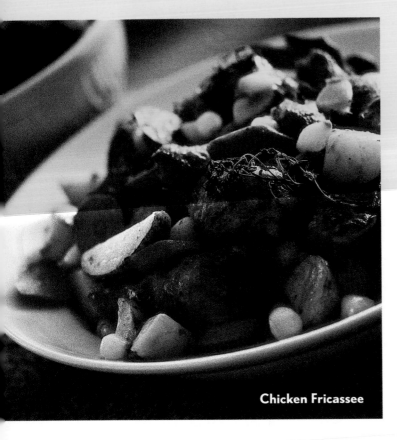

Chicken Fricassee

Chicken Fricassee

Make this dish the day before so the flavors blend together and party day becomes a lot easier for you.

PREP: 1 hour **COOK:** 30 minutes

2	3- to 3½-lb. cut-up broiler-fryer chickens	¼	cup red wine vinegar
	Salt	¼	cup champagne vinegar
	Ground black pepper	4	cups chicken broth
½	cup all-purpose flour	¼	cup snipped fresh thyme or 2 tsp. dried thyme, crushed, plus 2 Tbsp. snipped fresh parsley
¼	cup olive oil		
4	medium carrots, bias-sliced ¼ inch thick		
2	cups pearl onions, peeled*	1	lb. small Yukon gold potatoes, quartered
12	cloves garlic, peeled		

1. If desired, remove skin from chicken. Sprinkle chicken with salt and pepper. Place flour in a sturdy plastic bag. Add chicken pieces, a few at a time, shaking to coat. Heat two 10- to 12-inch skillets (or use one electric skillet and one 10- to 12-inch skillet) over medium-high heat. Add 2 tablespoons of the oil to each skillet. Cook chicken in hot oil for 10 to 15 minutes or until brown, turning occasionally to brown evenly. Remove the chicken from skillets; set one skillet aside.

2. Add carrots and onions to the other skillet, adding more oil if necessary. Cook and stir vegetables for 4 minutes. Add garlic cloves; cook for 1 minute. Add vinegars. Cook, uncovered, about 3 minutes more or until most of the liquid has evaporated, stirring occasionally. Transfer half of the vegetable mixture to the first skillet. Add 2 cups of the chicken broth and 1 tablespoon of the fresh thyme or parsley (or 1 teaspoon of the dried thyme) to each skillet. Bring mixture in each skillet to boiling.

3. Add light-meat chicken pieces to one skillet and dark-meat chicken pieces to other skillet. Divide potatoes between the 2 skillets. Return to boiling; reduce heat. Simmer, covered, for 30 to 40 minutes or until chicken is no longer pink (170° F for light-meat pieces, 180° F for dark-meat pieces). (Light-meat pieces may be done a few minutes before dark-meat pieces.)**

4. Transfer chicken pieces and vegetables to a serving platter; cover and keep warm. For sauce, boil mixture in both skillets, uncovered, until it reaches desired consistency. Skim off fat. Spoon sauce over chicken and vegetables. Sprinkle with remaining fresh thyme or parsley. Makes 10 servings.

***NOTE:** To peel onions, in a medium saucepan cook onions in boiling water for 30 seconds; drain. Rinse under cold running water; drain again. When cool enough to handle, cut a small slice from the root end of each onion. Squeeze from the other end to remove onion from peel.

****TO FINISH IN OVEN:** Use 2 oven-going skillets and preheat oven to 350° F. After adding potatoes and returning mixture to boiling in step 3, cover skillets and place in oven. Bake for 35 to 45 minutes or until chicken is no longer pink (170° F for light-meat pieces, 180° F for dark-meat pieces). Transfer chicken and vegetables to platter; cook sauce in skillets as directed.

Each serving: 535 cal., 33 g total fat (9 g sat. fat), 138 mg chol., 517 mg sodium, 19 g carbo., 2 g fiber, 38 g pro. Daily Values: 128% vit. A, 26% vit. C, 5% calcium, 16% iron.

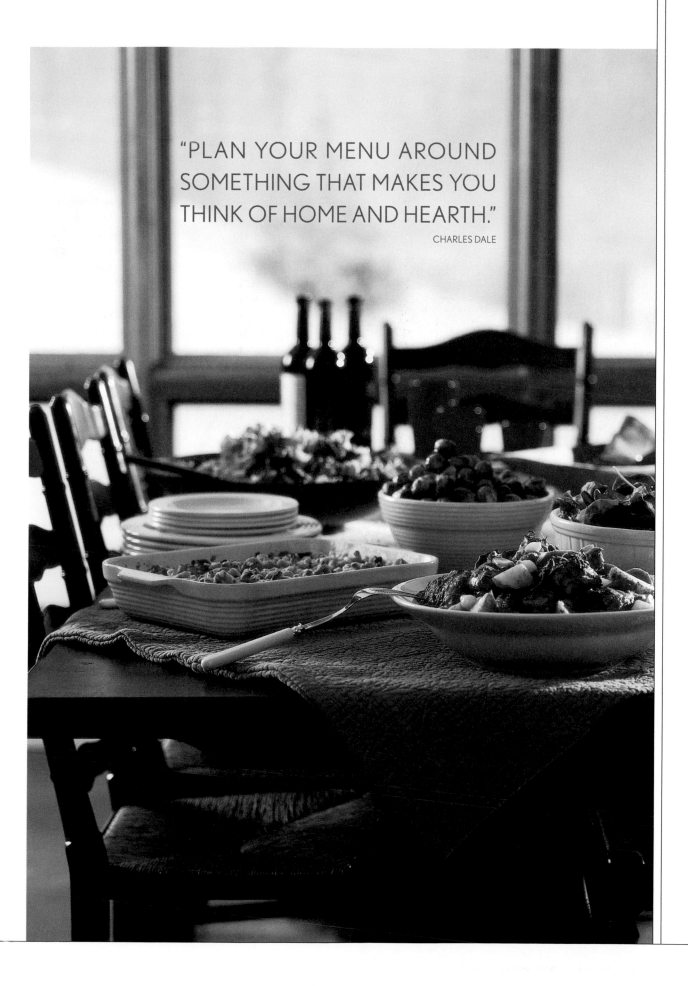

"PLAN YOUR MENU AROUND SOMETHING THAT MAKES YOU THINK OF HOME AND HEARTH."

CHARLES DALE

Cornmeal Buns

Serve this big batch of homespun buns warm with softened butter and you'll be glad this recipe makes so many.

PREP: 45 minutes **RISE:** 1 hour 50 minutes **BAKE:** 12 minutes

6	to 6½ cups all-purpose flour	½	cup butter
1	pkg. active dry yeast	1	tsp. salt
2¼	cups milk	2	eggs
½	cup sugar	1½	cups cornmeal

1. In a large mixing bowl stir together 3 cups of the flour and the yeast. In a medium saucepan heat and stir milk, sugar, butter, and salt just until warm (120° F to 130° F) and butter almost melts. Add milk mixture to flour mixture; add eggs. Beat with an electric mixer on low speed for 30 seconds, scraping the side of the bowl constantly. Beat on high speed for 3 minutes. Add cornmeal, beating on low speed until combined. Using a wooden spoon, stir in as much of the remaining flour as you can.

2. Turn dough out onto a lightly floured surface. Knead in enough of the remaining flour to make a moderately stiff dough that is smooth and elastic (6 to 8 minutes total). Shape into a ball. Place in a lightly greased bowl; turn once to grease surface. Cover and let rise in a warm place until double (1 to 1¼ hours).

3. Meanwhile, grease thirty-six 2½-inch muffin cups; set aside. Punch dough down. Turn dough out onto a lightly floured surface. Shape into 72 balls. Place 2 balls in each prepared muffin cup. Cover and let rise in a warm place until nearly double (50 to 60 minutes).

4. Preheat oven to 375° F. Bake for 12 to 15 minutes or until buns are golden brown. Immediately transfer from pans to wire racks. Serve warm or cool. Makes 36 buns.

*NOTE: If you don't have 36 muffin cups, place dough balls on a waxed-paper-lined baking sheet; cover with plastic wrap and chill while the first pan rises and bakes. After removing the baked buns from pan, wash pan, grease, and refill with chilled dough. Cover, let rise, and bake as directed.

low fat Each bun: 144 cal., 4 g total fat (2 g sat. fat), 20 mg chol., 106 mg sodium, 24 g carbo., 1 g fiber, 4 g pro. Daily Values: 3% vit. A, 2% calcium, 7% iron.

Macaroni and Cheese with Mushrooms

Not only will kids love this double cheese version of one of their favorite foods, but adults will enjoy it too.

PREP: 35 minutes **BAKE:** 30 minutes **STAND:** 15 minutes

12	oz. dried cavatappi or penne pasta	1	Tbsp. porcini mushroom powder* (optional)
5	Tbsp. butter	⅛	tsp. salt
3	Tbsp. all-purpose flour		Dash ground nutmeg
1½	cups half-and-half or light cream	12	oz. assorted fresh mushrooms, sliced, such as porcini, chanterelle, hedgehog, shiitake, or button
4	oz. Gruyère cheese, shredded (1 cup)		
3	Tbsp. finely shredded Parmigiano-Reggiano cheese	¼	cup dry white wine
		2	Tbsp. snipped fresh parsley

1. Preheat oven to 350° F. Cook pasta according to package directions; drain. Rinse under cold running water; drain again. Return pasta to pan; set aside.

2. Meanwhile, in a medium saucepan heat 3 tablespoons of the butter over medium heat until melted. Stir in flour. Add half-and-half all at once. Cook and stir until thickened and bubbly. Add ¾ cup of the Gruyère cheese, the Parmigiano-Reggiano cheese, porcini mushroom powder (if desired), salt, and nutmeg, stirring until cheeses are melted. Set aside.

3. In a large skillet cook mushrooms in the remaining 2 tablespoons butter over medium heat about 6 minutes or until tender and most of the liquid has evaporated, stirring occasionally. Add wine and cook, uncovered, until wine has nearly evaporated. Stir in parsley.

4. Add cheese mixture and mushroom mixture to the cooked pasta; stir to coat. Transfer pasta mixture to a 2- to 2½-quart shallow baking dish. Top with remaining ¼ cup Gruyère cheese. Bake, uncovered, about 30 minutes or until light brown and heated through. Let stand for 15 minutes before serving. Makes 10 servings.

MAKE-AHEAD TIP: Prepare pasta dish up to 24 hours in advance. Store tightly covered in the refrigerator. To serve, bake, covered, for 25 minutes. Uncover and bake about 30 minutes more or until light brown and heated through. Let stand as directed.

*NOTE: If you can't find porcini mushroom powder, use a spice mill to grind dried mushrooms into a powder.

Each serving: 336 cal., 18 g total fat (10 g sat. fat), 49 mg chol., 317 mg sodium, 30 g carbo., 1 g fiber, 14 g pro. Daily Values: 13% vit. A, 2% vit. C, 29% calcium, 8% iron.

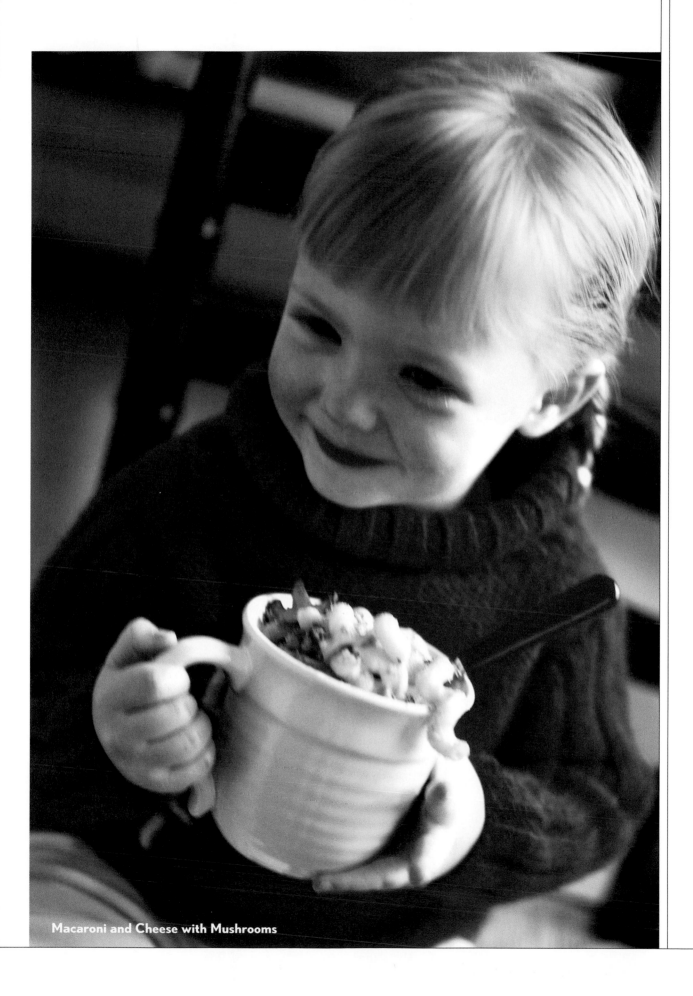

Macaroni and Cheese with Mushrooms

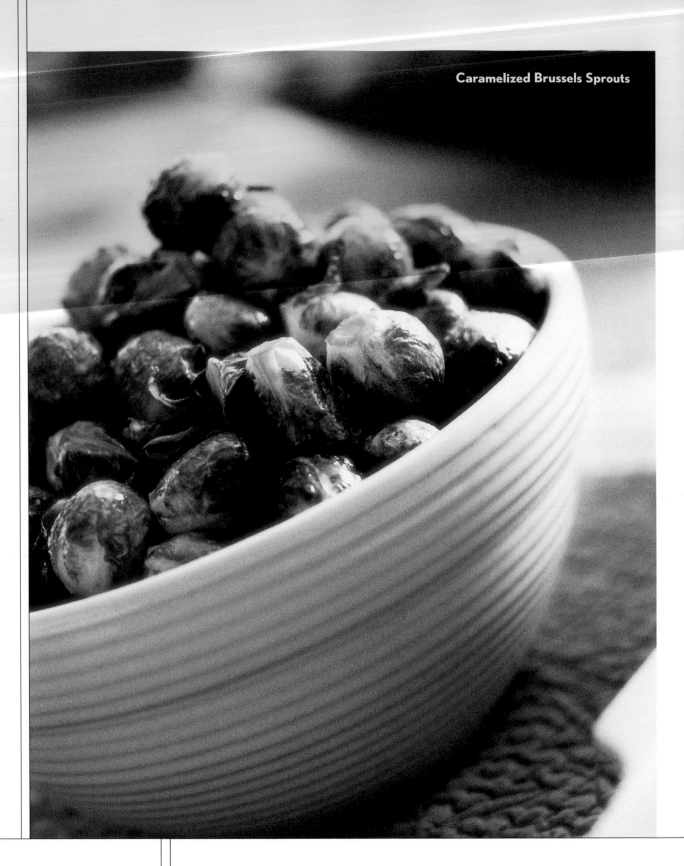

Caramelized Brussels Sprouts

"WE WANT PEOPLE TO REMEMBER THE COZY
FEELING OF SHARING A GOOD MEAL."

AIMEE DALE

Spinach with Sweet Red Onion

Simple spinach salad takes a surprising twist when punctuated with onions sautéed in grenadine syrup.

PREP: 15 minutes **COOK:** 15 minutes

2	large red onions, halved lengthwise and sliced (3 cups)	¼	cup grenadine syrup or boysenberry syrup
2	Tbsp. butter	2	Tbsp. sugar
1	cup dry or sweet red wine	¼	tsp. salt
		2	5- to 6-oz. pkg. fresh baby spinach (16 cups)

1. In a large nonstick skillet cook onions in hot butter for 5 to 8 minutes or until tender, stirring occasionally. Add wine, syrup, sugar, and salt. Bring to boiling; reduce heat. Simmer gently, uncovered, about 15 minutes or until most of the liquid has evaporated and liquid is syrupy.

2. Meanwhile, place the baby spinach in a very large serving bowl. Spoon the onion mixture over spinach; toss to combine. Season to taste with salt and pepper. Serve immediately. Makes 10 servings.

low fat Each serving: 88 cal., 3 g total fat (2 g sat. fat), 7 mg chol., 153 mg sodium, 12 g carbo., 3 g fiber, 1 g pro. Daily Values: 32% vit. A, 15% vit. C, 3% calcium, 12% iron.

Caramelized Brussels Sprouts

Spoon up homey Brussels sprouts to serve alongside the root vegetables in Chicken Fricassee.

PREP: 25 minutes **COOK:** 21 minutes

10	cups small, firm fresh Brussels sprouts (about 2¾ lb.)	¼	cup butter
		½	cup red wine vinegar
½	cup sugar	¾	cup water
		¾	tsp. salt

1. Prepare Brussels sprouts by peeling off 2 or 3 of the dark outer leaves; trim stem ends.

2. In a Dutch oven or 12-inch skillet heat the sugar over medium-high heat until it begins to melt, shaking pan occasionally to heat sugar evenly. Once sugar starts to melt, reduce heat and cook until sugar starts to turn brown. Add butter; stir until melted. Add vinegar. Cook and stir for 1 minute.

3. Carefully add the water and salt. Bring to boiling. Add the Brussels sprouts. Return to boiling; reduce heat. Simmer, covered, for 6 minutes. Uncover and cook about 15 minutes more or until most of the liquid has been absorbed and Brussels sprouts are coated with a golden glaze, gently stirring occasionally. Makes 16 servings.

low fat Each serving: 76 cal., 3 g total fat (2 g sat. fat), 8 mg chol., 155 mg sodium, 11 g carbo., 2 g fiber, 2 g pro. Daily Values: 11% vit. A, 66% vit. C, 2% calcium, 5% iron.

ROCKY MOUNTAIN SUPPER

Chicken Fricassee *(page 246)*
Caramelized Brussels Sprouts *(above)*
Cornmeal Buns *(page 248)*
Chocolate-Cherry Bread Pudding *(page 253)*
Coffee or tea

Spinach with Sweet Red Onion

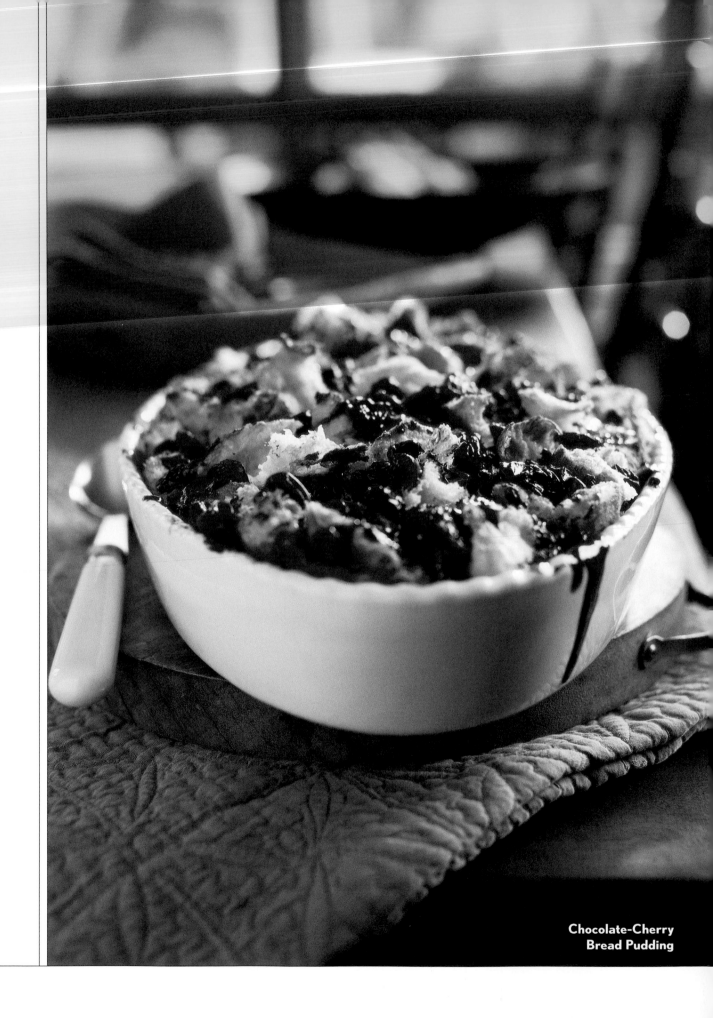

**Chocolate-Cherry
Bread Pudding**

Caramel Apple Crepes

Make the crepes ahead so you simply reheat them before serving.

START TO FINISH: 30 minutes

1 recipe Blender Crepes (below)	1 cup whipping cream
1 recipe Candied Nuts (below) or toasted pecan halves (optional)	2 Tbsp. apple brandy, brandy, or apple juice
1 cup packed brown sugar	1 Tbsp. butter softened
4 tsp. cornstarch	2 cups thinly sliced apples
	Vanilla ice cream (optional)

1. Prepare Blender Crepes. To reheat or to keep warm, place stack of crepes in a 300° F oven until serving time. Prepare Candied Nuts, if using.

2. In a large saucepan stir together brown sugar and cornstarch. Stir in whipping cream, brandy, and butter. Add apples. Cook and stir over medium heat until thickened and bubbly. Cook and stir for 2 minutes more.

3. To serve, fold each crepe in half, brown side out. Fold in half again, forming a triangle. Place 2 crepes on each of 6 dessert plates. Pour warm apple mixture onto crepes. Sprinkle with some of the Candied Nuts. If desired, serve with vanilla ice cream. Makes 6 servings.

BLENDER CREPES: In a blender combine 3/4 cup all-purpose flour, 1/3 cup water, 1/3 cup milk, 2 eggs, 2 tablespoons sugar, and 4 teaspoons walnut oil or cooking oil. Cover and blend until smooth, stopping and scraping the sides as necessary. Heat a lightly greased 6-inch skillet over medium heat; remove from heat. Spoon 2 tablespoons of batter into skillet; lift and tilt skillet to spread batter evenly. Return skillet to heat; brown on 1 side only. Invert skillet over paper towels to remove crepe from pan. Repeat with remaining batter, making 12 crepes total.

CANDIED NUTS: Line a baking sheet with foil; butter the foil. Set aside. In a large heavy skillet combine 1 1/2 cups pecan halves, 1/2 cup sugar, 2 tablespoons butter, and 1/2 teaspoon vanilla. Cook over medium-high heat, shaking skillet occasionally, until sugar begins to melt; do not stir. Reduce heat to low; continue cooking until sugar is golden brown, stirring occasionally. Remove skillet from heat. Pour nut mixture onto the prepared baking sheet. Cool completely. Break into clusters.

MAKE-AHEAD TIP: To freeze crepes, stack with waxed paper between layers. Place in a moisture-proof freezer bag; freeze for up to 3 months. Thaw at room temperature for 1 hour before using. Before reheating, remove waxed paper. You can also store Candied Nuts tightly covered in the refrigerator for up to 3 weeks.

Each serving: 465 cal., 22 g total fat (11 g sat. fat), 132 mg chol., 79 mg sodium, 61 g carbo., 1 g fiber, 5 g pro. Daily Values: 16% vit. A, 4% vit. C, 9% calcium, 10% iron.

Chocolate-Cherry Bread Pudding

When guests lean back in their chairs, bring out this old-time dessert, studded with bits of dried cherries and bittersweet chocolate.

PREP: 25 minutes **STAND:** 1 hour **BAKE:** 1 hour **COOL:** 1 hour

2/3 cup Kirsch or orange juice	8 oz. bittersweet chocolate, coarsely chopped
1 1/2 cups dried tart cherries or dried plums (prunes), snipped (about 8 oz.)	6 eggs
1 16-oz. loaf country Italian bread or baguette, cut into 1- to 1 1/2-inch pieces (about 11 cups)	3 cups milk
	2 cups half-and-half or light cream
	1 cup sugar
1/4 cup butter, melted	1 tsp. vanilla

1. In a small saucepan heat Kirsch or orange juice over medium-low heat just to simmering; remove from heat. Stir in dried cherries or plums. Let stand, covered, for 1 hour. Do not drain.

2. Preheat oven to 350° F. In a very large bowl drizzle bread with melted butter; toss to coat. Divide bread evenly between two 1 1/2-quart casseroles or place in one 3-quart rectangular baking dish. Sprinkle half of the chocolate evenly over bread in casseroles or baking dish; reserve remaining half of chocolate. Spoon half of the fruit and liquid evenly over the chocolate layer; reserve remaining half of fruit and liquid. Top with remaining bread.

3. In a large bowl whisk eggs; whisk in milk, half-and-half, sugar, and vanilla until combined. Slowly pour egg mixture evenly over the layers in casseroles or baking dish. Press down lightly.

4. Bake, covered, for 45 minutes. Uncover and bake for 15 to 20 minutes more for the 1 1/2-quart casseroles or 30 minutes more for the baking dish or until egg portion in center appears set. Sprinkle with remaining chocolate and fruit with liquid. Let stand about 1 hour. Serve warm. Makes 12 servings.

Each serving: 506 cal., 20 g total fat (11 g sat. fat), 137 mg chol., 342 mg sodium, 67 g carbo., 3 g fiber, 11 g pro. Daily Values: 12% vit. A, 2% vit. C, 17% calcium, 12% iron.

Giant Ginger Cookies

Chewy and delicious, these cookies are giants in both size and snappy ginger flavor.

PREP: 20 minutes **BAKE:** 11 minutes per batch

4½	cups all-purpose flour	1½	cups shortening
4	tsp. ground ginger	2	cups granulated sugar
2	tsp. baking soda	2	eggs
1½	tsp. ground cinnamon	½	cup molasses
1	tsp. ground cloves	½	cup coarse or granulated
¼	tsp. salt		sugar

1. Preheat oven to 350° F. In a medium bowl stir together flour, ginger, baking soda, cinnamon, cloves, and salt; set aside.

2. In a large mixing bowl beat shortening with an electric mixer on medium to high speed for 30 seconds. Add the 2 cups sugar. Beat until combined, scraping side of bowl occasionally. Beat in eggs and molasses until combined. Beat in as much of the flour mixture as you can with the mixer. Stir in any remaining flour mixture.

3. Using ¼ cup dough for each cookie, shape dough into balls. Roll balls in the ½ cup sugar. Place 2½ inches apart on an ungreased cookie sheet.

4. Bake for 11 to 13 minutes or until bottoms are light brown and tops are puffed (do not overbake). Cool on the cookie sheet for 2 minutes. Transfer cookies to a wire rack; let cool. Makes about 24 cookies.

Each cookie: 306 cal., 13 g total fat (3 g sat. fat), 18 mg chol., 138 mg sodium, 45 g carbo., 1 g fiber, 3 g pro. Daily Values: 1% vit. A, 1% vit. C, 3% calcium, 10% iron.

Mitten Cookies

Plain big cookies become the talk of the sledding hill when Charles and Aimee sprinkle on mitten shapes with colored sugars.

PREP: 30 minutes **CHILL:** 2 hours **BAKE:** 14 minutes per batch

1½	cups butter, softened	½	tsp. vanilla
1⅔	cups granulated sugar	⅓	cup ground toasted
2	tsp. baking powder		almonds
½	tsp. salt	4	cups all-purpose flour
2	eggs		Coarse colored sugars
¼	cup buttermilk		

1. In a large mixing bowl beat butter with an electric mixer on medium to high speed for 30 seconds. Add granulated sugar, baking powder, and salt. Beat until combined, scraping side of bowl occasionally. Beat in eggs, buttermilk, and vanilla until combined. Beat in ground almonds. Beat in as much of the flour as you can with the mixer. Stir in any remaining flour. Cover and chill about 2 hours or until easy to handle.

2. Preheat oven to 375° F. Using ⅓ cup dough for each cookie, shape dough into balls. Place 3½ inches apart on an ungreased cookie sheet. Cover with plastic wrap and flatten with hand or bottom of a pie plate to 4- to 5-inch rounds.

3. Place a mitten cookie cutter or a stencil* on top of cookie; sprinkle colored sugar inside the cutter or stencil. Remove and repeat with remaining cookies. Bake about 14 minutes or until edges are firm and bottoms are brown. Cool on cookie sheet for 2 to 3 minutes. Transfer to a wire rack and let cool. Makes 16 large cookies.

***MITTEN STENCIL:** Draw a mitten shape about 3 inches long on heavy cardboard or on the back of a stiff paper plate. Cut out mitten with a sharp knife or scissors.

Each cookie: 426 cal., 21 g total fat (12 g sat. fat), 76 mg chol., 321 mg sodium, 57 g carbo., 1 g fiber, 5 g pro. Daily Values: 15% vit. A, 5% calcium, 10% iron.

ROCKY MOUNTAIN SUPPER TOO

Macaroni and Cheese with Mushrooms *(page 248)*
Spinach with Sweet Red Onion *(page 251)*
Cornmeal Buns *(page 248)*
Caramel Apple Crepes *(page 253)*
Milk

Mitten Cookies

Pack up some cookies for the car to see everyone home in good spirits. Little ones will giggle at the sugar-sprinkled mittens on cheery Mitten Cookies.

Prize Tested Recipes

OUR MONTHLY RECIPE CONTEST HAS BEEN GOING SINCE 1923.
SEE THE WINNERS FROM 2003, PLUS EARLIER FAVORITES

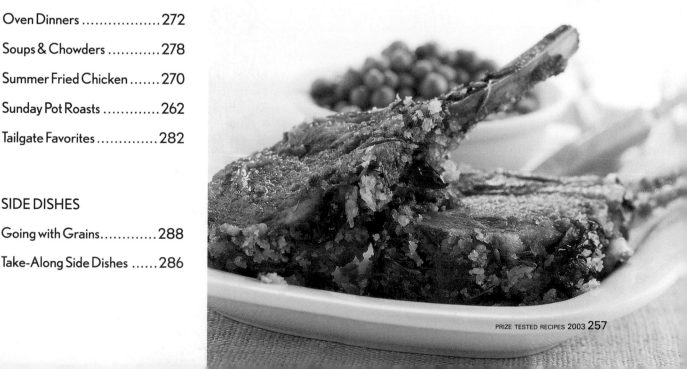

SEAFOOD APPETIZERS

L.D. MONTGOMERY, NASHVILLE, TENN.

DONNA FEUERSTEIN, NEENAH, WIS.

Calypso Shrimp Skewers

PREP: 30 minutes **GRILL:** 5 minutes

1/3	cup honey	1	3-oz. pkg. very thinly sliced prosciutto, cut into 7×1/2-inch strips
1	tsp. grated fresh ginger		
2/3	cup shredded coconut	1	7-oz. container crème fraîche
2/3	cup finely chopped peanuts		
1	lb. large shrimp, peeled and deveined (about 30)	1	tsp. finely shredded lime peel
			Lime juice

1. Soak 30 short wooden skewers in water for 30 minutes. Meanwhile, in a shallow dish combine honey and ginger. In another shallow dish combine coconut and peanuts. Set aside.

2. Drain skewers. Thread shrimp lengthwise on skewers, beginning at tail end. Brush each shrimp with honey mixture; roll in coconut mixture. Wrap a strip of prosciutto around each shrimp.

3. For a charcoal grill, arrange medium-hot coals around a drip pan. Test for medium heat above the pan. Place shrimp on grill rack over the drip pan. Cover and grill for 5 to 8 minutes or until shrimp turn opaque. (For a gas grill, preheat grill. Reduce heat to medium. Adjust for indirect cooking. Grill as above.)

4. Mix crème fraîche, peel, and enough juice to make of dipping consistency. Serve with shrimp. Makes 30 appetizers.

BAKING DIRECTIONS: Preheat oven to 375° F. Arrange the shrimp on a foil-lined baking sheet. Bake for 4 to 6 minutes or until shrimp turn opaque.

Each appetizer: 72 cal., 5 g total fat (2 g sat. fat), 25 mg chol., 111 mg sodium, 4 g carbo., 0 g fiber, 4 g pro. Daily Values: 1% vit. C, 2% calcium, 2% iron.

Smoked Salmon Roll-Ups

PREP: 30 minutes **CHILL:** 1 hour

2	cups cooked short grain rice, cooled	2	3-oz. pkg. thinly sliced, smoked salmon (lox-style)
2	Tbsp. toasted sesame seeds	1	medium avocado, halved, seeded, peeled, and sliced
2	Tbsp. rice vinegar		
2	tsp. sugar	1/2	of a medium cucumber, halved lengthwise, seeded, and cut into thin sticks
1	tsp. salt		
1/4	cup mayonnaise or salad dressing		
1/8	tsp. cayenne pepper		Shredded lettuce (optional)
4	10-inch spinach-flavored flour tortillas		

1. Combine rice and sesame seeds. Combine vinegar, sugar, and salt; stir until sugar is dissolved. Pour vinegar mixture over rice; toss to coat. Combine mayonnaise and cayenne. Set aside.

2. Spread 1 tablespoon mayonnaise mixture onto each tortilla. Top half of each tortilla with rice mixture, salmon, avocado, and cucumber. Carefully roll each tortilla tightly, starting at the filled sides. Wrap each in plastic wrap. Chill for 1 to 4 hours.

3. To serve, trim ends. Cut rolls crosswise into 1-inch-thick slices. If necessary, secure with toothpicks. If desired, arrange on shredded lettuce. Makes 28 appetizers.

Each appetizer: 77 cal., 4 g total fat (1 g sat. fat), 5 mg chol., 146 mg sodium, 8 g carbo., 1 g fiber, 2 g pro. Daily Values: 1% vit. A, 1% vit. C, 2% calcium, 3% iron.

Peppered Shrimp over Spicy Cheese Grits

PREP: 25 minutes **BAKE:** 25 minutes

1 recipe Spicy Cheese Grits (below)
8 oz. medium shrimp, peeled and deveined (about 24)
½ tsp. chili powder
¼ tsp. ground black pepper
2 slices bacon
4 cups crimini mushrooms, quartered
2 cloves garlic, minced
2 Tbsp. dry white wine or chicken broth
1 Tbsp. olive oil
¼ cup sliced green onions

1. Preheat oven to 350° F. Prepare Spicy Cheese Grits. Spoon the grits into a 1-quart casserole. Bake for 25 minutes; keep warm.

2. Meanwhile, toss shrimp with chili powder and black pepper; set aside. In a large skillet cook bacon until crisp. Remove bacon; drain on paper towels. Reserve 2 tablespoons of the drippings in skillet.

3. Add mushrooms and garlic to drippings; cook and stir until mushrooms are tender. Stir in wine or broth. Meanwhile, in a medium skillet cook shrimp in hot oil 4 to 5 minutes or until shrimp turn opaque.

4. Divide grits among 8 appetizer plates; top with mushroom and shrimp mixtures. Crumble bacon on top; sprinkle with green onion. Makes 8 appetizer servings.

SPICY CHEESE GRITS: In a medium saucepan bring 2½ cups water to boiling. Slowly add ¾ cup quick-cooking (hominy) grits, stirring constantly. Gradually stir ½ cup of the hot mixture into 1 beaten egg. Return egg mixture to saucepan; stir to combine. Remove from heat. Stir in 4 ounces Monterey Jack cheese with jalapeño peppers, shredded (1 cup); 2 tablespoons butter or margarine; ⅛ teaspoon salt; and, if desired, ⅛ teaspoon cayenne pepper.

Each serving: 247 cal., 15 g total fat (7 g sat. fat), 97 mg chol., 353 mg sodium, 14 g carbo., 1 g fiber, 14 g pro. Daily Values: 9% vit. A, 2% vit. C, 13% calcium, 10% iron.

Mahi Mahi Spring Rolls

PREP: 40 minutes
GRILL: 4 minutes per ½-inch thickness

2 tsp. sesame oil
1 tsp. cooking oil
12 oz. mahi mahi, monkfish, or red snapper fillets
12 8-inch rice papers
1 recipe Hoisin Dipping Sauce (below)
1½ cups shredded cabbage
⅔ cup shredded carrot
⅓ cup shredded coconut
¼ cup thinly sliced green onions

1. In a bowl combine sesame oil and cooking oil; brush onto both sides of fish. Place fish in a well-greased grill basket. Place on rack of an uncovered grill directly over medium coals. Grill for 4 to 6 minutes per ½-inch thickness or until fish flakes easily, turning fish once halfway through grilling. (Or, place on greased unheated rack of a broiler pan. Broil 4 to 6 minutes per ½-inch thickness, turning once.) Cool slightly.

2. Pour 1 cup warm water into a pie plate. Carefully dip rice papers into water, 1 at a time. Place papers, without touching, on clean dry kitchen towels. Let soften a few minutes until pliable.

3. For filling, prepare Hoisin Dipping Sauce. Gently flake fish; place in a large bowl. Add 6 tablespoons of the dipping sauce. Gently fold in cabbage, carrot, coconut, and green onion.

4. Spoon about ⅓ cup of the fish mixture onto a softened rice paper, just below center of paper. Tightly roll rice paper up from bottom around filling, tucking in opposite sides as you roll. Repeat with remaining papers and fish mixture, covering rolls as you make them to prevent drying. Serve with remaining Hoisin Dipping Sauce. Makes 12 appetizers.

HOISIN DIPPING SAUCE: Combine ½ cup hoisin sauce, 3 tablespoons unsweetened pineapple juice, 1 tablespoon rice vinegar, and ⅛ teaspoon cayenne pepper.

low fat Each appetizer: 120 cal., 3 g total fat (1 g sat. fat), 21 mg chol., 160 mg sodium, 16 g carbo., 1 g fiber, 7 g pro. Daily Values: 42% vit. A, 7% vit. C, 2% calcium, 4% iron.

Seafood-Melon Cocktail

PREP: 35 minutes **CHILL:** 1 hour

1 recipe Cilantro-Lime Salad Dressing (below)
8 oz. sea scallops
8 oz. medium shrimp, peeled and deveined (about 24)
2 cups cubed cantaloupe and/or honeydew melon
¼ of a medium English cucumber (3 oz.), quartered lengthwise and sliced (about 1 cup)
1 medium avocado, halved, seeded, peeled, and chopped (about 1 cup)
¼ cup finely chopped red onion
Red leaf lettuce
Lime slices (optional)
Fresh cilantro sprigs (optional)

1. Prepare Cilantro-Lime Salad Dressing; set aside. Quarter the scallops. In a large saucepan cook the scallops and shrimp in boiling water for 1 to 2 minutes or until opaque. Drain and rinse with cold water; drain again.

2. In a large bowl stir together the scallops, shrimp, melon, cucumber, avocado, and onion. Add dressing; gently toss until coated. Cover and chill for 1 to 4 hours.

3. To serve, line martini or margarita glasses with lettuce. Stir seafood mixture; spoon into glasses. If desired, garnish with lime slices and cilantro sprigs. Makes 8 to 10 appetizer servings.

CILANTRO-LIME SALAD DRESSING: In a small bowl combine ½ cup mayonnaise; 2 tablespoons snipped fresh cilantro; 1 fresh jalapeño chile pepper, seeded and finely chopped; ½ teaspoon finely shredded lime peel; 1 tablespoon lime juice; 1 clove garlic, minced; ½ teaspoon salt; ¼ teaspoon ground cumin; and ⅛ teaspoon ground black pepper.

Each serving: 207 cal., 15 g total fat (2 g sat. fat), 57 mg chol., 316 mg sodium, 8 g carbo., 2 g fiber, 12 g pro. Daily Values: 34% vit. A, 44% vit. C, 4% calcium, 7% iron.

SUMMER COOLERS

White Strawberry Sangria

For unbeatable flavor, select a white wine such as Pinot Grigio or Sauvignon Blanc.

PREP: 10 minutes **CHILL:** 1 hour

1 750-ml bottle dry white wine	2 cups sliced fresh strawberries
½ cup strawberry schnapps	Ice cubes
¼ cup sugar	Whole fresh strawberries (optional)

1. In a 2-quart pitcher stir together wine, strawberry schnapps, and sugar until sugar is dissolved. Add sliced strawberries; chill for 1 to 4 hours.

2. Serve over ice in 5 or 6 glasses. If desired, garnish each serving with a whole strawberry. Makes 5 or 6 servings.

low fat Each serving: 221 cal., 0 g total fat. 0 mg chol., 8 mg sodium, 22 g carbo., 1 g fiber, 1 g pro. Daily Values: 54% vit. C, 2% calcium, 4% iron.

Cranberry-Pineapple Cooler

PREP: 10 minutes **CHILL:** 1 hour

½ cup sugar	¾ cup lemon juice, chilled (about 4 lemons)
½ cup water	
2 cups cranberry juice, chilled	1 2-liter bottle ginger ale, chilled
1 cup orange juice, chilled (about 3 oranges)	Fresh cranberries (optional)
1 cup unsweetened pineapple juice, chilled	Lemon slices (optional)

1. For syrup, in a small saucepan combine sugar and the water. Cook and stir over medium heat until sugar is dissolved. Transfer to a 1-cup glass measure. Cover and chill for 1 hour.

2. In a large punch bowl stir together cranberry juice, orange juice, pineapple juice, lemon juice, and chilled syrup. Slowly add ginger ale, pouring down side of bowl; stir gently to mix. Serve immediately. If desired, garnish with cranberries and lemon slices. Makes 14 servings.

low fat Each serving: 118 cal., 0 g total fat, 0 mg chol., 12 mg sodium, 30 g carbo., 0 g fiber, 0 g pro. Daily Values: 1% vit. A, 49% vit. C, 1% calcium, 2% iron.

Mango-Ginger Coladas

START TO FINISH: 15 minutes

3/4 cup ginger brandy
3/4 cup mango or apricot nectar
1/2 cup cream of coconut
3 Tbsp. lime juice
4 1/2 to 5 cups ice cubes
    Fresh mango wedges (optional)

1. In a blender combine ginger brandy, mango nectar, cream of coconut, and lime juice. Cover; blend until combined.

2. Add ice, 1 cup at a time, blending well after each addition. Blend until mixture becomes slushy. Pour into 6 tall glasses. If desired, garnish with mango wedges. Makes 6 servings.

low fat Each serving: 160 cal., 7 g total fat, 0 mg chol., 4 mg sodium, 7 g carbo., 0 g fiber, 1 g pro. Daily Values: 11% vit. C, 1% calcium, 3% iron.

Raspberry Delight Punch

START TO FINISH: 15 minutes

1 qt. raspberry sorbet or sherbet
1 12-oz. can frozen raspberry juice blend concentrate, thawed
3 cups unsweetened pineapple juice, chilled
1/4 cup lemon juice
1/2 of a 2-liter bottle club soda, chilled

1. In a chilled large bowl stir 1 cup of the raspberry sorbet to soften; stir in thawed juice concentrate. Add pineapple juice and lemon juice.

2. Transfer to a punch bowl. Add remaining sorbet in small scoops. Slowly add club soda, pouring down side of bowl; stir gently to mix. Serve immediately. Makes 10 servings.

MAKE-AHEAD TIP: Scoop the sorbet or sherbet ahead onto a 15×10×1-inch baking pan or into a large freezer container. Cover and freeze until just before serving.

low fat Each serving: 200 cal., 0 g total fat, 0 mg chol., 25 mg sodium, 50 g carbo., 2 g fiber, 0 g pro. Daily Values: 93% vit. C, 2% calcium, 1% iron.

Frozen Strawberry-Mango Margaritas

PREP: 10 minutes **FREEZE:** 1 hour

2 medium mangoes*
1/2 cup gold (oro) tequila
1/3 cup orange liqueur
1/4 cup lime juice
2 Tbsp. sugar
2 cups frozen unsweetened whole strawberries
2 cups ice cubes

1. Seed, peel, and cube mangoes. Place cubes in a single layer in a shallow baking pan lined with plastic wrap. Cover and freeze for 1 hour. Transfer to a freezer bag or container for longer storage.

2. In a blender combine tequila, orange liqueur, lime juice, sugar, strawberries, and mango chunks. Cover; blend until smooth. With blender running, add ice cubes, 1 at a time, through opening in lid, blending until mixture becomes slushy. Pour mixture into 5 glasses. Makes 5 servings.

***NOTE:** If mangoes are not available, use 2 cups frozen unsweetened peach slices and skip step 1.

low fat Each serving: 176 cal., 0 g total fat, 0 mg chol., 3 mg sodium, 26 g carbo., 3 g fiber, 1 g pro. Daily Values: 52% vit. A, 91% vit. C, 2% calcium, 2% iron.

Icy Cranberry Margaritas

START TO FINISH: 10 minutes

1/2 cup frozen cranberry-raspberry juice cocktail concentrate, thawed
1/2 cup tequila
1/4 cup orange liqueur
3 Tbsp. melon liqueur
5 cups ice cubes

1. In a blender combine juice concentrate, tequila, orange liqueur, and melon liqueur. Cover; blend until combined.

2. With blender running, add ice cubes, 1 at a time, through opening in lid, blending until slushy. Pour into 6 margarita glasses. Makes 6 servings.

low fat Each serving: 147 cal., 0 g total fat, 0 mg chol., 2 mg sodium, 18 g carbo., 0 g fiber, 0 g pro. Daily Values: 19% vit. C.

Peaches and Cream Sunrise

This frosty dessert resembles soft-serve ice cream.

PREP: 15 minutes **FREEZE:** 1 hour

2 medium fresh peaches,* peeled, pitted, and sliced, or 2 cups frozen unsweetened peach slices
1 15 1/2-oz. can pineapple chunks (juice pack)
1 8-oz. carton vanilla yogurt
1/4 cup mascarpone cheese
1 cup milk
2 Tbsp. honey
2 tsp. grenadine syrup
    Fresh peach slices, strawberries, and/or peeled kiwifruit slices (optional)

1. Place the 2 sliced fresh peaches on a plastic wrap-lined 15×10×1-inch baking pan. Drain pineapple, reserving juice. Add pineapple chunks to the baking pan. Cover; freeze for 1 to 2 hours or until frozen. Cover and chill juice.

2. In a blender combine reserved pineapple juice, yogurt, mascarpone, milk, and honey. Add half of the frozen peaches and half of the pineapple. Cover and blend until smooth. Add the remaining frozen fruit; cover and blend until smooth.

3. Place 1/2 teaspoon of the grenadine in each of 4 glasses; swirl slightly to coat glasses. Pour in peach mixture. If desired, garnish each with fresh fruit on a skewer. Serve immediately. Makes 4 servings.

***NOTE:** If using fresh peaches, brush with lemon juice before freezing.

Each serving: 270 cal., 9 g total fat (5 g sat. fat), 26 mg chol., 79 mg sodium, 45 g carbo., 2 g fiber, 9 g pro. Daily Values: 9% vit. A, 25% vit. C, 19% calcium, 3% iron.

SUNDAY POT ROASTS

PRIZE TESTED RECIPES® $400 WINNER

GAIL L. JENNER, ETNA, CALIF.

PRIZE TESTED RECIPES® $200 WINNER

CONSTANCE MOYLAN, WILMETTE, ILL.

"Can't Be Beat" Pot Roast
PREP: 20 minutes **ROAST:** 1½ hours + 45 minutes

1	3- to 4-lb. boneless beef chuck pot roast
1	Tbsp. cooking oil
⅓	cup sweet Marsala wine
2	tsp. dried basil, crushed
1	tsp. garlic salt
½	cup plum preserves
4	medium potatoes, peeled and cut lengthwise into sixths
4	medium carrots, peeled, halved lengthwise, and halved crosswise
1	large rutabaga, peeled and cut into 1-inch chunks
1	medium onion, cut into large wedges
1	Tbsp. cold water
2	tsp. cornstarch

1. Preheat oven to 350° F. Trim fat from meat. In a 6- to 8-quart Dutch oven brown meat in hot oil. Drain off fat. In a small bowl stir together ⅓ cup water, wine, basil, garlic salt, and ½ teaspoon ground black pepper; pour over meat. Cover; roast for 1½ hours.

2. In a small saucepan melt preserves; pour over roast. Arrange vegetables around meat. Cover; roast 45 minutes to 1 hour more or until meat and vegetables are tender, stirring vegetables once.

3. Transfer meat and vegetables to a platter; cover to keep warm. For gravy, measure pan juices and skim off fat. If necessary, add enough water to juices to equal 1½ cups. Return to Dutch oven. Stir together the cold water and cornstarch. Stir into juices in Dutch oven. Cook and stir until thickened and bubbly; cook and stir for 2 minutes more. Serve with meat and vegetables. Makes 8 to 10 servings.

low fat Each serving: 388 cal., 10 g total fat (3 g sat. fat), 108 mg chol., 222 mg sodium, 33 g carbo., 4 g fiber, 38 g pro. Daily Values: 160% vit. A, 36% vit. C, 6% calcium, 29% iron.

Mediterranean Pot Roast
PREP: 20 minutes **COOK:** 2 + 1 hour

1	3-lb. fresh beef brisket
3	Tbsp. all-purpose flour
1	tsp. dried oregano, crushed
1	tsp. dried thyme, crushed
¾	tsp. salt
½	tsp. ground black pepper
2	Tbsp. olive oil
1	28-oz. can crushed tomatoes
¾	cup beef broth
1	large onion, chopped
4	cloves garlic, minced
½	tsp. sugar
2	medium fennel bulbs, cut into wedges
¼	cup pitted ripe and/or green olives
½	tsp. finely shredded lemon peel
	Hot cooked noodles or rice (optional)
	Pitted ripe and/or green olives (optional)

1. Trim fat from meat. In a small bowl combine flour, oregano, thyme, salt, and black pepper. Rub onto both sides of meat. In a 4- to 6-quart Dutch oven brown meat in hot oil. Combine undrained tomatoes, broth, onion, garlic, and sugar. Pour over meat. Bring to boiling; reduce heat. Cover; simmer for 2 hours.

2. Add fennel wedges and the ¼ cup olives. Simmer, covered, about 1 hour more or until meat is tender.

3. Transfer meat to a platter. For sauce, stir lemon peel into fennel mixture. Serve sauce and vegetables with meat and noodles or rice, if desired. If desired, garnish with additional olives. Makes 8 to 10 servings.

Each serving: 520 cal., 36 g total fat (13 g sat. fat), 110 mg chol., 689 mg sodium, 13 g carbo., 8 g fiber, 32 g pro. Daily Values: 1% vit. A, 24% vit. C, 7% calcium, 21% iron.

Beef and Sweet Potato Pot Roast

PREP: 20 minutes
COOK: 1¾ hours + 15 minutes

1   3-lb. boneless beef chuck pot roast
2   Tbsp. cooking oil
1   14-oz. can beef broth
1   Tbsp. Worcestershire sauce
3   medium sweet potatoes, peeled and cut into ½-inch-thick slices
1   14-oz. pkg. frozen whole green beans
1   large onion, cut into wedges
¼   tsp. ground cinnamon
    Apple juice
2   Tbsp. cornstarch
¼   tsp. salt

1. Trim fat from meat. Season with salt and ground black pepper. In a 4- to 6-quart Dutch oven brown roast in hot oil. Drain off fat. Pour broth and Worcestershire over roast. Bring to boiling; reduce heat. Simmer, covered, for 1¾ hours. Add vegetables and cinnamon. Return to boiling; reduce heat. Simmer, covered, 15 to 20 minutes or until meat and vegetables are tender.

2. Transfer meat and vegetables to a platter. For gravy, measure juices; skim off fat. Add enough apple juice to equal 1¾ cups; add to Dutch oven. Stir together ¼ cup apple juice, cornstarch, and salt. Stir into juices in Dutch oven. Cook and stir over medium heat until thickened and bubbly. Cook and stir for 2 minutes more. Serve over roast and vegetables. Makes 8 servings.

Each serving: 456 cal., 25 g total fat (9 g sat. fat), 109 mg chol., 441 mg sodium, 21 g carbo., 3 g fiber, 34 g pro. Daily Values: 180% vit. A, 23% vit. C, 5% calcium, 26% iron.

Reuben Pot Roast

PREP: 20 minutes **ROAST:** 1 + 1 hours
STAND: 10 minutes

1   3-lb. corned beef brisket
⅓   cup bottled Russian salad dressing
1   16-oz. can sauerkraut, drained
4   medium russet potatoes, peeled and quartered
2   cups packaged peeled baby carrots
2   oz. Swiss cheese, shredded (½ cup)
    Crusty rye bread (optional)

1. Preheat oven to 350° F. Discard seasoning packet from corned beef brisket. Trim fat from meat; place meat in a roasting pan. Spread dressing onto meat. Spoon sauerkraut around meat. Pour 1 cup water into pan. Cover; roast for 1 hour.

2. Arrange potatoes and carrots around the roast. Cover; roast for 1 to 1¼ hours more or until meat and vegetables are tender.

3. Transfer meat and vegetables to a platter; sprinkle vegetables with cheese. Let stand 10 minutes. Thinly slice meat across the grain. If desired, serve with bread. Serves 8.

Each serving: 407 cal., 27 g total fat (8 g sat. fat), 95 mg chol., 610 mg sodium, 10 g carbo., 4 g fiber, 29 g pro. Daily Values: 156% vit. A, 91% vit. C, 11% calcium, 25% iron.

Balsamic Pork Pot Roast

PREP: 15 minutes **COOK:** 2 hours

1   2½- to 3-lb. boneless pork shoulder roast
1   Tbsp. olive oil
1   large onion, sliced
2   cloves garlic, minced
1   14½-oz. can Italian-style stewed tomatoes
¼   cup dry red wine
¼   cup balsamic vinegar
1½ tsp. fines herbes or dried basil, crushed
1   bay leaf
    Hot cooked spaetzle or pasta
¼   cup shredded Parmesan cheese (optional)

1. Trim fat from meat. Season with salt and ground black pepper. In a 4-quart Dutch oven brown roast in hot oil. Remove meat. Add onion and garlic to Dutch oven; cook about 5 minutes or until tender.

2. Stir in undrained tomatoes, wine, vinegar, herbs, and bay leaf. Return meat to the Dutch oven. Bring to boiling; reduce heat. Simmer, covered, about 2 hours or until meat is tender.

3. Transfer meat to a platter; cover to keep warm. Skim fat from pan juices. Discard bay leaf.

4. For sauce, in a blender blend juices, half at a time, until smooth. Top spaetzle with meat, sauce, and cheese, if desired. Makes 8 servings.

Each serving: 420 cal., 15 g total fat (5 g sat. fat), 136 mg chol., 590 mg sodium, 27 g carbo., 3 g fiber, 38 g pro. Daily Values: 5% vit. A, 12% vit. C, 8% calcium, 19% iron.

Caribbean Pork Pot Roast

PREP: 20 minutes **ROAST:** 2½ hours

1   3½- to 4-lb. boneless pork shoulder roast
2   tsp. chili powder
1   tsp. packed brown sugar
½   tsp. salt
½   tsp. ground black pepper
¼   tsp. cayenne pepper
2   4-oz. cans whole green chile peppers, drained
1   20-oz. can pineapple tidbits
1   to 2 fresh jalapeño chile peppers, seeded and finely chopped (see note, page 302) (optional)
2   Tbsp. cornstarch
1   Tbsp. packed brown sugar
2   tsp. cider vinegar

1. Preheat oven to 325° F. Remove netting from roast, if present. Trim fat from meat. Combine chili powder, the 1 teaspoon brown sugar, the salt, and black and cayenne peppers; rub onto roast. Cut pocket down center of the roast. Stuff green chile peppers into pocket; tie with clean string, if necessary.

2. In a 6-quart Dutch oven arrange half of the undrained pineapple and, if desired, jalapeños. Add meat, stuffed side up. Cover; roast about 2½ hours or until tender.

3. Transfer meat to a platter. Skim fat from pan juices. Measure juices; add water, if necessary, to equal 1½ cups. Combine the 2 tablespoons cornstarch and remaining pineapple; stir into pan juices. Stir in the 1 tablespoon brown sugar and the vinegar. Cook and stir until thickened and bubbly. Cook and stir for 2 minutes more. Serve with meat. Makes 10 to 12 servings.

Each serving: 391 cal., 24 g total fat (8 g sat. fat), 111 mg chol., 287 mg sodium, 13 g carbo., 1 g fiber, 29 g pro. Daily Values: 5% vit. A, 23% vit. C, 8% calcium, 12% iron.

MOTHER'S DAY ENTRÉES

PRIZE TESTED RECIPES® $400 WINNER

JACQUELYN CLARK, SAN ANTONIO, TEXAS

PRIZE TESTED RECIPES® $200 WINNER

TINA FERDINAND, TAMARAC, FLA.

Roast Rack of Lamb

PREP: 20 minutes **MARINATE:** 4 hours
ROAST: 25 minutes **STAND:** 15 minutes

2	1-lb. French-style lamb rib roasts (each rack about 8 ribs)	3	Tbsp. olive oil
		1	Tbsp. butter
1	cup Merlot or other dry red wine	1	Tbsp. snipped fresh rosemary
2	cloves garlic, minced	2	cups soft bread crumbs
½	tsp. ground nutmeg	3	Tbsp. dried cranberries
		1	Tbsp. dried lavender*

1. Peel off the lamb's layer of fell (membrane) and fat, if present, down to the silver skin. Place lamb in a large resealable plastic bag set in a shallow dish. Add wine, 1 clove of the garlic, and the nutmeg. Seal bag. Refrigerate for 4 to 24 hours; turn bag occasionally.

2. In a skillet heat 1 tablespoon oil and butter. Add rosemary and remaining garlic; cook for 1 minute. Add crumbs; cook and stir for 3 minutes. Remove from heat. Stir in remaining oil, cranberries, lavender, ½ teaspoon salt, and ½ teaspoon ground black pepper.

3. Preheat oven to 450° F. Remove lamb from marinade; reserve marinade. Place lamb, bone side down, in a foil-lined shallow roasting pan. Pat crumb mixture evenly onto lamb. Insert a meat thermometer. Pour reserved marinade into roasting pan.

4. Roast for 25 to 30 minutes or until meat thermometer registers 140° F (medium-rare) or 155° F (medium). Cover loosely with foil for last 5 minutes of roasting. Let stand 15 minutes. Serves 8.

*NOTE: Look for dried lavender at health food stores.

Each serving: 212 cal., 11 g total fat (3 g sat. fat), 36 mg chol., 255 mg sodium, 9 g carbo., 1 g fiber, 11 g pro. Daily Values: 4% vit. A, 1% vit. C, 3% calcium, 10% iron.

Sausage and Apple Torta

PREP: 25 minutes **BAKE:** 35 minutes **STAND:** 10 minutes

½	of a 15-oz. pkg. folded refrigerated unbaked piecrust (1 crust)	1	clove garlic, minced
		2	eggs
2	large tart apples, peeled and thinly sliced	2	cups shredded Italian-style cheese blend (8 oz.)
½	cup chopped onion	1	cup ricotta cheese
1	Tbsp. sugar (optional)	1	oz. garlic-and-herb feta cheese, crumbled (¼ cup)
3	Tbsp. butter		
12	oz. bulk sweet Italian sausage		

1. Preheat oven to 450° F. Unfold piecrust and use to line a 9-inch pie plate. Bake according to package directions. Set aside. Reduce oven temperature to 350° F.

2. In a large skillet cook apples, onion, and sugar (if using) in hot butter over medium heat about 5 minutes or until tender. Transfer to a medium bowl. In the same skillet cook sausage and garlic until done. Drain in a colander; pat dry with clean paper towels.

3. Spoon sausage into prebaked crust. Top with the cooked apple mixture. In a bowl beat eggs; stir in cheeses. Spoon evenly over apple mixture.

4. Bake for 35 to 40 minutes or until a knife inserted near the center comes out clean. Let stand for 10 minutes on a wire rack before serving. Makes 8 servings.

Each serving: 486 cal., 34 g total fat (17 g sat. fat), 138 mg chol., 641 mg sodium, 23 g carbo., 2 g fiber, 19 g pro. Daily Values: 9% vit. A, 7% vit. C, 27% calcium, 5% iron.

Portobello and Spinach Brunch Tart

PREP: 25 minutes **BAKE:** 12 minutes

- 1 recipe Thyme Pastry (right)
- 3 cups fresh baby portobello mushrooms, quartered
- 2 cloves garlic, minced
- 1 Tbsp. butter
- 5 cups torn fresh spinach
- 1/2 cup sliced green onions
- 2 Tbsp. butter
- 5 eggs
- 1/4 cup half-and-half, light cream, or milk
- 1 tsp. snipped fresh thyme
- 1/4 tsp. ground nutmeg
- 1/4 tsp. salt
- 1/8 tsp. ground black pepper
- 4 oz. Gruyère cheese, cut into small cubes
- 1/4 cup shredded Parmesan cheese

1. Prepare and bake Thyme Pastry. Reduce oven temperature to 325° F.

2. Meanwhile, in a large skillet cook and stir mushrooms and garlic in 1 tablespoon butter over medium heat about 4 minutes or until tender. Add spinach and green onion; cover and cook about 2 minutes or until spinach is wilted. Drain in a colander.

3. In the same skillet melt the 2 tablespoons butter over medium heat. In a large bowl beat eggs; stir in half-and-half, thyme, nutmeg, salt, and pepper. Add to skillet. Cook, without stirring, until mixture begins to set on the bottom and around edges. With a spatula or large spoon, lift and fold the partially cooked egg mixture so the uncooked portion flows underneath. Continue cooking over medium heat for 2 to 3 minutes or until egg mixture is cooked through but still glossy and moist.

4. Remove from heat; fold in mushroom mixture and Gruyère cheese. Spoon into baked pastry shell. Sprinkle Parmesan cheese atop egg mixture. Bake for 12 to 15 minutes or until filling is heated through and cheese is melted. Makes 6 servings.

THYME PASTRY: Preheat oven to 450° F. Stir together 1 1/4 cups all-purpose flour, 2 teaspoons snipped fresh thyme, and 1/4 teaspoon salt; cut in 1/2 cup butter until pieces are pea-size. Add 4 to 5 tablespoons cold water, 1 tablespoon at a time, until dough forms, tossing with a fork to moisten evenly. Form dough into a ball. On a lightly floured surface, roll dough to 12-inch circle. Ease into 9-inch pie plate. Trim to 1/2 inch beyond edge of pie plate. Fold under extra pastry; flute as desired. Prick bottom and sides with a fork. Line pastry with double thickness of foil. Bake 8 minutes. Remove foil. Bake 5 to 6 minutes more or until golden. Cool on a wire rack.

Each serving: 438 cal., 36 g total fat (20 g sat. fat), 265 mg chol., 657 mg sodium, 22 g carbo., 4 g fiber, 18 g pro. Daily Values: 57% vit. A, 15% vit. C, 32% calcium, 23% iron.

Smothered Chicken

PREP: 30 minutes **BAKE:** 45 minutes

- 4 chicken breast halves (2 1/2 lb. total)
- 1/2 cup crumbled feta cheese (2 oz.)
- 1/4 cup pitted kalamata olives, chopped
- 2 Tbsp. snipped fresh basil
- 1/2 tsp. lemon-pepper seasoning
- 1 large onion, thinly sliced
- 2 cloves garlic, minced
- 1 Tbsp. olive oil
- 1 green sweet pepper, cut into strips
- 1 cup cherry tomatoes, halved

1. Preheat oven to 375° F. Loosen skin from chicken. In a small bowl combine half of the cheese, olives, and half of the basil; spread under skin of each breast half. Place chicken, skin sides up, in a lightly greased 2-quart rectangular baking dish. Sprinkle with seasoning. Bake, uncovered, for 40 minutes.

2. Meanwhile, in a large skillet cook onion and garlic in hot oil until onion is tender. Add sweet pepper, tomatoes, and remaining basil; cook for 1 minute more.

3. Drain fat. Top with onion mixture and remaining cheese. Bake 5 minutes more or until done (170° F). Makes 4 servings.

Each serving: 491 cal., 27 g total fat (8 g sat. fat), 156 mg chol., 506 mg sodium, 9 g carbo., 2 g fiber, 51 g pro. Daily Values: 14% vit. A, 60% vit. C, 11% calcium, 12% iron.

Warm Gorgonzola and Beef Salad

PREP: 35 minutes **FREEZE:** 1 hour

- 4 oz. Gorgonzola cheese
- 1 Tbsp. honey
- 1 1/2 tsp. packed brown sugar
- 1/4 cup toasted panko (Japanese-style) bread crumbs
- 1 recipe Dijon Vinaigrette (below)
- 12 oz. boneless beef sirloin steak, cut 1 inch thick
- 6 cups torn mixed salad greens
- 1/4 cup thinly sliced red onion, separated into rings
- 1/3 cup hazelnuts (filberts), toasted and chopped

1. Slice cheese into 4 pieces. In a small microwave-safe bowl combine honey and brown sugar. Microwave on 100% power (high) for 30 seconds. Brush honey mixture onto both sides of each slice of cheese; coat slices with crumbs. Place on a baking sheet. Freeze for 1 hour.

2. Prepare Dijon Vinaigrette. Set aside half for the dressing. Brush remaining vinaigrette onto steak.

3. Preheat oven to 375° F. Preheat a large nonstick skillet over medium-high heat until very hot. Add steak. Reduce heat to medium and cook for 15 to 18 minutes or until medium-rare (145° F), turning once. Remove from skillet; thinly slice.

4. Meanwhile, bake cheese for 4 to 5 minutes or just until cheese starts to melt. Toss salad greens and red onion with the reserved vinaigrette. Divide dressed greens among 4 dinner plates. Top with steak slices, warmed cheese, and nuts. Serve immediately. Makes 4 servings.

DIJON VINAIGRETTE: In a bowl whisk together 1/3 cup hazelnut or walnut oil, 1/4 cup balsamic vinegar, 2 teaspoons Dijon-style mustard, 1/2 teaspoon ground black pepper, and 1/4 teaspoon sea salt.

Each serving: 506 cal., 36 g total fat (8 g sat. fat), 61 mg chol., 620 mg sodium, 18 g carbo., 3 g fiber, 27 g pro. Daily Values: 10% vit. A, 7% vit. C, 20% calcium, 17% iron.

MAIN DISHES FROM THE GRILL

PRIZE TESTED RECIPES® $400 WINNER

CATHERINE A. BODI, WESTERVILLE, OHIO

PRIZE TESTED RECIPES® $200 WINNER

SHARON ROBERTSON, RENTON, WASH.

Burgers with Jicama Slaw
PREP: 30 minutes **GRILL:** 10 minutes

1	recipe Jicama Slaw (below)	½	tsp. salt
¼	cup bottled fire-roasted chunky salsa	¼	tsp. ground black pepper
		1½	lb. lean ground beef
1	clove garlic, minced	½	cup canned black beans, rinsed and drained
2	tsp. chili powder	6	kaiser rolls, split and toasted

1. Prepare Jicama Slaw; cover and set aside. In a small bowl combine salsa, garlic, chili powder, salt, and black pepper; add beef and beans. Mix well. Shape into six ½-inch-thick patties.

2. For a charcoal grill, grill patties on the rack of an uncovered grill directly over medium coals for 10 to 13 minutes or until an instant-read thermometer registers 160° F, turning once halfway through grilling. (For a gas grill, preheat grill. Reduce heat to medium. Place patties on rack over heat. Cover and grill as above.) Place burger on bottom half of each roll. Add about ¼ cup of the slaw and the top half of roll. Makes 6 servings.

JICAMA SLAW: In a small food processor or blender combine 1 canned chipotle pepper in adobo sauce, ¼ cup lime juice, and ½ teaspoon salt. Cover; process or blend until smooth. Transfer to a bowl; stir in ⅓ cup snipped fresh cilantro, ¼ cup dairy sour cream, and 2 tablespoons mayonnaise or salad dressing. Add 2 cups shredded peeled jicama; toss to combine.

Each serving: 448 cal., 19 g total fat (6 g sat. fat), 77 mg chol., 870 mg sodium, 41 g carbo., 3 g fiber, 29 g pro. Daily Values: 12% vit. A, 33% vit. C, 9% calcium, 28% iron.

Grilled Teriyaki Tuna Wraps
PREP: 25 minutes **MARINATE:** 1 hour **GRILL:** 8 + 2 minutes

3	8-oz. tuna steaks, cut 1 inch thick	1	Tbsp. cooking oil
⅓	cup soy sauce	¾	cup fat-free dairy sour cream
2	cloves garlic, minced	¾	cup bottled honey-Dijon salad dressing
1½	tsp. packed brown sugar	2	cups arugula leaves
1½	tsp. grated fresh ginger	1	large red onion, sliced
8	10-inch flour tortillas	1	medium tomato, chopped

1. Place fish in resealable plastic bag set in shallow dish. Combine soy sauce, garlic, brown sugar, and ginger; pour over fish. Seal bag. Marinate in refrigerator 1 to 2 hours, turning often.

2. Drain; discard marinade. For a charcoal grill, grill fish on greased rack of uncovered grill directly over medium coals for 8 to 12 minutes or until fish flakes easily (may be slightly pink in center), turning once. (For gas grill, preheat grill. Reduce heat to medium. Place fish on greased rack over heat. Cover; grill as above.) Brush both sides of each tortilla with cooking oil; place 2 at a time on grill rack for 30 to 45 seconds or just until warm.

3. In a medium bowl stir together sour cream and salad dressing. Spread 3 tablespoons sour cream mixture onto each tortilla. Cut tuna into ½-inch chunks; place some near an edge of each tortilla. Top each with arugula, onion, and tomato. Fold edges over filling; fold in the sides and roll up. Makes 8 wraps.

low fat Each wrap: 384 cal., 15 g total fat (3 g sat. fat), 42 mg chol., 610 mg sodium, 35 g carbo., 2 g fiber, 25 g pro. Daily Values: 46% vit. A, 11% vit. C, 10% calcium, 14% iron.

Grilled Salmon with Citrus Sauce

PREP: 15 minutes **MARINATE:** 1 hour
GRILL: 4 to 6 minutes per ½-inch thickness

1½ lb. boneless salmon fillet (with skin)
1 recipe Citrus Marinade (below)
1 Tbsp. orange peel cut into thin strips* (set aside)
1 Tbsp. lemon peel cut into thin strips* (set aside)
½ cup orange juice
3 Tbsp. lemon juice
1 Tbsp. olive oil

1. Place salmon in a shallow glass dish. Prepare Citrus Marinade; pour over fish. Cover and marinate in the refrigerator for 1 hour, turning often.

2. For sauce, in a small saucepan combine peel strips, orange juice, and lemon juice. Bring to boiling; reduce heat to medium. Simmer, uncovered, about 10 minutes or until mixture is reduced by half and slightly syrupy.

3. Remove salmon from marinade, reserving marinade. Measure thickness of fish. Brush salmon with olive oil. For a charcoal grill, place fish, skin side up, on the greased rack of an uncovered grill directly over medium coals; grill for 4 to 6 minutes per ½-inch thickness or until fish flakes easily when tested with a fork, brushing once with reserved marinade and gently turning halfway through grilling. (For a gas grill, preheat grill. Reduce heat to medium. Place fish on greased grill rack over heat. Cover and grill as above.)

4. Use a large spatula to transfer fish from grill to a platter, leaving skin behind; discard skin. Discard any remaining marinade. To serve, pour sauce over fish. Makes 6 servings.

CITRUS MARINADE: Combine 1 tablespoon shredded orange peel, ¼ cup orange juice, 1 tablespoon shredded lemon peel, 2 tablespoons lemon juice, 2 tablespoons snipped fresh basil, 1 tablespoon snipped fresh lemon thyme, 1 tablespoon snipped fresh chives, ½ teaspoon salt, and ⅛ teaspoon ground black pepper.

*NOTE: To make orange and lemon peel strips, use a vegetable peeler to peel orange and lemon. Use a sharp knife to cut peels into thin strips.

low fat Each serving: 172 cal., 6 g total fat (1 g sat. fat), 59 mg chol., 270 mg sodium, 5 g carbo., 1 g fiber, 23 g pro. Daily Values: 5% vit. A, 46% vit. C, 3% calcium, 6% iron.

Tennessee Pork Ribs

PREP: 20 minutes **CHILL:** 6 hours
GRILL: 1½ hours

1 Tbsp. paprika
1 Tbsp. packed brown sugar
1 tsp. ground black pepper
1 tsp. ground cumin
1 tsp. dry mustard
½ tsp. garlic powder
½ tsp. cayenne pepper
¼ tsp. celery seeds
4 to 5 lb. pork loin back ribs or meaty pork spareribs
1½ cups hickory wood chips
½ cup cider vinegar
2 Tbsp. prepared mustard
¼ tsp. salt

1. In a small bowl combine paprika, brown sugar, black pepper, cumin, dry mustard, garlic powder, cayenne pepper, and celery seeds. Sprinkle evenly over all sides of ribs; rub onto the surface of the meat. Wrap with plastic wrap; refrigerate for 6 to 24 hours.

2. Meanwhile, at least 1 hour before grilling, soak wood chips in enough water to cover. Drain wood chips. For a charcoal grill, arrange medium-hot coals around a drip pan. Test for medium heat above the pan. Sprinkle drained wood chips over coals. Place ribs, bone sides down, on grill rack over drip pan. Cover and grill for 1 hour, adding additional charcoal as necessary.

3. Meanwhile, stir together vinegar, prepared mustard, and salt. Brush onto ribs. Grill for 30 to 45 minutes more or until tender, brushing with mustard mixture every 10 minutes. Makes 4 to 6 servings.

Each serving: 485 cal., 21 g total fat (7 g sat. fat), 135 mg chol., 336 mg sodium, 8 g carbo., 1 g fiber, 63 g pro. Daily Values: 23% vit. A, 4% vit. C, 5% calcium, 18% iron.

Grilled Pork Tenderloin with Blackberry Sauce

PREP: 40 minutes **MARINATE:** 2 hours
GRILL: 30 minutes

1 1-lb. pork tenderloin
¼ cup olive oil
⅓ cup dry white wine
3 Tbsp. balsamic vinegar
2 Tbsp. Dijon-style mustard
½ tsp. soy sauce
2 cloves garlic, minced
1 tsp. snipped fresh rosemary
¼ tsp. ground black pepper
   Dash cayenne pepper
¼ cup seedless blackberry jam
1 tsp. finely shredded lemon peel

1. Trim fat from meat. Place meat in a resealable plastic bag set in a shallow dish. For marinade, combine olive oil, white wine, vinegar, mustard, soy sauce, garlic, rosemary, black pepper, and cayenne pepper. Pour over meat; seal bag. Marinate in the refrigerator for 2 to 4 hours, turning bag occasionally.

2. Drain meat, reserving marinade. For a charcoal grill, arrange medium-hot coals around a drip pan. Test for medium heat above the pan. Place meat on the grill rack over the drip pan. Cover and grill for 30 to 45 minutes or until done (160° F). (For a gas grill, preheat grill. Reduce heat to medium. Adjust for indirect cooking. Place meat on a rack in a roasting pan; place on grill rack and grill as above.)

3. Meanwhile, in small saucepan bring reserved marinade to boiling; reduce heat. Simmer, uncovered, for 8 to 10 minutes or until reduced by about half. Strain mixture. Return strained mixture to saucepan. Stir in jam and lemon peel; heat through.

4. To serve, arrange sliced meat on a platter; spoon jam mixture over meat. Makes 4 servings.

Each serving: 347 cal., 17 g total fat (3 g sat. fat), 73 mg chol., 266 mg sodium, 18 g carbo., 0 g fiber, 24 g pro. Daily Values: 6% vit. C, 2% calcium, 10% iron.

WINTER GRILLING

Blue Cheese Vidalia Onions

Grill burgers or steaks alongside the vegetable packet.

PREP: 15 minutes **GRILL:** 25 minutes

2 large Vidalia onions or other sweet onions, cut into ½-inch-thick slices	½ of an 8-oz. pkg. cream cheese, cut up
1 Tbsp. butter	2 tsp. Worcestershire sauce
4 oz. blue cheese, crumbled (1 cup)	½ tsp. ground black pepper
	½ tsp. dried dill weed

1. Fold a 36×18-inch piece of heavy-duty foil in half to make an 18-inch square. Place onion slices in center of foil. Dot with butter. Bring up opposite edges of the foil; seal with a double fold. Seal remaining edges with double folds to completely enclose the onions, leaving space for steam to build.

2. For a charcoal grill, place the packet on the rack of a covered grill directly over medium coals. Cover and grill for 25 to 30 minutes or until onions are just tender, turning packet once or twice during cooking. (For a gas grill, preheat the grill. Reduce heat to medium. Grill as above.)

3. Meanwhile, in a large bowl combine the crumbled blue cheese, cream cheese, Worcestershire sauce, pepper, and dill weed. Use a slotted spoon to add onions to the cheese mixture; toss to coat. Makes 8 servings.

Each serving: 130 cal., 11 g total fat (7 g sat. fat), 30 mg chol., 273 mg sodium, 5 g carbo., 1 g fiber, 5 g pro. Daily Values: 7% vit. A, 4% vit. C, 10% calcium, 3% iron.

Football Chicken Fajitas

PREP: 20 minutes **MARINATE:** 1 hour **GRILL:** 12 minutes

4 skinless, boneless chicken breast halves (about 1¼ lb.)	2 small sweet peppers
½ cup bottled Italian salad dressing	1 small red onion
	8 10-inch flour tortillas
½ tsp. chili powder	1 recipe Jicama Relish (below)
½ tsp. ground cumin	1 16-oz. jar salsa

1. Place chicken in resealable plastic bag. For marinade, combine dressing, chili powder, and cumin. Pour over chicken; seal bag. Marinate in refrigerator 1 to 24 hours; turn bag often.

2. Drain chicken, reserving marinade. Quarter and seed sweet peppers. Slice onion ½ inch thick. Brush with marinade.

3. For a charcoal grill, place chicken, peppers, and onion on the rack of an uncovered grill directly over medium coals. Grill until chicken is no longer pink (170° F) and vegetables are crisp-tender, turning once halfway through grilling (allow 12 to 15 minutes for chicken and 8 to 10 minutes for vegetables).

4. Meanwhile, prepare Jicama Relish. Warm tortillas. Slice chicken and vegetables into bite-size strips; spoon onto tortillas. Top with Jicama Relish and salsa. Roll up. Makes 8 servings.

JICAMA RELISH: In a large bowl toss together one 15-ounce can black beans, rinsed and drained; 1 cup chopped, peeled jicama; 1 large tomato, chopped; 1 medium avocado, halved, seeded, peeled, and chopped; and ½ cup snipped fresh cilantro.

Each serving: 396 cal., 16 g total fat (3 g sat. fat), 41 mg chol., 720 mg sodium, 42 g carbo., 6 g fiber, 25 g pro. Daily Values: 38% vit. A, 91% vit. C, 11% calcium, 22% iron.

Grilled Steak House Salad

PREP: 45 minutes **MARINATE:** 8 hours
GRILL: 17 minutes

1   1½-lb. beef flank steak
2   Tbsp. soy sauce
2   Tbsp. toasted sesame oil
1   Tbsp. grated fresh ginger
2   tsp. finely shredded lemon peel
2   cloves garlic, minced
½   tsp. ground black pepper
1   recipe Honey-Lemon Dressing
      (right)
1   large Vidalia onion or other sweet
      onion, cut into ½-inch-thick slices
1   Tbsp. cooking oil
2   hearts of romaine lettuce, torn
      (about 8 cups)
1   5-oz. pkg. arugula
½   cup chopped walnuts, toasted
2   oz. Gorgonzola cheese, crumbled

1. Trim fat from steak. Score steak on both sides by making shallow cuts at 1-inch intervals in a diamond pattern. Place steak in a resealable plastic bag set in a shallow dish. For marinade, combine soy sauce, sesame oil, ginger, lemon peel, garlic, and pepper. Pour over steak; seal bag. Marinate in the refrigerator for 8 to 24 hours, turning the bag occasionally. Prepare Honey-Lemon Dressing; chill.

2. Remove steak from marinade; discard marinade. Brush onion slices with cooking oil. For a charcoal grill, grill steak and onion slices on the rack of an uncovered grill directly over medium coals for 17 to 21 minutes for medium doneness (160° F), turning once halfway through grilling. (For a gas grill, preheat grill. Reduce heat to medium. Place steak on grill rack over heat. Cover and grill as above.)

3. Remove onion slices when they are tender and slightly charred. Thinly slice the steak diagonally across the grain.

4. In a very large bowl toss together the torn romaine and arugula. Drizzle with half of the Honey-Lemon Dressing; toss to coat. Add sliced steak, grilled onion, walnuts, and remaining dressing; toss to coat. Divide among 8 plates. Sprinkle with cheese. Makes 8 servings.

HONEY-LEMON DRESSING: In a small bowl whisk ¾ cup olive oil, ¼ cup white balsamic vinegar, 3 tablespoons lemon juice, 2 tablespoons finely chopped shallots, 1 tablespoon honey, 1 tablespoon Dijon-style mustard, ½ teaspoon ground black pepper, and ¼ teaspoon salt.

Each serving: 482 cal., 39 g total fat (8 g sat. fat), 39 mg chol., 502 mg sodium, 11 g carbo., 2 g fiber, 24 g pro. Daily Values: 39% vit. A, 35% vit. C, 11% calcium, 16% iron.

Cheesy Meat Loaf

PREP: 30 minutes **GRILL:** 60 minutes

1   egg
1¼   cups soft bread crumbs
¼   cup milk
1   cup shredded taco cheese (4 oz.)
½   cup shredded carrot
¼   cup bottled steak sauce
1   to 2 Tbsp. prepared horseradish
½   tsp. seasoned salt
½   tsp. ground black pepper
1   lb. ground beef
8   oz. ground pork

1. In a large bowl beat egg; stir in bread crumbs, milk, cheese, carrot, 2 tablespoons of the steak sauce, the horseradish, seasoned salt, and pepper. Add ground meats; mix well. Shape meat mixture into an 8×4-inch loaf.

2. Fold a 24×18-inch piece of heavy-duty foil in half crosswise. Trim to a 12-inch square. Cut several large slits in the foil. Place the meat loaf on foil.

3. For a charcoal grill, arrange medium coals around a drip pan. Test for medium-low heat above pan. Place foil with meat loaf on grill rack over pan. Cover; grill for 60 to 70 minutes or until meat is done (160° F), brushing with remaining 2 tablespoons steak sauce during the last 5 minutes. To check doneness, insert an instant-read thermometer through the side of the loaf to a depth of 2 to 3 inches. (For a gas grill, preheat grill. Reduce heat to medium-low. Adjust for indirect cooking. Cover and grill as above.)

4. Carefully remove meat loaf from grill. Cover with foil; let stand for 15 minutes before serving. Makes 6 to 8 servings.

Each serving: 305 cal., 13 g total fat (9 g sat. fat), 117 mg chol., 534 mg sodium, 8 g carbo., 1 g fiber, 22 g pro. Daily Values: 64% vit. A, 6% vit. C, 14% calcium, 12% iron.

Marinated Mint Lamb

PREP: 25 minutes **MARINATE:** 8 hours
GRILL: 1½ hours **STAND:** 15 minutes

1   3- to 4-lb. boneless leg of lamb,
        rolled and tied
¾   cup snipped fresh mint
½   cup white wine vinegar
¼   cup cooking oil
2   Tbsp. honey
1   Tbsp. Worcestershire sauce
3   cloves garlic, minced
½   tsp. salt
½   tsp. ground black pepper

1. Untie roast and trim fat. Place lamb in a resealable plastic bag set in a shallow dish. For marinade, combine mint, vinegar, oil, honey, Worcestershire sauce, garlic, salt, and pepper. Pour marinade over lamb; seal bag. Marinate in the refrigerator for 8 to 24 hours, turning bag occasionally.

2. Drain lamb; discard marinade. Retie meat with butcher's string. Insert an oven-going meat thermometer into center.

3. For a charcoal grill, arrange medium coals around a drip pan. Test for medium-low heat above pan. Place meat on a grill rack over drip pan. Cover and grill until meat thermometer registers 140° F for medium-rare doneness (1½ to 2¼ hours) or 155° F for medium doneness (1¾ to 2½ hours). (For a gas grill, preheat grill. Reduce heat to medium. Adjust for indirect cooking. Cover and grill as above, except place meat on rack in a roasting pan.)

4. Remove meat from grill. Cover with foil; let stand for 15 minutes (the meat's temperature will rise 5° F during standing). To serve, remove string and thinly slice meat. Makes 8 servings.

Each serving: 358 cal., 23 g total fat (9 g sat. fat), 111 mg chol., 158 mg sodium, 3 g carbo., 0 g fiber, 32 g pro. Daily Values: 4% vit. C, 2% calcium, 20% iron.

SUMMER FRIED CHICKEN

Green Chile Fried Chicken

PREP: 25 minutes **MARINATE:** 8 hours **COOK:** 40 minutes

1 2½- to 3-lb. cut-up broiler-fryer chicken, skinned, if desired	2 Tbsp. lime juice
	1 clove garlic, minced
	¾ tsp. ground cumin
1 8-oz. carton dairy sour cream	½ tsp. salt
¼ cup milk	¼ tsp. ground black pepper
1 4-oz. can diced green chile peppers	¾ cup all-purpose flour
	Cooking oil
2 Tbsp. snipped fresh cilantro	Bottled hot pepper sauce (optional)
	Lime wedges (optional)

1. Place chicken in resealable plastic bag set in shallow dish. For marinade, in a medium bowl combine sour cream, milk, chile peppers, cilantro, lime juice, garlic, cumin, salt, and black pepper. Pour over chicken; seal bag. Refrigerate for 8 to 24 hours, turning bag occasionally. Place flour in a shallow dish. Remove chicken from bag; discard marinade. Add chicken pieces to flour, a few at a time, turning to coat.

2. Add oil to a 12-inch heavy skillet to a depth of ¼ to ½ inch. Heat over medium-high heat until hot (350° F). Reduce heat. Carefully add chicken to the skillet. Cook, uncovered, over medium heat about 40 minutes or until chicken is no longer pink (170° F for breasts; 180° F for thighs and drumsticks), turning occasionally to brown evenly. Drain on paper towels. If desired, serve with bottled hot pepper sauce and lime wedges. Serves 4 to 6.

Each serving: 608 cal., 42 g total fat (14 g sat. fat), 125 mg chol., 501 mg sodium, 22 g carbo., 1 g fiber, 36 g pro. Daily Values: 12% vit. A, 25% vit. C, 15% calcium, 15% iron.

Pecan Crust Chicken

Marmalade and maple syrup lend a hint of sweetness while pecans provide the crunch.

PREP: 20 minutes **COOK:** 12 minutes

2 Tbsp. orange marmalade	¼ tsp. salt
2 Tbsp. pure maple syrup	4 skinless, boneless chicken breast halves (1¼ lb. total)
1 cup finely chopped pecans	
	2 Tbsp. cooking oil
3 Tbsp. all-purpose flour	1 Tbsp. butter

1. In a small bowl stir together orange marmalade and maple syrup; set aside. In a shallow dish combine pecans, flour, and salt. Brush marmalade mixture onto both sides of each chicken breast half. Dip chicken into pecan mixture, turning to coat; press pecan mixture onto chicken, if necessary.

2. In a 12-inch skillet heat oil and butter over medium heat until butter is melted and mixture begins to bubble. Carefully add chicken to skillet. Cook for 6 minutes. Turn chicken. Cook for 6 to 9 minutes more or until golden brown and no longer pink (170° F). Watch closely and reduce heat if chicken browns too quickly. Makes 4 servings.

Each serving: 506 cal., 32 g total fat (5 g sat. fat), 90 mg chol., 279 mg sodium, 21 g carbo., 3 g fiber, 36 g pro. Daily Values: 4% vit. A, 4% vit. C, 5% calcium, 12% iron.

Dilled Chicken and Jicama-Potato Salad

PREP: 45 minutes **CHILL:** 4 hours

- 1 recipe Jicama-Potato Salad (below)
- 1 lb. skinless, boneless chicken breasts
- 1 egg
- 1 Tbsp. dill mustard or Dijon-style mustard
- 1 Tbsp. water
- 1/4 cup all-purpose flour
- 1/4 cup seasoned fine dry bread crumbs
- 2 Tbsp. finely chopped almonds
- 3 Tbsp. garlic-flavored olive oil or olive oil Fresh dill sprigs (optional)

1. Prepare Jicama-Potato Salad; cover and chill for 4 to 24 hours.

2. Cut chicken into bite-size strips. In a shallow bowl beat egg; stir in mustard and water. Place flour in a second shallow bowl. In a third shallow bowl combine bread crumbs and almonds. Coat chicken with flour; dip into egg mixture, then into bread crumb mixture, turning to coat.

3. In a 12-inch skillet cook chicken in hot oil over medium-high heat about 6 minutes or until tender and no longer pink, turning once. Serve chicken with Jicama-Potato Salad. If desired, garnish with dill sprigs. Makes 6 servings.

JICAMA-POTATO SALAD: In a large saucepan place 5 medium potatoes, peeled and cubed, and 1/2 teaspoon salt; add enough water to cover. Bring to boiling; reduce heat. Simmer, covered, for 10 to 15 minutes or just until tender. Drain well; cool slightly. In a large bowl combine potatoes; 1/2 of a small jicama, peeled and cut into 3/4-inch pieces; 2 stalks celery, sliced; and 3 green onions, sliced. Gently fold in 3/4 cup bottled cucumber ranch salad dressing and 1 tablespoon snipped fresh dill or 1 teaspoon dried dill weed.

Each serving: 462 cal., 26 g total fat (4 g sat. fat), 79 mg chol., 673 mg sodium, 34 g carbo., 3 g fiber, 24 g pro. Daily Values: 2% vit. A, 45% vit. C, 5% calcium, 17% iron.

Parmesan-Sesame Chicken Strips

START TO FINISH: 30 minutes

- 1 lb. chicken breast tenderloins or skinless, boneless chicken breasts
- 1 egg
- 2 Tbsp. light mayonnaise dressing or salad dressing
- 3/4 cup fine dry bread crumbs
- 1/4 cup grated Parmesan cheese
- 3 Tbsp. sesame seeds, toasted
- 1/4 tsp. salt
- 1/4 tsp. ground black pepper
- 1 1/2 cups cooking oil
- 1 recipe Tahini-Lemon Dipping Sauce (below)

1. With a sharp knife, cut the white membrane away from each of the chicken tenderloins or breasts; cut chicken into bite-size strips. Set aside.

2. In a small bowl beat egg; stir in mayonnaise dressing. In a shallow bowl combine bread crumbs, Parmesan cheese, sesame seeds, salt, and pepper. Dip each chicken strip into egg mixture, then into bread crumb mixture, turning to coat.

3. In a large skillet heat cooking oil and sesame oil to 350° F. Add chicken strips, a few at a time, to hot oil. Cook for 4 to 5 minutes or until no longer pink. Remove chicken with a slotted spoon; drain on paper towels.

4. Make Tahini-Lemon Dipping Sauce; serve with chicken. Makes 4 to 6 servings.

TAHINI-LEMON DIPPING SAUCE: In a small bowl combine 1/3 cup light mayonnaise dressing or salad dressing, 2 tablespoons tahini (sesame seed paste), 2 tablespoons toasted sesame oil, and 1 1/2 teaspoons lemon juice.

Each serving: 633 cal., 48 g total fat (9 g sat. fat), 133 mg chol., 900 mg sodium, 18 g carbo., 2 g fiber, 35 g pro. Daily Values: 3% vit. A, 4% vit. C, 14% calcium, 15% iron.

Curried Oven-Fried Chicken

PREP: 30 minutes **BAKE:** 45 minutes

- 1/3 cup all-purpose flour
- 1 tsp. onion powder
- 1/2 tsp. salt
- 1/2 tsp. ground coriander
- 1/2 tsp. curry powder
- 1/2 tsp. cayenne pepper
- 1/2 tsp. ground black pepper
- 1/4 tsp. ground cinnamon
- 1/4 tsp. garlic powder
- 1/8 tsp. ground allspice
- 1/3 cup orange juice
- 2 Tbsp. honey
- 2 1/2 lb. meaty chicken pieces (breast halves, thighs, and drumsticks), skinned
- 2 Tbsp. butter, melted
- 1 recipe Yogurt Curry Sauce (below)

1. Preheat oven to 375° F. Line a 15×10×1-inch baking pan with foil; grease the foil. In a shallow dish stir together flour, onion powder, salt, coriander, curry powder, cayenne pepper, black pepper, cinnamon, garlic powder, and allspice; set aside. Pour orange juice into another shallow bowl; whisk in honey. Dip chicken pieces into orange juice mixture, then into flour mixture, turning to coat.

2. Arrange the chicken on the prepared baking pan, bone sides down, so pieces aren't touching. Drizzle chicken with the melted butter.

3. Bake chicken, uncovered, for 45 to 55 minutes or until no longer pink (170° F for breasts; 180° F for thighs and drumsticks). Do not turn chicken pieces while baking. Prepare Yogurt Curry Sauce; serve with chicken. Makes 4 servings.

YOGURT CURRY SAUCE: In a small bowl stir together one 8-ounce carton plain yogurt, 1/2 cup seeded and chopped cucumber, 1/2 teaspoon curry powder, and 1/4 teaspoon salt. Cover and chill until serving time.

Each serving: 414 cal., 16 g total fat (7 g sat. fat), 135 mg chol., 644 mg sodium, 24 g carbo., 1 g fiber, 41 g pro. Daily Values: 9% vit. A, 20% vit. C, 14% calcium, 13% iron.

OVEN DINNERS

PRIZE TESTED RECIPES® $400 WINNER

DARLENE GODSCHALX, PRESCOTT, ARIZ.

PRIZE TESTED RECIPES® $200 WINNER

KATHY BERKEY, WHITEHOUSE, OHIO

Moroccan-Style Short Ribs

PREP: 30 minutes **ROAST:** 1 hour + 45 minutes

1 Tbsp. dried thyme, crushed	4 cloves garlic, minced
1 tsp. salt	1 15-oz. can chickpeas
1 tsp. ground ginger	(garbanzo beans), rinsed
1 tsp. ground black pepper	and drained
1/2 tsp. ground cinnamon	1 large onion, cut into wedges
5 lb. beef short ribs	1 medium fennel bulb,
2 Tbsp. olive oil	trimmed and cut into wedges
3 cups beef broth	1 cup chopped carrot
1 14½-oz. can diced	1 recipe Nut-Olive
tomatoes	Couscous (below)

1. Preheat oven to 350° F. In a small bowl combine thyme, salt, ginger, pepper, and cinnamon. Sprinkle over ribs; rub in. In a 4-quart Dutch oven brown ribs, half at a time, in hot oil over medium-high heat. Drain off fat. Add beef broth, undrained tomatoes, and garlic. Bring to boiling. Cover; roast for 1 hour.

2. Add chickpeas, onion, fennel, and carrot; stir. Cover; roast 45 to 60 minutes more or until meat and vegetables are tender.

3. Prepare Nut-Olive Couscous; spoon couscous onto a platter. Transfer ribs to platter. Pour remaining mixture into a colander, reserving liquid. Top ribs and couscous with vegetables. If desired, moisten with cooking liquid. Makes 8 servings.

NUT-OLIVE COUSCOUS: Prepare one 10-ounce package quick-cooking couscous according to package directions. Stir in 1/2 cup sliced almonds, toasted, and 1/2 cup pitted kalamata olives, halved.

Each serving: 506 cal., 20 g total fat (5 g sat. fat), 53 mg chol., 1,046 mg sodium, 46 g carbo., 10 g fiber, 34 g pro. Daily Values: 79% vit. A, 17% vit. C, 11% calcium, 23% iron.

Pork with Parsnips and Pears

PREP: 45 minutes **ROAST:** 2 hours

1 3½- to 4-lb. boneless	2 lb. parsnips and/or carrots,
pork top loin roast (double	peeled and cut into
loin, tied)	1½- to 2-inch-long pieces
2 Tbsp. cooking oil	5 to 6 medium fresh pears,
6 cloves garlic, minced	peeled, quartered, and
1 tsp. snipped fresh rosemary	cored
1 tsp. snipped fresh thyme	1½ cups port wine
1/2 tsp. salt	2 Tbsp. cold water
1/4 tsp. ground black pepper	1 Tbsp. cornstarch

1. Preheat oven to 325° F. In a large skillet brown meat on all sides in hot oil. Transfer to a shallow roasting pan. Sprinkle meat with garlic, rosemary, thyme, salt, and pepper. Place parsnips and/or carrots and pears around meat. Pour wine over all. Loosely cover with foil; roast 2 to 2½ hours or until meat is done (160° F).

2. Transfer meat to a platter, reserving cooking liquid; transfer parsnips and pears to platter. Cover with foil; set aside.

3. For sauce, measure 1½ cups of the cooking liquid; skim off fat. In a medium saucepan stir together cold water and cornstarch; add cooking liquid. Cook and stir over medium heat until thickened and bubbly; cook and stir for 2 minutes more. Season to taste with additional salt and pepper. Remove string from roast; slice meat. Serve sauce with meat and vegetables. Makes 10 to 12 servings.

low fat Each serving: 417 cal., 12 g total fat (3 g sat. fat), 93 mg chol., 238 mg sodium, 33 g carbo., 6 g fiber, 35 g pro. Daily Values: 1% vit. A, 27% vit. C, 7% calcium, 15% iron.

Ham-Spinach Lasagna

The classic French sauce known as béchamel is commonly referred to as white sauce in the U.S. Here whipping cream adds richness to the simple sauce.

PREP: 45 minutes **BAKE:** 35 minutes
STAND: 10 minutes

12 dried lasagna noodles
 1 recipe Béchamel Sauce (below)
 1 lb. fresh mushrooms, sliced
 3 cloves garlic, minced
 2 Tbsp. olive oil
 6 cups torn fresh spinach leaves
 2 cups diced cooked ham (about 10 oz.)
1 1/2 cups grated Parmesan cheese

1. Preheat oven to 375° F. Cook noodles according to package directions. Prepare Béchamel Sauce; set aside.

2. Meanwhile, in a large skillet cook mushrooms and garlic in hot oil until mushrooms are tender. Add spinach; cook and stir for 1 to 2 minutes or just until spinach is wilted. Drain off excess liquid.

3. Drain noodles; rinse with cold water. Drain well. Spread 1/2 cup of the Béchamel Sauce in the bottom of an ungreased 3-quart rectangular baking dish. Arrange 3 of the noodles over sauce. Layer a third of the mushroom mixture, a third of the ham, 1/2 cup of the Béchamel Sauce, and 1/3 cup of the Parmesan cheese. Repeat layers twice. Top with remaining noodles and remaining sauce.

4. Bake, covered, about 35 minutes or until heated through. Uncover and top with remaining cheese. Let stand 10 minutes before serving. Makes 8 servings.

BÉCHAMEL SAUCE: In a medium saucepan melt 2 tablespoons butter or margarine over medium-high heat. Add 1/4 cup chopped shallots; cook and stir for 1 minute. Stir in 3 tablespoons all-purpose flour. Stirring constantly, gradually add 2 cups milk and 1/2 cup whipping cream, half-and-half, or light cream. Cook and stir over medium heat until slightly thickened and bubbly.

Each serving: 407 cal., 23 g total fat (11 g sat. fat), 65 mg chol., 825 mg sodium, 31 g carbo., 3 g fiber, 21 g pro. Daily Values: 38% vit. A, 12% vit. C, 32% calcium, 21% iron.

Tijuana Taco Beef Borracho

PREP: 40 minutes **ROAST:** 1 + 1 hours

 1 1.25-oz. pkg. taco seasoning mix
 1 2 1/2- to 3- lb. boneless beef chuck pot roast
 2 Tbsp. cooking oil
 2 dried New Mexico chile peppers (see note, page 302)
1/2 cup tequila
 2 medium onions, sliced
 1 14 1/2-oz. can diced tomatoes
 2 fresh poblano chile peppers, seeded and chopped (see note, page 302)
1/2 cup tequila
1/4 cup raisins
 2 Tbsp. snipped fresh cilantro
 6 cloves garlic, peeled and thinly sliced
 1 15-oz. can black beans, rinsed and drained
 4 fresh ears of corn, husked and cut into quarters
 4 fresh tomatillos, husks removed and chopped
    Flour tortillas (optional)
 1 lime, cut into wedges

1. Preheat oven to 350° F. Sprinkle 2 tablespoons of the taco seasoning evenly over roast; rub in. In a 4- to 6-quart Dutch oven heat oil over medium heat; brown roast on all sides. Remove pan from heat. Drain off fat.

2. Remove seeds and stems from New Mexico chile peppers and discard. Crumble the dried peppers; add to Dutch oven along with onions, undrained tomatoes, poblano peppers, tequila, raisins, 1 tablespoon of the cilantro, the garlic, and remaining taco seasoning mix. Cover and roast for 1 hour.

3. Add black beans, corn, and tomatillos. Cover and roast for 1 hour more.

4. To serve, slice meat. Serve with vegetables, juices, flour tortillas (if desired), and lime wedges. Sprinkle with remaining 1 tablespoon cilantro. Makes 8 servings.

low fat Each serving: 392 cal., 10 g total fat (3 g sat. fat), 84 mg chol., 690 mg sodium, 32 g carbo., 5 g fiber, 36 g pro. Daily Values: 11% vit. A, 131% vit. C, 5% calcium, 31% iron.

Herb-Crusted Cornish Hens with Fennel and Orzo

A trio of herbs—sage, thyme, and rosemary—deliciously seasons the Cornish hens and the pasta mixture.

PREP: 20 minutes **BAKE:** 40 + 20 minutes

 1 cup dried orzo
 1 Tbsp. dried sage, crushed
 2 tsp. dried thyme, crushed
 1 tsp. salt
 1 tsp. dried rosemary, crushed
1/4 tsp. ground black pepper
 2 medium fennel bulbs, trimmed, halved, and sliced
 2 Tbsp. olive oil
 2 1- to 1 1/2-lb. Cornish game hens, split lengthwise
 2 Tbsp. balsamic vinegar

1. Preheat oven to 375° F. Cook orzo according to package directions.

2. In a small bowl stir together sage, thyme, salt, rosemary, and pepper. Drain orzo; toss with fennel, olive oil, and half of the herb mixture. Transfer orzo mixture to a greased 3-quart rectangular baking dish.

3. Brush hens with balsamic vinegar; sprinkle with remaining herb mixture. Place hens, skin side up, on top of orzo.

4. Bake, covered, for 40 minutes; uncover and bake 20 to 30 minutes more or until an instant-read thermometer inserted into center of an inside thigh muscle of each hen registers 180° F (the thermometer should not touch the bone). Makes 4 servings.

Each serving: 607 cal., 30 g total fat (7 g sat. fat), 173 mg chol., 731 mg sodium, 43 g carbo., 5 g fiber, 37 g pro. Daily Values: 10% vit. A, 25% vit. C, 11% calcium, 24% iron.

COMPANY CASSEROLES

Tuscan Mac 'n' Cheese

PREP: 45 minutes **BAKE:** 35 + 15 minutes **STAND:** 15 minutes

8 oz. sweet or hot Italian sausage	4 oz. mozzarella cheese, shredded (1 cup)
8 oz. dried gemelli or elbow macaroni (2 cups), cooked and drained	1 Tbsp. butter
	1 Tbsp. all-purpose flour
	1 Tbsp. snipped fresh sage
1 8-oz. pkg. cream cheese, cut into cubes and softened	1 tsp. snipped fresh thyme
	⅛ tsp. cayenne pepper
4 oz. crusty Italian bread, cut into 1-inch cubes (2 cups)	1½ cups milk
	1 medium tomato, sliced
1 cup pitted kalamata olives, halved	½ cup shredded Asiago or Parmesan cheese (2 oz.)

1. Preheat oven to 350° F. Remove casings, if present, from sausage. In a skillet crumble and cook sausage; drain. In a very large bowl combine sausage, cooked pasta, cream cheese, bread cubes, olives, and mozzarella cheese. Set aside.

2. In a medium saucepan melt butter over medium heat. Stir in flour, sage, thyme, cayenne pepper, and ½ teaspoon salt. Add milk all at once. Cook and stir until slightly thickened and bubbly. Pour over pasta mixture; stir gently. Transfer to an ungreased 2-quart casserole. Bake, covered, for 35 minutes.

3. Uncover; top with tomato and Asiago. Bake, uncovered, about 15 minutes more or until heated through. Let stand 15 minutes before serving. Makes 8 servings.

Each serving: 478 cal., 29 g total fat (14 g sat. fat), 76 mg chol., 890 mg sodium, 35 g carbo., 2 g fiber, 18 g pro. Daily Values: 15% vit. A, 7% vit. C, 26% calcium, 12% iron.

Mexican Polenta Pie

PREP: 35 minutes **BAKE:** 35 minutes **STAND:** 15 minutes

1 medium onion, chopped	1 14½-oz. can diced tomatoes
1 medium green sweet pepper, chopped	1 cup bottled salsa
3 cloves garlic, minced	2 16-oz. tubes refrigerated cooked polenta
2 Tbsp. olive oil	
1 lb. uncooked ground turkey	8 oz. Monterey Jack cheese, shredded (2 cups)
3 Tbsp. chili powder	
1 Tbsp. ground cumin	⅔ cup chopped fresh tomato
¼ tsp. cayenne pepper	¼ cup snipped fresh cilantro
1 15-oz. can black beans, rinsed and drained	

1. Preheat oven to 375° F. In a 12-inch skillet cook onion, sweet pepper, and garlic in 1 tablespoon hot oil until tender. Add turkey, chili powder, cumin, and cayenne. Cook until turkey is no longer pink. Add beans, undrained tomatoes, and salsa. Bring to boiling; reduce heat. Simmer gently, uncovered, for 15 minutes.

2. Meanwhile, grease a 3-quart rectangular baking dish with the remaining 1 tablespoon oil. Cut 1 tube of the polenta into ½-inch cubes; press evenly into prepared baking dish. Sprinkle with 1 cup of the cheese; top with meat mixture. Halve remaining polenta lengthwise; cut into ½-inch-thick slices. Arrange sliced polenta over meat; sprinkle with remaining cheese and fresh tomato. Bake, uncovered, about 35 minutes or until bubbly. Sprinkle with cilantro. Let stand for 15 minutes. Makes 12 servings.

Each serving: 264 cal., 12 g total fat (5 g sat. fat), 47 mg chol., 633 mg sodium, 24 g carbo., 5 g fiber, 16 g pro. Daily Values: 23% vit. A, 30% vit. C, 19% calcium, 10% iron.

Mexican Fiesta Casserole

PREP: 30 minutes **BAKE:** 23 minutes
STAND: 5 minutes

1 recipe Cornmeal Pastry (below)
12 oz. uncooked chorizo sausage
8 oz. lean ground beef
1 small onion, chopped (1/3 cup)
1 small red sweet pepper, chopped
2 cloves garlic, minced
1 16-oz. jar fire-roasted salsa or salsa
1 15-oz. can black beans,
   rinsed and drained
1 cup frozen whole kernel corn
1 tsp. chili powder
   Dash bottled hot pepper sauce
2 oz. sharp cheddar cheese, shredded
   (1/2 cup)

1. Prepare Cornmeal Pastry; set aside. In a large skillet crumble chorizo and beef. Add onion, sweet pepper, and garlic; cook until meat is brown. Drain off fat. Stir in salsa, beans, corn, chili powder, hot pepper sauce, and 1/4 teaspoon salt. Cook and stir for 5 minutes. Spoon into baked pastry shell. Lay pastry strips atop. Bake for 20 to 25 minutes or until pastry is golden.

2. Sprinkle with cheese. Bake about 3 minutes more or until cheese is melted. Let stand 5 minutes before serving. Serves 8.

CORNMEAL PASTRY: Preheat oven to 425° F. In a large bowl stir together 2 cups all-purpose flour, 2/3 cup yellow cornmeal, and 1/2 teaspoon salt. Cut in 3/4 cup butter until pieces are pea-size. Using 1/3 to 1/2 cup cold water total, sprinkle water over flour mixture, 1 tablespoon at a time, gently tossing with a fork until all of the flour mixture is moistened. Form dough into a ball. Set aside one-third of the dough. On a lightly floured surface, roll remaining dough to 12×7-inch rectangle; place in lightly greased 2-quart rectangular baking dish. Bake for 8 minutes. Meanwhile, on a lightly floured surface, roll reserved dough to a 10×6-inch rectangle; cut into 8 strips. Cover strips.

Each serving: 650 cal., 41 g total fat (20 g sat. fat), 112 mg chol., 1,366 mg sodium, 48 g carbo., 6 g fiber, 26 g pro. Daily Values: 36% vit. A, 46% vit. C, 11% calcium, 22% iron.

Baked Chicken And Artichoke Risotto

PREP: 30 minutes **BAKE:** 1 hour + 5 minutes
STAND: 5 minutes

3 cups sliced fresh mushrooms, such as
   crimini, oyster, shiitake (stems
   removed), and/or button
1 small onion, chopped (1/3 cup)
2 cloves garlic, minced
1 Tbsp. olive oil
3/4 cup arborio or long grain rice
2 9-oz. pkg. frozen artichoke hearts,
   thawed, drained, and halved
1 14 1/2-oz. can Italian-style stewed
   tomatoes
1 tsp. dried thyme, crushed
1/4 tsp. ground black pepper
1 cup chicken broth
2/3 cup milk, half-and-half, or light cream
3 cups cubed cooked chicken
   (about 1 lb.)
1/2 cup finely shredded Parmesan or
   Romano cheese (2 oz.)
1/4 cup seasoned fine dry bread crumbs
1 Tbsp. olive oil
1/2 tsp. finely shredded lemon peel

1. Preheat oven to 350° F. In a 12-inch skillet cook mushrooms, onion, and garlic in 1 tablespoon hot oil over medium-high heat until onion is tender. Add uncooked rice; cook and stir for 1 minute more.

2. Add artichoke hearts, tomatoes, thyme, and pepper. Stir in broth and milk. Bring just to boiling. Stir in chicken and 1/4 cup of the Parmesan cheese. Transfer to a 2 1/2-quart ungreased casserole. Bake, covered, about 1 hour or until rice is tender.

3. Meanwhile, for topping, combine remaining 1/4 cup cheese, the bread crumbs, 1 tablespoon oil, and lemon peel. Uncover casserole and sprinkle with topping; bake for 5 minutes more. Let stand for 5 minutes before serving. Makes 6 servings.

Each serving: 563 cal., 25 g total fat (10 g sat. fat), 96 mg chol., 1,316 mg sodium, 38 g carbo., 6 g fiber, 45 g pro. Daily Values: 10% vit. A, 12% vit. C, 67% calcium, 19% iron.

Orange-Spinach Stuffed Snapper

PREP: 30 minutes **BAKE:** 10 + 8 minutes

8 oz. fresh mushrooms, sliced (3 cups)
1 large onion, chopped (1 cup)
2 cloves garlic, minced
2 Tbsp. butter
2 10-oz. pkg. frozen chopped spinach,
   thawed and well drained
2 cups herb-seasoned stuffing mix
1 tsp. finely shredded orange peel
   (set aside)
1/3 cup orange juice
2 lb. red snapper fillets, skinned and cut
   into 8 serving-size portions
1 cup whipping cream
2 Tbsp. Dijon-style mustard
1/2 cup thinly sliced green onions
1 Tbsp. butter, melted
1/4 cup finely shredded Parmesan cheese

1. Preheat oven to 375° F. Grease a 3-quart rectangular baking dish; set aside.

2. In a large skillet cook mushrooms, onion, and garlic in the 2 tablespoons hot butter until mushrooms and onion are tender. Remove from heat; set aside half of the onion mixture (about 1/2 cup). Stir spinach, 1 1/2 cups of the stuffing mix, and the orange juice into mixture remaining in skillet. Heat through.

3. Transfer to prepared baking dish. Top with fish fillets; sprinkle fish with salt and pepper. Bake, uncovered, for 10 minutes.

4. Meanwhile, for sauce, in the same skillet combine the reserved onion mixture, the whipping cream, mustard, and orange peel. Bring to boiling; reduce heat. Simmer, uncovered, about 2 minutes or until slightly thickened. Stir in green onion.

5. For topping, crush remaining stuffing mix; place in a small bowl. Add melted butter; stir to coat.

6. Spoon sauce over fish. Sprinkle with topping and Parmesan. Bake, uncovered, about 8 minutes more or until fish flakes easily with a fork. Makes 8 servings.

Each serving: 426 cal., 23 g total fat (13 g sat. fat), 107 mg chol., 837 mg sodium, 18 g carbo., 4 g fiber, 35 g pro. Daily Values: 223% vit. A, 25% vit. C, 34% calcium, 9% iron.

BAKED PASTA & LASAGNA

MARY ALCIERE, HINGHAM, MASS.

CATHERINE MARTIN, PERRIS, CALIF.

Mexican-Style Pasta Bake

PREP: 35 minutes **BAKE:** 15 minutes **STAND:** 5 minutes

12 oz. dried bow tie pasta	3 cups milk
½ cup chopped onion	6 oz. colby cheese, cubed
½ cup chopped red sweet pepper	1½ cups shredded Monterey Jack cheese (6 oz.)
3 Tbsp. butter	1 cup bottled salsa
⅓ cup all-purpose flour	⅔ cup halved pitted green and/or ripe olives
1 tsp. dried cilantro, crushed	Chili powder
½ tsp. ground cumin	

1. Preheat oven to 350° F. Butter six 12- to 16-ounce individual casserole dishes or one 3-quart baking dish; set aside. In a 4-quart Dutch oven cook pasta according to package directions. Drain; return to pan. In a large saucepan cook onion and sweet pepper in hot butter over medium heat about 5 minutes or until tender. Stir in flour, cilantro, cumin, and 1 teaspoon salt. Add milk all at once. Cook and stir until thickened and bubbly. Reduce heat to low. Stir in colby cheese and 1 cup of the Monterey Jack cheese; stir until cheese is melted. Pour over pasta; stir to combine.

2. Layer half of the pasta mixture, all of the salsa, and remaining pasta mixture in prepared casserole(s). Sprinkle with remaining ½ cup Jack cheese, the olives, and chili powder. Bake for 15 to 20 minutes or until bubbly around the edges and heated through. (If using large casserole, bake in a 400° F oven about 20 minutes.) Let stand for 5 minutes. Makes 6 servings.

Each serving: 604 cal., 31 g total fat (17 g sat. fat), 132 mg chol., 1,293 mg sodium, 56 g carbo., 3 g fiber, 27 g pro. Daily Values: 40% vit. A, 42% vit. C, 59% calcium, 19% iron.

Cheese 'n' Nut Stuffed Shells

PREP: 45 minutes **BAKE:** 45 minutes

24 dried jumbo shell macaroni*	1 cup chopped walnuts
2 eggs	1 Tbsp. snipped fresh parsley
1 15-oz. carton ricotta cheese	½ tsp. salt
1½ cups shredded mozzarella cheese (6 oz.)	¼ tsp. ground black pepper
1 cup shredded Parmesan cheese (4 oz.)	⅛ tsp. ground nutmeg
	1 26-oz. jar thick-and-chunky pasta sauce

1. Preheat oven to 350° F. Cook shells according to package directions. Drain shells; rinse with cold water and drain well.

2. Meanwhile, for filling, in a large bowl beat eggs; stir in ricotta cheese, 1 cup of the mozzarella cheese, ¾ cup of the Parmesan cheese, the walnuts, parsley, salt, pepper, and nutmeg.

3. Spread 1 cup of the pasta sauce in the bottom of a 3-quart baking dish. Spoon a heaping tablespoon of the filling into each cooked shell. Arrange filled shells in the baking dish. Pour remaining sauce over shells. Sprinkle with the remaining mozzarella and Parmesan cheeses. Bake, covered, about 45 minutes or until heated through. Makes 6 servings.

***NOTE:** Cook a few extra shells so you can replace any that tear during cooking.

Each serving: 549 cal., 32 g total fat (12 g sat. fat), 132 mg chol., 1,072 mg sodium, 36 g carbo., 4 g fiber, 30 g pro. Daily Values: 18% vit. A, 19% vit. C, 60% calcium, 15% iron.

Greek Orzo and Pepper Casserole

PREP: 50 minutes **BAKE:** 45 minutes
STAND: 5 minutes

6 oz. dried orzo (1 cup)
½ of a 10-oz. pkg. frozen chopped
   spinach, thawed
3 medium red and/or green sweet
   peppers, halved lengthwise, seeded,
   and membranes removed
8 oz. bulk pork sausage
1 cup sliced fresh mushrooms
1 small onion, chopped (⅓ cup)
1 clove garlic, minced
2 cups shredded Italian-style cheese
   blend (8 oz.)
½ cup ricotta cheese
2 oz. feta or kasseri cheese, crumbled
   (½ cup)
2 Tbsp. seasoned fine dry bread
   crumbs
1 egg, slightly beaten
6 pitted kalamata olives, chopped
   (1 Tbsp.)
1 26-oz. jar marinara sauce

1. Preheat oven to 350° F. Grease 6 individual au gratin or casserole dishes; set aside. Cook orzo according to package directions; drain. Stir in spinach. Divide evenly among prepared dishes. Place a sweet pepper half, cut side up, in each dish. Set aside.

2. In a large skillet cook sausage, mushrooms, onion, and garlic until meat is done and onion is tender. Drain off fat. Stir 1 cup of the Italian cheese, the ricotta, feta, bread crumbs, egg, and olives into mushroom-sausage mixture. Spoon mixture into pepper halves. Pour marinara sauce evenly over stuffed peppers and orzo mixture.

3. Cover with foil. Bake about 45 minutes or until heated through. Uncover; sprinkle with remaining 1 cup Italian cheese. Let stand for 5 minutes before serving. Makes 6 servings.

Each serving: 526 cal., 28 g total fat (13 g sat. fat), 102 mg chol., 1,200 mg sodium, 42 g carbo., 5 g fiber, 25 g pro. Daily Values: 126% vit. A, 168% vit. C, 39% calcium, 17% iron.

Green Lasagna

PREP: 30 minutes **BAKE:** 25 + 10 minutes
STAND: 10 minutes

1 10-oz. pkg. frozen cut broccoli,
   thawed
1 9-oz. pkg. frozen artichoke hearts,
   thawed and cut up
1 recipe Basil Cream Sauce (below)
6 no-boil lasagna noodles
6 oz. mozzarella cheese, shredded
   (1½ cups)
¼ cup grated Parmesan cheese (1 oz.)

1. Preheat oven to 375° F. In a medium bowl stir together broccoli and artichoke hearts; set aside.

2. Prepare Basil Cream Sauce. In a 2-quart square baking dish spread about ½ cup of Basil Cream Sauce. Arrange 2 of the lasagna noodles on the sauce. Top with half of the broccoli mixture, a third of the remaining sauce, and half of the mozzarella cheese. Add 2 more noodles, the remaining broccoli mixture, a third of the remaining sauce, and the remaining mozzarella cheese. Top with the remaining noodles and the remaining sauce. Sprinkle with Parmesan cheese.

3. Bake, covered, for 25 minutes. Uncover; bake about 10 minutes more or until top begins to brown. Let stand for 10 minutes before serving. Serves 6.

BASIL CREAM SAUCE: In a medium saucepan melt 3 tablespoons butter or margarine over medium heat. Add ½ cup sliced green onions and 6 cloves garlic, minced; cook and stir about 5 minutes or until green onion is almost tender. Stir in ¼ cup all-purpose flour and ½ teaspoon salt; cook and stir for 1 minute. Add 2½ cups milk all at once; cook and stir until thickened and bubbly. Remove from heat. Stir in ½ cup snipped fresh basil.

Each serving: 313 cal., 14 g total fat (9 g sat. fat), 43 mg chol., 541 mg sodium, 30 g carbo., 5 g fiber, 17 g pro. Daily Values: 35% vit. A, 49% vit. C, 42% calcium, 11% iron.

Nutty Gorgonzola Roll-Ups

Two convenient products—Italian cheese blend and bottled pasta sauce—make these cheesy roll-ups extra easy.

PREP: 45 minutes **BAKE:** 40 minutes

8 dried lasagna noodles
12 oz. cream cheese (four 3-oz.
   or 1½ 8-oz. pkg.), softened
2 cups shredded Italian-style cheese
   blend (8 oz.)
4 oz. Gorgonzola or other blue cheese,
   crumbled (1 cup)
1 cup chopped walnuts, toasted
2 Tbsp. snipped fresh basil
   or 2 tsp. dried basil, crushed
1 26-oz. jar tomato-basil pasta sauce
6 cups shredded fresh spinach

1. Preheat oven to 375° F. Cook lasagna noodles according to package directions; drain well. Rinse with cold water; drain.

2. In a large bowl combine cream cheese, Italian cheese, Gorgonzola, ¾ cup of the walnuts, and the basil. Spread some of the cheese mixture onto one side of each lasagna noodle. Roll up noodles; place, seam sides down, in an ungreased 2-quart rectangular baking dish. Pour pasta sauce over all.

3. Cover and bake about 40 minutes or until heated through.

4. Divide spinach evenly among 8 dinner plates. Place a roll-up on top of spinach on each plate. Spoon sauce evenly over lasagna rolls. Sprinkle with remaining ¼ cup walnuts. Makes 8 servings.

Each serving: 513 cal., 37 g total fat (17 g sat. fat), 77 mg chol., 813 mg sodium, 28 g carbo., 4 g fiber, 21 g pro. Daily Values: 49% vit. A, 17% vit. C, 37% calcium, 17% iron.

SOUPS & CHOWDERS

CAMILLA SORENSON, ADA, MINN.

STEPHEN ALEXANDER, CINCINNATI, OHIO

Curried Butternut Chicken Bisque
PREP: 30 minutes **BAKE:** 30 + 20 minutes

2 lb. butternut squash	1/4 cup water
1 medium onion, chopped	2 to 3 tsp. curry powder
1 Tbsp. olive oil	1/2 tsp. salt
2 cloves garlic, minced	1/8 tsp. ground black pepper
2 Tbsp. grated fresh ginger	2 cups hot cooked brown rice
2 cups cubed cooked chicken	1/4 cup snipped fresh cilantro
1 14-oz. can chicken broth	1/4 cup chopped cashews
1 13 1/2-oz. can unsweetened coconut milk	

1. Preheat oven to 350° F. Cut squash in half lengthwise; remove and discard seeds. Arrange squash halves, cut sides down, in a 3-quart rectangular baking dish. Bake for 30 minutes. Turn squash cut sides up. Bake, covered, for 20 to 25 minutes more or until tender. Cool slightly. Carefully scoop squash pulp into bowl; discard shells. Use a potato masher to mash squash slightly; set aside.

2. In a large saucepan cook onion in hot oil for 3 to 4 minutes or until tender. Add garlic and ginger; cook and stir for 1 minute more. Carefully stir in mashed squash, chicken, broth, coconut milk, water, curry powder, salt, and pepper. Cook over medium heat until heated through, stirring occasionally.

3. To serve, spoon hot rice and chicken mixture into bowls. Sprinkle with cilantro and cashews. Makes 5 or 6 servings.

Each serving: 465 cal., 26 g total fat (15 g sat. fat), 50 mg chol., 684 mg sodium, 37 g carbo., 4 g fiber, 24 g pro. Daily Values: 103% vit. A, 32% vit. C, 7% calcium, 18% iron.

Zydeco Soup
PREP: 25 minutes **COOK:** 30 minutes

2 stalks celery, chopped (1 cup)	1/2 tsp. dried oregano, crushed
1 large onion, chopped (1 cup)	1/2 tsp. dried thyme, crushed
1 medium green sweet pepper, chopped (3/4 cup)	1/4 tsp. ground cloves
2 cloves garlic, minced	1/4 tsp. ground black pepper
2 Tbsp. olive oil	1/8 tsp. cayenne pepper
6 oz. cooked ham, diced (1 1/4 cups)	1 15-oz. can black-eyed peas, rinsed and drained
1 tsp. paprika	1 14 1/2-oz. can golden hominy, rinsed and drained
1/2 tsp. dry mustard	1 14 1/2-oz. can diced tomatoes
1/2 tsp. ground cumin	1 14-oz. can chicken broth
1/2 tsp. sugar	1 Tbsp. snipped fresh parsley
1/2 tsp. dried basil, crushed	1 Tbsp. mild-flavored molasses

1. In a 4-quart Dutch oven cook celery, onion, sweet pepper, and garlic in hot oil over medium heat for 5 minutes. Stir in ham, paprika, mustard, cumin, sugar, basil, oregano, thyme, cloves, black pepper, and cayenne pepper. Cook and stir 5 minutes more.

2. Stir in black-eyed peas, hominy, undrained tomatoes, chicken broth, parsley, and molasses. Bring to boiling; reduce heat. Cover and simmer for 30 minutes. Makes 4 servings.

low fat Each serving: 384 cal., 14 g total fat (3 g sat. fat), 24 mg chol., 1,627 mg sodium, 47 g carbo., 10 g fiber, 17 g pro. Daily Values: 16% vit. A, 69% vit. C, 13% calcium, 15% iron.

Brie, Crab, and Mushroom Soup

Serve this elegant soup as a first course for a dinner party or a main dish for a luncheon.

START TO FINISH: 35 minutes

8 oz. fresh mushrooms, thinly sliced
1 medium onion, finely chopped
3 Tbsp. butter or margarine
¼ cup all-purpose flour
¼ tsp. ground white pepper
⅛ tsp. salt
1 14-oz. can vegetable broth
2 cups milk
1 4½-oz. round Brie cheese, rind removed and cut into 1-inch pieces
3 plum tomatoes, chopped
2 6-oz. cans crabmeat, drained, flaked, and cartilage removed
2 Tbsp. snipped fresh parsley
4 tsp. finely shredded Romano cheese

1. In large saucepan cook mushrooms and onion in hot butter about 5 minutes or until tender. Stir in flour, pepper, and salt. Add vegetable broth all at once. Cook and stir until thickened and bubbly.

2. Stir in milk, Brie, and tomatoes. Cook and stir about 7 minutes more or until Brie is melted. Stir in crabmeat; heat through.

3. To serve, spoon into 4 bowls; top with parsley and shredded Romano cheese. Makes 4 main-dish servings or 8 first-course servings.

Each serving: 419 cal., 24 g total fat (13 g sat. fat), 150 mg chol., 1,183 mg sodium, 19 g carbo., 2 g fiber, 35 g pro. Daily Values: 28% vit. A, 33% vit. C, 33% calcium, 12% iron.

Dilly Dijon Salmon Bisque

Bisques are noted for being rich and creamy. This one lives up to that reputation, even though it uses evaporated fat-free milk.

START TO FINISH: 35 minutes

1 medium onion, chopped
1 Tbsp. olive oil
1¼ cups water
½ cup long grain rice
1 14-oz. can chicken broth
8 oz. salmon fillet, cut into 1-inch pieces
2 cups fresh or frozen whole kernel corn

1 12-oz. can (1½ cups) evaporated fat-free milk
1 Tbsp. Dijon-style mustard
1 tsp. snipped fresh dill or ½ tsp. dried dill weed
½ tsp. salt
½ tsp. ground black pepper
Fresh dill sprigs (optional)

1. In a large saucepan cook onion in hot olive oil over medium heat until tender. Add the water; bring to boiling. Stir in uncooked rice. Reduce heat. Simmer, covered, for 15 minutes.

2. Add chicken broth; return to boiling. Add salmon and corn; simmer about 5 minutes or until rice is tender and salmon flakes easily with a fork.

3. Stir in evaporated milk, mustard, dill, salt, and pepper; heat through. To serve, spoon into 4 bowls. If desired, garnish with fresh dill sprigs. Makes 4 main-dish servings.

low fat Each serving: 348 cal., 8 g total fat (1 g sat. fat), 33 mg chol., 944 mg sodium, 48 g carbo., 3 g fiber, 23 g pro. Daily Values: 13% vit. A, 14% vit. C, 27% calcium, 13% iron.

Seafood Salsa Soup

For a little extra kick, opt for medium salsa instead of mild.

PREP: 30 minutes **COOK:** 25 minutes

1 cup chopped peeled potato
1 cup chopped onion
1 cup chopped carrot
½ cup chopped celery
1 clove garlic, minced
2 Tbsp. olive oil
1 14-oz. can chicken or vegetable broth
1¼ cups bottled mild salsa
½ tsp. lemon-pepper seasoning
12 oz. orange roughy fillets, cut into 1-inch pieces
2 cups shredded fresh spinach
Snipped fresh cilantro or parsley

1. In a large saucepan cook potato, onion, carrot, celery, and garlic in hot oil for 5 minutes. Stir in broth, salsa, and lemon-pepper seasoning. Bring to boiling; reduce heat. Cover and simmer for 15 minutes.

2. Add the orange roughy and spinach. Cook, uncovered, about 5 minutes more or until fish flakes easily with a fork. To serve, spoon into 4 bowls. Top with cilantro or parsley. Makes 4 main-dish servings.

Each serving: 206 cal., 9 g total fat (1 g sat. fat), 17 mg chol., 818 mg sodium, 17 g carbo., 5 g fiber, 16 g pro. Daily Values: 178% vit. A, 36% vit. C, 8% calcium, 13% iron.

Cheesy Cream of Roasted Red Pepper and Jalapeño Soup

PREP: 45 minutes **COOK:** 15 minutes

1 7-oz. jar roasted red pepper, drained and chopped
1 cup finely chopped sweet onion
½ cup finely chopped celery
2 cloves garlic, minced
2 14-oz. cans chicken broth
⅛ tsp. seasoned salt
⅛ tsp. ground black pepper
4 tsp. finely chopped seeded jalapeño peppers (see note, page 302)
3 Tbsp. butter or margarine
3 Tbsp. all-purpose flour
1 cup milk
6 oz. smoked cheddar or Swiss cheese, shredded
1 cup half-and-half, light cream, or milk
½ cup finely chopped cooked ham

1. In a large saucepan combine sweet pepper, onion, celery, garlic, broth, seasoned salt, black pepper, and half of the finely chopped jalapeño peppers. Bring to boiling; reduce heat. Cover and simmer for 7 minutes or until onion and celery are tender. Remove from heat; cool slightly.

2. Place broth mixture, half at a time, in a blender or food processor. Cover and blend or process until smooth.

3. In same pan melt butter. Stir in flour. Add milk and pureed mixture; cook and stir until thickened and bubbly. Add cheese, half-and-half, remaining jalapeño, and ham; cook and stir until cheese is melted. Makes 4 main-dish servings.

Each serving: 473 cal., 35 g total fat (21 g sat. fat), 105 mg chol., 1,549 mg sodium, 20 g carbo., 2 g fiber, 21 g pro. Daily Values: 89% vit. A, 171% vit. C, 47% calcium, 7% iron.

COOKING WITH WINE

Croatian Nut Tart

Wine in the pastry is a delightfully delicious surprise.
PREP: 30 minutes **BAKE:** 40 minutes

1	recipe White Wine Pastry (see recipe, opposite)	¼	cup packed brown sugar
3	egg whites	3	egg yolks, slightly beaten
1¼	cups finely chopped walnuts (about 5 oz.)	1½	tsp. finely shredded lemon peel
¼	cup granulated sugar	½	tsp. vanilla

1. Prepare the White Wine Pastry. Let egg whites stand at room temperature for 30 minutes. Preheat oven to 350° F.

2. For filling, in a medium bowl combine walnuts, granulated sugar, and brown sugar. Stir in egg yolks, lemon peel, and vanilla. Set aside. In a small bowl beat egg whites with an electric mixer on medium to high speed until stiff peaks form (tips stand straight). Fold beaten egg whites, a third at a time, into walnut mixture.

3. Pour filling into partially baked pastry, spreading evenly. Roll remaining dough ball into a circle about 11 inches in diameter. Cut slits to allow steam to escape. Place pastry on filling; trim edges even with edges of pan.

4. Bake for 40 to 45 minutes or until pastry is golden. Cool completely in pan on a wire rack. To serve, remove sides of pan; cut into wedges. Makes 12 servings.

Each serving: 354 cal., 26 g total fat (11 g sat. fat), 97 mg chol., 232 mg sodium, 25 g carbo., 1 g fiber, 6 g pro. Daily Values: 14% vit. A, 1% vit. C, 3% calcium, 9% iron.

Wine-Balsamic Glazed Steak
START TO FINISH: 30 minutes

2	tsp. cooking oil	2	cups sliced fresh mushrooms
1	lb. boneless beef top loin or top sirloin steak, cut ½ to ¾ inch thick	3	Tbsp. balsamic vinegar
3	cloves garlic, minced	2	Tbsp. soy sauce
⅛	tsp. crushed red pepper	4	tsp. honey
¾	cup dry red wine	2	Tbsp. butter

1. In a large skillet heat oil over medium-high heat until very hot. Add steak(s). Do not add any liquid and do not cover the skillet. Reduce heat to medium; cook for 10 to 13 minutes or until desired doneness (145° F for medium-rare doneness or 160° F for medium doneness), turning meat occasionally. If meat browns too quickly, reduce heat to medium-low. Transfer meat to a platter; keep warm.

2. For sauce, add garlic and crushed red pepper to skillet; cook for 10 seconds. Remove skillet from heat. Carefully add wine. Return to heat. Boil, uncovered, about 5 minutes or until most of the liquid is evaporated. Add mushrooms, balsamic vinegar, soy sauce, and honey; return to simmer. Cook and stir about 4 minutes or until mushrooms are tender. Stir in butter until melted. Spoon sauce over steak. Makes 4 servings.

Each serving: 377 cal., 21 g total fat (9 g sat. fat), 82 mg chol., 588 mg sodium, 12 g carbo., 0 g fiber, 27 g pro. Daily Values: 5% vit. A, 1% vit. C, 2% calcium, 15% iron.

White Wine Pastry

Prep: 10 minutes **Bake:** 8 + 4 minutes

2   cups all-purpose flour
1/4   tsp. salt
1   cup cold butter
7   to 9 Tbsp. dry or sweet white wine, chilled

1. In a large bowl stir together flour and salt. Using a pastry blender, cut in butter until mixture resembles coarse cornmeal. Sprinkle 1 tablespoon of the wine over part of the flour mixture; gently toss with a fork. Push moistened dough to side of bowl. Repeat, using 1 tablespoon wine at a time, until all the flour mixture is moistened. Divide dough in half; form each half into a ball. If necessary, wrap dough in plastic wrap and chill for 30 minutes until easy to handle.

2. Preheat oven to 450° F. On a floured surface, slightly flatten 1 dough ball. Roll dough from center to edges into a circle 11 inches in diameter. Transfer pastry to a 9-inch round tart pan with a removable bottom. Ease pastry into pan without stretching it. Press pastry into fluted sides of tart pan; trim edges even with pan. Prick bottom and sides of pastry with tines of a fork. Line pastry with a double thickness of foil. Bake for 8 minutes. Remove foil; bake 4 to 5 minutes more or until set and dry. Cool slightly on wire rack. Use tart shell and remaining dough for Croatian Nut Tart (see recipe, opposite). Makes 12 servings.

Swiss Cheese and Olive Spread

Prep: 10 minutes
Stand: 30 minutes + 1 hour **Chill:** 2 hours

12   oz. Swiss cheese, shredded (3 cups)
1   3-oz. pkg. cream cheese, cubed
1/4   cup dry sherry or dry white wine
3   Tbsp. mayonnaise or salad dressing
1   tsp. Worcestershire sauce
1/3   cup chopped pitted ripe olives, drained
3   Tbsp. snipped flat-leaf parsley
3   Tbsp. finely chopped green onions
    Toasted baguette slices or crackers

1. Place cheeses in a large bowl; let stand, covered, at room temperature for 30 minutes. Add sherry, mayonnaise, and Worcestershire. Beat with electric mixer until combined. Stir in olives, parsley, and green onion. Transfer to serving bowl. Cover; chill for 2 to 24 hours.

2. Let stand at room temperature for 1 hour. Serve with baguette slices. Makes 2 1/2 cups (10 to 12 servings).

Each serving: 201 cal., 16 g total fat (8 g sat. fat), 42 mg chol., 181 mg sodium, 2 g carbo., 0 g fiber, 10 g pro. Daily Values: 10% vit. A, 3% vit. C, 34% calcium, 3% iron.

Spiced Pork and Sweet Potatoes

Prep: 20 minutes
Cook: 10 hours (low) or 5 hours (high)

1   3- to 3 1/2-lb. boneless pork shoulder roast
2   cloves garlic, minced
1   Tbsp. cooking oil
1   lb. sweet potatoes, peeled and cut into 1-inch cubes (3 1/2 cups)
2   stalks celery, sliced (1 cup)
1   cup dried cranberries
1   medium onion, cut into thin wedges
1   small cooking apple, coarsely chopped
2   Tbsp. quick-cooking tapioca
1/2   cup chicken broth
1/2   cup Merlot or other dry red wine
1/2   teaspoon apple pie spice
1/4   teaspoon ground sage

1. Trim fat from meat. If necessary, cut meat to fit into a 4- to 6-quart electric slow cooker. Sprinkle pork with salt and black pepper; rub with garlic. In a large skillet brown meat on all sides in hot oil; drain.

2. Place sweet potatoes, celery, cranberries, onion, and apple in the slow cooker. Sprinkle with tapioca. In a medium bowl combine broth, wine, apple pie spice, and sage; pour over mixture in cooker. Place meat on top of mixture. Cover; cook on low-heat setting for 10 to 12 hours or on high-heat setting for 5 to 6 hours.

3. To serve, transfer meat and vegetable mixture to a platter. Drizzle with some of the cooking liquid. Makes 8 servings.

low fat Each serving: 381 cal., 12 g total fat (4 g sat. fat), 110 mg chol., 260 mg sodium, 29 g carbo., 3 g fiber, 35 g pro. Daily Values: 148% vit. A, 17% vit. C, 3% calcium, 15% iron.

Five-Spice Beef Soup

Prep: 25 minutes **Cook:** 1 1/4 hours

1 1/2   lb. beef stew meat
2   Tbsp. cooking oil
1   tsp. Five-Spice Powder (below)
2   green onions, sliced
4   cloves garlic, minced
1   1-inch piece fresh ginger
1/2   tsp. crushed red pepper
3   medium tomatoes, chopped (1 lb.)
1   cup chopped daikon
1   cup chopped carrot
1 1/3   cups rice wine
1   cup water
3   Tbsp. soy sauce
4   cups hot cooked rice

1. In a 4-quart Dutch oven brown meat, half at a time, in the hot oil. Meanwhile, prepare Five-Spice Powder. Remove meat from Dutch oven. Cook green onion, garlic, ginger, and crushed red pepper in drippings for 1 minute. Stir in tomatoes, daikon, carrot, and browned meat. Stir in rice wine, the water, soy sauce, and Five-Spice Powder.

2. Bring to boiling; reduce heat. Simmer, covered, about 1 1/4 hours or until meat and vegetables are tender. Skim off fat. Discard fresh ginger. Serve over hot cooked rice. Makes 6 servings.

FIVE-SPICE POWDER: In a blender combine 3 tablespoons ground cinnamon; 2 teaspoons anise seeds or 6 star anise; 1 1/2 teaspoons fennel seeds; 1 1/2 teaspoons whole Szechwan pepper or whole black peppercorns; and 3/4 teaspoon ground cloves. Cover and process until powdery. Store in a covered container.

low fat Each serving: 480 cal., 10 g total fat (3 g sat. fat), 68 mg chol., 608 mg sodium, 51 g carbo., 2 g fiber, 31 g pro. Daily Values: 111% vit. A, 24% vit. C, 16% calcium, 34% iron.

TAILGATE FAVORITES

Hot and Spicy Sloppy Joes
PREP: 25 minutes **COOK:** 40 + 10 minutes

2 lb. ground beef	2 tsp. paprika
4 medium green sweet peppers, chopped (3 cups)	½ tsp. salt
	½ tsp. ground black pepper
2 medium red sweet peppers, chopped (1½ cups)	1 fresh Scotch bonnet chile pepper, seeded and finely chopped (see note, page 302), or ¼ tsp. cayenne pepper
4 medium onions, chopped (2 cups)	
2 cups strong coffee	
1 cup cider vinegar	14 to 16 hamburger or hot dog buns, split
1½ cups ketchup	
2 tsp. chili powder	

1. In a 4-quart Dutch oven cook ground beef, green and red sweet peppers, and onions until meat is brown and vegetables are tender. Drain off fat.

2. Stir in coffee and vinegar. Bring to boiling. Boil gently, uncovered, over medium heat about 40 minutes or until liquid is almost all evaporated, stirring occasionally.

3. Stir in ketchup, chili powder, paprika, salt, black pepper, and Scotch bonnet or cayenne pepper. Cook and stir for 10 to 15 minutes more or until desired consistency. Keep hot while transporting. If desired, toast hamburger or hot dog buns. Serve meat in buns. Makes 14 to 16 servings.

low fat Each serving: 283 cal., 9 g total fat (3 g sat. fat), 41 mg chol., 658 mg sodium, 36 g carbo., 3 g fiber, 17 g pro. Daily Values: 35% vit. A, 111% vit. C, 8% calcium, 18% iron.

Carrot Dip
Serve a colorful assortment of vegetable dippers alongside the horseradish-sparked dip.
PREP: 15 minutes **CHILL:** 4 hours

½ of an 8-oz. carton dairy sour cream	1½ tsp. prepared horseradish (optional)
½ of an 8-oz. pkg. cream cheese, softened	¼ tsp. salt
	¼ tsp. ground black pepper
¼ cup mayonnaise or salad dressing	1½ cups shredded carrots
	⅓ cup chopped green onions
2 tsp. soy sauce	

1. In a medium mixing bowl combine sour cream, cream cheese, mayonnaise, soy sauce, horseradish (if using), salt, and pepper; beat with an electric mixer until smooth. Stir in shredded carrot and green onion.

2. Cover and chill for 4 to 24 hours. Keep chilled while transporting. Stir before serving. Makes 2 cups.

Each tablespoon: 110 cal., 10 g total fat (4 g sat. fat), 19 mg chol., 195 mg sodium, 3 g carbo., 1 g fiber, 2 g pro. Daily Values: 107% vit. A, 4% vit. C, 3% calcium, 2% iron.

Hearty Sausage Gumbo

Smoked turkey sausage stars in this hearty Cajun-style stew.

PREP: 45 minutes **COOK:** 30 minutes

1	medium Vidalia onion or other sweet onion, chopped (1 cup)
1	small red sweet pepper, chopped
1	small green sweet pepper, chopped
1	stalk celery, chopped
1	clove garlic, minced
1	Tbsp. olive oil
5½	cups water
1	lb. smoked turkey sausage links, quartered lengthwise and sliced
1	16-oz. pkg. frozen cut okra
1	14½-oz. can diced tomatoes
1	7-oz. pkg. gumbo mix with rice
1	tsp. snipped fresh rosemary
½	tsp. snipped fresh thyme
⅛	tsp. cayenne pepper (optional)

1. In a 4-quart Dutch oven cook onion, red and green sweet pepper, celery, and garlic in hot oil over medium heat until tender, stirring frequently.

2. Stir in the water, sausage, okra, undrained tomatoes, gumbo mix, rosemary, thyme, and, if desired, cayenne pepper. Bring to boiling; reduce heat. Simmer, covered, about 20 minutes or until rice is tender. Keep stew hot while transporting. Makes 8 servings.

Each serving: 224 cal., 7 g total fat (1 g sat. fat), 38 mg chol., 1,329 mg sodium, 29 g carbo., 3 g fiber, 13 g pro. Daily Values: 13% vit. A, 53% vit. C, 8% calcium, 11% iron.

Mushroom Deluxe Hamburgers

Set up a grill at your tailgate site and bring on the burgers.

PREP: 25 minutes **GRILL:** 14 minutes

1	cup assorted fresh mushrooms, chopped
¼	cup chopped green sweet pepper
¼	cup chopped onion
1	Tbsp. butter
1	egg
3	Tbsp. garlic-flavored fine dry bread crumbs
3	Tbsp. grated Parmesan cheese
2	Tbsp. ketchup
½	tsp. celery salt
⅛	tsp. ground coriander
⅛	tsp. cayenne pepper
1	lb. ground beef
1	medium onion, cut into 4 slices
1	Tbsp. olive oil
4	hamburger buns, split and toasted
	Sliced Swiss cheese (optional)
	Sliced tomatoes (optional)

1. In a medium skillet cook mushrooms, green sweet pepper, and onion in hot butter until tender; cool.

2. In a large bowl beat egg; stir in bread crumbs, Parmesan cheese, ketchup, celery salt, coriander, and cayenne pepper. Add mushroom mixture and ground beef; mix well. Shape into four ³/₄-inch-thick patties. Brush onion slices with olive oil.

3. At the party, grill patties and onion slices on the rack of an uncovered grill directly over medium coals for 14 to 18 minutes or until an instant-read thermometer inserted in the burgers registers 160° F, turning once halfway through grilling. Serve burgers topped with onion slices on buns. If desired, add cheese and tomato slices. Makes 4 servings.

Each serving: 483 cal., 26 g total fat (10 g sat. fat), 136 mg chol., 845 mg sodium, 32 g carbo., 2 g fiber, 31 g pro. Daily Values: 8% vit. A, 19% vit. C, 14% calcium, 22% iron.

Onion Chili Sauce

Adjust the heat to suit your taste by using small, medium, or large jalapeños and your favorite Louisiana hot sauce.

PREP: 20 minutes **COOK:** 30 minutes

1½	lb. Vidalia onions or other sweet onions, halved lengthwise and sliced (about 6 cups)
1	Tbsp. cooking oil
1	medium green sweet pepper, cut into thin strips (1 cup)
2	fresh jalapeño chile peppers, halved, seeded, and thinly sliced (see note, page 302)
³/₄	cup bottled chili sauce
1	Tbsp. bottled Louisiana hot sauce
1	Tbsp. honey
½	tsp. salt
½	tsp. ground cinnamon
¼	tsp. ground black pepper
⅛	tsp. ground cloves

1. In a large skillet cook onion slices, covered, in hot oil over medium heat for 20 minutes, stirring occasionally. (Reduce heat to medium-low if onion slices begin to brown.)

2. Add sweet and hot peppers; cover and cook about 5 minutes more or just until peppers are tender. Stir in chili sauce, Louisiana hot sauce, honey, salt, cinnamon, black pepper, and cloves. Bring to boiling; reduce heat. Simmer, uncovered, for 5 minutes. Cool; chill to store. Keep cold while transporting.

3. Serve chili sauce over grilled bratwurst, hot dogs, or burgers. Makes about 3 cups sauce (enough sauce for 12 sandwiches).

low fat Each serving: 54 cal., 1 g total fat (0 g sat. fat), 0 mg chol., 307 mg sodium, 10 g carbo., 2 g fiber, 1 g pro. Daily Values: 4% vit. A, 23% vit. C, 2% calcium, 2% iron.

BAG LUNCH SPECIALS

PRIZE TESTED RECIPES® $400 WINNER

SHOBA HAVALAD, GLENVIEW, ILL.

PRIZE TESTED RECIPES® $200 WINNER

ELLEN BURR, LOS ANGELES, CALIF.

Cucumber Sandwiches

START TO FINISH: 20 minutes

1 cup packed fresh cilantro leaves	2 Tbsp. grated Parmesan cheese
½ cup packed fresh mint leaves	4 slices whole wheat or white bread
1 Tbsp. lime juice	2 Tbsp. butter, softened
1 fresh jalapeño pepper, quartered (seeded, if desired) (see note, page 302)	4 1-oz. slices provolone cheese
1 clove garlic, quartered	½ of a medium cucumber, thinly sliced (1 cup)

1. In a food processor combine cilantro, mint, lime juice, jalapeño pepper, and garlic. Cover and process until finely chopped. (If you do not have a food processor, finely chop the herbs, jalapeño, and garlic; combine with the lime juice.) Stir in Parmesan cheese.

2. If desired, remove crusts from bread. Spread one side of each bread slice with softened butter. Top 2 of the bread slices with 2 of the cheese slices. Top with cucumber slices. Carefully top with cilantro mixture, remaining cheese slices, and remaining bread slices, buttered sides down. Cut sandwiches in half. Serve immediately or wrap in plastic wrap and pack with an ice pack and chill up to 4 hours before eating. Makes 2 sandwiches.

Each sandwich: 485 cal., 31 g total fat (19 g sat. fat), 75 mg chol., 992 mg sodium, 30 g carbo., 4 g fiber, 23 g pro. Daily Values: 53% vit. A, 104% vit. C, 62% calcium, 43% iron.

Stuffed Focaccia

Mascarpone cheese, artichoke hearts, capers, salami, and arugula layered on focaccia add up to one tremendous sandwich.

START TO FINISH: 20 minutes

½ of a 9- to 10-inch garlic-flavored, onion-flavored, or plain Italian flatbread (focaccia), split horizontally	1 6-oz. jar marinated artichoke hearts, drained and chopped
½ of an 8-oz. container mascarpone cheese	1 Tbsp. capers, drained
	4 oz. thinly sliced Genoa salami
	1 cup arugula leaves

1. Spread cut sides of focaccia with mascarpone cheese. Sprinkle bottom half of focaccia with artichoke hearts and capers; top with salami and arugula leaves. Add top of focaccia, mascarpone side down.

2. Cut sandwich into thirds. Serve immediately or wrap in plastic wrap and pack with an ice pack and chill up to 4 hours before eating. Makes 3 sandwiches.

Each sandwich: 545 cal., 36 g total fat (16 g sat. fat), 83 mg chol., 970 mg sodium, 43 g carbo., 3 g fiber, 23 g pro. Daily Values: 3% vit. A, 24% vit. C, 10% calcium, 8% iron.

Asian-Style Pork and Noodle Salad

Look for bottled Thai peanut sauce in your supermarket's Asian foods section or at an Asian market.

PREP: 30 minutes **BROIL:** 9 minutes
CHILL: 4 hours

1 3-oz. pkg. pork- or chicken-flavored ramen noodles
1/2 cup salad oil
1/3 cup rice vinegar
3 cloves garlic, minced
3 Tbsp. Thai peanut sauce
1/4 tsp. crushed red pepper
12 oz. boneless pork loin chops, cut 3/4 inch thick
4 cups shredded cabbage
1 cup broccoli florets
1/2 cup sliced almonds, toasted
1/2 cup sliced green onions

1. Measure out 3/4 teaspoon of the seasoning packet (half of the packet); reserve the remaining for another use. In a medium bowl whisk together the 3/4 teaspoon seasoning, salad oil, rice vinegar, garlic, peanut sauce, and red pepper. Remove 2 tablespoons of the mixture; brush onto pork chops.

2. Preheat broiler. Place pork on the unheated rack of a broiler pan. Broil 3 to 4 inches from the heat for 9 to 12 minutes or until meat juices run clear (160° F), turning chops once. Cool slightly. Thinly slice across the grain into bite-size strips.

3. Meanwhile, cook noodles in a large saucepan in boiling water for 2 minutes; drain. Transfer to a large bowl. Add the pork, cabbage, broccoli, almonds, green onion, and remaining oil mixture. Toss to coat. Cover and chill for 4 to 24 hours.

4. To tote, spoon into 5 individual containers; pack each with an ice pack. Eat within 5 hours. Makes 5 servings.

Each serving: 505 cal., 38 g total fat (6 g sat. fat), 40 mg chol., 490 mg sodium, 22 g carbo., 4 g fiber, 22 g pro. Daily Values: 8% vit. A, 63% vit. C, 10% calcium, 11% iron.

Cucumber and Corn Chicken Salad

Transform leftover cooked chicken into a refreshing main-dish salad. No leftovers on hand? Use frozen diced cooked chicken.

PREP: 25 minutes **BAKE:** 6 minutes
CHILL: 4 hours

1 10-oz. pkg. frozen whole kernel corn
1 large cucumber, seeded and chopped
1 1/2 cups cubed cooked chicken (about 8 oz.)
1/2 of a medium red, yellow, or green sweet pepper, seeded and chopped
1/3 cup bottled creamy Italian salad dressing
1 Tbsp. snipped fresh dill or 1 tsp. dried dill weed
1/4 tsp. salt
1 recipe Toasted Wheat Pita Triangles (below)

1. Cook corn according to package directions; drain well. In a large bowl combine corn, cucumber, chicken, sweet pepper, salad dressing, dill, and salt. Toss to mix. Cover and chill for 4 to 24 hours.

2. To tote, spoon into 4 individual containers; pack each with an ice pack. Pack pita wedges separately. Eat within 5 hours. Makes 4 servings.

TOASTED WHEAT PITA TRIANGLES: Preheat oven to 375° F. Split 2 whole wheat pita rounds in half horizontally. Cut each half into 6 wedges. Place, cut sides up, on a large baking sheet. Brush with 1 tablespoon olive oil. In a small bowl stir together 1/4 cup finely shredded Parmesan cheese; 1/4 teaspoon dried Italian seasoning, crushed; and 1/8 teaspoon cayenne pepper. Sprinkle Parmesan mixture over pita wedges. Bake for 6 to 8 minutes or until wedges are toasted.

Each serving: 379 cal., 17 g total fat (4 g sat. fat), 50 mg chol., 614 mg sodium, 37 g carbo., 4 g fiber, 23 g pro. Daily Values: 22% vit. A, 57% vit. C, 9% calcium, 11% iron.

Greek Chicken Salad Sub with Olive Salsa

Another time, serve the Olive Salsa as a dip with tortilla chips.

START TO FINISH: 20 minutes

1 recipe Olive Salsa (below)
1 16-oz. loaf French bread
1 9-oz. pkg. frozen cooked chicken breast strips, thawed
3/4 cup thinly sliced cucumber
3 oz. feta cheese, coarsely crumbled (3/4 cup)

1. Prepare Olive Salsa; set aside. Horizontally split loaf of bread. Hollow out inside of each half, leaving a 3/4-inch-thick shell. Fill the bottom half of the loaf with chicken, cucumber, feta, and the Olive Salsa. Top with hollowed-out top half.

2. To serve, cut sandwich into 4 to 6 pieces. To tote, wrap each slice in plastic wrap. Pack each with an ice pack. Eat within 5 hours. Makes 4 to 6 servings.

OLIVE SALSA: In a food processor* combine 1/2 cup pitted kalamata olives; 1/2 cup pepperoncini salad peppers, stems and seeds removed; 1/4 cup chopped red onion; 1/4 cup olive oil; 2 tablespoons red wine vinegar; 2 teaspoons snipped fresh oregano; 1/8 teaspoon salt; and 1/8 teaspoon ground black pepper. Cover and process until coarsely chopped. Stir in 1 medium tomato, diced; set aside.

*NOTE: If you don't have a food processor, finely chop the ingredients and combine by hand.

Each serving: 611 cal., 24 g total fat (6 g sat. fat), 60 mg chol., 2,206 mg sodium, 65 g carbo., 5 g fiber, 13 g pro. Daily Values: 7% vit. A, 13% vit. C, 20% calcium, 21% iron.

TAKE-ALONG SIDE DISHES

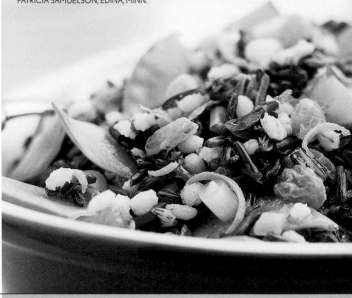

Squash Gratin with Spinach
PREP: 40 minutes **BAKE:** 10 minutes

1³/4 to 2 lb. butternut squash	1 Tbsp. cornstarch
1 Tbsp. olive oil	1 cup finely shredded
Salt	Parmesan cheese
Ground black pepper	½ cup purchased crème
16 cups fresh spinach	fraîche
1 cup half-and-half or	
light cream	

1. Preheat oven to 425° F. Lightly grease a 2-quart rectangular baking dish; set aside. Peel squash; slice ¼ inch thick. Discard seeds; halve large slices. Brush both sides with olive oil. Arrange in a 15×10×1-inch baking pan. Sprinkle with salt and pepper. Bake, uncovered, for 20 minutes.

2. In a 4- to 6-quart Dutch oven cook spinach, half at a time, in lightly salted boiling water for 1 minute or until wilted. Drain and cool slightly; squeeze out excess liquid. Coarsely chop the spinach; set aside.

3. Meanwhile, in a medium saucepan stir together half-and-half and cornstarch; cook and stir until thickened and bubbly. Stir in spinach. Spread in prepared dish; arrange squash on top.

4. Increase oven temperature to 475° F. In a small bowl stir together Parmesan and crème fraîche; spread onto squash. Bake, uncovered, for 10 to 15 minutes or until squash is tender and Parmesan mixture is light brown. Makes 8 servings.

Each serving: 408 cal., 28 g total fat (17 g sat. fat), 72 mg chol., 1,297 mg sodium, 11 g carbo., 7 g fiber, 29 g pro. Daily Values: 130% vit. A, 28% vit. C, 95% calcium, 28% iron.

Buffet Wild Rice
PREP: 30 minutes **COOK:** 45 minutes

2 14-oz. cans chicken or	6 green onions, sliced
vegetable broth	(³/4 cup)
³/4 cup uncooked wild rice,	2 tsp. finely shredded
rinsed and drained	orange peel
⅓ cup regular barley	½ cup orange juice
1 cup fresh pea pods,	¼ cup snipped fresh mint
halved crosswise	2 Tbsp. olive oil
1 cup golden raisins	½ tsp. curry powder

1. In a large saucepan bring broth to boiling; stir in wild rice and barley. Return to boiling; reduce heat. Simmer, covered, about 40 minutes or until rice and barley are tender. Drain off liquid. Return rice and barley to pan.

2. Stir in pea pods, raisins, green onions, orange peel, orange juice, mint, olive oil, and curry powder. Cook and stir over medium heat until heated through. Serve warm or at room temperature. Makes 6 to 8 servings.

Each serving: 271 cal., 6 g total fat (1 g sat. fat), 0 mg chol., 562 mg sodium, 50 g carbo., 6 g fiber, 7 g pro. Daily Values: 3% vit. A, 30% vit. C, 5% calcium, 13% iron.

Roasted Potatoes with Goat Cheese Sauce

PREP: 25 minutes **BAKE:** 40 + 45 minutes

3   lb. tiny red potatoes, scrubbed and quartered, or medium round red potatoes, cut into eighths
3   cloves garlic, minced
3   Tbsp. olive oil
1/2   tsp. salt
1/2   tsp. ground black pepper
4   oz. chèvre (soft goat cheese)
3/4   cup milk
1   Tbsp. all-purpose flour
2   tsp. snipped fresh rosemary or 1/2 tsp. dried rosemary, crushed
1   recipe Walnut-Rosemary Topper (below)

1. Preheat oven to 450° F. In an extra-large mixing bowl toss together potatoes, garlic, olive oil, 1/4 teaspoon of the salt, and 1/4 teaspoon of the pepper. Spread mixture in a greased 15×10×1-inch baking pan. Place pan on bottom oven rack; roast for 40 to 45 minutes or until golden brown and tender, turning once. Transfer to a 2-quart baking dish. If making ahead, cool slightly, then cover and chill.

2. Meanwhile, for sauce, in a blender combine cheese, milk, flour, rosemary, remaining 1/4 teaspoon salt, and 1/4 teaspoon pepper. Cover and blend until smooth. If making ahead, transfer to a container; cover and chill. Prepare Walnut-Rosemary Topper; cover and chill.

3. To serve, bake potatoes, covered, at 350° F for 30 minutes. Pour sauce onto potatoes; stir gently. Sprinkle with topper. Bake, uncovered, about 15 minutes or until heated through. Makes 6 to 8 servings.

WALNUT-ROSEMARY TOPPER: In a small bowl combine 1/4 cup finely chopped walnuts, 1/4 cup fine dry bread crumbs, and 1 teaspoon fresh rosemary or 1/4 teaspoon crushed dried rosemary. Toss with 2 teaspoons olive oil. Cover and chill until needed.

Each serving: 318 cal., 16 g total fat (5 g sat. fat), 11 mg chol., 379 mg sodium, 34 g carbo., 3 g fiber, 10 g pro. Daily Values: 2% vit. A, 43% vit. C, 10% calcium, 17% iron.

Paradise Bread

PREP: 30 minutes **RISE:** 2 hours
BAKE: 30 minutes

5   to 5 1/2 cups all-purpose flour
2   pkg. active dry yeast
2   tsp. finely shredded orange peel
1/3   cup butter
1/3   cup honey
3   Tbsp. granulated sugar
1 1/2   tsp. anise seeds, crushed
1   tsp. salt
1   tsp. ground mace
1   egg
1   cup raisins
1   cup coarsely chopped pecans
1   Tbsp. butter, melted
1/2   cup sifted powdered sugar
1   to 2 tsp. orange juice

1. In a large bowl combine 2 1/2 cups flour, the yeast, and orange peel; set aside.

2. In a medium saucepan heat and stir 1 1/4 cups water, 1/3 cup butter, honey, granulated sugar, anise seeds, salt, and mace just until warm (120° F to 130° F) and butter almost melts. Add butter mixture and egg to flour mixture. Beat with an electric mixer on low to medium speed for 30 seconds, scraping bowl constantly. Beat on high speed for 3 minutes. Stir in raisins, pecans, and as much remaining flour as you can.

3. Turn dough out onto a lightly floured surface. Knead in enough of the remaining flour to make a moderately stiff dough that is smooth and elastic (6 to 8 minutes total). Shape into a ball. Place in a lightly greased bowl; turn once. Cover; let rise in a warm place until double (1 1/4 to 1 1/2 hours).

4. Punch dough down. Turn dough out onto a lightly floured surface; divide in half. Cover; let rest for 10 minutes.

5. Lightly grease two 8×4×2-inch loaf pans. Shape dough into loaves; place in pans. Cover; let rise in a warm place until nearly double in size (about 45 minutes).

6. Preheat oven to 350° F. Bake for 30 to 35 minutes or until bread sounds hollow when lightly tapped (if necessary, cover loosely with foil the last 10 minutes of baking). Remove from pans. Brush with melted butter. Cool on wire racks.

7. In a small bowl combine powdered sugar and enough orange juice to make of drizzling consistency. Drizzle onto cooled loaves. Makes 2 loaves (24 servings).

Each serving: 198 cal., 9 g total fat (2 g sat. fat), 17 mg chol., 134 mg sodium, 32 g carbo., 1 g fiber, 4 g pro. Daily Values: 3% vit. A, 1% vit. C, 1% calcium, 9% iron.

Corn and Fig Spoon Bread

PREP: 35 minutes **BAKE:** 45 minutes

3   egg whites
   Nonstick cooking spray
1/2   cup chopped dried figs
1/2   cup apple juice
2   cups milk
1 1/2   cups buttermilk
1 1/4   cups cornmeal
1   Tbsp. sugar
1   tsp. salt
1 1/2   cups frozen whole kernel corn, thawed
1/4   cup butter, cut up
3   egg yolks
1   tsp. baking powder

1. Let egg whites stand at room temperature for 30 minutes. Preheat oven to 375° F. Lightly coat a 2 1/2-quart casserole with nonstick cooking spray; set aside. In a small saucepan combine figs and apple juice. Bring to boiling; remove from heat. Set aside.

2. In a large saucepan combine milk, buttermilk, cornmeal, sugar, and salt. Cook and stir over medium heat for 10 to 15 minutes or until very thick and bubby, stirring often. Remove from heat. Stir in corn, butter, and fig-apple juice mixture.

3. In a small bowl combine egg yolks and baking powder. Slowly stir in 1 cup hot cornmeal mixture. Return mixture to pan.

4. In a large bowl beat egg whites until stiff peaks form. Fold egg whites into the corn mixture. Transfer to the prepared dish.

5. Bake, uncovered, for 45 minutes or until slightly puffed and center appears set. Makes 8 servings.

Each serving: 272 cal., 11 g total fat (6 g sat. fat), 103 mg chol., 514 mg sodium, 38 g carbo., 4 g fiber, 9 g pro. Daily Values: 13% vit. A, 5% vit. C, 19% calcium, 8% iron.

GOING WITH GRAINS

MELISSA BARTON, TALLAHASSEE, FLA.

DAWN K. MURPHY, RENO, NEV.

Mom's Bread

PREP: 30 minutes **RISE:** 1½ hours **BAKE:** 30 minutes

1. Place ½ cup bulgur in a small bowl. Add boiling water to cover. Let stand 15 minutes; drain well. Meanwhile, in a large mixing bowl combine 2 cups all-purpose flour and 1 package active dry yeast; set aside. In medium saucepan heat and stir 1¼ cups milk, ¼ cup honey, ¼ cup butter, and 1 teaspoon salt just until warm (120° F to 130° F) and butter almost melts. Add milk mixture to flour mixture. Add 1 egg. Beat with electric mixer on low to medium speed for 30 seconds, scraping sides of bowl. Beat on high speed 3 minutes. Using a wooden spoon, stir in bulgur, 1 cup whole wheat flour, ½ cup all-purpose flour, ½ cup rolled oats, ½ cup wheat cereal flakes, and ½ cup toasted wheat germ.

2. Turn out onto lightly floured surface. Knead in ¼ to ¾ cup whole wheat flour to make a moderately stiff dough that is smooth and elastic (6 to 8 minutes total). Shape dough into a ball. Place in lightly greased bowl; turn once. Cover; let rise in warm place until double in size (about 1 hour). Punch down dough. Turn out onto lightly floured surface; divide in half. Cover; let rest 10 minutes. Lightly grease two 8×4×2-inch loaf pans. Shape dough into 2 loaves; place in prepared pans. Mix 1 egg white and 1 tablespoon water; brush onto loaves. Sprinkle with coarsely crushed wheat cereal flakes. Cover; let rise until nearly double (about 30 minutes).

3. Preheat oven to 375° F. Bake about 30 minutes or until bread sounds hollow when lightly tapped. If desired, cover with foil the last 10 minutes of baking to prevent overbrowning. Remove from pans; cool on wire racks. Makes 2 loaves (24 slices).

low fat Each slice: 134 cal., 3 g total fat (2 g sat. fat), 15 mg chol., 136 mg sodium, 23 g carbo., 2 g fiber, 4 g pro. Daily Values: 3% vit. A, 3% vit. C, 3% calcium, 10% iron.

Orzo and Bulgur Salad

PREP: 30 minutes **STAND:** 45 minutes **CHILL:** 4 hours

1 cup dried orzo	½ cup dried cranberries
1 cup bulgur	¼ cup bias-sliced green
1 recipe Parsley-Fennel	onions
Vinaigrette (below)	¼ cup crumbled feta cheese
½ cup finely chopped celery	(1 oz.)
½ cup shredded carrot	
½ cup chopped, seeded	
cucumber	

1. Cook orzo according to package directions. Drain orzo, reserving cooking water. Place bulgur in a 2-cup glass measure. Add enough of the hot cooking water to bulgur to equal 2 cups total mixture. Let bulgur stand about 45 minutes or until all liquid is absorbed. Meanwhile, prepare Parsley-Fennel Vinaigrette.

2. In a large bowl combine orzo, bulgur, celery, carrot, cucumber, and cranberries. Add Parsley-Fennel Vinaigrette; toss to coat. Cover and chill for 4 to 24 hours. Stir before serving. Top with green onion and feta cheese. Makes 10 to 12 servings.

PARSLEY-FENNEL VINAIGRETTE: In a bowl whisk together ½ cup snipped fresh parsley, ⅓ cup olive oil, ¼ cup balsamic vinegar, 2 tablespoons finely chopped shallot, 1 teaspoon sugar, 1 teaspoon salt, 1 teaspoon dry mustard, ½ teaspoon crushed fennel seeds, and ¼ teaspoon ground black pepper.

Each serving: 217 cal., 9 g total fat (2 g sat. fat), 3 mg chol., 288 mg sodium, 31 g carbo., 4 g fiber, 5 g pro. Daily Values: 35% vit. A, 10% vit. C, 4% calcium, 8% iron.

Asparagus Barley Pilaf

START TO FINISH: 50 minutes

- 1 cup quick-cooking barley
- 1 Tbsp. olive oil
- ½ cup finely chopped onion
- 1 Tbsp. butter
- 1 large clove garlic, minced
- 1 14-oz. can chicken broth or vegetable broth
- 8 oz. fresh asparagus, cut into 1-inch pieces
- ½ cup shredded carrot
- ¼ cup shredded Asiago cheese or Parmesan cheese (1 oz.)
- ¼ cup snipped fresh basil

1. In a large saucepan cook barley in hot olive oil over medium heat about 5 minutes or until lightly toasted, stirring often. Add onion, butter, and garlic; cook until onion is tender.

2. In a small saucepan heat broth. Slowly add ³/4 cup of the broth to barley mixture, stirring constantly. Continue to cook and stir over medium heat until liquid is absorbed. Add another ½ cup of the broth, stirring constantly. Continue to cook and stir until the liquid is absorbed. Add another ½ cup of the broth; cook and stir until liquid is almost all absorbed.

3. Add asparagus and carrot; continue cooking until all the liquid is absorbed and the barley is tender. (Should take about 30 minutes total.)

4. Remove from heat. Stir in cheese and basil; season to taste with salt and ground black pepper. Makes 3 main-dish servings or 6 side-dish servings.

Each main-dish serving: 334 cal., 15 g total fat (6 g sat. fat), 21 mg chol., 836 mg sodium, 44 g carbo., 7 g fiber, 10 g pro. Daily Values: 103% vit. A, 14% vit. C, 9% calcium, 9% iron.

Fiesta Quinoa Salad

PREP: 30 minutes **CHILL:** 2 hours

- 1 cup quinoa
- 1 15-oz. can black beans, rinsed and drained
- 1 medium jicama, peeled and cut into bite-size strips (2 cups)
- 1 medium yellow or red sweet pepper, chopped (³/4 cup)
- ⅓ cup chopped red onion
- ¼ cup snipped fresh cilantro
- 1 fresh jalapeño chile pepper, seeded and finely chopped (see note, page 302)
- 1 recipe Spiced Lime Dressing (below)

1. Place quinoa in a fine-mesh strainer. Rinse under cold running water; drain. In a medium saucepan bring 2½ cups water to boiling. Add quinoa. Return to boiling; reduce heat. Cover; simmer for 10 minutes. Drain in fine-mesh strainer. Rinse with cold water; drain again. Place in large bowl.

2. Stir in beans, jicama, sweet pepper, onion, cilantro, and jalapeño. Prepare Spiced Lime Dressing; add to quinoa mixture. Toss to coat. Cover and chill for 2 to 24 hours. Makes 4 main-dish servings or 8 side-dish servings.

SPICED LIME DRESSING: In a small bowl stir together ¼ cup olive oil, 1 teaspoon finely shredded lime peel, 3 tablespoons lime juice, 1 teaspoon salt, and 1 teaspoon ground cumin.

Each main-dish serving: 406 cal., 17 g total fat (2 g sat. fat), 0 mg chol., 858 mg sodium, 57 g carbo., 9 g fiber, 14 g pro. Daily Values: 6% vit. A, 188% vit. C, 8% calcium, 35% iron.

Feta Tabbouleh Salad

PREP: 20 minutes **CHILL:** 30 minutes

- 1 5.25-oz. pkg. tabbouleh (wheat salad) mix
- 1 cup boiling water
- 1½ cups chopped tomato
- 4 oz. feta cheese with garlic and herb, crumbled (1 cup)
- 1 cup chopped yellow, red, and/or green sweet pepper
- 2 oz. hard salami, chopped (½ cup)
- ½ cup sliced green onions
- ½ cup snipped fresh parsley
- ½ cup snipped fresh mint
- 3 Tbsp. lemon juice
- 2 Tbsp. olive oil
- ½ tsp. ground black pepper
   Lettuce leaves

1. In a large bowl combine tabbouleh mix with spice packet. Stir in the boiling water. Cover and chill for 30 minutes or up to 24 hours.

2. Stir in tomato, ½ cup of the feta cheese, the sweet pepper, salami, green onion, parsley, mint, lemon juice, olive oil, and black pepper.

3. To serve, spoon onto lettuce leaves. (Or cover and chill up to 24 hours.) Sprinkle with remaining feta cheese. Makes 6 side-dish servings or 4 main-dish servings.

Each side-dish serving: 229 cal., 12 g total fat (5 g sat. fat), 24 mg chol., 627 mg sodium, 25 g carbo., 6 g fiber, 9 g pro. Daily Values: 21% vit. A, 135% vit. C, 14% calcium, 11% iron.

Jeweled Bulgur Salad

PREP: 10 minutes **COOK:** 20 minutes
STAND: 30 minutes **CHILL:** 2 hours

- 1³/4 cups water
- ²/3 cup bulgur
- ½ cup dried cranberries
- ½ cup dried apricot halves, quartered
- 1 8-oz. can pineapple tidbits
- 1 recipe Apricot-Dijon Dressing (below)
- 1 cup seedless green grapes, halved
- ¼ cup broken pecans, toasted

1. In a medium saucepan combine the water and bulgur. Bring to boiling; reduce heat. Simmer, covered, about 20 minutes or until liquid is absorbed. Remove from heat. Stir in cranberries and apricots; let stand, covered, for 30 minutes. Transfer bulgur to a medium bowl.

2. Stir in undrained pineapple. Cover and chill for 2 to 24 hours. Prepare Apricot-Dijon Dressing; add to salad. Add grapes and pecans. Toss to coat. Makes 6 side-dish servings.

APRICOT-DIJON DRESSING: In a screw-top jar combine ¼ cup apricot nectar, 3 tablespoons cider vinegar, 3 tablespoons salad oil, 1 teaspoon Dijon-style mustard, and ¼ teaspoon salt. Cover and shake well to mix.

Each serving: 253 cal., 11 g total fat (1 g sat. fat), 0 mg chol., 125 mg sodium, 41 g carbo., 6 g fiber, 3 g pro. Daily Values: 19% vit. A, 12% vit. C, 3% calcium, 8% iron.

TOMATO IDEAS

Tomato-Cucumber Soup
START TO FINISH: 25 minutes

3	medium cucumbers, peeled, seeded, and cut up (1½ lb.)
3	medium tomatoes, cored, seeded, and cut up (1 lb.)
½	cup coarsely sliced green onions or scallions
¼	cup snipped fresh parsley
3	Tbsp. cider vinegar
1	clove garlic, minced
1	cup chicken broth
2	8-oz. cartons dairy sour cream
½	tsp. salt
½	tsp. ground black pepper
	Cucumber slices (optional)
	Cherry tomato or grape tomato wedges (optional)

1. In a food processor or blender combine cut-up cucumbers, tomatoes, green onion, parsley, vinegar, and garlic; cover and process until nearly smooth. (If using a blender, blend half of the vegetables at a time.) Transfer puree to a bowl; stir in chicken broth.

2. Serve immediately or cover and chill for up to 4 hours. Before serving, add sour cream, salt, and pepper; whisk until smooth. Spoon into 6 bowls. If desired, garnish with cucumber slices and tomato wedges. Makes 6 side-dish servings.

Each serving: 203 cal., 17 g total fat (10 g sat. fat), 33 mg chol., 413 mg sodium, 11 g carbo., 2 g fiber, 4 g pro. Daily Values: 29% vit. A, 43% vit. C, 12% calcium, 6% iron.

Tomato-Corn Pudding
PREP: 45 minutes **BAKE:** 25 minutes **COOL:** 10 minutes

12	small tomatoes (about 4 oz. each)
	Nonstick cooking spray
½	cup light dairy sour cream
½	cup milk
2	eggs
1	Tbsp. butter, melted
¼	cup finely crushed saltine crackers (7)
1	Tbsp. all-purpose flour
1	Tbsp. sugar
½	tsp. baking powder
1	cup fresh corn kernels or frozen whole kernel corn, thawed
1	Tbsp. finely chopped onion
2	oz. Havarti cheese with dill, shredded (½ cup)
	Fresh dill sprigs (optional)

1. Cut a ¼-inch slice from stem end of each tomato. Using a spoon, scoop out pulp of each, leaving about a ¼-inch-thick shell. Sprinkle cavities with salt and pepper. Turn upside down on a paper towel-lined baking sheet; let drain for 30 minutes.

2. Meanwhile, lightly coat twelve 2½-inch muffin cups with cooking spray; set aside. Preheat oven to 350° F. In a medium bowl whisk together sour cream, milk, eggs, and butter. Whisk in crackers, flour, sugar, baking powder, and ¼ teaspoon salt until smooth. Stir in corn and onion.

3. Place tomatoes, cut sides up, in prepared muffin cups. Fill each with about 3 tablespoons corn mixture. Top with cheese. Bake, uncovered, for 25 to 30 minutes or until puffed and set.

4. Cool in pan on a wire rack for 10 minutes. Use a large spoon to remove from cups. Serve warm. If desired, trim with dill sprigs. Makes 12 side-dish servings.

Each serving: 107 cal., 5 g total fat (2 g sat. fat), 48 mg chol., 204 mg sodium, 11 g carbo., 2 g fiber, 5 g pro. Daily Values: 17% vit. A, 35% vit. C, 8% calcium, 4% iron.

Cheesy Cavatappi with Tomatoes and Olives

START TO FINISH: 35 minutes

- 12 oz. dried cavatappi or mostaccioli pasta
- 4 cups red pear tomatoes, yellow pear tomatoes, and/or cherry tomatoes, halved
- 1 tsp. kosher salt or salt
- 1½ cups half-and-half or light cream
- 3 oz. Gorgonzola cheese, crumbled (³/4 cup)
- ³/4 cup finely shredded Parmesan cheese (3 oz.)
  Dash ground white pepper
  Dash cayenne pepper
- ¼ cup snipped fresh parsley
- 2 Tbsp. snipped fresh basil
- 1 Tbsp. snipped fresh lemon thyme or thyme
- ²/3 cup pitted kalamata olives, halved
- ¼ cup sliced green onions
- ¼ cup shredded fresh basil

1. In a 4-quart Dutch oven cook pasta according to package directions; drain. Return to Dutch oven.

2. Meanwhile, in a large bowl toss together tomatoes and salt; set aside. In a small saucepan bring half-and-half just to boiling. Reduce heat; stir in Gorgonzola cheese, Parmesan cheese, white pepper, and cayenne pepper until cheese is melted. Stir in parsley, the 2 tablespoons snipped basil, and the thyme.

3. Add the tomato mixture and cheese mixture to the pasta; toss gently to coat. Transfer the pasta mixture to a platter. Sprinkle with olives, green onion, and shredded basil. Makes 8 side-dish servings.

Each serving: 182 cal., 13 g total fat (7 g sat. fat), 32 mg chol., 724 mg sodium, 9 g carbo., 2 g fiber, 9 g pro. Daily Values: 22% vit. A, 36% vit. C, 25% calcium, 5% iron.

Rosemary Potatoes and Tomatoes

PREP: 10 minutes **BAKE:** 25 minutes

- 1 lb. tiny new potatoes, scrubbed and quartered (10 to 12)
- 2 Tbsp. olive oil
- 1 tsp. snipped fresh rosemary
- ¼ tsp. salt
- ¼ tsp. ground black pepper
- 4 plum tomatoes, quartered lengthwise (2 cups)
- ½ cup pitted kalamata olives, halved
- 3 cloves garlic, minced
- ¼ cup grated Parmesan cheese

1. Preheat oven to 450° F. Lightly grease a 15×10×1-inch baking pan; place potatoes in pan. In a small bowl combine oil, rosemary, salt, and pepper; drizzle over potatoes, tossing to coat.

2. Bake for 20 minutes, stirring once. Add tomatoes, olives, and garlic, tossing to combine. Bake for 5 to 10 minutes more or until potatoes are tender and brown on the edges and tomatoes are soft. Transfer to a serving dish. Sprinkle with Parmesan cheese. Makes 6 to 8 side-dish servings.

Each serving: 144 cal., 7 g total fat (1 g sat. fat), 3 mg chol., 295 mg sodium, 17 g carbo., 2 g fiber, 4 g pro. Daily Values: 8% vit. A, 39% vit. C, 6% calcium, 8% iron.

Tomatoes with Smoked Salmon

START TO FINISH: 15 minutes

- 2 small yellow or red tomatoes (6 to 8 oz. total)
- 3 oz. thinly sliced, smoked salmon (lox-style), cut into strips
- 1 recipe Horseradish Dill Cream (right)
- 4 small fresh dill sprigs

1. Core tomatoes; cut a thin slice from top and bottom ends so tomato slices will be even thickness. Cut tomatoes in half crosswise to make 4 thick slices. Arrange tomato slices on a platter; set aside.

2. Arrange smoked salmon on tomatoes. Prepare Horseradish Dill Cream; spoon onto salmon. Top with dill sprigs. Makes 4 appetizer servings.

HORSERADISH DILL CREAM: In a small bowl stir together ¼ cup dairy sour cream, 1½ teaspoons snipped fresh dill or ¼ teaspoon dried dill weed, 1 teaspoon finely chopped shallot, ½ teaspoon prepared horseradish, ½ teaspoon white wine Worcestershire sauce, dash salt, and dash ground white pepper.

Each serving: 61 cal., 4 g total fat (2 g sat. fat), 10 mg chol., 479 mg sodium, 3 g carbo., 0 g fiber, 5 g pro. Daily Values: 8% vit. A, 13% vit. C, 2% calcium, 2% iron.

Sweet Summer Tomato Relish

PREP: 15 minutes **CHILL:** 4 hours

- 3 medium plum tomatoes, chopped
- 1 small zucchini, chopped
- 1 stalk celery, chopped
- 4 tsp. lemon juice
- 1 Tbsp. sugar
- 1 Tbsp. finely chopped red onion
- 1 Tbsp. strawberry balsamic vinegar or balsamic vinegar
- 1½ tsp. olive oil
- ½ tsp. salt
- ½ tsp. dry mustard
- ½ tsp. poppy seeds

1. In a medium bowl combine the tomatoes, zucchini, and celery; set aside.

2. In a screw-top jar combine lemon juice, sugar, onion, vinegar, olive oil, salt, mustard, and poppy seeds. Cover; shake well. Pour over vegetable mixture. Cover; chill for 4 to 24 hours.

3. Serve with a slotted spoon as a relish for bratwurst, burgers, or ham. Makes 2½ cups relish.

low fat Each ¼-cup serving: 23 cal., 1 g total fat (0 g sat. fat), 0 mg chol., 125 mg sodium, 4 g carbo., 1 g fiber, 0 g pro. Daily Values: 4% vit. A, 12% vit. C, 1% calcium, 1% iron.

ZUCCHINI FROM APPETIZERS TO DESSERTS

CHRISTINE FORTNEY, CARMICHAELS, PA.

LILLIAN KAYTE, GAINESVILLE, FLA.

Zucchini Alfredo
PREP: 30 minutes **STAND:** 1 hour

5 large zucchini (about 2½ lb. total)	¾ cup half-and-half or light cream
1 tsp. salt	½ cup finely shredded Parmesan cheese (2 oz.)
2 to 3 cloves garlic, minced	Ground black pepper
2 Tbsp. olive oil	Ground nutmeg
1 8-oz. pkg. cream cheese, cubed and softened	Finely shredded Parmesan cheese

1. Cut zucchini in half crosswise. Cut lengthwise into ¼-inch-thick slices; cut slices lengthwise into long, thin strips about ¼ inch wide (resembling strips of fettuccine). You should have about 8 cups. In a large colander toss the zucchini with the salt. Let stand to drain for 1 hour. Rinse and drain. Pat dry.

2. In a 12-inch skillet cook zucchini and garlic in hot oil over medium-high heat for 2 to 4 minutes or until crisp-tender. Transfer mixture to a large bowl.

3. In the same skillet heat and stir the cream cheese and half-and-half over medium-low heat until smooth. Stir in the ½ cup Parmesan cheese. Stir in zucchini; heat through. Transfer to a serving dish. Sprinkle with pepper, nutmeg, and additional Parmesan cheese. Makes 8 side-dish servings.

Each serving: 351 cal., 27 g total fat (16 g sat. fat), 69 mg chol., 876 mg sodium, 7 g carbo., 2 g fiber, 20 g pro. Daily Values: 25% vit. A, 21% vit. C, 59% calcium, 7% iron.

Zucchini-Olive Couscous
START TO FINISH: 30 minutes

2 cloves garlic, minced	2 tsp. finely shredded lemon peel
1 Tbsp. olive oil	¼ tsp. ground black pepper
3 cups chicken broth	4 green onions, sliced
1 cup pimiento-stuffed green olives, pitted green olives, and/or pitted ripe olives, cut up	2 Tbsp. snipped fresh parsley
3 medium zucchini, halved lengthwise and thinly sliced (about 3¾ cups)	Thin strips lemon peel (optional)
1 10-oz. pkg. quick-cooking couscous	Lemon wedges

1. In a large saucepan cook garlic in hot oil for 1 minute, stirring frequently. Add broth and olives; bring to boiling. Stir in zucchini, couscous, shredded lemon peel, and pepper. Cover; remove from heat. Let stand for 5 minutes.

2. To serve, gently stir in green onion and parsley. If desired, top with thin strips of lemon peel. Serve with lemon wedges. Makes 8 side-dish servings.

low fat Each serving: 190 cal., 5 g total fat (1 g sat. fat), 0 mg chol., 762 mg sodium, 31 g carbo., 3 g fiber, 6 g pro. Daily Values: 7% vit. A, 18% vit. C, 4% calcium, 6% iron.

Shrimp and Zucchini with Basil-Chive Cream Sauce

PREP: 40 minutes **GRILL:** 8 minutes

- 1 recipe Basil-Chive Cream Sauce (below)
- 1¼ lb. large shrimp in shells
- 2 medium zucchini, halved lengthwise and cut into 1-inch-thick slices (about 1 lb. total)
- 2 Tbsp. olive oil
- ½ tsp. finely shredded orange peel or lime peel
- 1 Tbsp. orange juice or lime juice
- ¼ tsp. salt
- ¼ tsp. cayenne pepper
- 5 cups shredded fresh spinach, arugula, and/or romaine

1. Prepare Basil-Chive Cream Sauce. Cover and store in the refrigerator until ready to serve.

2. Peel and devein shrimp, leaving tails intact. Rinse shrimp; pat dry. Thread shrimp and zucchini alternately onto 6 long metal skewers, leaving ½-inch space between pieces. In a small bowl combine olive oil, orange or lime peel, orange or lime juice, salt, and cayenne pepper; brush evenly onto shrimp and zucchini.

3. For a charcoal grill, grill kabobs on the greased rack of an uncovered grill directly over medium coals for 8 to 10 minutes or until shrimp turn opaque, turning once. (For a gas grill, preheat grill. Reduce heat to medium. Cover and grill as above.)

4. Arrange shredded greens on a platter. Top with shrimp and zucchini; serve with sauce. Makes 4 to 6 servings.

BASIL-CHIVE CREAM SAUCE: In a food processor or blender combine one 8-ounce carton dairy sour cream, ½ cup snipped fresh basil, 3 tablespoons snipped fresh chives, ½ teaspoon salt, and ⅛ teaspoon ground black pepper. Cover and process or blend until nearly smooth.

Each serving: 283 cal., 20 g total fat (9 g sat. fat), 174 mg chol., 670 mg sodium, 7 g carbo., 3 g fiber, 20 g pro. Daily Values: 76% vit. A, 41% vit. C, 16% calcium, 23% iron.

Zucchini Spoon Bread

PREP: 20 minutes **BAKE:** 35 minutes

- 3 cups shredded zucchini
- 1 8½-oz. pkg. corn muffin mix
- 1⅓ cups shredded Italian-style or Mexican-style cheese blend
- 4 eggs
- ½ cup cooking oil
- ½ cup finely chopped onion
- ¼ cup buttermilk or sour milk*
- ½ tsp. dried Italian seasoning
  - Dash bottled hot pepper sauce
- ⅔ cup chopped almonds

1. Preheat oven to 350° F. In a large bowl combine zucchini, dry muffin mix, 1 cup of the cheese, the eggs, oil, onion, buttermilk, Italian seasoning, and hot pepper sauce. Spoon into a greased 2- to 2½-quart baking dish. Sprinkle with almonds and remaining ⅓ cup cheese.

2. Bake, uncovered, about 35 minutes or until a wooden toothpick inserted in the center comes out clean.

3. To serve, spoon warm spoon bread onto plates. Makes 12 side-dish servings.

*NOTE: To make ¼ cup sour milk, place 1 teaspoon lemon juice or vinegar in a glass measuring cup. Add enough milk to make ¼ cup total liquid; stir. Let mixture stand for 5 minutes before using.

Each serving: 277 cal., 20 g total fat (4 g sat. fat), 80 mg chol., 250 mg sodium, 17 g carbo., 1 g fiber, 9 g pro. Daily Values: 4% vit. A, 4% vit. C, 11% calcium, 6% iron.

Triple-Nut Zucchini Cake

PREP: 35 minutes **BAKE:** 35 minutes
COOL: 1 hour **BROIL:** 1½ minutes

- ¾ cup chopped walnuts
- ¾ cup chopped pecans
- ¾ cup slivered almonds, chopped
- ¾ cup rolled oats
- 2 cups all-purpose flour
- 2 cups granulated sugar
- 1 tsp. baking powder
- 1 tsp. salt
- ¼ tsp. baking soda
- 3 cups shredded zucchini
- 1 cup cooking oil
- 3 eggs, slightly beaten
- 1 tsp. vanilla
- ⅓ cup butter
- 3 Tbsp. half-and-half, light cream, or milk
- ⅔ cup packed brown sugar

1. Preheat oven to 350° F. Grease a 13×9×2-inch baking pan; set aside. In a 15×10×1-inch baking pan combine ½ cup of the walnuts, ½ cup of the pecans, ½ cup of the almonds, and all of the rolled oats. Bake about 12 minutes or until toasted, stirring several times. Set aside on a wire rack.

2. In a large bowl stir together the flour, granulated sugar, baking powder, salt, and baking soda. Stir in zucchini, oil, eggs, and vanilla until combined. Stir in toasted nut mixture. Spread in prepared baking pan.

3. Bake for 35 to 40 minutes or until a wooden toothpick inserted near the center comes out clean. Cool in pan on a wire rack for 1 hour.

4. In a small saucepan combine butter and half-and-half. Cook and stir until butter is melted. Add brown sugar; stir until sugar is dissolved. Remove from heat. Stir in remaining nuts.

5. Spread nut mixture onto cake in pan. Broil 4 inches from the heat for 1½ to 2 minutes or until topping is bubbly and golden. Cool in pan on wire rack before serving. Makes 20 servings.

Each serving: 388 cal., 24 g total fat (5 g sat. fat), 41 mg chol., 199 mg sodium, 41 g carbo., 2 g fiber, 5 g pro. Daily Values: 5% vit. A, 4% vit. C, 6% calcium, 9% iron.

FRESH FRUIT DESSERTS

Lemon-Blackberry Mini Tarts

PREP: 20 minutes **BAKE:** 10 minutes
COOL: 30 minutes **CHILL:** 2 hours

½ of a 15-oz. pkg. folded refrigerated unbaked piecrust (1 crust)	1 cup fresh blackberries
	2 Tbsp. seedless blackberry spreadable fruit
½ of an 8-oz. pkg. cream cheese, softened	2 tsp. lemon juice
¼ cup lemon curd	Fresh mint sprigs (optional)
	Powdered sugar

1. Let piecrust stand at room temperature for 15 minutes. Preheat oven to 400° F. Unfold piecrust. Cut four 4½- to 5-inch rounds from piecrust. Press rounds firmly onto bottom and up sides of four 3½- to 4-inch individual tart pans with removable bottoms. Trim crusts even with tops of tart pans. Prick bottom of each crust several times with tines of a fork. Place tart pans on a baking sheet. Bake for 10 to 12 minutes or until golden brown. Cool in pan on a wire rack.

2. For filling, in a small mixing bowl beat cream cheese and lemon curd with an electric mixer on medium speed until smooth. Divide filling among pastry shells, spreading evenly. Cover and chill for 2 to 24 hours.

3. Before serving, remove tarts from pans; place on 4 plates. Arrange berries in each tart. Combine spreadable fruit and lemon juice; spoon over tarts. If desired, garnish with mint sprigs. Sift powdered sugar over tops. Makes 4 servings.

Each serving: 448 cal., 25 g total fat (13 g sat. fat), 56 mg chol., 299 mg sodium, 54 g carbo., 4 g fiber, 3 g pro. Daily Values: 9% vit. A, 15% vit. C, 3% calcium, 3% iron.

Minty Summer Shortcake

PREP: 25 minutes **BAKE:** 12 minutes **STAND:** 30 minutes

1²/₃ cups all-purpose flour	3 Tbsp. finely chopped crystallized ginger
¼ cup sugar	
1½ tsp. baking powder	1 recipe Minty Fruit Topper (below)
¼ tsp. baking soda	
¼ tsp. salt	1 7-oz. container purchased crème fraîche
½ cup butter	
²/₃ cup buttermilk	1 Tbsp. sugar

1. Preheat oven to 425° F. Stir together flour, the ¼ cup sugar, the baking powder, soda, and salt. Cut in butter until coarse crumbs. Make a well in center of flour mixture. Add buttermilk all at once. Using a fork, stir in ginger. Stir just until moistened. Turn out onto lightly floured surface. Knead gently 4 to 6 strokes or just until dough holds together. Lightly roll to a 7½×6-inch rectangle (about ¾ inch thick). Cut into six 3×2½-inch rectangles. Place 1 inch apart on ungreased baking sheet. Bake about 12 minutes or until golden. Cool on wire rack; split biscuits.

2. Prepare Minty Fruit Topper. Place biscuit bottom halves on 6 dessert plates. Combine crème fraîche and the 1 tablespoon sugar; spoon onto biscuit bottoms. Spoon on Minty Fruit Topper; add biscuit tops. Makes 6 servings.

MINTY FRUIT TOPPER: Combine 3 cups chopped, seeded, and peeled mangoes or peaches; 1½ cups sliced fresh strawberries; ¼ cup lightly packed fresh mint, finely chopped; 2 tablespoons honey; and 2 teaspoons lemon juice. Let stand for 30 minutes.

Each serving: 553 cal., 32 g total fat (20 g sat. fat), 98 mg chol., 460 mg sodium, 64 g carbo., 3 g fiber, 5 g pro. Daily Values: 98% vit. A, 74% vit. C, 12% calcium, 11% iron.

Tropical Fruit Strudel

PREP: 40 minutes **BAKE:** 25 minutes
COOL: 1¼ hours

2   medium fresh pears, peeled and chopped
⅔   cup apricot or mango nectar
⅓   cup tropical blend mixed dried fruit bits
1   3-oz. pkg. cream cheese, softened
2   Tbsp. packed brown sugar
½   tsp. vanilla
⅓   cup chopped macadamia nuts, toasted
1   to 2 Tbsp. finely chopped crystallized ginger
1   tsp. finely shredded lemon peel
12   sheets frozen phyllo dough (14×9-inch rectangles), thawed
⅓   cup butter, melted
2   tsp. granulated sugar

1. Preheat oven to 375° F. In a medium saucepan combine pears, nectar, and dried fruit bits. Bring to boiling; reduce heat. Cover; simmer for 5 minutes. Drain well. Cool completely.

2. For filling, in a medium bowl stir together cream cheese, brown sugar, and vanilla. Stir in cooled pear mixture, nuts, ginger, and lemon peel; set aside.

3. Line a baking sheet with parchment paper or foil; set aside. On a work surface, place 1 sheet of phyllo. (Keep remaining covered with plastic wrap to keep it from drying.) Brush phyllo sheet with some of the melted butter. Repeat layering, using 5 more sheets and most of the remaining butter. Spoon half of the filling about 2 inches from a long side of phyllo. Fold in short sides; roll into a spiral. Repeat with remaining phyllo and filling. Place, seam side down, on prepared baking sheet. Brush with remaining butter; sprinkle with granulated sugar.

4. Bake for 25 to 30 minutes or until golden. Cool on baking sheet on a wire rack for 45 minutes. Serve warm. Serves 8.

Each serving: 273 cal., 17 g total fat (8 g sat. fat), 33 mg chol., 219 mg sodium, 28 g carbo., 2 g fiber, 3 g pro. Daily Values: 16% vit. A, 4% vit. C, 3% calcium, 6% iron.

Macaroon Fruit Tart

PREP: 30 minutes **BAKE:** 15 minutes
CHILL: 2 hours

Nonstick cooking spray
1   13-oz. pkg. soft macaroon cookies (16)
1   cup ground pecans
⅓   cup miniature semisweet chocolate pieces (2 oz.)
¾   cup whipping cream
12   oz. cream cheese (four 3-oz. pkg. or 1½ 8-oz. pkg.), softened
½   cup sugar
1   Tbsp. orange juice
1½   tsp. vanilla
2   cups strawberries, halved
2   medium kiwifruit, peeled, halved lengthwise, and sliced
⅓   cup apricot preserves or jam

1. Chill a medium mixing bowl and beaters of an electric mixer. Preheat oven to 350° F.

2. For crust, lightly coat the bottom and sides of a 12-inch tart pan with removable bottom with nonstick cooking spray. Set aside. In a medium bowl crumble cookies. Add pecans; mix well. Press onto bottom of prepared tart pan. Bake for 15 to 20 minutes or until golden. Immediately sprinkle with chocolate pieces; cool.

3. In chilled bowl beat whipping cream with the chilled beaters on medium speed until soft peaks form (tips curl); set aside. In large mixing bowl beat cream cheese and sugar until smooth; beat in orange juice and vanilla. Fold in whipped cream. Spread in prepared crust. Cover surface with plastic wrap; chill for 2 to 24 hours.

4. Arrange fruit on tart. Melt preserves or jam; gently brush onto fruit. Serve immediately or chill for up to 2 hours. Makes 12 servings.

Each serving: 442 cal., 28 g total fat (15 g sat. fat), 52 mg chol., 170 mg sodium, 47 g carbo., 3 g fiber, 5 g pro. Daily Values: 14% vit. A, 46% vit. C, 5% calcium, 6% iron.

Blackberry-Coconut Dessert

PREP: 30 minutes **FREEZE:** 4 hours
STAND: 10 minutes

1   recipe Nut Crust (below)
3   cups fresh or frozen blackberries, thawed and drained
⅓   cup sugar
1½   tsp. cornstarch
¼   cup orange juice
¾   cup flaked coconut
¾   cup chopped walnuts
1   qt. vanilla bean ice cream

1. Prepare and bake Nut Crust. Meanwhile, in a blender place half of the blackberries; cover and blend until smooth. In a small saucepan combine sugar and cornstarch; add berry puree and orange juice. Cook and stir until thickened and bubbly; cook and stir for 2 minutes more. Cool slightly. Stir in remaining whole blackberries. Cover and cool.

2. In a shallow baking pan combine coconut and walnuts. Bake in the 350° F oven about 8 minutes or until toasted, stirring once. Cool.

3. In a large chilled bowl stir ice cream to soften; swirl in ¾ cup of the blackberry mixture and 1 cup of the coconut mixture. Spoon over baked crust. Sprinkle with remaining coconut mixture. Cover and freeze at least 4 hours or until firm. Cover and chill remaining berry mixture.

4. Before serving, let stand at room temperature for 10 minutes. Spoon some of the remaining blackberry mixture onto each serving. Makes 12 servings.

NUT CRUST: Preheat oven to 350° F. In large bowl combine ½ cup all-purpose flour, ⅓ cup chopped walnuts, and ¼ cup sugar. Add ⅓ cup softened butter; beat with an electric mixer on low to medium speed until mixture resembles fine crumbs. Press onto the bottom of a 2-quart rectangular baking dish. Bake about 20 minutes or until golden.

Each serving: 348 cal., 23 g total fat (11 g sat. fat), 45 mg chol., 105 mg sodium, 34 g carbo., 3 g fiber, 5 g pro. Daily Values: 12% vit. A, 18% vit. C, 8% calcium, 4% iron.

LEMON DESSERTS

Citrus Shortbread Torte

PREP: 30 minutes **BAKE:** 20 minutes **CHILL:** 2 hours

1 recipe Nut Shortbread (below)	1½ tsp. finely shredded lime peel
1½ cups whipping cream	3 Tbsp. lemon juice
1 14-oz. can sweetened condensed milk	2 Tbsp. lime juice
1½ tsp. finely shredded lemon peel	2 drops yellow food coloring
	1 10-oz. jar (about ¾ cup) lemon curd

1. Prepare and bake Nut Shortbread. Whip cream to stiff peaks. Stir together milk, 1 teaspoon of each peel, lemon and lime juices, and food coloring. Fold in 2 cups of the whipped cream.

2. To assemble, on a platter layer shortbread rounds with lemon curd and cream mixture. Spread remaining cream mixture on top. Sprinkle with remaining peels. Cover and refrigerate for 2 to 6 hours before serving. Makes 12 servings.

NUT SHORTBREAD: Preheat oven to 325° F. In large bowl beat ¾ cup softened butter and ¾ cup sifted powdered sugar until combined. Gradually beat in 1¼ cups all-purpose flour and 2 tablespoons cornmeal. Stir in ½ cup macadamia nuts, toasted and finely chopped. Divide dough in half. On 2 large ungreased baking sheets, press each half of dough into an 8-inch circle. Prick each circle several times with tines of a fork. Bake about 20 minutes or until edges are light brown. Cool on baking sheets for 10 minutes. Transfer to wire racks; cool completely.

Each serving: 513 cal., 32 g total fat (18 g sat. fat), 103 mg chol., 210 mg sodium, 55 g carbo., 3 g fiber, 5 g pro. Daily Values: 20% vit. A, 7% vit. C, 12% calcium, 5% iron.

Good Thyme Lemon Cups

PREP: 25 minutes **BAKE:** 35 minutes

½ cup sugar	2 egg yolks
2 Tbsp. all-purpose flour	3 Tbsp. lemon juice
2 tsp. snipped fresh thyme or ½ tsp. dried thyme, crushed	1 Tbsp. butter, melted
	¾ cup milk
1 tsp. finely shredded lemon peel	2 egg whites
	Whipped cream
⅛ tsp. salt	Fresh thyme sprigs (optional)

1. Preheat oven to 325° F. For batter, in a medium bowl combine sugar, flour, thyme, lemon peel, and salt. In a small bowl beat egg yolks; stir in lemon juice and butter. Stir in milk until combined. Stir milk mixture into flour mixture; set aside.

2. In another medium bowl beat egg whites with an electric mixer on medium to high speed until stiff peaks form (tips stand straight). Fold egg whites into batter (batter will be thin).

3. Place four 6-ounce custard cups in a 9×9×2-inch baking pan. Divide batter evenly among custard cups. Place pan on oven rack. Pour hot water into pan around cups to depth of 1 inch. Bake 35 to 40 minutes or until tops are light brown and puffed (tops may be cracked).

4. Carefully transfer cups to a wire rack. Serve warm, or cover and chill for up to 24 hours. Top with whipped cream. If desired, garnish with fresh thyme sprigs. Makes 4 servings.

Each serving: 250 cal., 12 g total fat (7 g sat. fat), 139 mg chol., 164 mg sodium, 31 g carbo., 0 g fiber, 5 g pro. Daily Values: 12% vit. A, 12% vit. C, 8% calcium, 3% iron.

Lemon-Lime Mascarpone Trifle

PREP: 25 minutes **CHILL:** 1 + 4 hours

- 1 recipe Citrus Curd (below)
- 2 8-oz. cartons mascarpone cheese
- 3/4 cup sugar
- 1/2 cup milk
- 1 10 3/4-oz. frozen pound cake, thawed and cubed
- 1/2 cup orange juice or 1/4 cup orange liqueur plus 1/4 cup orange juice
- 1/3 cup sliced almonds, toasted, or purchased glazed nuts

1. Prepare Citrus Curd. In a medium bowl beat mascarpone cheese, sugar, and milk with a wooden spoon until smooth.

2. In a 2-quart clear straight-sided bowl layer half of the cake cubes. Sprinkle with half of the orange juice (or a mixture of the juice and liqueur). Add half of the Citrus Curd and half of the mascarpone mixture. Repeat layers. Cover and chill for 4 to 24 hours.

3. Before serving, sprinkle with nuts. Makes 12 servings.

CITRUS CURD: In a medium saucepan stir together 1 cup sugar and 2 tablespoons cornstarch. Stir in 2/3 cup water, 2 teaspoons finely shredded lemon peel, 1/4 cup lemon juice, 1 teaspoon finely shredded lime peel, and 2 tablespoons lime juice. Cook and stir over medium heat until thickened and bubbly. Stir half of the lemon mixture into 4 egg yolks. Return the egg yolk mixture to the saucepan. Cook and stir over medium heat until mixture comes to a gentle boil. Cook and stir for 2 minutes more. Remove from heat. Add 1/2 cup butter, cut up, stirring until melted. Cover surface with plastic wrap. Chill for 1 to 2 hours.

Each serving: 511 cal., 34 g total fat (19 g sat. fat), 170 mg chol., 206 mg sodium, 47 g carbo., 1 g fiber, 11 g pro. Daily Values: 12% vit. A, 15% vit. C, 4% calcium, 4% iron.

Lemon Cream Coffee Cake

PREP: 25 minutes **BAKE:** 45 minutes

- 1 recipe Lemon Cream (below)
- 3 cups all-purpose flour
- 1 cup sugar
- 1 Tbsp. baking powder
- 1/4 tsp. salt
- 1/4 tsp. ground nutmeg or mace
- 1 cup butter
- 2 eggs
- 1 cup milk
- 1/2 tsp. almond extract
- 1/2 cup sugar
- 1/2 cup all-purpose flour
- 1/4 cup butter
- 1/2 cup chopped pecans or sliced almonds

1. Prepare Lemon Cream; set aside. Preheat oven to 350° F. Grease a 13×9×2-inch baking pan; set aside.

2. In a large mixing bowl stir together the 3 cups flour, the 1 cup sugar, the baking powder, salt, and nutmeg. Using a pastry blender, cut in the 1 cup butter until mixture resembles fine crumbs. Beat eggs; stir in milk and almond extract. Add to flour mixture, stirring until mixed. Spread half of the batter in the prepared pan.

3. Spoon Lemon Cream onto batter. Spoon remaining batter into small mounds on cream, spreading as much as possible.

4. For topping, combine the 1/2 cup sugar and the 1/2 cup flour; cut in the 1/4 cup butter until mixture resembles coarse crumbs. Stir in nuts. Sprinkle over batter.

5. Bake for 45 to 50 minutes or until cake is golden and toothpick inserted in dough mounds comes out clean. Cool on a wire rack at least 45 minutes before serving. Chill to store. Makes 12 servings.

LEMON CREAM: In a medium mixing bowl beat one 8-ounce package cream cheese, softened, with an electric mixer on medium speed until fluffy. Beat in 1/4 cup sugar. Fold in one 8-ounce carton lemon yogurt and 1 1/2 teaspoons finely shredded lemon peel.

Each serving: 559 cal., 32 g total fat (18 g sat. fat), 114 mg chol., 447 mg sodium, 61 g carbo., 1 g fiber, 8 g pro. Daily Values: 23% vit. A, 1% vit. C, 15% calcium, 12% iron.

Strawberry-Lemon Bars

PREP: 20 minutes **BAKE:** 35 minutes
CHILL: 1 hour

- 1 cup all-purpose flour
- 1/4 cup sifted powdered sugar
- 1/2 cup butter
- 2 eggs
- 3/4 cup granulated sugar
- 2 tsp. finely shredded lemon peel (set aside)
- 3 Tbsp. lemon juice
- 2 Tbsp. all-purpose flour
- 1/4 tsp. baking soda
- 1/3 cup strawberry jelly
- 1 tsp. lemon juice
- 5 whole fresh strawberries, hulled and quartered

1. Preheat oven to 350° F. In a medium bowl stir together the 1 cup flour and the powdered sugar. Using a pastry blender, cut in the butter until mixture resembles coarse crumbs (mixture will be dry). Press mixture onto the bottom of an ungreased 8×8×2-inch baking pan. Bake for 15 to 18 minutes or just until golden.

2. Meanwhile, for filling, in a large mixing bowl beat the eggs, the granulated sugar, the 3 tablespoons lemon juice, the 2 tablespoons flour, and the baking soda with an electric mixer on medium speed about 2 minutes or until combined. Stir in lemon peel. Pour filling over hot crust. Bake about 20 minutes more or until light brown around the edges and center is set. Cool on a wire rack.

3. In a small saucepan heat and stir jelly and the 1 teaspoon lemon juice just until jelly is melted; spoon over bars in pan and spread evenly. Arrange berry quarters on top of bars so that each cut bar will have a berry on top. Cover and chill for 1 to 2 hours. Cut into bars. Makes 20 bars.

Each bar: 125 cal., 5 g total fat (3 g sat. fat), 34 mg chol., 73 mg sodium, 18 g carbo., 0 g fiber, 1 g pro. Daily Values: 4% vit. A, 5% vit. C, 1% calcium, 2% iron.

EASTER DESSERTS

Orange Chiffon Cake

PREP: 30 minutes **BAKE:** 30 minutes **CHILL:** 1 hour

2 eggs	2 tsp. baking powder
3 medium oranges	1/2 cup milk
1 1/2 cups sugar	1/3 cup cooking oil
2 1/4 cups all-purpose flour	1 recipe Fluff Frosting (below)

1. Let eggs stand at room temperature for 30 minutes. Preheat oven to 350° F. Grease and flour two 9×1 1/2-inch round cake pans. Finely shred 1 tablespoon peel. Squeeze juice from 2 oranges to measure 1/2 cup. Section remaining orange; set aside.

2. Separate eggs; set yolks aside. Beat egg whites to soft peaks. Gradually add 1/2 cup of the sugar, beating to stiff peaks.

3. In another large mixing bowl combine remaining 1 cup sugar, the flour, baking powder, and 1 teaspoon salt. Add milk and oil. Beat on until combined. Add orange juice and egg yolks; beat for 1 minute. Gently fold in egg white mixture until combined. Fold in peel. Divide batter between pans. Bake for 30 to 35 minutes or until toothpick inserted near centers comes out clean.

4. Cool in pans on wire racks; remove from pans. Frost with Fluff Frosting. Top with orange sections. Chill. Makes 12 servings.

FLUFF FROSTING: Finely shred 2 tablespoons orange peel; set aside. In a small saucepan stir together 1/3 cup sugar and 4 teaspoons cornstarch. Stir in 1/2 cup orange juice. Cook and stir until thickened. Cook and stir for 2 minutes more. Remove from heat; stir in reserved peel. Cover and chill for 1 hour. Beat 2 cups whipping cream to stiff peaks; fold into chilled mixture.

Each serving: 417 cal., 22 g total fat (11 g sat. fat), 91 mg chol., 292 mg sodium, 51 g carbo., 1 g fiber, 5 g pro. Daily Values: 14% vit. A, 26% vit. C, 9% calcium, 7% iron.

Coconut-Lemon Puffs

PREP: 35 minutes **BAKE:** 25 minutes

5 eggs, separated	1/3 cup sugar
1/4 cup butter	1/3 cup shredded coconut
1/4 cup all-purpose flour	2 Tbsp. finely shredded lemon peel
1/8 tsp. salt	1/4 cup lemon juice
1 cup canned unsweetened coconut milk or whole milk	Shredded coconut, toasted

1. Let egg whites stand at room temperature for 30 minutes. Preheat oven to 350° F. Butter sides of six 6-ounce soufflé dishes or custard cups; set aside. In small saucepan melt the 1/4 cup butter over medium heat. Stir in flour and salt. Add coconut milk all at once. Cook and stir until very thick and bubbly around edges; set aside.

2. In a medium bowl beat egg yolks and sugar with an electric mixer on high speed about 3 minutes or until light and lemon-colored. Stir in the 1/3 cup coconut, the lemon peel, and lemon juice. Stir in flour mixture.

3. Wash beaters. In a large mixing bowl beat egg whites with electric mixer on medium speed until stiff peaks form (tips stand straight). Fold about 1 cup of the beaten egg white into lemon mixture. Fold lemon mixture into remaining beaten white. Transfer to prepared dishes (dishes will be full). Bake, uncovered, for 25 to 30 minutes or until a knife inserted near centers comes out clean. Serve immediately. If desired, sprinkle with toasted coconut. Makes 6 servings.

Each serving: 337 cal., 25 g total fat (18 g sat. fat), 199 mg chol., 221 mg sodium, 23 g carbo., 2 g fiber, 8 g pro. Daily Values: 11% vit. A, 14% vit. C, 3% calcium, 9% iron.

Easter Ricotta Pie

PREP: 45 minutes **BAKE:** 30 minutes
COOL: 1 hour **CHILL:** 2 hours

- 1 cup water
- 1/4 cup long grain rice
- 1 recipe Lemon Pastry (right)
- 1 15-oz. carton ricotta cheese
- 2/3 cup granulated sugar
- 1 1/2 tsp. finely shredded lemon peel
- 3/4 tsp. vanilla
  Dash ground cinnamon
- 4 eggs, slightly beaten
- 1/3 cup dried tart cherries
- 1/4 cup dried apricot halves, snipped
  Milk
  Coarse sugar

1. In a small saucepan bring the water and rice to boiling; reduce heat. Simmer, covered, about 25 minutes or until rice is very tender. Pour into a fine-mesh sieve; rinse with cold water. Drain well; let cool.

2. Preheat oven to 375° F. Prepare Lemon Pastry. On lightly floured surface, roll half of the pastry to 12-inch circle. Transfer to 9-inch pie plate. Trim pastry to 1/2 inch beyond edge of pie plate; set aside.

3. For filling, in a large bowl combine ricotta, the 2/3 cup sugar, the lemon peel, vanilla, and cinnamon. Add eggs; mix well. Fold rice and dried fruit into ricotta mixture. Pour filling into pastry-lined pie plate.

4. On a lightly floured surface, roll remaining pastry to 12-inch circle. Cut into 1/2-inch-wide strips. Dampen edge of the pie with water and place strips over the filling in lattice-fashion, laying a strip in one direction, then overlapping in the other direction; repeat until pie is covered. Press edges of strips into bottom pastry rim. Fold pastry under; seal and crimp edge. Brush pastry strips with milk. Sprinkle with coarse sugar. To prevent overbrowning, cover edge of pie with foil.

5. Bake for 30 to 35 minutes or until filling is set, removing foil for the last 15 minutes of baking. Cool on a wire rack for 1 hour. Cover and chill before serving. Makes 10 servings.

LEMON PASTRY: In a medium bowl stir together 2 1/4 cups all-purpose flour and 2 tablespoons sugar. Cut in 2/3 cup cold butter until pieces are pea-size. Stir in 1 1/2 teaspoons finely shredded lemon peel. Beat 1 egg yolk and 6 tablespoons ice water; stir into flour mixture with a fork. Using your fingers, gently knead dough just until a ball forms. Divide in half. Cover with plastic wrap; let rest for 15 minutes.

Each serving: 423 cal., 21 g total fat (12 g sat. fat), 163 mg chol., 197 mg sodium, 47 g carbo., 1 g fiber, 11 g pro. Daily Values: 22% vit. A, 1% vit. C, 11% calcium, 12% iron.

Italian Cheesecake

PREP: 25 minutes **BAKE:** 50 minutes
COOL: 2 hours **CHILL:** 4 hours

- 1 recipe Crumb Crust (right)
- 1 15-oz. carton ricotta cheese
- 1 8-oz. pkg. cream cheese, softened
- 3/4 cup sugar
- 1/2 cup dairy sour cream
- 2 Tbsp. all-purpose flour
- 4 eggs, slightly beaten
- 2 tsp. vanilla
- 1 1/2 tsp. finely shredded orange peel
- 1/3 cup golden raisins
- 1/2 cup semisweet chocolate pieces
- 1/2 cup pistachio nuts, chopped

1. Preheat oven to 350° F. Prepare Crumb Crust. Set aside.

2. In a large mixing bowl combine the ricotta and cream cheese. Beat with an electric mixer on medium speed until smooth. Add sugar, sour cream, and flour; beat on low speed until combined. Stir in eggs, vanilla, and orange peel. Stir in raisins. Spoon over crust in pan. Place the roasting pan on the oven rack. Add boiling water to roasting pan to a depth of 1 inch.

3. Bake for 50 to 55 minutes or until center appears nearly set when gently shaken. Remove roasting pan from oven. Remove springform pan; place on a wire rack. Remove foil. Cool for 15 minutes. Loosen from sides of pan; cool for 30 minutes more. Remove sides of pan; cool completely. Cover and chill at least 4 hours before serving.

4. An hour before serving, in a small saucepan heat chocolate pieces over low heat, stirring until smooth. Sprinkle pistachio nuts over cheesecake; drizzle with melted chocolate. Return to refrigerator. Makes 12 to 16 servings.

CRUMB CRUST: Lightly grease a 9-inch springform pan. Wrap outside of the pan with heavy foil. Place springform pan in a large roasting pan; set aside. In a medium bowl combine 3/4 cup crushed zwieback (9 slices), 1/4 cup sugar, and 2 tablespoons all-purpose flour. Stir in 1/4 cup butter, melted. Press onto bottom of prepared springform pan.

Each serving: 374 cal., 23 g total fat (13 g sat. fat), 125 mg chol., 165 mg sodium, 34 g carbo., 2 g fiber, 10 g pro. Daily Values: 16% vit. A, 2% vit. C, 12% calcium, 7% iron.

Hazelnut Poached Pears and Strawberries

PREP: 30 minutes **COOL:** 2 hours

- 1 cup dark-colored corn syrup
- 1/4 cup hazelnut liqueur (Frangelico)
- 1/2 tsp. ground cinnamon
- 1/2 tsp. ground nutmeg
- 4 small pears, peeled, cored, and sliced
- 3 cups small fresh strawberries, halved
- 1 qt. vanilla ice cream
- 1/2 cup hazelnuts (filberts) or almonds, toasted and finely chopped

1. In a medium saucepan combine corn syrup, hazelnut liqueur, cinnamon, and nutmeg. Bring mixture to boiling. Add pears; cook, covered, about 5 minutes or just until pears are tender. Use a slotted spoon to transfer pears to a large bowl. Boil mixture in saucepan, uncovered, for 5 to 7 minutes or until syruplike (about 1 cup); pour over pears. Cover and cool about 2 hours or until room temperature.

2. To serve, stir strawberries into pear mixture. Divide evenly among 8 serving bowls. Top with ice cream and hazelnuts. Makes 8 servings.

Each serving: 396 cal., 14 g total fat (5 g sat. fat), 25 mg chol., 98 mg sodium, 66 g carbo., 4 g fiber, 4 g pro. Daily Values: 9% vit. A, 56% vit. C, 10% calcium, 6% iron.

CHOCOLATE CHIPS BEYOND THE COOKIE

Terrific Toffee

PREP: 15 minutes **COOK:** 15 minutes **COOL:** 1 hour

1 cup unblanched whole almonds, toasted and coarsely chopped	1/3 cup white baking pieces
	2 Tbsp. instant malted milk powder
3/4 cup semisweet chocolate pieces	1 cup butter
3/4 cup milk chocolate pieces	1 cup sugar
	3 Tbsp. water

1. Line a 13×9×2-inch baking pan with foil, extending foil over edges of pan. In a bowl combine almonds, semisweet and milk chocolate pieces, and white baking pieces. Sprinkle half (about 1 1/2 cups) of the mixture onto prepared baking pan. Sprinkle malted milk powder over mixture.

2. In a heavy 2-quart saucepan combine butter, sugar, and water. Cook over medium heat until boiling, stirring to dissolve sugar. Clip a candy thermometer to side of pan. Cook, stirring often, until thermometer registers 290° F, soft-crack stage (about 15 minutes). Mixture should boil at a steady rate over the entire surface. (Adjust heat as necessary to maintain a steady boil.)

3. Remove from heat; remove thermometer. Quickly pour mixture over nuts and chocolate pieces in pan. Immediately sprinkle remaining nut-chocolate piece mixture over toffee. Cool for 1 hour; break into pieces. If necessary, chill about 15 minutes or until chocolate is firm. Makes about 2 pounds (36 servings).

Each serving: 137 cal., 10 g total fat (5 g sat. fat), 16 mg chol., 65 mg sodium, 12 g carbo., 1 g fiber, 2 g pro. Daily Values: 4% vit. A, 2% calcium, 2% iron.

Chocolate-Kissed Date Puffs

PREP: 30 minutes **BAKE:** 12 minutes

1 egg	1/2 cup coarsely chopped hazelnuts (filberts), toasted
1 Tbsp. water	
1 17 1/4-oz. pkg. frozen puff pastry (2 sheets), thawed	1/3 cup chopped pitted dates
1 13-oz. jar chocolate-hazelnut spread	1/3 cup large milk chocolate pieces

1. Preheat oven to 400° F. Lightly grease 2 baking sheets; set aside. In a small bowl beat egg and the water; set aside. On a lightly floured surface unfold each pastry sheet. Roll each into a 12-inch square. Cut each into nine 4-inch squares (18 total).

2. Spread the center of each square with about 1 tablespoon of the chocolate-hazelnut spread, leaving a 1-inch border around edges. Divide hazelnuts, dates, and chocolate pieces evenly among the prepared pastry squares, placing atop spread. Brush edges of squares with egg mixture. Fold each to form a triangle; crimp edges with a fork to seal. Prick tops with the fork. Transfer to prepared baking sheets. Brush with egg mixture.

3. Bake for 12 to 15 minutes or until golden brown. Cool slightly on wire racks. Serve warm. Makes 18 puffs.

Each puff: 282 cal., 18 g total fat (1 g sat. fat), 13 mg chol., 128 mg sodium, 27 g carbo., 1 g fiber, 4 g pro. Daily Values: 1% calcium, 2% iron.

Coffee and Chocolate Gingerbread

PREP: 20 minutes **BAKE:** 40 minutes

2¼ cups all-purpose flour
1 Tbsp. finely chopped crystallized ginger
2 tsp. ground cinnamon
1 tsp. baking soda
1 tsp. ground ginger
½ cup butter, softened
⅓ cup sugar
1 egg
¾ cup mild-flavored molasses
1 cup strong coffee, cooled
1 cup semisweet chocolate pieces
1 recipe Coffee Whipped Cream (below)
Finely chopped crystallized ginger (optional)

1. Preheat oven to 350° F. Grease an 8×8×2-inch baking pan; set aside. In a bowl stir together flour, 1 tablespoon crystallized ginger, the cinnamon, soda, ground ginger, and ¼ teaspoon salt; set aside.

2. In a large bowl beat butter with an electric mixer on medium speed for 30 seconds. Add sugar; beat until combined. Add egg and molasses; beat for 1 minute on medium speed. Alternately add flour mixture and coffee to beaten mixture, beating on low speed after each addition until combined. Stir in chocolate pieces. Pour batter into prepared pan.

3. Bake about 40 minutes or until a wooden toothpick inserted near center comes out clean. Cool slightly in pan on a wire rack. Serve warm with Coffee Whipped Cream. If desired, sprinkle with crystallized ginger. Makes 9 servings.

COFFEE WHIPPED CREAM: In a chilled medium mixing bowl combine 1 cup whipping cream, 1 tablespoon sugar, and ½ teaspoon instant coffee crystals. Beat with chilled beaters of an electric mixer on low to medium speed until soft peaks form (tips curl).

Each serving: 510 cal., 27 g total fat (17 g sat. fat), 89 mg chol., 345 mg sodium, 65 g carbo., 2 g fiber, 5 g pro. Daily Values: 17% vit. A, 1% vit. C, 10% calcium, 20% iron.

Nutty Berry-Chip Squares

PREP: 30 minutes **BAKE:** 50 minutes

1⅓ cups all-purpose flour
½ cup ground almonds
1¼ tsp. baking powder
⅛ tsp. salt
¼ cup butter, softened
1 cup sugar
1 tsp. vanilla
1 egg
⅔ cup half-and-half, light cream, or milk
1 cup white baking pieces
1 cup dried blueberries or dried cranberries
1 recipe Creamy Frosting (below)
¼ cup sliced almonds, toasted

1. Preheat oven to 350° F. Grease and lightly flour an 8×8×2-inch or 9×9×2-inch baking pan. In a bowl stir together flour, ground almonds, baking powder, and salt. Set aside.

2. In a large mixing bowl beat butter with an electric mixer on medium to high speed for 30 seconds. Add sugar and vanilla; beat until combined. Beat in egg. Alternately add flour mixture and half-and-half to beaten mixture, beating on low speed after each addition just until combined. Fold in white baking pieces and dried fruit. Spread batter in prepared pan.

3. Bake for 50 to 55 minutes for 8-inch pan, 40 to 45 minutes for 9-inch pan, or until wooden toothpick inserted in center comes out clean. Cool in pan on a wire rack.

4. Spread Creamy Frosting onto cooled cake. Sprinkle with sliced almonds. Chill to store. Makes 12 servings.

CREAMY FROSTING: In a medium mixing bowl combine one 3-ounce package softened cream cheese, ¼ cup softened butter, and 1 teaspoon vanilla; beat for 30 seconds. Gradually beat in 2¼ to 2½ cups sifted powdered sugar until mixture reaches spreading consistency.

Each serving: 490 cal., 22 g total fat (11 g sat. fat), 55 mg chol., 197 mg sodium, 69 g carbo., 2 g fiber, 6 g pro. Daily Values: 10% vit. A, 9% calcium, 6% iron.

Frozen Praline Chocolate Torte

PREP: 25 minutes **COOL:** 30 minutes
FREEZE: 4 hours **STAND:** 15 minutes

1⅓ cups crushed chocolate wafers (about 24)
3 Tbsp. butter, melted
1 12-oz. pkg. miniature semisweet chocolate pieces
2 cups whipping cream
1 8-oz. pkg. cream cheese or mascarpone cheese
¼ cup sugar
½ cup caramel ice cream topping
1½ tsp. vanilla
¾ cup coarsely chopped pecans, toasted

1. For crust, lightly butter an 8- or 9-inch springform pan. In a small bowl combine crushed wafers and melted butter. Sprinkle half of the crumb mixture onto bottom of prepared pan; set aside.

2. In a small saucepan combine 1½ cups of the chocolate pieces and ½ cup of the whipping cream. Cook and stir over low heat until chocolate is melted. Cool for 30 minutes.

3. Chill a medium bowl and beaters of an electric mixer. Beat remaining 1½ cups whipping cream until soft peaks form (tips curl); fold into chocolate mixture.

4. In a large bowl beat cream cheese, sugar, ¼ cup of the caramel ice cream topping, and the vanilla. Stir in remaining chocolate and ½ cup of the pecans.

5. Drop half of the chocolate mixture by spoonfuls into the prepared pan; spread carefully. Spoon the cheese mixture over top. Sprinkle with remaining crumbs. Top with remaining chocolate mixture.

6. Cover; freeze for 4 to 24 hours. Before serving, remove sides of pan. Let stand for 15 minutes. To serve, cut into wedges. Top with remaining ¼ cup caramel topping and ¼ cup pecans. Makes 12 servings.

Each serving: 514 cal., 38 g total fat (20 g sat. fat), 85 mg chol., 227 mg sodium, 44 g carbo., 3 g fiber, 6 g pro. Daily Values: 20% vit. A, 5% calcium, 8% iron.

FROZEN HOMEMADE TREATS

Frozen Berry-Melon Pops
PREP: 20 minutes **FREEZE:** several hours

2½ cups cubed, seeded watermelon, cantaloupe, or honeydew melon
½ cup fresh or frozen red raspberries, thawed
¼ cup sugar
5 tsp. lemon juice
1 Tbsp. light-colored corn syrup

1. In a blender combine melon, berries, sugar, lemon juice, and corn syrup. Cover and blend until smooth. Press fruit mixture through a fine-mesh sieve, holding sieve over a bowl to catch juices. Discard solids. Pour strained juices into 3-ounce paper or plastic drink cups or pop molds. Cover cups with foil; cut a slit in the foil over each cup and insert wooden sticks. Freeze several hours or overnight until pops are firm.

2. To serve, remove from cups or molds. Makes 8 pops.

low fat Each pop: 50 cal., 0 g total fat, 0 mg chol., 4 mg sodium, 12 g carbo., 1 g fiber, 0 g pro. Daily Values: 4% vit. A, 13% vit. C, 1% calcium, 1% iron.

Cucumber-Chile Granité
PREP: 20 minutes **FREEZE:** 3 + 2 hours

2 14-oz. cucumbers, peeled, seeded, and cut into 1-inch chunks (3 cups)
1 fresh jalapeño pepper, seeded and cut up*
⅔ cup sugar
⅓ cup lemon juice
¼ of a small cucumber, cut into matchstick-size pieces (optional)

1. In a food processor or blender combine cucumber chunks, jalapeño pepper, sugar, and lemon juice. Cover and process or blend until nearly smooth. Press mixture through a fine-mesh sieve, one-third at a time, holding sieve over a bowl to catch juices (you should have about 1⅔ cups strained juices). Discard solids. Transfer strained juices to a shallow 2-quart freezer container. Cover and freeze for 3 to 4 hours or until firm.

2. Break up frozen mixture. Transfer mixture to a chilled large mixing bowl. Beat with an electric mixer until slushy, but not melted. Return to freezer container; cover and freeze for 2 to 3 hours or until firm.

3. To serve, scoop into 8 small dessert dishes. If desired, top with cucumber pieces. Makes 8 servings.

***NOTE:** Because hot peppers contain volatile oils that can burn your skin and eyes, avoid direct contact with chile peppers as much as possible. When working with chile peppers, wear plastic or rubber gloves. If your bare hands do touch the chile peppers, wash your hands well with soap and water.

low fat Each serving: 70 cal., 0 g total fat, 0 mg chol., 1 mg sodium, 18 g carbo., 0 g fiber, 0 g pro. Daily Values: 2% vit. A, 12% vit. C, 1% calcium, 1% iron.

Frozen White Chocolate Cranberry Cheese Pie

PREP: 20 minutes **COOL:** 30 minutes
FREEZE: 15 minutes + 6 hours
STAND: 15 minutes

2   oz. white chocolate baking squares or white baking bars, coarsely chopped
1   3-oz. pkg. cream cheese, cut up
1   butter-flavored crumb pie shell
1   qt. vanilla ice cream
½   cup dried cranberries, chopped
¼   cup chopped pecans, toasted
    Dried cranberries (optional)
    Chopped pecans, toasted (optional)

1. In a small saucepan combine white chocolate and cream cheese; cook and stir over low heat until melted and smooth. Cool to room temperature. Spread white chocolate mixture onto bottom of the pie shell. Freeze about 15 minutes or until firm.

2. In a chilled medium bowl stir ice cream to soften; fold in the ½ cup chopped cranberries and the ¼ cup chopped pecans. Spoon ice cream mixture into pie shell. Cover and freeze about 6 hours or until firm.

3. Before serving, let stand at room temperature for 15 minutes. If desired, top with additional dried cranberries and pecans. To serve, slice into 8 wedges. Makes 8 servings.

Each serving: 419 cal., 28 g total fat (13 g sat. fat), 67 mg chol., 195 mg sodium, 38 g carbo., 1 g fiber, 5 g pro. Daily Values: 17% vit. A, 1% vit. C, 12% calcium, 4% iron.

Lemon-Avocado Sorbet

Serve this refreshing sorbet as a palate cleanser between courses.

PREP: 10 minutes **FREEZE:** 4 hours
STAND: 15 minutes

1   large avocado, halved, seeded, peeled, and coarsely chopped
1   cup half-and-half or light cream
⅔   cup sifted powdered sugar
½   tsp. finely shredded lemon peel
⅓   cup lemon juice

1. In a blender combine avocado, half-and-half, powdered sugar, lemon peel, and lemon juice. Cover and blend until smooth. Pour mixture into a shallow 2-quart freezer container. Cover and freeze at least 4 hours or until firm.

2. Before serving, let stand at room temperature for 15 minutes. To serve, scrape mixture with a small scoop into 8 small dishes. Makes 8 servings.

Each serving: 112 cal., 7 g total fat (3 g sat. fat), 11 mg chol., 15 mg sodium, 12 g carbo., 1 g fiber, 1 g pro. Daily Values: 5% vit. A, 11% vit. C, 3% calcium, 2% iron.

Pistachio-Coconut Sorbet

PREP: 20 minutes **FREEZE:** 5 + 8 hours

1   recipe Glazed Pistachios (right)
1   13½-oz. can unsweetened coconut milk
1   cup cream of coconut
1   cup half-and-half or light cream
1   tsp. finely shredded lemon peel

1. Prepare Glazed Pistachios; set aside. In a large bowl whisk together the coconut milk, cream of coconut, half-and-half, and lemon peel. Pour into a shallow 2-quart freezer container. Cover; freeze for 5 to 6 hours or until nearly firm, stirring once.

2. Break up frozen mixture. Transfer to a chilled large mixing bowl. Beat with an electric mixer on low to medium speed until smooth but not melted. Stir in glazed pistachio pieces. Return to freezer container. Cover and freeze about 8 hours or overnight until firm.

3. To serve, scoop into 8 small dessert dishes. Makes 8 servings.

GLAZED PISTACHIOS: Butter a 12-inch piece of foil; set aside. In a heavy medium skillet combine ½ cup pistachio nuts, coarsely chopped; ¼ cup sugar; and 1 tablespoon butter. Cook and stir over medium heat for 4 to 6 minutes or until sugar melts and turns a rich brown color. Spread on prepared foil. Cool. Break apart and coarsely crush.

Each serving: 307 cal., 28 g total fat (21 g sat. fat), 15 mg chol., 41 mg sodium, 13 g carbo., 2 g fiber, 4 g pro. Daily Values: 5% vit. A, 3% vit. C, 4% calcium, 8% iron.

Tropical Sorbet

PREP: 30 minutes **FREEZE:** 4 hours
STAND: 10 minutes

½   cup water
⅓   cup sugar
¼   cup light-colored corn syrup
½   of a small pineapple, peeled, cored, and chopped (1½ cups)
1   medium papaya, peeled, seeded, and chopped (1½ cups)
1   medium mango, seeded, peeled, and chopped (1 cup)
1   cup unsweetened pineapple juice
2   Tbsp. lemon juice

1. In a small saucepan combine the water, sugar, and corn syrup. Bring just to boiling, stirring to dissolve sugar; remove from heat. Cool to room temperature.

2. In a food processor or blender combine half of the fruits and half of the pineapple juice; cover and process or blend until smooth. Transfer to a shallow 3-quart freezer container. Repeat with remaining fruits and pineapple juice; add to container. Stir in the cooled syrup mixture and the lemon juice. Cover and freeze for 4 to 5 hours or just until firm.

3. For a fluffier texture, break up frozen mixture and transfer to a chilled large mixing bowl. Beat with an electric mixer until fluffy but not melted. Return to freezer container. Cover and freeze until firm.

4. Before serving, let stand at room temperature for 10 minutes. To serve, scoop fruit mixture into 8 small dessert dishes. Makes 8 servings.

low fat Each serving: 131 cal., 0 g total fat, 0 mg chol., 17 mg sodium, 34 g carbo., 2 g fiber, 1 g pro. Daily Values: 22% vit. A, 70% vit. C, 2% calcium, 2% iron.

CANDY & FUDGE

Spiced Brandy Truffles

PREP: 30 minutes **CHILL:** 2 hours **STAND:** 30 minutes

1	11½-oz. pkg. milk chocolate pieces
½	cup chopped walnuts, toasted
¼	cup dairy sour cream
2	tsp. brandy or ¼ tsp. brandy extract
½	tsp. ground nutmeg
¼	cup sifted powdered sugar
¼	tsp. ground cinnamon

1. In a small heavy saucepan melt chocolate pieces over low heat, stirring constantly. Remove from heat. Stir in walnuts, sour cream, brandy, and ¼ teaspoon of the ground nutmeg. Transfer mixture to a bowl. Cover and chill for at least 2 hours or until chocolate mixture is firm enough to shape into balls.

2. Line a baking sheet with waxed paper; set aside. In a small bowl stir together powdered sugar, cinnamon, and remaining ¼ teaspoon ground nutmeg; set aside.

3. Shape chilled truffle mixture into ³/₄-inch balls. Roll each ball in the powdered sugar mixture; place on the prepared baking sheet. Cover and chill until firm. Store truffles tightly covered in the refrigerator for up to 2 weeks. Before serving, let stand at room temperature about 30 minutes. Makes about 30 truffles.

Each truffle: 79 cal., 5 g total fat (2 g sat. fat), 3 mg chol., 9 mg sodium, 7 g carbo., 1 g fiber, 1 g pro. Daily Values: 2% iron.

Pretzel Yummies

PREP: 40 minutes **COOK:** 10 minutes

2	cups walnuts (8 oz.)
1	cup peanut butter-flavored pieces
1	cup milk chocolate pieces
1	cup packed brown sugar
½	cup light-colored corn syrup
¼	cup butter
½	of a 14-oz. can (²/₃ cup) sweetened condensed milk
½	tsp. vanilla
20	to 25 pretzels

1. In a food processor combine walnuts, peanut butter pieces, and chocolate pieces. Cover; process until coarsely chopped. Transfer nut mixture to a large bowl; set aside.

2. In a heavy small saucepan combine brown sugar, corn syrup, and butter. Cook over medium heat until boiling, stirring constantly. Stir in condensed milk. Return to boiling, stirring constantly. Reduce heat to medium-low. Clip a candy thermometer to side of pan. Cook, stirring constantly, until 236° F, soft-ball stage (about 10 minutes). (Adjust heat to maintain a steady boil.) Remove from heat; remove thermometer. Stir in vanilla. Cool for 15 to 20 minutes or until slightly thickened.

3. Dip each pretzel into caramel mixture, covering about ²/₃ of the pretzel. Let caramel drip off slightly. Spoon nut mixture onto caramel, pressing lightly with back of a spoon. Let stand on nonstick foil until set. Store in an airtight container between layers of waxed paper in refrigerator for up to 4 days or freeze for up to 1 month. Makes about 25 pretzels.

Each pretzel: 298 cal., 15 g total fat (7 g sat. fat), 10 mg chol., 192 mg sodium, 37 g carbo., 1 g fiber, 6 g pro. Daily Values: 2% vit. A, 1% vit. C, 1% calcium, 2% iron.

Coconut Cashew Pralines

PREP: 15 minutes **COOK:** 21 minutes
COOL: 30 minutes

1½ cups granulated sugar
1½ cups packed brown sugar
1   cup half-and-half or light cream
3   Tbsp. butter
2   cups lightly salted roasted cashews
1   cup flaked coconut, toasted*

1. Butter the sides of a heavy 2-quart saucepan. In the saucepan combine the granulated sugar, brown sugar, and half-and-half. Cook over medium-high heat until boiling, stirring to dissolve sugar. Clip a candy thermometer to side of pan. Reduce heat to medium-low; continue boiling at a moderate steady rate, stirring occasionally, until thermometer registers 234° F, soft-ball stage (16 to 18 minutes).

2. Remove saucepan from heat. Add butter, but do not stir. Cool, without stirring, to 150° F (about 30 minutes).

3. Remove thermometer from pan. Stir in cashews and coconut. Beat vigorously with a clean wooden spoon until mixture just begins to thicken but is still glossy (about 3 minutes).

4. Working quickly, drop candy by spoonfuls onto waxed paper. Let stand until firm. Store tightly covered for up to 1 week. Makes about 60 candies.

*NOTE: To toast coconut, spread the coconut in a single layer in a shallow baking pan. Bake in a 350° F oven for 5 to 8 minutes or until light golden brown, watching carefully and stirring once or twice so the coconut doesn't burn.

Each candy: 83 cal., 4 g total fat (2 g sat. fat), 3 mg chol., 23 mg sodium, 12 g carbo., 0 g fiber, 1 g pro. Daily Values: 1% vit. A, 1% calcium, 2% iron.

Peanut Granola Balls

PREP: 1 hour **FREEZE:** 40 minutes

2   cups low-fat granola (without raisins), coarsely crushed
1   cup creamy peanut butter
¼   cup honey
1   lb. vanilla-flavored candy wafers or candy coating, chopped
3   cups finely chopped lightly salted peanuts

1. In a medium bowl stir together granola, peanut butter, and honey. Drop from a teaspoon onto a waxed paper-lined cookie sheet. Freeze for 20 minutes.

2. Meanwhile, in a medium saucepan melt candy wafers or candy coating over very low heat, stirring constantly. Remove from heat.

3. Shape granola mixture into smooth balls. Dip balls in melted candy to coat; lift with a fork, allowing excess candy to drip off. Roll balls in peanuts; return to waxed paper-lined cookie sheet. Freeze for 20 minutes more or until set. Store tightly covered in the refrigerator for up to 1 week or in the freezer for up to 1 month. Makes about 60 pieces.

Each piece: 128 cal., 8 g total fat (3 g sat. fat), 0 mg chol., 28 mg sodium, 11 g carbo., 1 g fiber, 3 g pro. Daily Values: 1% vit. A, 1% calcium, 2% iron.

Coconut-Cranberry Bark

PREP: 15 minutes **CHILL:** 10 minutes

1   11- to 12-oz. pkg. white baking pieces
⅓   cup coconut
⅓   cup toasted slivered almonds
¼   cup raisins
¼   cup dried cranberries or coarsely chopped dried tart cherries

1. Line a baking sheet with foil. Melt baking pieces according to package directions. Quickly stir in coconut, almonds, raisins, and dried fruit. Spread on prepared baking sheet. If necessary, place in the refrigerator about 10 minutes or until set.

2. When ready to serve, break candy into irregular pieces. Store tightly covered at room temperature for up to 1 week. Makes about 1 pound (36 pieces).

Each piece: 67 cal., 4 g total fat (2 g sat. fat), 2 mg chol., 13 mg sodium, 7 g carbo., 0 g fiber, 1 g pro. Daily Values: 2% calcium.

Double-Chocolate Raspberry Creams

PREP: 40 minutes **CHILL:** 3 hours
STAND: 15 minutes

1   lb. vanilla-flavored candy coating, chopped
½   of a 14-oz. can (⅔ cup) sweetened condensed milk
¼   cup seedless raspberry preserves
4   drops raspberry oil or ¼ tsp. raspberry flavoring
14 oz. chocolate-flavored candy coating, chopped

1. In a medium saucepan combine vanilla-flavored candy coating, sweetened condensed milk, and preserves. Cook and stir over low heat until melted. Remove from heat; stir in raspberry oil or flavoring. Transfer to a bowl. Cover and chill for 2 to 3 hours or until just firm.

2. Line a 15×10×1-inch baking pan with waxed paper. With damp hands, shape candy mixture into ¾-inch balls; place on the prepared pan. Chill for 1 hour.

3. In a small saucepan melt chocolate-flavored candy coating over low heat until smooth. Dip raspberry balls into chocolate mixture to coat; allow excess chocolate to drip off. Arrange on the waxed paper-lined baking sheet; let stand until chocolate is set, about 15 minutes. Makes 4 dozen.

Each candy: 118 cal., 6 g total fat (5 g sat. fat), 1 mg chol., 6 mg sodium, 15 g carbo., 0 g fiber, 0 g pro. Daily Values: 2% calcium.

Menus

FOR PARTY AND MEAL IDEAS TO MARK YOUR MILESTONES
ANY TIME OF YEAR, TRY OUR MENUS OF WINNING RECIPES.

Winning Menus for Family and Friends

Menus often suit the mood of the season, as you've seen throughout this book, but other times a menu must rise to the occasion, no matter what time of year. On the following pages, you'll find timeless party and meal suggestions for special celebrations, for dietary concerns, and for the adventurous, all based on 2003 Prize Tested Recipes from *Better Homes and Gardens*® magazine. The planning's been done. All you need to do is shop, cook a little, and enjoy good meal times.

celebration menus

WE ALL HAVE REASONS TO CELEBRATE, NO MATTER WHAT THE SEASON. PERHAPS IT'S A PROMOTION, A NEW HOUSE, OR A BIG ANNIVERSARY. OR MAYBE JUST GETTING EVERYONE TOGETHER IS REASON ENOUGH.

TROPICAL BUFFET
Mahi Mahi Spring Rolls *(page 259)*
Calypso Shrimp Skewers *(page 258)*
Asian-Style Pork and Noodle Salad *(page 285)*
Tropical fruit platter (pineapple, mango, papaya, kiwifruit)
Tropical Fruit Strudel *(page 295)*
Pistachio Coconut Sorbet *(page 303)*
Mango-Ginger Coladas *(page 261)*

SOUTHERN-STYLE COOKOUT
Tennessee Pork Ribs *(page 267)*
Blue Cheese Vidalia Onions *(page 268)*
Jicama-Potato Salad *(page 271)*
Baked beans
Corn and Fig Spoon Bread *(page 287)*
Coconut Cashew Pralines *(page 305)*
Iced tea

TAILGATE TIME-OUT
Carrot Dip *(page 282)*
Assorted snack chips, crackers, vegetable dippers
Hot and Spicy Sloppy Joes *(page 282)*
Orzo and Bulgur Salad *(page 288)*
Triple-Nut Zucchini Cake *(page 293)*
Hot or cold cider or beer

AUTUMN CANDLELIGHT DINNER
Brie, Crab, and Mushroom Soup *(page 279)*
Roast Rack of Lamb *(page 264)*
Butternut Squash Gratin with Creamed Spinach *(page 286)*
Buffet Wild Rice *(page 286)*
Dinner rolls
Frozen White Chocolate Cranberry Cheese Pie *(page 303)*
Merlot or other red wine
Coffee

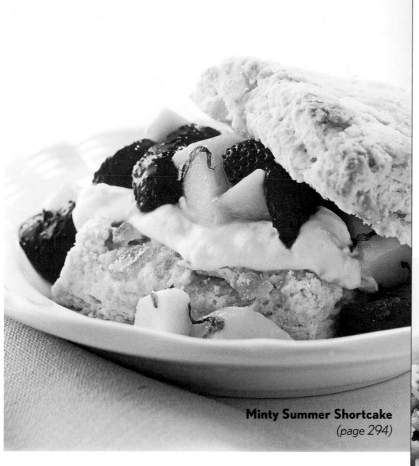

Minty Summer Shortcake
(page 294)

Orzo and Bulgur Salad
(page 288)

Roast Rack of Lamb
(page 264)

shower &wedding menus

ADDING PEOPLE WE LOVE TO OUR LIVES IS CAUSE FOR GREAT JOY AND
LOTS OF PARTIES, WHETHER IT'S A BRIDE OR A BABY WE'RE WELCOMING.
YOU PICK HOW AND WHEN, THEN CHOOSE THE MENU TO SUIT.

RECEPTION BUFFET
Smoked Salmon Roll-Ups *(page 258)*
Swiss Cheese and Olive Spread *(page 281)* with crackers
Grilled Pork Tenderloin with Blackberry Sauce *(page 267)*
Rosemary Potatoes and Tomatoes *(page 291)* with mixed greens
Spiced Brandy Truffles *(page 304)*
Double-Chocolate Raspberry Creams *(page 305)*
Champagne or other sparkling wine
Cranberry-Pineapple Cooler *(page 260)*

SHOWER FOR BUSY HOSTS
Antipasto tray (olives, sausages, cheeses, marinated peppers)
Focaccia or crackers
Baked Chicken and Artichoke Risotto *(page 275)*
Mixed green salad
Lemon-Lime Mascarpone Trifle *(page 297)*
Red or white wine
Cappuccino or espresso

AFTERNOON HIGH TEA
Cucumber Sandwiches *(page 284)*
Tomatoes with Smoked Salmon *(page 291)*
Assorted tea breads
Lemon-Blackberry Mini Tarts *(page 294)*
Citrus Shortbread Torte *(page 296)*
Hot tea or iced tea

WEEKEND BRUNCH
Portobello and Spinach Brunch Tart *(page 265)*
Sliced melons and berries
Paradise Bread *(page 287)*
Lemon Cream Coffee Cake *(page 297)*
White Strawberry Sangria *(page 260)*
Hot coffee or tea

Lemon-Blackberry Mini Tarts
(page 294)

White Strawberry Sangria *(page 260)*

Smoked Salmon Roll-Ups
(page 258)

birthday menus

IT'S SO EASY TO MAKE SPECIAL PEOPLE FEEL SPECIAL ON THEIR DAY, AS THE MENUS BELOW PROVE. YOUNG CHILDREN, TEENS, PARENTS, AND GRANDPARENTS WILL ALL BE AS PLEASED AS PUNCH.

BALLERINA BIRTHDAY
Pretzel Yummies *(page 304)*
Parmesan-Sesame Chicken Strips *(page 271)*
Carrot and celery sticks
Orange Chiffon Cake *(page 298)*
Raspberry Delight Punch *(page 261)*

BACKYARD BASH
Snack chips and dips
Mushroom Deluxe Hamburgers *(page 283)*
Onion Chili Sauce *(page 283)*
Sweet Summer Tomato Relish *(page 291)*
Corn on the cob
Frozen Praline Chocolate Torte *(page 301)*
Cranberry-Pineapple Cooler *(page 260)*

ON HER DAY
Tomato-Cucumber Soup *(page 290)*
Shrimp and Zucchini with Basil-Chive Cream Sauce *(page 293)*
Breadsticks
Blackberry Coconut Dessert *(page 295)*
Dry white wine
Hot tea or iced tea

ON HIS DAY
Wine-Balsamic Glazed Steak *(page 280)*
Roasted Potatoes with Goat Cheese Sauce *(page 287)*
Steamed green beans
Coffee and Chocolate Gingerbread *(page 301)*
Dry red wine
Coffee

Orange Chiffon Cake *(page 298)*

Tomato-Cucumber Soup *(page 290)*

Cranberry-Pineapple Cooler *(page 260)*

low-fat menus

EATING SMART CAN TASTE GREAT FOR THE WHOLE FAMILY, AS YOU CAN SEE FROM THE MENUS BELOW. THEY'RE SO CREATIVE, SATISFYING, AND FULL OF FLAVOR, YOU'LL NEVER MISS THE FAT!

TASTE OF THE NORTHWEST
Grilled Salmon with Citrus Sauce *(page 267)*
Asparagus and Barley Pilaf *(page 289)*
Dinner rolls
Hazelnut Poached Pears and Strawberries
over frozen low-fat yogurt *(page 299)*
Northwest wines

COMFORTING SOUP SUPPER
Hearty Sausage Gumbo *(page 283)*
Mom's Bread *(page 288)*
Frozen Berry-Melon Pops *(page 302)*
Fat-free milk

TEX-MEX FIESTA
Baked tortilla chips and salsa
Fiesta Quinoa Salad *(page 289)*
Tijuana Taco Beef Borracho *(page 273)*
Hot cooked rice
Cucumber-Chile Granité *(page 302)*
Frozen Strawberry-Mango Margaritas *(page 261)* and/or
Icy Cranberry Margaritas *(page 261)*

POT ROAST PLEASER
Pork with Parsnips and Pears *(page 272)*
Mashed potatoes
Dinner rolls
Tropical Sorbet *(page 303)*
Coffee or fat-free milk

Mom's Bread
(page 288)

Frozen Berry-Melon Pops
(page 302)

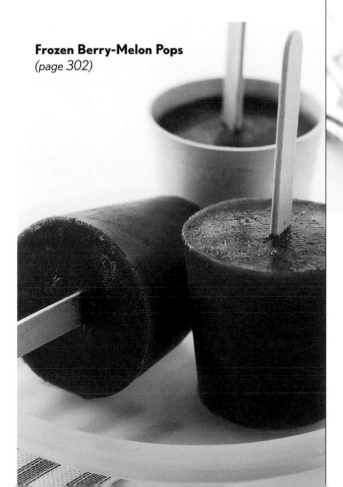

Cucumber-Chile Granité
(page 302)

global flavor menus

TAKE YOUR FAMILY AROUND THE WORLD JUST SITTING AT YOUR DINNER TABLE. THESE MENUS BORROW INSPIRATION FROM THE CUISINES OF FARAWAY PLACES. LET THEIR SEASONINGS TICKLE YOUR TASTE BUDS.

CARIBBEAN CAPER
Tropical fruit salad
Caribbean Pork Pot Roast (*page 263*)
Black beans
Hot cooked rice
Coconut-Lemon Puffs (*page 298*)
Caribbean Pork Pot Roast (*page 263*)
Mango-Ginger Coladas (*page 261*)

GREEK ODYSSEY
Feta Tabbouleh Salad (*page 289*)
Greek Orzo and Pepper Casserole (*page 277*)
Toasted pita bread
Good Thyme Lemon Cups (*page 296*)
Sparkling water

ITALIAN ARIA
Green salad with balsamic vinaigrette
Ham-Spinach Lasagna (*page 273*)
Italian bread with olive oil
Easter Ricotta Pie (*page 299*)
Red wine
Cappuccino or espresso

MOROCCAN CRUSADE
Orange-almond spinach salad
Moroccan-Style Short Ribs (*page 272*)
Zucchini-Olive Couscous (*page 292*)
Chocolate-Kissed Date Puffs (*page 300*)
Coffee or tea

Moroccan-Style Short Ribs
(page 272)

Coconut-Lemon Puffs
(page 298)

Zucchini-Olive Couscous
(page 292)

annualrecipesindex

a-b

ALMONDS
Almond-Cherry Trifles, 179
Almond Crumb Topping, 170
Almond Tart Shell, 179
Asian-Style Pork and Noodle
  Salad, 285
Coconut-Cranberry Bark, 305
Dilled Chicken and Jicama-Potato
  Salad, 271
Easter Rings, 54
Flourless Chocolate Torte with
  Apricot Filling, 75
Hazelnut Poached Pears and
  Strawberries, 299
Herbed Leek Tart, 152
Lemon Cream Coffee Cake, 297
Lemon-Lime Mascarpone Trifle, 297
Mitten Cookies, 254
Nut-Olive Couscous, 272
Nutty Berry-Chip Squares, 301
Orange-Champagne Cakes, 17
Orange-Saffron Bread, 54
Simple Fudge, 22
Spicy Garlic Chicken Pizza, 175
Terrific Toffee, 300
Toasted Almonds with Rosemary
  and Cayenne, 152
Triple-Nut Zucchini Cake, 293
Zucchini Spoon Bread, 293
Angel Food Cake, 40

APPETIZERS AND SNACKS
(see also **Dips and Spreads** and **Soups, Side-Dish**)
Calypso Shrimp Skewers, 258
Figs with Herbed Goat Cheese, 141
Fire and Ice Nut Mix, 237
Herbed Leek Tart, 152
Lemon-Scented Eggplant Tart, 43
Mahi Mahi Spring Rolls, 259
Pears and Brie in Phyllo, 162
Peppered Shrimp over Spicy
  Cheese Grits, 259
Pita Crisps, 11
Roasted Mushrooms
  with Fresh Sage, 14
Roasted Red Pepper and
  Black Olive Tapenade, 14
Seafood-Melon Cocktail, 259
Smoked Salmon Roll-Ups, 258
Smoked Trout with
  Mango-Avocado Salsa, 36
Toasted Almonds with Rosemary
  and Cayenne, 152
Toasted Wheat Pita Triangles, 285
Tomatoes with Smoked Salmon, 291

APPLES AND APPLE JUICE
Apple-and-Herb Syrup, 232
Apple Dumplings, 233
Buttery Cider-Glazed Turkey, 212
Caramel Apple Crepes, 253
Chunky Apple-Sage Sauce, 231
Cider Glaze, 212
Cinnamon Apple Syrup, 232
Hot Apple Cider with Calvados, 244
Sausage and Apple Torta, 264
Spiced Pork and Sweet Potatoes, 281
Spicy Apple Syrup, 232
Watermelon Lemonade, 106

APRICOTS
Apricot-Dijon Dressing, 289
Apricot Filling, 75
Easter Ricotta Pie, 299
Figs with Herbed Goat Cheese, 141
Jeweled Bulgur Salad, 289
Artichoke and Basil Hero, 201
Asian-Style Pork and Noodle Salad, 285

ASPARAGUS
Asparagus Barley Pilaf, 289
Asparagus-Salmon Scramble, 84
Roasted Asparagus Soup, 67
Spring Greens with Shortcut
  Lemon Sauce, 40
Strawberry-Spinach Salad, 125

AVOCADOS
Bacon-Avocado Deviled Eggs, 101
Citrus-Avocado Salad, 114
Double-Duty Salsa, 155
Jicama Relish, 268
Lemon-Avocado Sorbet, 303
Mango-Avocado Salsa, 36
Seafood-Melon Cocktail, 259
Smoked Salmon Roll-Ups, 258

BACON
Bacon-Avocado Deviled Eggs, 101
Baked Bean Quintet, 98
Beef and Cabbage Soup, 194
Creamy Macaroni and Cheese, 64
Farm-Style Green Beans, 127
Hearty Hodgepodge, 197
Peppered Shrimp over
  Spicy Cheese Grits, 259
Poor Boy Filets, 128
Potato-Onion Soup, 186
Rosemary Roasted Vegetables, 214

d-e

j-l

m

Macaroni and Cheese
    with Mushrooms, 248
Macaroon Fruit Tart, 295
Madeline's Lemonade, 136
Mahi Mahi Spring Rolls, 259
Maine Vichyssoise with Chive Oil, 142
MANGOES
    Double-Duty Salsa, 155
    Frozen Strawberry-Mango
        Margaritas, 261
    Ginger Fruit Salsa, 155
    Lamb and Black Bean Burritos, 241
    Lamb and Black Bean Quesadillas, 241
    Mango-Avocado Salsa, 36
    Mango-Ginger Coladas, 261
    Mango Sorbet with
        Ginger Fruit Salsa, 155
    Minty Fruit Topper, 294
    Tropical Sorbet, 303
Maple-Pumpkin Cheesecake, 218
Marinade, Citrus, 267
Marinated Mint Lamb, 269
Mashed Potatoes with
    Caramelized Onions, 217
Meat Loaf, Cheesy, 269
Mediterranean Pot Roast, 262
Melon-Tomato Tumble, 87
Mexican Fiesta Casserole, 275
Mexican Polenta Pie, 274
Mexican-Style Pasta Bake, 276
Milk Chocolate Mini Cookies, 26
Milk Chocolate-Sour Cream
    Frosting, 26
MINT
    Buffet Wild Rice, 286
    Cucumber Sandwiches, 284
    Double-Mint Brandy Cooler, 152
    Feta Tabbouleh Salad, 289

MINT *(continued)*
    Ginger Fruit Salsa, 155
    Marinated Mint Lamb, 269
    Melon-Tomato Tumble, 87
    Minted Hot Chocolate, 244
    Minty Fruit Topper, 294
    Minty Summer Shortcake, 294
    Pan-Seared Lamb Chops with
        Mint Salad, 35
    Peppermint Meringue, 105
    Watermelon Salad with Watercress, 122
Mitten Cookies, 254
Mom's Bread, 288
Moroccan-Style Short Ribs, 272
Moussaka, 203
Muffins, Lemon, 60
Mulled Cranberry Drink, 229
MUSHROOMS
    Baked Chicken and Artichoke Risotto, 275
    Brie, Crab, and Mushroom Soup, 279
    Cassoulet-Style Stew, 192
    Flash-Roasted Vegetables
        and Pasta, 83
    German Meatballs with Spaetzle, 89
    Greek Orzo and Pepper
        Casserole, 277
    Grilled Cheese Sandwich with
        Sautéed Onions and Mushrooms, 137
    Ham-Spinach Lasagna, 273
    Macaroni and Cheese
        with Mushrooms, 248
    Mushroom Deluxe Hamburgers, 283
    Orange-Spinach Stuffed Snapper, 275
    Pasta with Mushrooms and
        Aged Jack Cheese, 39
    Peppered Shrimp over
        Spicy Cheese Grits, 259
    Poor Boy Filets, 128
    Portobello and Lemon
        Thyme Bread Pudding, 225
    Portobello and Spinach Brunch Tart, 265
    Roasted Mushrooms with Fresh Sage, 14
    Wine-Balsamic Glazed Steak, 280
Mustard Barbecue Sauce, 87

n-o

New Potato Simmer, 80
N.Y. Steak with Pear Brandy-Black
    Pepper Sauce, 161
NUTS
(see also **Almonds**, **Peanuts**, **Pecans**, and **Walnuts**)
    Chicken with Lemon Thyme Pesto, 146
    Chocolate-Hazelnut Tart Shells, 29
    Chocolate-Kissed Date Puffs, 300
    Coconut Cashew Pralines, 305
    Curried Butternut Chicken Bisque, 278
    Fire and Ice Nut Mix, 237
    Glazed Pistachios, 303
    Hazelnut Poached Pears and
        Strawberries, 299
    Italian Cheesecake, 299
    Nut Crust, 295
    Nut-Olive Couscous, 272
    Nut Shortbread, 296
    Orange-Saffron Bread, 54
    Pistachio-Coconut Sorbet, 303
    Spicy Garlic Chicken Pizza, 175
    Tropical Fruit Strudel, 295
    Warm Gorgonzola and
        Beef Salad, 265
Nutty Berry-Chip Squares, 301
Nutty Gorgonzola Roll-Ups, 277
Oatmeal Jam Bars, 244
Olive Salsa, 285
Onion Chili Sauce, 283
ORANGES
    Candied Orange Slices and Syrup, 54
    Citrus-Avocado Salad, 114
    Citrus Salad with Honey
        Balsamic Vinaigrette, 243
    Fluff Frosting, 298
    Hibiscus Tea, 106
    Orange-Champagne Cakes, 17
    Orange Chiffon Cake, 298
    Orange-Saffron Bread, 54
    Orange-Spinach Stuffed Snapper, 275
    Orange-Yogurt Cheese Spread, 91

tips

menus

Nutrition information.
With each recipe, we give you useful nutrition information you easily can apply to your own needs. First, read "What you need" *(below)* to determine your dietary requirements. Then refer to the nutrition information listed after each recipe. You'll find the calorie count and the amount of fat, saturated fat, cholesterol, sodium, carbohydrates, fiber, and protein for each serving. You'll find the amount of vitamin A, vitamin C, calcium, and iron noted as a percentage of the Daily Values, if they are present. The Daily Values are dietary standards set by the Food and Drug Administration. To stay in line with the nutrition breakdown of each recipe, follow the suggested number of servings.

How we analyze.
The *Better Homes and Gardens®* Test Kitchen computer analyzes each recipe for the nutritional value of a single serving.
- The analysis does not include optional ingredients.
- We use the first serving size listed when a range is given. For example: If we say a recipe "Makes 4 to 6 servings," the nutrition information is based on 4 servings.
- When ingredient choices (such as margarine or butter) appear in a recipe, we use the first one mentioned for analysis. The ingredient order does not mean we prefer one ingredient over another.
- When milk and eggs are recipe ingredients, the analysis is calculated using 2-percent (reduced-fat) milk and large eggs.

What you need.
The dietary guidelines below suggest nutrient levels that moderately active adults should strive to eat each day. As your calorie levels change, adjust your fat intake too. Try to keep the percentage of calories from fat to no more than 30 percent. There's no harm in occasionally going over or under these guidelines, but the key to good health is maintaining a balanced diet most of the time.

Calories: About 2,000
Total fat: Less than 65 grams
Saturated fat: Less than 20 grams
Cholesterol: Less than 300 milligrams
Carbohydrates: About 300 grams
Sodium: Less than 2,400 milligrams
Dietary fiber: 20 to 30 grams

Low-fat recipes.
For recipes that meet our low-fat criteria, each serving must contain three or fewer grams of fat for every 100 calories. These recipes are flagged with a low-fat symbol.

Emergency substitutions.

If you don't have:	Substitute:
Bacon, 1 slice, crisp-cooked, crumbled	1 tablespoon cooked bacon pieces
Baking powder, 1 teaspoon	$^1/_2$ teaspoon cream of tartar plus $^1/_4$ teaspoon baking soda
Balsamic vinegar, 1 tablespoon	1 tablespoon cider vinegar or red wine vinegar plus $^1/_2$ teaspoon sugar
Bread crumbs, fine dry, $^1/_4$ cup	$^3/_4$ cup soft bread crumbs, or $^1/_4$ cup cracker crumbs, or $^1/_4$ cup cornflake crumbs
Broth, beef or chicken, 1 cup	1 teaspoon or 1 cube instant beef or chicken bouillon plus 1 cup hot water
Butter, 1 cup	1 cup shortening plus $^1/_4$ teaspoon salt, if desired
Buttermilk, 1 cup	1 tablespoon lemon juice or vinegar plus enough milk to make 1 cup (let stand 5 minutes before using), or 1 cup plain yogurt
Chocolate, semisweet, 1 ounce	3 tablespoons semisweet chocolate pieces, or 1 ounce unsweetened chocolate plus 1 tablespoon granulated sugar, or 1 tablespoon unsweetened cocoa powder plus 2 teaspoons sugar and 2 teaspoons shortening
Chocolate, sweet baking, 4 ounces	$^1/_4$ cup unsweetened cocoa powder plus $^1/_3$ cup granulated sugar and 3 tablespoons shortening
Chocolate, unsweetened, 1 ounce	3 tablespoons unsweetened cocoa powder plus 1 tablespoon cooking oil or shortening, melted
Cornstarch, 1 tablespoon (for thickening)	2 tablespoons all-purpose flour
Corn syrup (light), 1 cup	1 cup granulated sugar plus $^1/_4$ cup water
Egg, 1 whole	2 egg whites, or 2 egg yolks, or $^1/_4$ cup refrigerated or frozen egg product, thawed
Flour, cake, 1 cup	1 cup minus 2 tablespoons all-purpose flour
Flour, self-rising, 1 cup	1 cup all-purpose flour plus 1 teaspoon baking powder, $^1/_2$ teaspoon salt, and $^1/_4$ teaspoon baking soda
Garlic, 1 clove	$^1/_2$ teaspoon bottled minced garlic or $^1/_8$ teaspoon garlic powder
Ginger, grated fresh, 1 teaspoon	$^1/_4$ teaspoon ground ginger
Half-and-half or light cream, 1 cup	1 tablespoon melted butter or margarine plus enough whole milk to make 1 cup
Molasses, 1 cup	1 cup honey
Mustard, dry, 1 teaspoon	1 tablespoon prepared (in cooked mixtures)
Mustard, prepared, 1 tablespoon	$^1/_2$ teaspoon dry mustard plus 2 teaspoons vinegar
Onion, chopped, $^1/_2$ cup	2 tablespoons dried minced onion or $^1/_2$ teaspoon onion powder
Sour cream, dairy, 1 cup	1 cup plain yogurt
Sugar, granulated, 1 cup	1 cup packed brown sugar or 2 cups sifted powdered sugar
Sugar, brown, 1 cup packed	1 cup granulated sugar plus 2 tablespoons molasses
Tomato juice, 1 cup	$^1/_2$ cup tomato sauce plus $^1/_2$ cup water
Tomato sauce, 2 cups	$^3/_4$ cup tomato paste plus 1 cup water
Vanilla bean, 1 whole	2 teaspoons vanilla extract
Wine, red, 1 cup	1 cup beef or chicken broth in savory recipes; cranberry juice in desserts
Wine, white, 1 cup	1 cup chicken broth in savory recipes; apple juice or white grape juice in desserts
Yeast, active dry, 1 package	about $2^1/_4$ teaspoons active dry yeast

Seasonings

Apple pie spice, 1 teaspoon	$^1/_2$ teaspoon ground cinnamon plus $^1/_4$ teaspoon ground nutmeg, $^1/_8$ teaspoon ground allspice, and dash ground cloves or ginger
Cajun seasoning, 1 tablespoon	$^1/_2$ teaspoon white pepper, $^1/_2$ teaspoon garlic powder, $^1/_2$ teaspoon onion powder, $^1/_2$ teaspoon ground red pepper, $^1/_2$ teaspoon paprika, and $^1/_2$ teaspoon black pepper
Herbs, snipped fresh, 1 tablespoon	$^1/_2$ to 1 teaspoon dried herb, crushed, or $^1/_2$ teaspoon ground herb
Poultry seasoning, 1 teaspoon	$^3/_4$ teaspoon dried sage, crushed, plus $^1/_4$ teaspoon dried thyme or marjoram, crushed
Pumpkin pie spice, 1 teaspoon	$^1/_2$ teaspoon ground cinnamon plus $^1/_4$ teaspoon ground ginger, $^1/_4$ teaspoon ground allspice, and $^1/_8$ teaspoon ground nutmeg